THE ANNUAL DIRECTORY OF AMERICAN
AND CANADIAN BED & BREAKFASTS

# The South

*Includes*

**PUERTO RICO** AND **VIRGIN ISLANDS**

2000 EDITION • VOLUME III

# THE ANNUAL DIRECTORY OF AMERICAN AND CANADIAN BED & BREAKFASTS

# The South

*Includes*

## PUERTO RICO AND VIRGIN ISLANDS

2000 EDITION • VOLUME III

Tracey Menges, *Compiler*

BARBOUR
PUBLISHING, INC.
Uhrichsville, Ohio

Published by Barbour Publishing, Inc., P.O. Box 719, Uhrichsville, Ohio 44683
http://www.barbourbooks.com

Cover design and book design by Harriette Bateman
Page composition by Roger A. DeLiso, Rutledge Hill Press®

*Printed in the United States of America.*

1 2 3 4 5 6—02 01 00 99

# Contents

# Introduction

The 2000 edition of *The Annual Directory of Southern Bed & Breakfasts* is one of the most comprehensive directories available today. Whether planning your honeymoon, a family vacation or reunion, or a business trip (many bed and breakfasts provide conference facilities), you will find what you are looking for at a bed and breakfast. They are all here just waiting to be discovered.

Once you know your destination, look for it, or one close by, to see what accommodations are available. Each state has a general map with city locations to help you plan your trip efficiently. There are listings for all 50 states, Canada, Puerto Rico, and the Virgin Islands. Don't be surprised to find a listing in the remote spot you thought only you knew about. Even if your favorite hideaway isn't listed, you're sure to discover a new one.

## How to Use This Guide

The sample listing below is typical of the entries in this directory. Each bed and breakfast is listed alphabetically by city and establishment name. The description provides an overview of the bed and breakfast and may include nearby activities and attractions. *Please note that the descriptions have been provided by the hosts. The publisher has not visited these bed and breakfasts and is not responsible for inaccuracies.*

Following the description are notes that have been designed for easy reference. Looking at the sample, a quick glance tells you that this bed and breakfast has four guest rooms, two with private baths (PB) and two that share a bath (SB). The rates are for two people sharing one room. Tax may or may not be included. The specifics of "Credit Cards" and "Notes" are listed at the bottom of each page.

**GREAT TOWN**_____

### *Favorite Bed and Breakfast*

123 Main Street, 12345
(800) 555-1234

This quaint bed and breakfast is surrounded by five acres of award-winning landscaping and gardens. There are four guest rooms, each individually decorated with antiques. It is close to antique shops, restaurants, and outdoor activities. Breakfast includes homemade specialties and is served in the formal dining room at guests' leisure. Minimum stay of two nights.

Hosts: Sue and Jim Smith
Rooms: 4 (2 PB; 2 SB) $65-80
Full Breakfast
Credit Cards: A, B
Notes: 2, 5, 8, 10, 11, 12, 13

For example, the letter A means that MasterCard is accepted. The number 10 means that tennis is available on the premises or within 10 to 15 miles.

In many cases, a bed and breakfast is listed with a reservation service that represents several houses in one area. This service is responsible for bookings and can answer other questions you may have. They also inspect each listing and can help you choose the best place for your needs.

## Before You Arrive

Now that you have chosen the bed and breakfast that interests you, there are some things you need to find out. You should always make reservations in advance, and while you are doing so you should ask about the local taxes. City taxes can be an unwelcome surprise. Make sure there are accommodations for your children. If you have dietary needs or prefer nonsmoking rooms, find out if these requirements can be met. Ask about check-in times and cancellation policies. Get specific directions. Most bed and breakfasts are readily accessible, but many are a little out of the way.

## When You Arrive

In many instances you are visiting someone's home. Be respectful of their property, their schedules, and their requests. Don't smoke if they ask you not to, and don't show up with pets without prior arrangement. Be tidy in shared bathrooms, and be prompt. Most places have small staffs or may be run single-handedly and cannot easily adjust to surprises.

With a little effort and a sense of adventure you will learn firsthand the advantages of bed and breakfast travel. You will rediscover hospitality in a time when kindness seems to have been pushed aside. With the help of this directory, you will find accommodations that are just as exciting as your traveling plans.

We would like to hear from you about any experiences you have had or any inns you wish to recommend. Please write us at the following address:

Barbour Publishing, Inc.
P.O. Box 719
Uhrichsville, Ohio 44683

THE ANNUAL DIRECTORY OF AMERICAN
AND CANADIAN BED & BREAKFASTS

# The South

*Includes*

**PUERTO RICO** AND **VIRGIN ISLANDS**

2000 EDITION  •  VOLUME III

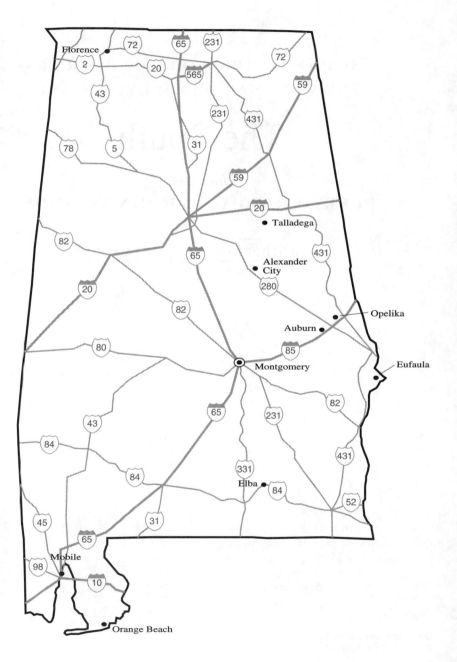

Alabama

# Alabama

Mistletoe Bough

## ALEXANDER CITY

### Mistletoe Bough Bed & Breakfast

497 Hillabee Street, 35010
(256) 329-3717; (877) 330-3707
www.bbonline.com/al/mistletoe

Mistletoe Bough offers guests a retreat into years gone by with all the comforts and conveniences of modern days. The moment guests enter, they will sense the elegance and charm of this lovely Victorian home. A distinctive decorating style creates a relaxing environment that is perfect for lingering and unwinding. Enjoy the elegant parlors and bedrooms decorated in an eclectic collection of traditional, Victorian, and European antiques. Stroll through the beautiful gardens or relax on one of the porches.

Hosts: Jean and Carlice Payne
Rooms: 5 (PB) $85-110

Full Breakfast
Credit Cards: None
Notes: 2, 5, 7, 9, 10, 11, 12

## AUBURN

### The Crenshaw Guest House

371 North College Street, 36830
(334) 821-1131; (800) 950-1131
FAX (334) 826-8123
e-mail: crenshaw-gh@mindspring.com
www.auburnalabama.com

A gracious bed and breakfast in Auburn's historic district, rich in history and late- Victorian detail. Spacious rooms include private baths, touch-tone telephones, cable TV, VCR, and clock/radio cassette players. Gleaming porcelain, brass, and ornately carved mantels provide the perfect setting for a collection of comfortable antiques. Suite or kitchenette units available. Room service breakfast. Just a short drive to world-class golf, three blocks to campus, downtown, and restaurants. AAA-rated three diamonds and Mobil Travel Guide.

The Crenshaw Guest House

NOTES: Credit cards accepted: A MasterCard; B Visa; C American Express; D Discover; E Diner's Club; F Other; 2 Personal checks accepted; 3 Lunch available; 4 Dinner available; 5 Open all year; 6 Pets welcome; 7 No smoking; 8 Children welcome; 9 Social drinking allowed; 10 Tennis nearby; 11 Swimming nearby; 12 Golf nearby; 13 Skiing nearby; 14 May be booked through a travel agent; 15 Handicapped accessible.

Take exit 51 from I-85, four miles north on College Street.

Hosts: Fran and Peppi Verma
Rooms: 6 (PB) $58-75
Continental Breakfast
Credit Cards: A, B, C
Notes: 2, 5, 7, 8, 9, 10, 11, 12, 14

## ELBA

### Aunt B's Bed & Breakfast

717 West Davis Street (Highway 84 West), 36323
(334) 897-6918

This historic country Victorian home, built in 1910, has survived three floods—1929, 1990, and again in 1998. Guests are surrounded by the serenity of days gone by while enjoying the wicker rocking chairs and swing on the large front porch or lazing in the hammock in shaded back yard. Three guest rooms: Angel—decorated in battenburg lace with king-size bed; Cowboy—two full-size beds decorated with handmade quilts; Mayberry—queen-size bed decorated with special warmth of country.

Hosts: Bobby and Barbara Hudson
Rooms: 3 (PB) $50
Full Breakfast
Credit Cards: A, B
Notes: 2, 3, 4, 5, 7, 8, 12

Aunt B's

## EUFAULA

### Kendall Manor Inn

534 West Broad Street, 36021
(334) 687-8847; FAX (334) 616-0678

Kendall Manor Inn

e-mail: kmanorinn@aol.com
www.bbonline.com/al/kendall

Capture a memory in an elegant antebellum home with a warm and friendly atmosphere. The six spacious guest rooms are well appointed, and the wraparound veranda, upstairs sitting porch, and deck in the rear offer opportunities to relax and unwind. A welcome beverage served on arrival. Wonderful breakfasts and tour of the historic home with a trip to the belvedere (cupola) and opportunity to add your name to the walls where generations have signed. Fishing, antique shops, and historic district nearby.

Hosts: Barbara and Tim Lubsen
Rooms: 6 (PB) $89-125
Full Breakfast
Credit Cards: A, B, C, D
Notes: 2, 4, 5, 7, 9, 10, 11, 12, 14

## FLORENCE

### Natchez Trace Bed & Breakfast Reservation Service

P.O. Box 193, Hampshire, TN 38461
(931) 285-2777; (800) 377-2770
e-mail: natcheztrace@worldnet.att.net
www.bbonline.com/natcheztrace

**Limestone Manor.** This 1915 Georgian Revival home is 12 miles from the trace. Built from blocks of local limestone and one of Florence's most treasured landmarks. Previous

---

NOTES: Credit cards accepted: A MasterCard; B Visa; C American Express; D Discover; E Diner's Club; F Other; 2 Personal checks accepted; 3 Lunch available; 4 Dinner available; 5 Open all year; 6 Pets welcome;

guests in the home include Henry Ford, Thomas Edison, and Humphrey Bogart! Two guest rooms, one with private sitting room, large sun porch, library with games. $80-85.

**Wood Avenue Inn.** Milepost 332. This magnificent Queen Anne Victorian mansion, circa 1889, is in the historic district of Florence, just 12 miles from the trace. Its octagonal and square towers, wraparound porch, 10 fireplaces, 14-foot ceilings, and antique furnishings provide elegance at its best. Full English breakfast. A suite available for $64-97.

Wood Avenue Inn

## Wood Avenue Inn

658 North Wood Avenue, 35630
(205) 766-8441; e-mail: woodaveinn@aol.com

Enjoy legendary hospitality in this 111-year-old Victorian mansion just 12 miles off Natchez Trace Parkway. Located in historical downtown Florence, walk to fine restaurants, museum, shopping, theaters, and art galleries. Port of Florence and Florence Marina is three miles away on the Tennessee River. The wisteria garden is a favorite while guests wake-up with hot muffins and fresh coffee. Romantic, elegant, and unforgettable.

Hosts: Gene and Alvern Greeley
Rooms: 5 (4 PB; 1 SB) $66-98
Full Breakfast
Credit Cards: A, B
Notes: 2, 4, 5, 8, 10, 11, 12

## MOBILE

## *Towle House*

1104 Montauk Avenue, 36604
(334) 432-6440; (800) 938-6953
FAX (334) 433-4381; e-mail: jfvereen@aol.com

Lovely home, circa 1874, in the heart of Mobile's historic Old Dauphin Way District. Only minutes away from the convention center, Mobile Auditorium, historic homes, antique shopping and the revitalized downtown area. The location also offers convenient access to the City of Mobile Museum, Fort Condé, the battleship USS *Alabama*. Within easy walking distance of the parade routes for Mardi Gras visitors. Gourmet breakfast served daily.

Hosts: Felix and Carolyn Vereen
Rooms: 3 (PB) $70-85
Full Breakfast
Credit Cards: A, B, C, D
Notes: 2, 5, 7, 9, 10, 12, 14

## MONTGOMERY

## *Red Bluff Cottage*

551 Clay Street, P.O. Box 1026, 36101
(334) 264-0056; (888) 551-2529
FAX (334) 263-3054
e-mail: redbluffbnb@aol.com
www.bbonline.com/al/redbluff

The Waldos built Red Bluff Cottage in 1987 high above the Alabama River in the historic Cottage Hill district. A raised cottage, it has all guest rooms on the ground floor, with easy access to off-street parking, gazebo, and fenced playyard. Upstairs, guests will enjoy pleasantly

Red Bluff Cottage

7 No smoking; 8 Children welcome; 9 Social drinking allowed; 10 Tennis nearby; 11 Swimming nearby; 12 Golf nearby; 13 Skiing nearby; 14 May be booked through a travel agent; 15 Handicapped accessible.

light and airy public rooms, including dining, living, music (piano and harpsichord), and sitting (TV) rooms. A deep porch overlooks downtown, the state capitol, and the river plain.

Hosts: Anne and Mark Waldo
Rooms: 4 (PB) $75
Full Breakfast
Credit Cards: A, B, C, D
Notes: 2, 5, 7, 8, 9, 14

## OPELIKA

### The Heritage House Inn

714 Second Avenue, 36801
(334) 705-0485

Spacious accommodations in a comfortably elegant home in one of Opelika's historic neighborhoods and just blocks from the downtown area. Championship golf, Auburn University, fine restaurants, and other area attractions are minutes away. Facilities are also available for meetings and special events. Touch-tone telephone, TV, clock/radio in every room. Room rates include a full gourmet breakfast. Gift shop in Old Carriage House on premises. Take exit 62 from I-85.

Hosts: Richard Patton and Barbara Patton
Rooms: 5 (PB) $65-85
Full Breakfast
Credit Cards: A, B, C
Notes: 2, 5, 7, 9, 10, 11, 12, 14

## ORANGE BEACH

### The Original Romar House

23500 Perdido Beach Boulevard, 36561
(334) 974-1625; (800) 487-6627
FAX (334) 974-1163
e-mail: original@gulftel.com
www.bbonline.com/al/romarhouse/

The Original Romar House is Alabama's first seaside bed and breakfast inn. This 1920s beach house has a romantic feeling with its Art Deco furniture, stained glass, and charmingly historic atmosphere. Enjoy complimentary wine and cheese at sundown in the Purple Parrot bar. Enjoy the private beach for an early morning walk or fast tan, the hot tub for a midnight dip, or a brief drive to the Gulf Coast's finest seafood restaurants, nightclub entertainment, or seven golf courses.

Host: Darrell Finley
Owner: Jerry M. Gilbreath
Rooms: 6 (PB) $79-129
Cottage: 1 (PB) $89-185
Full Breakfast
Credit Cards: A, B, C
Notes: 2, 5, 9, 10, 11, 12

## TALLADEGA

### Historic Oakwood Bed & Breakfast

715 North Street East, 35160
(256) 362-0662; FAX (256) 362-7168

This antebellum home was commissioned in 1847 and completed in 1849. Oakwood is one of the finest examples of Federal-style architecture remaining in Alabama. Enjoy a retreat into the quiet elegance of a bygone era. Just 20 miles southwest of Anniston on Highway 21, 10 miles south of I-20 on Highway 77, 50 miles east of Birmingham, and 4 blocks east of Talladega Courthouse Square. Closed Thanksgiving and Christmas.

Hosts: The Woods Family and Sam, the cat
Rooms: 3 (1 PB; 2 SB) $59-95
Full and Continental Breakfast
Credit Cards: None
Notes: 2, 7, 9, 12

Historic Oakwood

---

NOTES: Credit cards accepted: A MasterCard; B Visa; C American Express; D Discover; E Diner's Club; F Other; 2 Personal checks accepted; 3 **Lunch** available; 4 Dinner available; 5 Open all year; 6 Pets welcome;

# Arkansas

## The Inn at Bella Vista

1 Chelsea Road, 72714
(501) 876-5645; (877) 876-5645
e-mail: innkeeper@iabv.com

Built of native fieldstone, cedar, and glass, the inn is in the beautiful Ozark Mountains in northwest Arkansas. The 9,000-square-foot inn sits on 14 acres and offers incredible views. Access to seven golf courses, eight lakes, and lots to do.

Hosts: Bill and Beverly Williams
Rooms: 5 (PB) $95-140
Full Breakfast
Credit Cards: A, B, C, D
Notes: 2, 5, 7, 9, 10, 11, 12, 14

## Angel at Rose Hall

56 Hillside, 72632
(501) 253-5405; (800) 828-4255
www.the-angel.com

Step back into time and enjoy the romantic ambiance of breathtaking Victorian furnishings, grand fireplaces, and Jacuzzis for two. Twenty-eight century-old stained-glass windows invite glorious streams of light into the Angel where rich fabrics, designer linens, and fresh flowers splash vibrant colors into rooms. Specializing in weddings, honeymoons, anniversaries, and special getaways. Adults only. No smoking.

Host: Sandy Latimer
Rooms: 5 (PB) $125-160

Angel at Rose Hall

Full Breakfast
Credit Cards: A, B, C, D, E
Notes: 2, 5, 7, 9, 10, 11, 12, 14

## Antiques & Lace at Evening Shade Inn

Highway 62 East, 72632
(501) 253-6264; (800) 992-1224
e-mail: eveshade@ipa.net
www.eveningshade.com

Antiques and Lace is the newest honeymoon cottage at Evening Shade Inn. Two exceptional honeymoon suites filled with antiques make this cottage very special and romantic. Fireplace, Jacuzzi for two, king-size bed, and private deck are just some of the luxuries guests will enjoy. All cottages and rooms have private baths, TV with HBO, VCR with free movies, in-room telephones, breakfast at guests' leisure, champagne and snacks each evening. In the heart of Eureka Springs, on the trolley route, yet quiet and serene in the woods. The best of both worlds! Small weddings. AAA-rated three diamonds.

---

7 No smoking; 8 Children welcome; 9 Social drinking allowed; 10 Tennis nearby; 11 Swimming nearby; 12 Golf nearby; 13 Skiing nearby; 14 May be booked through a travel agent; 15 Handicapped accessible.

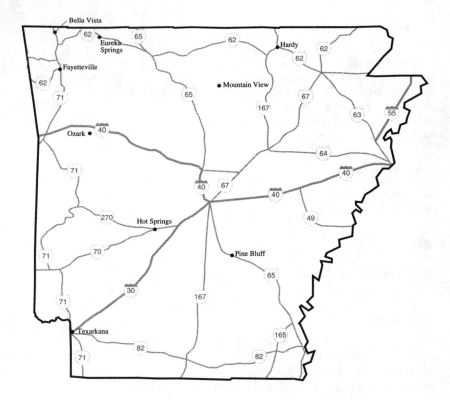

Arkansas

Hosts: Ed and Shirley Nussbaum
Rooms: 7 (PB) $120-160
Continental Breakfast
Credit Cards: A, B, C, D, E
Notes: 2, 5, 7, 9, 12, 14

## Arbour Glen Bed & Breakfast Victorian Inn & Guest House

7 Lema, 72632
(501) 253-9010; (800) 515-GLEN

The Arbour Glen (circa 1896) offers cottage-style lodging with Victorian romantic charm complete with Jacuzzis for two, fireplaces, and antique furnishings. This inn on Eureka Springs's historic district loop and trolley route, is only a five-minute walk from downtown shops and cafés. Completely renovated with guests' comfort in mind. Enjoy the picturesque setting while relaxing on the veranda.

Rooms: 5 (PB) $75-125
Full Breakfast
Credit Cards: A, B, C, D
Notes: 2, 3, 4, 5, 7, 9, 10, 11, 12, 14

## Arsenic & Old Lace Bed & Breakfast Inn

60 Hillside Avenue, 72632
(800) 243-5223; FAX (501) 253-2246
e-mail: arseniclace@prodigy.net
www.eureka~usa.com/arsenic

Victorian mansion in the historic district within easy walking distance of shopping, dining, and attractions. In-room Jacuzzis, fireplaces, balconies, cable TV and VCRs, antiques, fresh flowers, full gourmet breakfasts, 24-hour snack and beverage bar. Surrounded by trees, flower gardens, and wicker-filled verandas. Mobil and AAA three-diamond-rated. Featured in Gail Greco's *Romance of Country Inns*, *Houston Chronicle* travel section, *Oklahoma Living* TV show, and *Kiplinger's* magazine.

Hosts: Gary and Phyllis Jones
Rooms: 5 (PB) $125-165
Full Breakfast

Arsenic and Old Lace

Credit Cards: A, B, C, D
Notes: 2, 5, 7, 9, 10, 11, 12, 14, 15

## Beaver Lake Bed & Breakfast

1234 County Road 120, 72631
(501) 253-9210; (888) 253-9210
www.bbonline.com/ar/beaverlake/

Secluded nine acres on pristine Beaver Lake in the Ozark mountains. Fifteen minutes from the many attractions in historic Eureka Springs. Four guest rooms all with incredible lake views and private bathrooms. Full breakfast every morning. Sorry, no smoking, children, or pets permitted.

Hosts: David and Elaine Reppel
Rooms: 4 (PB) $75-95
Full Breakfast
Credit Cards: A, B, D
Notes: 2, 7, 9, 11, 12, 14

## Bonnybrooke Farm Atop Misty Mountain

361 CR 117 Misty Mountain Drive, 72631
(501) 253-6903
www.bonnybrooke.apexhosting.com

If guests' hearts are in the country—or long to be—the hosts invite them to come share in the sweet quiet and serenity that await them in their home away from home. Five cottages are

NOTES: Credit cards accepted: A MasterCard; B Visa; C American Express; D Discover; E Diner's Club; F Other; 2 Personal checks accepted; 3 Lunch available; 4 Dinner available; 5 Open all year; 6 Pets welcome; 7 No smoking; 8 Children welcome; 9 Social drinking allowed; 10 Tennis nearby; 11 Swimming nearby; 12 Golf nearby; 13 Skiing nearby; 14 May be booked through a travel agent; 15 Handicapped accessible.

distinctly different in their tempting pleasures: fireplace and Jacuzzi for two, full glass fronts, mountaintop views, shower under the stars in the glass shower, wicker porch swing in front of the fireplace, and a waterfall Jacuzzi. Guests are going to love it! In order to preserve privacy, the location is not made public and is given to registered guests only. Featured in *Country Heart* magazine as the Most Romantic Accommodation in Arkansas.

Hosts: Bonny and Josh
Cottages: 5 (PB) $115 and up
Credit Cards: None
Notes: 2, 5, 7, 9, 11, 14

Bonnybrooke Farm

# Bridgeford House Bed & Breakfast

263 Spring Street, 72632
(888) 567-2422
e-mail: bridgefordbb@earthlink.net
www.bridgefordhouse.com

Nestled in the heart of Eureka Springs's historic residential district, Bridgeford House is an 1884 Victorian delight. Hailed by many guests as "the best bed and breakfast in Eureka Springs." Outside are shady porches that invite guests to pull up a chair and watch the world go by on Spring Street. Each room has a private entrance, antique furnishings, and private bath. Fresh coffee in the suite, a selection of fine teas, color TV, air conditioning, and a

Bridgeford House

gourmet southern-style breakfast. Jacuzzis, private decks, and fireplaces!

Hosts: Linda and Henry Thornton
Rooms: 4 (PB) $85-105
Full Breakfast
Credit Cards: A, B, C, D
Notes: 2, 5, 7, 8, 9, 10, 11, 12, 14

# Brownstone Inn

75 Hillside Avenue, 72632
(800) 973-7505
www.eureka-usa.com/brownstone

Built in 1895, for 70 years it served as the site for the Ozarka Water Company. The two-story limestone structure retains the original façade while the interior has been converted into the uniquely finished Victorian decor with modern

Brownstone Inn

NOTES: Credit cards accepted: A MasterCard; B Visa; C American Express; D Discover; E Diner's Club; F Other; 2 Personal checks accepted; 3 Lunch available; 4 Dinner available; 5 Open all year; 6 Pets welcome;

amenities, along with ample off-street parking. Beverage basket delivered to guests' doorstep before full breakfast in the morning. Featured in "Best Places to Stay in the South." A member of PAII and the state Bed and Breakfast Association.

Hosts: Marvin and Donna Shepard
Rooms: 4 (PB) $85-105
Full Breakfast
Credit Cards: A, B, D
Notes: 2, 7, 9, 10, 12, 14

## 1881 Crescent Cottage Inn

211 Spring Street, 72632
(501) 253-6022; e-mail: raphael@ipa.net
www.eureka-usa.com/crescott/index.html

Landmark 1881 Victorian is in the national register and was built for the first governor of Arkansas after the Civil War. Oldest, most historic and photographed bed and breakfast has beautiful gardens and mountain-panoramic views. All with queen-size beds and private Jacuzzis and baths. Fireplaces, verandas, and antiques. Newly redecorated. Great breakfasts! Area known for arts, crafts, lakes, and forests. AAA-rated three diamonds. No smoking indoors. Children over 12 welcome.

Hosts: Ralph and Phyllis Becker
Rooms: 4 (PB) $97-145
Full Breakfast
Credit Cards: A, B, D
Notes: 2, 5, 7, 9, 11, 12, 14

1881 Crescent Cottage Inn

11 Singleton House

## 11 Singleton House Bed & Breakfast

11 Singleton Street, 72632
(501) 253-9111; (800) 833-3394

This country Victorian home in the historic district is an old-fashioned place with a touch of magic. Each guest room is whimsically decorated with a delightful collection of antiques and folk art. Breakfast is served on the balcony overlooking the fantasy wildflower garden below, with its goldfish pond and curious birdhouse collection. Guests park and walk a scenic wooded pathway to Eureka's shops and cafés. Innkeeper apprenticeship program available.

Host: Barbara Gavron
Rooms: 5 (PB) $65-110
Full Breakfast
Credit Cards: A, B, C, D
Notes: 2, 7, 8, 9, 11, 12, 14

## Enchanted Cottages

18 Nut Street, 72632
(501) 253-6790; (800) 862-2788

Secluded parklike setting in Eureka Springs historic district. Romantic private cottages just three blocks to shops and restaurants. Storybook cottages surrounded by woods with neighborhood family of deer. Each cottage has either an indoor Jacuzzi for two or a private hot tub under the stars, wood or gas fireplace, king- or queen-size bed, antique furnishings, cable TV, kitchens, and patios with grills. Special honeymoon and anniversary packages. Weekday discounts. Special Y2K rates!

Hosts: Barbara Kellogg and David Pettit
Cottages: 3 (PB) $79-149
Continental Breakfast
Credit Cards: A, B
Notes: 2, 5, 7, 9, 11, 12, 14

## Eureka Sunset

10 Dogwood Ridge, 72632
(501) 253-9565

Create fairytale memories to last a lifetime in the mystical, magical kingdom of Eureka Springs. Two luxury suites created for couples offer relaxing romantic getaways. Hosts offer two-person Jacuzzi spas, queen-size beds, separate baths with showers, entertainment centers, and kitchens stocked with snacks and beverages. Balconies overlook a wooded ravine where deer can be spotted.

Hosts: Jack and Ada Dozier
Rooms: 2 (PB) $90-125
Full Breakfast
Credit Cards: A, B, D
Notes: 2, 5, 6, 7, 9, 10, 12, 14

## The Gardener's Cottage

11 Singleton Street, 72632
(501) 253-9111; (800) 833-3394

Tucked away in a private, wooded, historic district location, this delightful cottage is deco-

The Gardener's Cottage

rated in charming country decor with romantic touches and a Jacuzzi for two. This cozy retreat features a beamed cathedral ceiling, skylights, full kitchen, TV, VCR, and gas log fireplace. Relax and listen to the local wildlife from the porch with its swing and hammock or walk to the shops and cafés. Open April through November. Breakfast not included, but can be prearranged for $12 at Singleton House.

Host: Barbara Gavron
Cottage: 1 (PB) $95-125
Credit Cards: A, B, C, D
Notes: 2, 7, 8, 9, 11, 12, 14

Harvest House

## Harvest House

104 Wall Street, 72632
(501) 253-9363; (800) 293-5665
FAX (501) 253-2912; e-mail: harvest@ipa.net
www.eureka-usa.com/harvest

Vintage Victorian house filled with lovely antiques, collectibles, and family favorites. The guest rooms have private entrances and private baths. A full breakfast is served in the dining room or, weather permitting, in the screened-in gazebo overlooking pine and oak trees. Bill is a native Arkansan and knows all the hidden treasures of the area. Patt is the shopper with a particular interest in antiques and the local attractions.

Hosts: Bill and Patt Carmichael
Rooms: 4 (PB) $89-129
Full Breakfast
Credit Cards: A, B, D
Notes: 2, 5, 6, 7, 9, 14

NOTES: Credit cards accepted: A MasterCard; B Visa; C American Express; D Discover; E Diner's Club; F Other; 2 Personal checks accepted; 3 Lunch available; 4 Dinner available; 5 Open all year; 6 Pets welcome;

"Heartstone Inn", Eureka Springs, AR

The Heartstone Inn

## The Heartstone Inn & Cottages

35 Kings Highway, 72632
(501) 253-8916; www.heartstoneinn.com

The nationally acclaimed historic district Victorian inn combines nostalgic charm with all modern conveniences. Inviting rooms filled with antiques, all with king- or queen-size beds plus private entrances and bathrooms. Experience the luxury of on-site therapeutic massage; savor gourmet breakfasts; laze awhile on tree-shaded verandas; enjoy the golf privileges; or indulge in bountiful shopping, entertainment, and restaurants nearby. AAA-, Mobil-, Fodor's-approved. Recommended by all.

Hosts: Iris and Bill Simantel
Rooms: 10 (PB) $73-129
Cottages: 2 (PB)
Full Breakfast
Credit Cards: A, B, C, D
Notes: 2, 7, 8, 9, 11, 12, 14

## 1908 Ridgeway House Bed & Breakfast

28 Ridgeway, 72632
(501) 253-6618; (800) 477-6618
www.eureka-usa.com/ridgeway

Gracious southern hospitality makes this lovely, immaculately restored bed and breakfast in the historic district the perfect place to have that much-needed getaway, or to celebrate that spe-

cial occasion. Built in 1908 by W. O. Perkins, the inn has large porches and decks, robes in each room, high ceilings, guest kitchens, and other amenities. Excellent location, quiet street within walking distance of downtown. Jacuzzi suites available. Smoking allowed on porches and decks. Small weddings.

Hosts: Becky and "Sony" Taylor
Rooms: 5 (PB) $89-149
Full Breakfast
Credit Cards: A, B, D
Notes: 2, 5, 9, 11, 12, 14

## FAYETTEVILLE

## Eton House

1485 Eton Street, 72703
(501) 443-7517

This buff brick, ranch-style home has a cathedral ceiling and is furnished in delicate pastels, Victorian wicker, and more staid European pieces. Guests are welcome to relax in the living room by a cozy fireplace during winter months, but the screened-in patio overlooking a parklike setting is a spring and summer delight. A gazebo can be used for weddings. Fayetteville boasts the University of Arkansas and Walton Arts Center, plus arts and crafts. A Continental breakfast is included in the rates or guests may choose waffles with fruit and whipped cream.

Host: Patricia Parks
Rooms: 3 (PB) $55-72
Continental Breakfast
Credit Cards: None
Notes: 5, 9, 10, 11, 12

## Hill Avenue Bed & Breakfast

131 South Hill Avenue, 72701
(501) 444-0865

In a residential neighborhood, this home is near the University of Arkansas, Walton Arts Center, the town square, and Bud Walton Arena. Guests will find immaculate and

7 No smoking; 8 Children welcome; 9 Social drinking allowed; 10 Tennis nearby; 11 Swimming nearby; 12 Golf nearby; 13 Skiing nearby; 14 May be booked through a travel agent; 15 Handicapped accessible.

comfortable accommodations with king-size beds and private baths.

Hosts: Dale and Cecelia Thompson
Room: 3 (PB) $60
Full Breakfast
Credit Cards: None
Notes: 5, 7

## Inn at the Mill

3906 Greathouse Springs Road, Johnson, 72741-0409
(501) 443-1800; (501) 521-8091
(800) CLARION

Timeless elegance awaits guests at the Inn at the Mill. Nestled in the Ozark Mountains between the communities of Fayetteville and Springdale, guests will feel worlds apart from the hassles of the city while being only minutes away. The Inn at the Mill embraces a historic landmark, listed in the National Register of Historic Places, formerly known as the Johnson Mill. The water wheel is powered by four million gallons of fresh spring water daily, rushing down the falls. The elegantly appointed guest rooms marry with the serenity of the Ozarks to afford guests the ultimate lodging experience.

Hosts: James and Joyce Lambeth
Rooms: 48 (PB) $89-225
Continental Breakfast
Credit Cards: A, B, C, D, E
Notes: 3, 4, 5, 7, 8, 9, 12, 14, 15

## HARDY

## Hideaway Inn

84 West Firetower Road, 72542-9598
(870) 966-4770; (888) 966-4770

Modern bed and breakfast on 376 acres, three guest rooms, queen-size beds, central heat and air. Gourmet full breakfast and evening dessert snack. Log cabin with a Continental breakfast for those seeking solitude. Playground, gardens, and swimming pool for guests' enjoyment. Available packages include honeymoon,

fly-fishing, anniversary, birthday, romance in the Ozarks, canoeing, and golfing. Hosts can also create special packages. Ten miles from antiques, fishing, parks, shopping, theater, and water sports. "If you are looking for a unique bed and breakfast experience, at a comfortable home, you've found it."

Host: Julia Baldridge
Rooms: 5 (3 PB; **2 SB**) $55-95
Full or Continental **Breakfast**
Credit Cards: A, B, Č, D
Notes: 2, 5, 7, 8, 9, 11, 12, 14

Olde Stonehouse

## Olde Stonehouse Bed & Breakfast Inn

511 Main Street, 72542
(870) 856-2983; (800) 514-2983 (reservations only)
FAX (870) 856-4036

Native Arkansas stone house listed in the National Register of Historic Places has large porches lined with jumbo rocking chairs. Comfortably furnished with antiques. Features zoned heat and air, ceiling fans, queen-size beds, and private baths. One block from Spring River and the shops of Old Hardy Town. Country music theaters, golf courses, horseback riding, canoeing, and fishing nearby. Local attractions include Mammoth Spring State

NOTES: Credit cards accepted: A MasterCard; B Visa; C American Express; D Discover; E Diner's Club; F Other; 2 Personal checks accepted; 3 Lunch available; 4 Dinner available; 5 Open all year; 6 Pets welcome;

Park, Grand Gulf, Evening Shade, Arkansas Traveller Theater, and country music and comedy theaters. Two-room "special occasion" suites are in a separate 1905 cottage. Smoking permitted on porches. Mystery, trout fishing, golf, and other packages available. Approved by AAA and BBAA.

Host: Peggy Volland
Rooms: 8 (PB) $69-125
Full Breakfast
Credit Cards: A, B, C, D
Notes: 2, 3, 5, 7, 9, 10, 11, 12, 14

## HOT SPRINGS NATIONAL PARK

### The Gables Inn Bed & Breakfast

318 Quapaw Avenue, 71901
(501) 623-7576; (800) 625-7576
www.gablesn.com

Featured in the *Dallas Morning News* travel section. Walk only four blocks to downtown historic district, shops, restaurants, and Bathhouse Row. Come enjoy the charm and history of this beautiful home and relax in the ambiance of a bygone era. This 1905 Victorian home with four romantic guest rooms each featuring antiques, cable TV, VCR, and private baths. Price includes a full breakfast served each morning in the elegant dining room. Scrumptious dessert always available with choice of coffee, tea, or soft drinks. Elegant

The Gables Inn

wedding, honeymoon, anniversary, and special occasion packages available. No facilities available for children. No smoking or pets.

Hosts: Judy and David Peters
Rooms: 4 (PB) $69-89
Full Breakfast
Credit Cards: A, B, C, E
Notes: 2, 5, 7, 9, 10, 11, 12, 14

Williams House

### Williams House Bed & Breakfast Inn

420 Quapaw Avenue, 71901
(501) 624-4275; (800) 756-4635 (reservations)
e-mail: willmtnb@ipa.net
www.bbonline.com/ar/williamshouse

The Williams House Inn is a nationally registered 1890 brownstone and brick Victorian mansion with carriage house. It has five antique-filled rooms with a romantic setting offering attention to comfort and detail. TV, VCR, and private bath in each room. Only five blocks to the national park visitor center, Bathhouse Row, hiking trails, art galleries, restaurants, antiques, and shopping. Spring water, wine, baby grand piano, upper and lower wraparound porches, common rooms, and patios for guests' enjoyment. Reservations preferred. Two-bedroom suites available. Spa tub available. Children 12 and older welcome. Gourmet breakfast offered 7:30-9:00 A.M.

Hosts: David and Karen Wiseman
Rooms: 5 (PB) $85-125
Full Breakfast
Credit Cards: A, B, C, D
Notes: 2, 5, 7, 9, 11, 12, 14

7 No smoking; 8 Children welcome; 9 Social drinking allowed; 10 Tennis nearby; 11 Swimming nearby; 12 Golf nearby; 13 Skiing nearby; 14 May be booked through a travel agent; 15 Handicapped accessible.

## MOUNTAIN VIEW

### Ozark Country Inn

219 South Peabody Street, P.O. Box 1201, 72560
(800) 379-8699

Just one block from downtown square at scenic
Mountain View. It was remodeled and turned
into a bed and breakfast in 1987. Its wonderful
wraparound porch offers a cool breeze and rest
for the weary traveller. A delicious, full country breakfast is served along with afternoon
snacks. "Come and enjoy our southern hospitality. We'll make you want to come back time
after time."

Rooms: 6 (PB) $59-69
Full Breakfast
Credit Cards: A, B
Notes: 2, 5, 7, 8, 11, 12

## OZARK

### The 1887 Inn

100 East Commercial Street, 72949
(501) 667-1121

Step back in time at this elegant century-old
inn, nestled at the foot of the Ozark Mountains.
Restored to its original beauty the stained-glass
windows, crown moldings, crystal chandeliers,
hardwood floors, and winding staircase grace
the spacious entryways and inviting rooms.
The charm of Southern hospitality will be
experienced with a luxurious breakfast. Also
an evening of romance can be enjoyed in the
Anniversary Suite. The evening can include a
romantic candlelight dinner with advance
reservations. Many extra amenities throughout
the inn are designed to make guests' stay here a
pleasurable experience. Dinner available with
advance reservation.

Rooms: 4 (2 PB; 2 SB) $60-75
Full Breakfast
Credit Cards: A, B
Notes: 2, 5, 7, 9, 10, 11, 12

## PINE BLUFF

### Margland Bed & Breakfast

703 West Second Street, 71601
(870) 536-6000; (800) 545-5383

Southern hospitality as it was meant to be—
four historic southern homes—each suite is
carefully furnished for the perfect combination
of atmosphere and comfort. Guests may savor
breakfast on the terrace or in the formal dining
room and have access to cable TV, private
baths, VCRs, fax machine, and whirlpools. Full
or queen-size beds; swimming pool; exercise
room. Margland II is handicapped accessible.
All buildings are equipped with sprinkler fire
protection system. Lunch and dinner reservations are required for groups of eight or more.

Host: Wanda Bateman
Rooms: 24 (PB) $90-110
Continental Breakfast
Credit Cards: A, B, C, D, E
Notes: 2, 5, 7, 8, 9, 10, 12, 14, 15

Margland

## TEXARKANA

### House of Wadley

618 Pecan, 71854
(870) 773-7019; FAX (870) 773-7093
e-mail: houseofwadley@cableone.net
www.cableone.net/houseofwadley

Elegant Queen Anne architecture bed and
breakfast with emphasis on singing supper club
in downstairs parlors. All waiters sing big band

---

NOTES: Credit cards accepted: A MasterCard; B Visa; C American Express; D Discover; E Diner's Club;
F Other; 2 Personal checks accepted; 3 Lunch available; 4 Dinner available; 5 Open all year; 6 Pets welcome;

music and love songs of long ago. Dinner theater is featured many months. Home of one of the 10 wealthiest men in the U.S. and guests such as Dwight D. Eisenhower, Byron Nelson, Conrad Hilton, Bob Hope, Bing Crosby, and most recently, the "Platters." Gazebo garden features symphonies and jazz bands. Four fireplaces, breakfast in room.

Hosts: Donna Gates
Rooms: 4 (2 PB; 2 SB) $69-129
Full Breakfast
Credit Cards: A, B
Notes: 2, 4, 5, 7, 9, 12, 14

House of Wadley

# Florida

# Florida

Amelia Island Williams House

## AMELIA ISLAND

### The Amelia Island Williams House

103 South 9th Street, 32034
(800) 414-9258; FAX (904) 321-1325
www.williamshouse.com

Winner of numerous national awards including "One of the Top 12 Inns of the Year" from *Country Inns* magazine and one of "Top 25 Inns of the South" from *National Geographic Traveler* magazine and named one of the "Most Romantic Inns in the Country" by *USA Today*. This 140-year-old antebellum mansion offers every possible amenity to please its guests. Eight magnificent rooms decorated in the style of different countries, with antiques dating from the 1600s. Jacuzzis, two-person showers, claw-foot soaking tubs, TVs, formal and informal gardens, and 240 feet of wicker-filled verandas.

Hosts: Dick Flitz and Chris Carter
Rooms: 8 (PB) $145-210
Full Breakfast
Credit Cards: A, B
Notes: 2, 5, 9, 10, 11, 12, 14, 15

### The Bailey House

28 South 7th Street, Fernandina Beach, 32034
(904) 261-5390

Completed in 1895, this fine old home is an outstanding example of the Queen Anne style. Filled with a vast collection of carefully chosen period antiques collected across the nation. The guest rooms are furnished with authentic antique furniture and decorator pieces, yet offer the modern conveniences of a private bath. Central heat and air for year-round comfort. Near Fort Clinch State Park, horseback riding, and beautiful beaches. Come enjoy the charm and history of this beautiful turn-of-the-century home and relax in the ambiance of a bygone era. In consideration of all guests, the hosts must say no to pets and children under eight years of age.

Hosts: Tom and Jenny Bishop
Rooms: 10 (PB) $105-160
Full Breakfast
Credit Cards: A, B, C
Notes: 2, 5, 7, 10, 11, 12

The Bailey House

NOTES: Credit cards accepted: A MasterCard; B Visa; C American Express; D Discover; E Diner's Club; F Other; 2 Personal checks accepted; 3 Lunch available; 4 Dinner available; 5 Open all year; 6 Pets welcome; 7 No smoking; 8 Children welcome; 9 Social drinking allowed; 10 Tennis nearby; 11 Swimming nearby; 12 Golf nearby; 13 Skiing nearby; 14 May be booked through a travel agent; 15 Handicapped accessible.

## 1857 Florida House Inn

22 South Third Street, 32034
(904) 261-3300; (800) 258-3301
e-mail: innkeepers@floridahouseinn.com
www.floridahouseinn.com

On Amelia Island in the heart of the 50-block historic district of Fernandina. Built in 1857 as a tourist hotel; today's guests can enjoy the same large porches and 15 rooms, some with fireplaces, all with private baths. Country pine and oak antiques, cheerful handmade rugs and quilts found in each room. Airport pickup available; bikes; fax machine; handicapped access.

Hosts: Bob and Karen Warner
Rooms: 15 (PB)
Full Breakfast
Credit Cards: A, B, C
Notes: 2, 3, 4, 5, 6, 7, 8, 9, 10, 11, 12, 14, 15

## The Fairbanks House

227 South Seventh Street, 32034
(904) 277-0500; (800) 261-4838

Elegant 1885 Italianate villa in Fernandina Beach. The mansion, its cottages, and swimming pool are on a full manicured acre in the historic district. Upscale rooms and suites are decorated with antiques, period pieces, and oriental rugs. All rooms have private baths, telephones, cable TV, and coffee makers. Full gourmet breakfast each morning, complimentary social hour each evening. Off-street parking and walking distance to shops and

Fairbanks House

restaurants. Completely non-smoking property, including grounds.

Hosts: Bill and Theresa Hamilton
Rooms: 12 (PB) $150-250
Full Breakfast
Credit Cards: A, B, C, D
Notes: 2, 5, 7, 9, 10, 11, 12, 14

## The 1735 House

584 South Fletcher Avenue, Fernandina Beach, 32034
(800) 872-8531; FAX (904) 261-9200
www.ameliaisland-fla.com/1735house/

Telephone jacks are installed, but unless requested, no telephones can be found in this unique bed and breakfast inn, the 1735 House. A New England style seaside inn, it offers one- or two-bedroom suites furnished in nautical decor with separate living and dining rooms and private baths. Guests are greeted with homemade Continental breakfast, complete with a complimentary newspaper, delivered to guests' suite in an antique wicker picnic basket. Amelia Island Lodging prides itself on providing the red carpet treatment to each of its guests. With no minimum length of stay required, guests can indulge economically in their fantasy vacation by visiting the unspoiled paradise that is Amelia Island.

Rooms: 6 (PB) $100-160
Continental Breakfast
Credit Cards: A, B, C, D, E, F
Notes: 2, 5, 7, 8, 9, 10, 11, 12, 14

# ARCADIA

## Historic Parker House

427 West Hickory Street, 34266-3703
(941) 494-2499; (800) 969-2499

The Historic Parker House, circa 1895, immediately transports guests back to a simpler, yet grander time. This 6,000-square-foot home is chock full of Victorian antiques, a wonderful clock collection, and bits of Florida's past. Within walking distance is downtown Arca-

Historic Parker House

dia's antique district, the Peace River for canoeing and fishing, and all of south-central Florida's attractions are nearby. Relax out back under the oak trees with the hosts as the garden railroad entertains guests before retiring to their elegantly furnished rooms.

Hosts: Bob and Shelly Baumann
Rooms: 4 (2 PB; 2 SB) $65-85
Continental Breakfast
Credit Cards: A, B, C
Notes: 2, 5, 7, 9, 10, 12, 14

# BROOKSVILLE

## Verona House Bed & Breakfast

201 South Main Street, 34601
(352) 796-4001; (800) 355-6717
FAX (352) 799-0612
www.bbhost.com/veronabb/

The Verona House is a unique 1925 Sears, Roebuck and Company catalog house in downtown

Verona House

Brooksville, among the rolling hills and the large oak tree-canopied streets of a historical town established in 1856. A truly cozy and quiet getaway with Jan's special baked casserole, fruit, and southern hospitality for breakfast. All four rooms, with queen-size beds and private baths are furnished in a warm atmosphere of antiques and collectible pieces. Proud to be in the National Register of Historic Places.

Hosts: Bob and Jan Boyd
Rooms: 4 (PB) $65-80
Full Breakfast
Credit Cards: A, B, C, D
Notes: 2, 5, 7, 8, 9, 10, 12, 14, 15

# CAPE CANAVERAL

## Beachside Bed & Breakfast

629 Adams Avenue, 32920
(407) 799-4320

See a space launch from the beach. The ocean is only a few yards from the guest suite with private entrance, bedroom with twin beds, one and one-half private baths, living room, and kitchen stocked for breakfast, which guests can enjoy at their leisure. Port Canaveral and Kennedy Space Center are minutes away. Walt Disney World and Orlando are just an hour's drive. Orlando International Airport (45 minutes) shuttle service available.

Hosts: Tony and Dorothy Dean Saccaro
Suite: 1 (PB) $65
Continental Breakfast
Credit Cards: None
Notes: 2, 5, 7, 9, 10, 11, 12

# CEDAR KEY

## The Island Hotel

P.O. Box 460, 32625
(352) 543-5111; (800) 432-4640
e-mail: ishotel@islandhotel-cedarkey.com
www.islandhotel-cedarkey.com

This pre-Civil War building with Jamaican-style architecture is rustic and authentic, with

7 No smoking; 8 Children welcome; 9 Social drinking allowed; 10 Tennis nearby; 11 Swimming nearby; 12 Golf nearby; 13 Skiing nearby; 14 May be booked through a travel agent; 15 Handicapped accessible.

The Island Hotel

much of the original structure. In the National Register of Historic Places. Gourmet seafood dining room, serving local Cedar Key specialties. Like stepping back in time, with muraled walls, paddle fans, French doors, and a wide wraparound porch which catches gulf breezes. A cozy lounge bar completes a perfect place to get away from it all. No smoking in bedrooms. Inquire about children being welcome.

Hosts: Dawn and Tony Cousins
Rooms: 13 (11 PB; 2 S1B) 75-120
Full Breakfast
Credit Cards: A, B, D
Notes: 4, 5, 9, 11, 12

## DAYTONA BEACH

### The Coquina Inn Bed & Breakfast

544 South Palmetto Avenue, 32114
(904) 254-4969; e-mail: coquinaBnB@aol.com

This charming coquina and cream-stucco house was built in 1912 in the old Daytona his-

The Coquina Inn

toric section, just south of the Beach Street business district. It sits on a tranquil shady street half-a-block west of the Halifax River. Five minutes to the beach. Beach cruiser bikes are available at no charge. Outdoor garden spa under a Victorian gazebo. An hour drive to Orlando, St. Augustine, or Cape Kennedy. Rates are slightly higher during special events.

Hosts: Ann Christoffersen and Dennis Haight
Rooms: 4 (PB) $80-110
Full Breakfast
Credit Cards: A, B, C
Notes: 2, 5, 7, 8, 9, 10, 11, 12

Live Oak Inn

### Live Oak Inn

444-448 South Beach, 32114
(904) 252-4667; (800) 881-4667

Relax and romance at one of Florida's top 10 historic inns. Live Oak Inn offers the best of Daytona. The restful atmosphere of the Intracoastal Waterway and the excitement of "the World's Most Famous Beach" only a mile away. In the historic district, guests are able to escape into the leisurely pace of days gone by. Twelve guest rooms with their own private baths, TVs, VCRs, and telephones. Some include balconies and in-room Jacuzzis. Enjoy lunch and dinner in the casual fine-dining restaurant.

Hosts: Del and Jessie Glock
Rooms: 12 (PB) $80-150
Continental Breakfast
Credit Cards: A, B
Notes: 2, 3, 4, 5, 9, 10, 11, 12, 14

NOTES: Credit cards accepted: A MasterCard; B Visa; C American Express; D Discover; E Diner's Club; F Other; 2 Personal checks accepted; 3 Lunch available; 4 Dinner available; 5 Open all year; 6 Pets welcome;

## The Villa Bed & Breakfast

801 North Peninsula Drive, 32118
(904) 248-2020

Private gated estate. Elegant accommodations in a historic Spanish mansion in the heart of Daytona Beach. Decorated with fine antiques, this lovely inn has richly detailed public areas, a formal living room, dining and breakfast rooms, and a library/entertainment room. Private walled flower gardens, the pool, and the sunning area. Guests are within walking distance of Daytona's famous beach, restaurants, shopping, nightlife, and the boardwalk and arcade area.

Host: Jim Camp
Rooms: 4 (PB) $90-170
Continental Breakfast
Credit Cards: A, B, C
Notes: 5, 7, 10, 11, 12, 14

Henderson Park Inn

conies and baths, some of which have Jacuzzis. Southern beachside breakfast, beach service, maid service, turndown service, room service, evening happy hour, heated pool, veranda, palm grove, and restaurant.

Host: Susie Nunnelley
Rooms: 20 (PB) $94-289
Full Breakfast
Credit Cards: A, B, C, D
Notes: 2, 3, 4  5, 9, 10, 11, 12, 14, 15

The Villa

## DESTIN

## Henderson Park Inn— A Beachside Bed & Breakfast

2700 Highway 98E-Beach Route, 32541
(800) 336-4853; www.hendersonparkinn.com

Destin's first and only beachside bed and breakfast combines the charm of a Queen Anne-style inn with the amenities of a modern resort. The perfect place for couples and romantics; rooms are decorated with cozy impressionistic themes, antique hand-crafted reproductions, high ceilings; some rooms have fireplaces and four-poster beds, private bal-

## DUNEDIN

## J. O. Douglas House

209 Scotland Street, 34698
(813) 735-9006; FAX (813) 736-0626
e-mail: hudson19@ix.netcom.com
www.jodouglashouse.com

Built in 1878, the J. O. Douglas House is the oldest home in historic Dunedin. This fully restored Victorian home is furnished with antiques and is listed in the National Register of Historic Places. A large swimming pool, hot

J. O. Douglas House

7 No smoking; 8 Children welcome; 9 Social drinking allowed; 10 Tennis nearby; 11 Swimming nearby; 12 Golf nearby; 13 Skiing nearby; 14 May be booked through a travel agent; 15 Handicapped accessible.

tub, and screened porch are available for relaxation. Smoke-free establishment. Walk to the marina, shops, galleries, restaurants. Biking, boating, and blading on the 42-mile Pinellas Trail. Continental plus breakfast served.

Hosts: Jeffrey and Sherril Melio
Rooms: 5 (1 PB; 4 SB) $85-110
Continental Breakfast
Credit Cards: A, B
Notes: 2, 5, 7, 9, 10, 11, 12, 15

## EVERGLADES CITY

### The Ivey House Bed & Breakfast

107 Camellia Street, P.O. Box 5038, 34139
(941) 695-3299; FAX (941) 695-4155
e-mail: sandee@iveyhouse.com
www.iveyhouse.com

This quaint bed and breakfast is for those who want to explore the Everglades National Park without leaving the comforts of home. There are 10 air-conditioned rooms with shared bathrooms and a large living room that includes an Everglades-area library. Cottage with private bath also available. Smoking and drinking are allowed only on the outside porches. Guided adventures, including canoeing, kayaking, boating, and sea shelling, are provided daily. Also available are canoe, kayak, and skiff rentals (bikes are complimentary for guests).

Hosts: The Harraden Family
Rooms: 11 (1 PB; 10 SB) $50-85
Full Breakfast
Credit Cards: A, B
Notes: 2, 3, 4, 7, 8, 10, 11, 14

## FORT LAUDERDALE

### Phoenix South Guest House

3609 NE 27th Street, 33308
(954) 733-7701 (Monday through Saturday)
(954) 563-6665 (Sundays and evenings)
FAX (954) 739-0282
e-mail: info@beachguesthouse.com
www.beachguesthouse.com

Phoenix South Guest House

Each guest apartment includes a queen-size bed, private bath, living area, kitchen, and upper patio terrace with beach access just footsteps away. At the Phoenix Guest House guests can enjoy warm sunny days and heavenly ocean breezes that rival any tropical paradise. World-class deep-sea fishing, scuba diving, sailing, or just basking in the sun are just some of activities available. Night-life and fine dining abound and are within walking distance. Take an early evening water taxi tour of the Intracoastal Waterway. Whatever guests decide to do, the friendly proprietors at the Phoenix Guest House will make sure a guest's stay will be a memorable one and they will leave wanting to come back soon. Continental breakfast is optional.

Hosts: Sandra and Tony
Apartments: 5 (PB) $125-175
Continental Breakfast
Credit Cards: None
Notes: 2, 5, 7, 11, 12, 13, 14

## FORT PIERCE

### The Mellon Patch Inn

3601 North A1A, 34949
(561) 461-5231; (800) 656-7824
www.sunet.net/mlnptch

Escape to a beach setting. "Let us pamper you." Wake up to freshly ground coffee and a full gourmet breakfast. The ocean is just across the street. Explore the parks and nature preserve. Play tennis, golf, and bicycle. Canoe and fish from the dock. Poke through little-known galleries and shop for antiques. Relax in the spa. Read while relaxing in the ham-

NOTES: Credit cards accepted: A MasterCard; B Visa; C American Express; D Discover; E Diner's Club; F Other; 2 Personal checks accepted; 3 Lunch available; 4 Dinner available; 5 Open all year; 6 Pets welcome;

mock or the swing. Two hours from Orlando and Pompano Beach.

Hosts: Andrea and Arthur Mellon
Rooms: 4 (PB) $85-140
Full Breakfast
Credit Cards: A, B, C, D
Notes: 2, 3, 5, 7, 9, 10, 11, 12, 14, 15

## HOMESTEAD

### Room at the Inn Bed & Breakfast

15830 SW 240 Street, 33031
(305) 246-0492; FAX (305) 246-0590

Room at the Inn Bed and Breakfast is a charming, relaxing retreat on two acres in the agricultural/grove area five miles north of Homestead and two miles west of US 1. From its convenient central location, guests can, within minutes, be exploring Everglades National Park, venturing into the Florida Keys, watching an exciting race at the Homestead Motorsports Complex, or relaxing in the pool and spa. Guests are invited to pick luscious tropical fruit in season. Visit one of the wonderful ethnic restaurants in the area for dinner, or use the back yard barbecue to do-it-yourself. Smoking permitted in designated areas only.

Host: Sally Robinson
Rooms: 4 (3 PB; 1 SB) $85-110
Full Breakfast
Credit Cards: None
Notes: 2, 5, 9, 10, 11, 12

## JACKSONVILLE

### Club Continental Suites

2143 Astor Street, P.O. Box 7059, Orange Park, 32073
(904) 264-6070; (800) 877-6070

The Club Continental Suites is a Mediterranean-style inn overlooking the broad St. Johns River, featuring romantic Continental

Club Continental Suites

dining with "Old Florida charm." The Club, built in 1923 as the Palmolive family estate, now hosts 22 river-view suites with expansive grounds, giant live oaks, lush gardens, and the pre-Civil War Riverhouse Pub with live entertainment. Sunday brunch available. Lunch and dinner available Tuesday through Friday. Inquire about accommodations for pets. Non-smoking rooms available.

Hosts: Caleb Massee and Karrie Stevens
Rooms: 22 (PB) $65-160
Continental Breakfast
Credit Cards: A, B, C, D, E
Notes: 2, 5, 8, 9, 10, 11, 12, 14, 15

### House on Cherry Street

1844 Cherry Street, 32205
(904) 384-1999; FAX (904) 384-5013
e-mail: houseoncherry@compuserve.com

Historic restored home on the St. Johns River near downtown Jacksonville features antiques, wine, snacks, and canoe, kayak, and bicycles for guest use. Children over nine welcome.

Host: Carol Anderson
Rooms: 4 (PB) $38.99-123.90
Continental Breakfast
Credit Cards: A, B, C
Notes: 2, 5, 7, 9, 10, 12, 14

---

7 No smoking; 8 Children welcome; 9 Social drinking allowed; 10 Tennis nearby; 11 Swimming nearby; 12 Golf nearby; 13 Skiing nearby; 14 May be booked through a travel agent; 15 Handicapped accessible.

## JUPITER

### *Innisfail*

17576 Bridle Court, 33478
(561) 744-5902; FAX (561) 744-3387
e-mail: kathie@vannoorden.com

Innisfail, in the farms of Jupiter, is a gracious
new home, framed with royal palms and pal-
mettos. Start the day with a dip in the heated
pool and enjoy a leisurely Continental breakfast on the lanai. Browse through the VanNoorden gallery or stroll out to the studio to observe
the sculpture studio in action. It helps to be a
pet lover as Innisfail is home to three royal
standard poodles and three cats. Children over
10 welcome. One night surcharge of $10.

Host: Katherine VanNoorden
Rooms: 2 (PB) $85-95
Continental Breakfast
Credit Cards: None
Notes: 2, 5, 7, 9, 10, 11, 12

Innisfail

## KEY WEST

### *Artist House Key West*

534 Eaton Street, 33040
(800) 582-7882; FAX (305) 296-3977
e-mail: artisthse@aol.com

World-famous Victorian mansion; elegant and
spacious rooms filled with antiques. Steps from
Key West's famous nightlife, restaurants, and
water attractions. Private baths, verandas, fireplaces, and intimate lush garden with fountain
whirlpool await. Continental plus breakfast
daily. Concierge service, unbeatable downtown
location and sparkling clean inside and out.

Hosts: Jim Davidzik and Mike Wright
Rooms: 6 (PB) $125-199

Artist House

Continental Breakfast
Credit Cards: A, B, C, D
Notes: 5, 7, 9, 10, 11, 14

### *Center Court*
### *Historic Inn & Cottages*

916 Center Street, 33040
(305) 296-9292; (800) 797-8787
FAX (305) 294-4104
www.centercourtkw.com

One-half block off famous Duval Street in the
very center of historic Old Town. Nestled in
lush tropical gardens, the beautifully renovated
1874 shipbuilder's home and cigar maker's
cottage are uniquely furnished with original
art, sculpture, and photos, air conditioning,
ceiling fan, cable TV, in-room safe, telephone,
and hair dryer. The guest house and cottages
surround the heated pool, Jacuzzi, exercise
pavilion, fish and lily pond, and gardens, which
extend along Center Street. Complimentary
evening happy hour.

Host: Naomi Van Steelandt
Rooms and Cottages: 18 (PB) $88-338
Continental Breakfast
Credit Cards: A, B, C, D
Notes: 2, 5, 6, 7, 8, 9, 10, 11, 12, 14, 15

---

NOTES: Credit cards accepted: A MasterCard; B Visa; C American Express; D Discover; E Diner's Club;
F Other; 2 Personal checks accepted; 3 Lunch available; 4 Dinner available; 5 Open all year; 6 Pets welcome;

Curry Mansion Inn

## Curry Mansion Inn

511 Caroline Street, 33040
(305) 294-5349; (800) 253-3466
FAX (305) 294-4093
e-mail: frontdesk@currymansion.com
www.currymansion.com

The Curry Mansion is an exquisitely restored Victorian landmark with beautiful modern guest rooms with private baths, air conditioning, ceiling fans, handmade quilts, telephones, and refrigerators. It is in the heart of Old Town Key West, steps from every attraction and 34 splendid restaurants. Complimentary Continental plus breakfast, cocktail party,. parking, laundry equipments, local calls, beach club. Inquire about accommodations for pets.

Rooms: 28 (PB) $140-274
Continental Breakfast
Credit Cards: A, B, C, D, E
Notes: 2, 5, 8, 9, 10, 11, 12, 14, 15

## The Cypress House

601 Caroline Street, 33040
(305) 294-6969; (800) 525-2488
FAX (305) 296-1174; e-mail: cypress@conch.net
www.cypresshousekw.com

Affordable luxury just one block from Duval Street. Grand Bahamian mansion, listed in the National Register of Historic Places. Spacious rooms feature air conditioning, color cable TV, telephone, and Bahama ceiling fans. A Continental plus breakfast is served daily. Lush tropical garden features a 40-foot lap pool and second-floor sun deck. Afternoon happy hour.

Free parking nearby for registered guests. Two blocks to historic seaport.

Host: Dave Taylor
Rooms: 16 (10 PB; 6 SB) $79-250
Continental Breakfast
Credit Cards: A, B, C, D
Notes: 5, 9 10, 14

## Duval House

815 Duval Street, 33040
(305) 294-1666; (800) 22 DUVAL
FAX (305) 292-1701

This beautifully restored century-old Victorian house has a special charm and deluxe amenities. Enjoy the swimming pool and quiet tropical gardens. Walk to any one of the many nearby restaurants and attractions. AAA- and Mobil Travel Guide-approved.

Host: Sarah Goldstein
Rooms: 28 (PB) $90-300
Continental Breakfast
Credit Cards: A, B, C, D, E
Notes: 5, 9, 10, 11, 12, 14

Duval House

## Heron House

512 Simonton Street, 33040
(305) 294-9227; (300) 294-1644
FAX (305) 294-5692

Key West's Heron House offers a refreshing new alternative. It has all of the intimacy of a quaint Key West guest house and all of the style of a small luxury hotel. Local artists have painstakingly handcrafted each room. Oak,

Heron House

redwood, and cedar adorn the walls of the guest rooms. Enjoy the coolness of Italian tile and marble under one's feet. Rest on huge oak beds as the morning sunlight filters through hand-crafted stained-glass transoms. Turn-down service, full concierge, morning newspaper, orchid gardens and tours, robes, and much more express a genuine caring. Everyone is treated as a friend. Rated four diamond by AAA.

Hosts: Fred Geibelt and Robert Framarin
Rooms: 23 (PB) $110.39-366.84
Continental Breakfast
Credit Cards: A, B, C, E
Notes: 5, 7, 9, 10, 11, 12, 14

## The Island City House Hotel

411 William Street, 33040
(305) 294-5702; (800) 634-8230
www.islandcityhouse.com

Three historic Victorian guest houses joined by brick pathways winding through a lush tropical garden. In the heart of Old Town Key West, this unique hotel offers one and two-bedroom parlor suites appointed with antiques, private baths, and shaded porches. Pool, Jacuzzi, widow's walk and complimentary Continental breakfast. Children welcome.

Hosts: Stanley and Janet Corneal
Rooms: 24 (PB) $95-225
Continental Breakfast
Credit Cards: A, B, C, D, E, F
Notes: 5, 8, 9, 10, 11, 12, 14

## Key West Bed & Breakfast— The Popular House

415 William Street, 33040
(305) 296-7274; (800) 438-6155
FAX (305) 293-0306; www.keywestbandb.com

The Key West Bed and Breakfast (circa 1898) is one of the oldest and more established guest houses in Old Town. On a quiet tree-lined street this historically registered Victorian is only three blocks from all Duval Street has to offer. With over a 20-year history in Key West, it houses an extensive collection of local art, and guests can learn about the folklore and the hidden Key West, the outrageous, the creative, and the truly laid back. Complimentary Continental plus breakfast at guests' leisure. Smoking permitted in designated areas only.

Host: Jody Carlson
Rooms: 8 (5 PB; 3 SB) $59-250
Continental Breakfast
Credit Cards: A, B, C
Notes: 5, 9, 10, 11, 12, 13

## The Paradise Inn

819 Simonton Street, 33040
(305) 293-8007; (800) 888-9648
FAX (305) 293-0807

In historic Old Town, just one block from Duval Street. Eighteen island-inspired luxury suites and one- and two-bedroom cottages with private marble baths, air conditioning, telephones, TVs, safes, bathrobes, and concierge services. Outdoor heated pool and Jacuzzi in a secluded, lushly landscaped tropical courtyard. Congenial multilingual staff. Convenient secured on-premise parking. Beaches, shopping, dining, and entertainment all within walking distance. Children over seven welcome.

Host: Shel Segel
Rooms: 18 (PB) $165-315
Continental Breakfast
Credit Cards: A, B, C, D, E
Notes: 5, 9, 10, 11, 12, 14, 15

NOTES: Credit cards accepted: A MasterCard; B Visa; C American Express; D Discover; E Diner's Club; F Other; 2 Personal checks accepted; 3 Lunch available; 4 Dinner available; 5 Open all year; 6 Pets welcome;

## Treetop Inn Historic Bed & Breakfast

806 Truman Avenue, 33040
(305) 293-0712; (800) 926-0712
FAX (305) 294-3668

Built at the turn of the century, Treetop Inn has been restored to provide modern comforts in a 1900s setting. It received the 1994 Key West Chamber of Commerce's Business for Beauty award. In central Old Town, Treetop Inn is within walking distance of beaches, restaurants, and shops. The hosts are knowledgeable about all Key West activities. The spacious rooms are graciously furnished and include private baths, cable TV, air conditioning, refrigerators, and telephones. A poolside breakfast is served.

Hosts: Sue and Fred Leake
Rooms: 3 (PB) $98-178
Full Breakfast
Credit Cards: A, B
Notes: 5, 7, 9, 10, 11, 12

## Whispers Bed & Breakfast Inn

409 William Street, 33040
(305) 294-5969; (800) 856-SHHH
FAX (305) 294-3899

The owner-managers take great pride in the service, hospitality, and romance of their historic 1866 inn. Each room is appointed with antiques. Included in the room rate is a full gourmet breakfast served in the tropical gardens and membership at a local beach club and health spa. Hot tub and sun deck on premises. Inquire about children.

Host: John Marburg
Rooms: 7 (PB) $80-175
Full Breakfast
Credit Cards: A, B, C, D
Notes: 2, 5, 7, 9, 10, 11, 12, 14

## The Wicker Guest House: An Island Bed & Breakfast

913 Duval Street, 33040
(305) 296-4275; (800) 880-4275
FAX (305) 294-7240

This spacious complex of six houses, 21 rooms, on colorful Duval Street, has been family owned and operated since 1984. The main house dates to 1890 and the guest house is within easy walking distance to all downtown attractions. A large variety of affordable accommodations is offered. Most rooms include kitchenettes and cable TV, off-street parking, and full concierge service on the property. A delicious Continental breakfast is served poolside in the lovely, tranquil tropical garden. Boasting the friendliest and most helpful staff. Families are always welcome.

Hosts: Mark and Libby Curtis
Rooms: 21 (18 PB: 3 SB) $63-205
Continental Breakfast
Credit Cards: A. B, C, D, E
Notes: 5, 8, 9, 10, 11, 12, 14, 15

## LAKE WALES

## Chalet Suzanne Country Inn & Restaurant

3800 Chalet Suzanne Drive, 33853-7060
(941) 676-6011; (800) 433-6011
FAX (941) 676-1814
e-mail: info@chaletsuzanne.com
www.chaletsuzanne.com

Discover Europe in the heart of Florida. Bordered by fragrant orange groves, this historic 30-room family-run inn has become an oasis for travelers, weary executives, and discriminating diners. The award-winning dining room is now open daily, including Mondays. Be sure

---

7 No smoking; 8 Children welcome; 9 Social drinking allowed; 10 Tennis nearby; 11 Swimming nearby; 12 Golf nearby; 13 Skiing nearby; 14 May be booked through a travel agent; 15 Handicapped accessible.

Chalet Suzanne

home provides a perfect backdrop for the small wedding or reception, corporate retreat, or romantic getaway. Bass fishing guide service also available.

Hosts: Jim and Kathy Dowling
Rooms: 5 (3 PB; 2 SB) $85-115
Continental Breakfast
Credit Cards: A, B
Notes: 2, 5, 7, 8, 9, 10, 12, 13

to ask about the Sunset Serenade summer packages.

Hosts: Vita Hinshaw and Family
Rooms: 30 (PB) $159-219
Full Breakfast
Credit Cards: A, B, C, D, E, F
Notes: 2, 3, 4, 5, 8, 9, 10, 11, 12, 14, 15

## The G.V. Tillman House Bed & Breakfast

301 East Sessoms Avenue, 33853-3789
(941) 676-5499 (phone/FAX); (800) 488-3315
e-mail: tillmanbb@aol.com
www.tillmanbb.com

The G.V. Tillman House, built in 1914, was the original home of Mr. George Vernon Tillman. Guests are invited to a traditional tea which may be enjoyed on the veranda overlooking Crystal Lake. Delightful feather beds and a bountiful breakfast, along with comfortable period antiques and turndown service are just a few of the amenities available. This historic

G.V. Tillman House

## LAKE WORTH

## Mango Inn Bed & Breakfast

128 North Lakeside Drive, 33460
(561) 533-6900 (phone/FAX); (888) 626-4619
www.mangoinn.com

The inn is a short 10-minute walk to the white sandy beaches of the Atlantic Ocean. Amenities include a heated pool, bicycles, guest rooms with central air conditioning, cable TV, refrigerators, private baths, queen-size beds, designer monogrammed bed linens, and plump down pillows. Deep-sea fishing, golfing, snorkeling, scuba-diving are within minutes of the inn. Two blocks from historic downtown Lake Worth, burgeoning with antique shops, art galleries, and sidewalk cafes. Ten minutes from Palm Beach International Airport and Palm Beach.

Hosts: Erin and Bo Allen
Rooms: 8 (PB) $65-145
Full and Continental Breakfast
Credit Cards: A, B, C, D, E
Notes: 5, 7, 9, 10, 11, 12, 14

## MIAMI

## Redland's Bed & Breakfast

19521 SW 128 Court, 33177
(305) 238-5285

The romantic tropical guest house is 750 square feet with a fully furnished kitchen, living room, bedroom, and private bath. It sleeps four (two private) and has private entrance, TV, air conditioning, pool, and Jacuzzi. Self-catered breakfast can be enjoyed poolside or at the garden gazebo. Bicycles also available for the nearby bike trails. Near Miami's farming community, 25 minutes from Florida Keys and Miami International Airport.

Hosts: Marianne and Tim Hamilton
Rooms: 1 (PB) $55
Continental Breakfast
Credit Cards: None
Notes: 2, 5, 7, 8, 9, 10, 11, 12

## MICANOPY

### Herlong Mansion

402 Northeast Cholokka Boulevard, P.O. Box 667, 32667
(352) 466-3322; (800) HERLONG

"Micanopy is the prettiest town in Florida. The Herlong Mansion is its crown jewel"—*Florida Trend*, November 1989. The brick Greek Revival structure has four Corinthian columns, 10 fireplaces, six different types of wood, and is decorated in period antiques. Built in 1845 and 1910, the three-story house has 12 bedrooms, all with private baths, on two acres with moss-draped oaks, pecans, dogwoods, and magnolias.

Host: H. C. "Sony" Howard Jr.
Rooms: 12 (PB) $80-175
Full Breakfast
Credit Cards: A, B
Notes: 2, 5, 7, 8, 9, 12, 14, 15

Herlong Mansion

## MOUNT DORA

The Emerald Hill Inn

### The Emerald Hill Inn

27751 Lake Jem Road, 32757
(352) 383-2777; (800) 366-9387
e-mail: Emeral hill@aol.com

On a country road in a natural, Old Florida setting, is this serene, sprawling 1941 lakefront estate amidst orange groves, on more than two acres with tall oaks, Spanish moss, broad sweeping lawn down to lake. Resembling a lodge, the stunning living room has a majestic coquina rock fireplace, wood cathedral ceiling, polished oak floors. Lake-view rooms have patio, TV/VCR. Ten minutes to Mount Dora antique shops, restaurants, festivals. Forty-five minutes to Orlando/Disney attractions. Many area lakes for water sports, boat cruises. AAA three-diamond rating. Children over 10 welcome.

Rooms: 4 (PB) $99-149
Full Breakfast
Credit Cards: A, B  D
Notes: 5, 7, 9, 12, 14

### Farnsworth House Bed & Breakfast

1029 East 5th Avenue, 32757
(352) 735-1894

On one and one-half acres in the historic town of Mount Dora with its many boutiques and antique shops, this home was built in 1886.

7 No smoking; 8 Children welcome; 9 Social drinking allowed; 10 Tennis nearby; 11 Swimming nearby; 12 Golf nearby; 13 Skiing nearby; 14 May be booked through a travel agent; 15 Handicapped accessible.

Three suites and two efficiencies, each decorated in a unique theme with private bath and kitchen. Guests can enjoy the large screened porch, living and dining room, and hot tub enclosed within a screened gazebo. Twenty-five miles northwest of Orlando.

Hosts: Dick and Sandy Shelton
Rooms: 5 (PB) $90-125
Credit Cards: A, B, D
Notes: 2, 5, 7, 8, 9, 10, 11, 12, 14

Magnolia Inn

## Magnolia Inn

347 East Third Avenue, 32757
(800) 776-2112; e-mail: magnolia@cde.com
www.magnolia.cde.com

A grand, historic, walled estate, circa 1926, in beautiful downtown Mount Dora. An elegant, romantic inn to provide peace and renew relationships. Furnished in antiques and collectibles. Every detail for guests' comfort and enjoyment is provided including a Jacuzzi in the gazebo. Guests walk to town, lounge in a hammock, or swing under the majestic Magnolia tree.

Hosts: Dave and Betty Cook
Rooms: 5 (PB) $125-185
Full Breakfast
Credit Cards: A, B, C
Notes: 5, 7, 11, 12, 14

## OCALA

### Seven Sisters Inn

820 SE Fort King Street, 34471
(352) 867-1170; FAX (352) 867-5266

"Florida's Enchantress" named Inn of the Month by *Country Inns* magazine. Featured in *Southern Living*, these circa 1888 mansions are in the historic district of Ocala. Fifteen rooms feature king- and queen-size suites, fireplaces, canopied beds, private baths, soaking tubs, Jacuzzis. Award-winning gourmet breakfast and afternoon tea are included. Murder mysteries and candlelight dinners are available. Canoeing, golf, horseback riding, hiking, antiquing, and famous Silver Springs attractions nearby.

Hosts: Bonnie and Ken Oden
Rooms: 15 (PB) $105-165
Full Breakfast
Credit Cards: A, B, C, D
Notes: 2, 4, 5, 7, 9, 10, 11, 12, 14, 15

## ORLANDO

### The Veranda Bed & Breakfast

115 North Summerlin Avenue, 32801
(800) 420-6822; e-mail: verandaBnB@aol.com
www.theverandaBandB.com

An Orlando bed and breakfast in historic Thornton Park. Five charming buildings house 11 sophisticated accommodations. All of the rooms welcome leisure and business travelers with private entrances, bathrooms, cable TV, and telephones. Enjoy a Continental breakfast in the beautiful landscaped courtyards or pool and hot tub terrance. Walking distance to restaurants, park, night life, and shopping.

Rooms: 11 (PB) $99-199
Continental Breakfast
Credit Cards: A, B, C, E
Notes: 2, 5, 7, 9, 10, 11, 12, 14, 15

## ORLANDO/LAKE BUENA VISTA

### Perri House
### Bed & Breakfast Inn

10417 Centurion Court, 32836
(407) 876-4830; (800) 780-4830
FAX (407) 876-0241
www.perrihouse.com

NOTES: Credit cards accepted: A MasterCard; B Visa; C American Express; D Discover; E Diner's Club; F Other; 2 Personal checks accepted; 3 Lunch available; 4 Dinner available; 5 Open all year; 6 Pets welcome;

Perri House is a quiet, private, country estate inn secluded on 16 acres of land adjacent to the Walt Disney World Resort. Bird sanctuary project, bird feeders, bird house museum. Outstanding location! Five minutes to Disney World. Upscale Continental breakfast buffet, pool, hot tub. Eight guest "nests" with private bath, entrance, TV, telephone. Four bird house cottages by late 1999, featuring king-size canopied beds, whirlpool tubs for two. Three-, five-, seven-day vacation packages will be offered.

Hosts: Nick and Angi Perretti
Rooms: 8 (PB) $99-139
Cottages: $225-399
Continental Breakfast
Credit Cards: A, B, C, D, E
Notes: 2, 5, 7, 8, 9, 10, 12, 14, 15

## ORLANDO (WINTER GARDEN)

## Meadow Marsh
## Bed & Breakfast

940 Tildenville School Road, Winter Garden, 34787
(407) 656-2064; (888) 656-2064
www.bbonline.com/fl/meadowmarsh

For a wonderful treat, visit this romantic getaway where the hectic pace of today fades into the sweet peace of yesteryears. Just 15 minutes west of downtown Orlando this Victorian farmhouse sits on 12 acres of Old Florida. Huge oaks and stately palms filter sunlight to the spacious lawn below. A leisurely stroll across the meadow takes guests to a "rails-to-trails" path for biking, skating, or an early morning walk. Close to all central Florida attractions yet far enough away to provide a haven from the fast lane. Guests can enjoy two-person whirlpools in the suites and cottage or old-fashioned tubs and showers in the smaller bedrooms. Cozy fireplaces and heart-pine floors add to the warmth and beauty of this country estate. A lovely one-room cottage sits just behind the main house for those seeking privacy in their own "little house." Southern hospitality is offered by the native Floridian, Cavelle, and her "transplanted" husband, John.

Hosts: Cavelle and John Pawlack
Rooms: 2 (PB) $95-199
Suites: 2 (PB)
Garden Cottage: $199
Full Breakfast
Credit Cards: A, B
Notes: 5, 7, 12, 14

## PALM BAY

## Casa Del Sol

Country Estates, 232 Rheine Road Northwest, 32907
(407) 728-4676

This award-winning home is on Florida's central east coast. Breakfast is served on the lanai, with breathtaking foliage. From here see a spaceship launched. Enjoy the luxury of a Roman tub. Minutes away from the space pad, all Disney attractions, and the Marlins' winter quarters. Closed April 16 through November 7. Smoking permitted outside only.

Host: Stanley Finkelstein
Rooms: 3 (1 PB; 2 SB) $55-135
Full Breakfast
Credit Cards: None
Notes: 2, 7, 8, 9, 10, 11, 12, 13, 14, 15

Casa del Sol

## RUSKIN

## Ruskin House Bed & Breakfast

120 Dickman Drive SW, 33570
(813) 645-3842

In rural Hillsborough County within easy driving distance of Tampa, St. Petersburg, and Sarasota, this landmarked Victorian house

Ruskin House

features columned verandas and a tower, a massive dogleg staircase, a fireplace, hardwood floors, high ceilings, and original wall coloring. Every room is furnished with period antiques and oriental rugs; rocking chairs and a hammock grace the upper veranda. The house looks over the Ruskin Inlet, which winds around three acres of lawn, tropical glades, and flower gardens.

Hosts: Melanie Hubbard and Mac Miller
Rooms: 3 (PB) $75-110
Continental Breakfast
Credit Cards: A, B, C
Notes: 2, 5, 7, 8, 9, 11, 12, 14, 15

## ST. AUGUSTINE

### Casa de la Paz Bayfront Bed & Breakfast

22 Avenida Menendez, 32084
(904) 829-2915; (800) 929-2915
www.casadelapaz.com

Enjoy views of Matanzas Bay from the elegant guest rooms or the second-story veranda at this Mediterranean-style inn decorated with antique furnishings. From the veranda, an open stairway leads to a beautiful walled garden courtyard. The inn is central to all historic sites, fine restaurants, and miles of ocean beaches. Complimentary wines and a full buffet breakfast. AAA-rated three diamonds. Listed in the National Register of Historic Places.

Hosts: Bob and Donna Marriott
Rooms: 6 (PB) $95-205
Full Breakfast
Credit Cards: A, B, D
Notes: 2, 5, 7, 9, 10, 11, 12, 14

### Casa de Solana Bed & Breakfast Inn

21 Aviles Street, 32084-4441
(904) 824-3555; e-mail: solana@aug.com
www.oldcity.com/solana

A lovingly renovated Colonial home, circa 1763, is in the heart of St. Augustine's historical area within walking distance of restaurants, museums, and quaint shops. There are four antique-filled guest accommodations. All are suites; some have fireplaces, others have balconies that overlook the beautiful garden, and others have a breathtaking view of Matanzas Bay. All have private baths. Tariff includes a full breakfast served in the formal guest dining room, cable TV, chocolates, decanter of sherry.

Host: Fayé Lang-McMurry
Rooms: 4 (PB) $125-175
Full Breakfast
Credit Cards: A, B, C, D
Notes: 2, 5, 7, 9, 10, 11, 12, 13, 14

Casa de Solana

### Castle Garden

15 Shenandoah Street, 32084
(904) 829-3839; FAX (904) 829-9049
e-mail: castleg@aug.com
www.castlegarden.com

"Stay at a Castle and be treated like royalty!" Relax and enjoy the peace and quiet of royal treatment at this newly restored 100-year-old castle of Moorish Revival design. Awaken to the aroma of freshly baked goodies as hosts prepare a full mouth-watering country breakfast just like Mom used to make! This former Castle Warden carriage house boasts three beautiful bridal rooms with sunken beds, soothing in-room Jacuzzis, and cathedral ceilings. Amenities include complimentary wine or champagne, chocolates, and bicycles. Packages and specialty gift baskets available. Children five and older are welcome.

Hosts: Bruce Kloeckner and Kimmy Van Kooten
    Kloeckner
Rooms: 7 (PB) $79-155
Full Breakfast
Credit Cards: A, B, C, D
Notes: 2, 5, 7, 8, 10, 11, 12

## The Cedar House Inn

79 Cedar Street, 32084
(904) 829-0079; (800) CEDAR-INN
FAX (904) 825-0916; e-mail: russ@aug.com
www.cedarhouseinn.com

Capture romantic moments at this 1893 Victorian home in the heart of the ancient city. Escape into a Jacuzzi suite or an antique-filled bedroom with claw-foot tub or enjoy the parlor with its fireplace, player piano, and antique Victrola. Elegant full breakfast, complimentary

Cedar House

beverages, evening snack, convenient on-premises parking. Garden Jacuzzi and bicycles. Walk to all historic sites. Easy drive to I-95, Atlantic Ocean beaches, tennis, and golf. Midweek specials. AAA three-diamond-rated. Picnic lunches available.

Hosts: Nina and Russ Thomas
Rooms: 6 (PB) $74-155
Full Breakfast
Credit Cards: A, B, C, D
Notes: 2, 4, 5, 7, 9, 10, 11, 12, 14

Kenwood Inn

## The Kenwood Inn

38 Marine Street, 32084
(904) 824-2116; (800) 824-8151
FAX (904) 824-1689

Local maps and early records show the inn was built between 1865 and 1885 and was functioning as a private guest house as early as 1886. In the historic district, the inn is within walking distance of many fine restaurants and all historic sights. One block from the Intracoastal Waterway, with its passing fishing trawlers, yachts at anchor, and the classic Bridge of Lions. Beautiful ocean beaches are just across the bridge. Children over eight welcome. Reduced rates Sunday through Thursday.

Hosts: Mark Kerrianne and Caitlin Constant
Rooms: 14 (PB) $100-135
Suite: $135-175
Continental Breakfast
Credit Cards: A, B, D
Notes: 2, 5, 7, 9, 10, 11, 12

## Old Powder House Inn

38 Cordova Street, 32084
(904) 824-4149: (800) 447-4149
e-mail: ahowes@aug.com
www.oldpowderhouse.com

High ceilings and wraparound verandas distinguish this Victorian home built in 1899 on the
site of an 18th-century Spanish powder magazine. It's in the heart of the historic area with
horse and buggies going right past the house.
Restaurants, antique stores, and quaint shops
are within walking distance. Full gourmet
breakfast, sparkling juice, wine, and hors
d'oeuvres each day. Single and tandem bicycles available. In-ground Jacuzzi and on-site
parking. Weddings and special packages.

Hosts: Al and Eunice Howes
Rooms: 8 (PB) $79-189
Full Breakfast
Credit Cards: A, B, D
Notes: 2, 5, 7, 9, 10, 11, 12, 14

St. Francis Inn

and peacefulness of the inn itself, its location,
and the kind of guests it attracts are all strong
assets. Buffet breakfast served. Inquire about
accommodations for children.

Host: Joe Finnegan
Rooms: 14 (PB) $80-180
Full Breakfast
Credit Cards: A, B, C, D, E
Notes: 2, 5, 7, 9, 10 ,11, 12, 14, 15

## Southern Wind Inn
## Bed & Breakfast

18 Cordova Street, 32084
(904) 825-3623; (800) 871-781-3338
FAX (904) 810-5215; e-mail: swind@aug.com
www.southerwindinn.com

Surrender yourself to gracious Southern hospitality at the inn renowned for her turn-of-the-
century elegance. Southern Wind Inn is set in
the heart of historic St. Augustine, America's
oldest city founded in 1565. From the inn
guests can easily explore beautiful St. Augustine, tour famous landmarks, dine at fine
restaurants, and shop for antiques and other
treasures. Spend a day relaxing at nearby
beaches, golf, try your luck at deep-sea fishing,
or enjoy many other attractions and activities.
Inquire about accommodations for children.

Hosts: Bob and Alana Indelicato
Rooms: 10 (PB) $79-185
Full Breakfast
Credit Cards: A, B, D
Notes: 5, 7, 9, 10, 11, 12, 14

Old Powder House

## St. Francis Inn

279 St. George Street, 32084
(904) 824-6068; (800) 824-6062
FAX (904) 810-5525; www.stfrancisinn.com

The St. Francis Inn, in the historic district, was
built as a private home for a Spanish soldier in
1791. It is a Spanish Colonial structure with a
private courtyard, fireplaces, balconies, and the
modern additions of a swimming pool, telephones, and some whirlpool tubs. The warmth

NOTES: Credit cards accepted: A MasterCard; B Visa; C American Express; D Discover; E Diner's Club;
F Other; 2 Personal checks accepted; 3 Lunch available; 4 Dinner available; 5 Open all year; 6 Pets welcome;

## Victorian House Bed & Breakfast

11 Cadiz Street, 32084
(904) 824-5214; (877) 703-0432

In the heart of the historic district, the Victorian House was built in 1897 and has been restored and furnished in period antiques. Enjoy canopied beds, handwoven coverlets, quilts, stenciled walls, and hand-hooked rugs on heart-pine floors. Featured in *Country Home, Better Homes and Gardens, Southern Homes, Country Almanac*, and *Innsider* magazines. Guests are within walking distance of fine restaurants, the waterfront, shops, museums, and the plaza. Weekly and monthly rates are available upon request.

Host: Ken and Marcia Cerotzke
Room: 8 (PB) $95-135
Full Breakfast
Credit Cards: A, B, C
Notes: 2, 5, 7, 9, 10, 11, 12, 14

Westcott House

## Westcott House

146 Avenida Menendez, 32084
(904) 824-4301

One of St. Augustine's most elegant guest houses overlooking Matanzas Bay. Circa 1890, restored in 1983, in the historic area and within walking distance to historic sites. All rooms have private baths, king-size beds, cable TV, private telephones, and are furnished in antiques. Year-round climate control. Complimentary afternoon wine. One-half block from the city's yacht pier. Evening brandy, chocolates, pastries, and turndown service.

Hosts: Robert and Janice Graubard
Rooms: 9 (PB) $95-225
Continental Breakfast
Credit Cards: A, B, C, D
Notes: 5, 7, 10, 12

## ST. PETE BEACH

## Beach Haven Villas

4980 Gulf Boulevard, 33706
(727) 367-8642

Directly on the sparkling Gulf of Mexico, Beach Haven harkens back to the days when much of Florida offered vacationers colorful Art Deco-style motels. Still in pink, Beach Haven retains its charming personality, while providing updated interiors and furnishings. Close to shopping, dining, and entertainment. Add the peaceful setting, a gulf-front pool, and a sandy beachfront setting and guests will know why Beach Haven is so popular. Non-smoking units available.

Hosts: Jone and Millard Gamble
Rooms: 18 (PB) $67-137
Continental Breakfast
Credit Cards: A, B
Notes: 2, 5, 8, 9, 11, 12

Beach Haven Villas

7 No smoking; 8 Children welcome; 9 Social drinking allowed; 10 Tennis nearby; 11 Swimming nearby; 12 Golf nearby; 13 Skiing nearby; 14 May be booked through a travel agent; 15 Handicapped accessible.

Island's End Resort

## Island's End Resort

1 Pass-A-Grille Way, 33706
(727) 360-5023; FAX (813) 367-7890

At the southernmost tip of St. Pete Beach, Island's End has a combination of sand, sea, and sky creating a unique atmosphere of rustic charm among gray weathered cottages. Experience the brilliant sunrises while sipping freshly squeezed orange juice. Later, enjoy the spectacular sunsets so famous along the Florida Suncoast. All cottages have modern kitchens and bathrooms. Furnishings are contemporary and extremely comfortable. Quality accommodations that enhance the beauty of the waterfront are at guests' disposal.

Hosts: Jone and Millard Gamble
Rooms: 6 (PB) $64-185
Continental Breakfast
Credit Cards: A, B
Notes: 2, 5, 8, 9, 11, 12

## ST. PETERSBURG

## Bay Gables Bed & Breakfast

340 Rowland Court, 33701
(813) 822-8855; (800) 822-8803
FAX (813) 824-7223; e-mail: solomio@msn.com

Nestled behind the tranquil garden and gazebo lies Bay Gables Bed and Breakfast, a three-story Key West-style building with nine spacious rooms that will suit guests' every need. Cheerfully decorated with antiques and an attention to detail, all rooms have private baths and separate entrances from spacious, covered, wide porches. A delicious Continental breakfast is offered in the breakfast room, garden, verandas or porches, or may be enjoyed in the privacy of the guest's room. Just one-half block from the bay, shopping, parks, and major museum.

Rooms: 9 (PB) $85-165
Continental Breakfast
Credit Cards: A, B
Notes: 2, 5, 7, 8, 10, 11, 12, 14, 15

## Mansion House

105 Fifth Avenue NE, 33701
(813) 821-9391 (phone/FAX); (800) 274-7520
e-mail: mansion1@ix.netcom.com
www.mansionbandb.com

Historic, award-winning Mansion House is the premier bed and breakfast in St. Petersburg. It has two Arts and Crafts-style homes separated by a lovely garden/courtyard and swimming pool/Jacuzzi area. All rooms have comfy beds, handmade bedding, private baths, cable TV; telephones with data ports. An ideal spot for business or leisure travelers; can host small, focus groups meetings; weddings and receptions, family reunions, and other large gatherings. Packages available. Boat cruises available with Robert Ray on Aussie Spirit. InnPoints airline/lodging incentive awards given. Portuguese, French, Czech, and Spanish spoken. Concierge services. Free use of beach amenities; bikes available. Complimentary wine, cheese, soft drinks, and snacks. AAA-three-diamond- and ABBA-three-crown-rated.

Mansion House

NOTES: Credit cards accepted: A MasterCard; B Visa; C American Express; D Discover; E Diner's Club; F Other; 2 Personal checks accepted; 3 Lunch available; 4 Dinner available; 5 Open all year; 6 Pets welcome;

Hosts: Robert and Rose Marie Ray
Rooms: 12 (PB) $95-165
Carriage House: $125-165
Full Breakfast
Credit Cards: A, B, C
Notes: 2, 3, 4, 5, 7, 8, 9, 10, 11, 12, 14

## SANIBEL ISLAND

### Sanibel's Seaside Inn

541 East Gulf Drive, 33957
(941) 472-1400; (800) 831-7384 (reservations)

Sanibel's Seaside Inn, a cozy beachfront inn that exudes Old Florida charm, offers newly renovated studios, one-bedroom cottages and apartments, and a three-bedroom suite. Guests will enjoy such complimentary amenities as a heated pool, shuffleboard, bicycles, library of videos and books, a daily Continental breakfast, and outdoor barbecue grills.

Host: Jack Reed
Rooms: 32 (PB) $150-350
Continental Breakfast
Credit Cards: A, B, C, D, E
Notes: 2, 5, 8, 9, 10, 11, 12, 14, 15

### Sanibel's Song of the Sea

863 East Gulf Drive, 33957
(941) 472-2220; (800) 231-1045 (reservations)

Song of the Sea, Sanibel Island's romantic European-style seaside inn, features luxurious studios and one-bedroom suites, each with a

Sanibel's Song of the Sea

fully equipped kitchenette, microwave, color cable TV, and screened patios. Guests enjoy complimentary wine and fresh flowers upon arrival, a heated gulfside pool and whirlpool, natural sandy beach, library of books and videos, bicycles, daily newspapers, and Continental plus breakfasts.

Host: Linda Logan
Rooms: 30 (PB) $160-350
Continental Breakfast
Credit Cards: A, B, C, D
Notes: 2, 5, 10, 12, 14

## SARASOTA

### The Crescent House

459 Beach Road, 34242
(941) 346-0857; www.crescenthouse.com

Completely renovated 100-year-old home directly across from the white sands of Siesta Beach in Siesta Key. Short walk to shops, restaurants. Sarasota's only bed and breakfast. Featuring many great antiques and artifacts. Exudes the Old Florida charm in today's beach house decor. New spa on rear sun deck and all the attention of new innkeepers.

Hosts: Matt and Cathy Ellis
Rooms: 6 (4 PB; 2 SB) $85-160
Full Breakfast
Credit Cards: A, B
Notes: 2, 5, 7, 9, 11, 12

---

7 No smoking; 8 Children welcome; 9 Social drinking allowed; 10 Tennis nearby; 11 Swimming nearby; 12 Golf nearby; 13 Skiing nearby; 14 May be booked through a travel agent; 15 Handicapped accessible.

## SEASIDE

### Josephine's French Country Inn

P.O. Box 4767, 32459
(850) 231-2446; (800) 848-1840
e-mail: judy@josephinesfl.com
www.josephinesfl.com

Josphine's has all the modern comforts of an upscale small luxury hotel. The southern 1840 replica of a Victorian home has private baths, TV, VCR, telephone, bar, sink, refrigerator, microwave, and coffee maker. The comfortable queen-size bedded rooms also have wood-burning fireplaces available November through April. Every morning, a scrumptious full breakfast is served. The brick streets, the sugar-white-sand beaches, and the incredible sunsets beckon the pampered guests for a stroll.

Rooms: 9 (PB) $135-215
Full Breakfast
Credit Cards: A, B, C
Notes: 2, 4, 5, 7, 9, 10, 11, 12, 14, 15

## SEBRING

### Kenilworth Lodge

836 SE Lakeview Drive, 33870
(800) 423-5939

Kenilworth Lodge, historic 130-room hotel. It was built in 1916 by George Sebring, the town's founder, as a winter vacation site for "the well to do." It retains its historic status, while adding air conditioning, color satellite TV, refrigerators in every room, and an 80-foot serpentine pool. The Lodge has two ballrooms with wood floors. It specializes in golf packages, bicycling, dance club events, retreats, nature watching, and just plain relaxing. All rooms have private baths.

Hosts: Mark and Madge Stewart
Rooms: 105 (PB) $43-75
Continental Breakfast
Credit Cards: A, B, C, D
Notes: 2, 5, 8, 9, 10, 11, 12, 14

## STEINHATCHEE

### Steinhatchee Landing Resort

Highway 51 North, 32359
(352) 498-3513; (800) 584-1709
e-mail: sli@dixie.4ez.com
www.steinhatcheelanding.com

Steinhatchee Landing is a unique resort dedicated to capturing the spirit and romance of Old Florida. It sits on the lush banks of the Steinhatchee River, just three miles from the Gulf of Mexico. Steinhatchee Landing offers the amenities of a fine resort, combined with untouched natural surroundings that make the dream of the perfect escape a reality.

Hosts: R. Dean Fowler and Gene Chapman
Rooms: 21 (PB) $120-367
Continental Breakfast
Credit Cards: A, B, D, F
Notes: 2, 4, 5, 6, 7, 8, 9, 10, 11, 12, 14, 15

## TALLAHASSEE

### Calhoun Street Inn Bed & Breakfast

525 North Calhoun Street, 32301
(850) 425-5095; e-mail: gailrei@juno.com

Turn-of-the-century house less than a mile from the capitol, government offices, and Florida

Calhoun Street Inn

---

NOTES: Credit cards accepted: A MasterCard; B Visa; C American Express; D Discover; E Diner's Club; F Other; 2 Personal checks accepted; 3 Lunch available; 4 Dinner available; 5 Open all year; 6 Pets welcome;

State University. Historic residential neighborhood with nearby parks for jogging and walking (inn's golden retriever available). From Tallahassee it's a short drive to gulf beaches and national forest recreation areas. Large, sunny, uncluttered rooms have good lights for reading. Breakfast served at small tables in the dining room. Rooms have TVs and telephone jacks.

Host: Gail Reinertsen
Rooms: 4 (PB) $65-95
Full Breakfast
Credit Cards: A, B, C, D
Notes: 2, 7, 9

Governors Inn

## Governors Inn

209 South Adams Street, 32301
(904) 681-6855

The Governors Inn combines original woodwork, exposed beams, and brilliant skylights to create a French country environment. The 41 guest rooms and suites are furnished with antique armoires and English pub tables. No two rooms are alike. Some have French fourposter beds and framed prints. Others have loft bedrooms and fireplaces, spiral staircases, and clerestory windows. The Spessard Holland Suite has a wet bar and vaulted ceilings. Conferences for up to 75 people can be arranged. One-half block from the state capitol.

Rooms: 40 (PB) $119-229
Continental Breakfast
Credit Cards: A, B, C, D, E
Notes: 5, 8, 14, 15

## TARPON SPRINGS

## East Lake Bed & Breakfast

421 Old East Lake Road, 34689
(727) 937-5487
e-mail: littleflower@prodigy.net

Private home on two and one-half acres, on a quiet road along Lake Tarpon. Bedroom and adjoining private bath are at the front of the house, away from the family quarters. Twenty-four-hour access. Room has color TV and telephone. The hosts are retired business people who enjoy new friends and are well informed about the area. A full home-cooked breakfast is served. Smoking allowed on porch or deck.

Hosts: Marie and Dick Fiorito
Room: 1 (PB) $35-40
Full Breakfast
Credit Cards: None
Notes: 2, 5, 9, 10, 11, 12

## Spring Bayou Inn Bed & Breakfast

32 West Tarpon Avenue, 34689
(727) 938-9333

A large, elegant home built in 1905 is in the center of the historical district. Enjoy the beautiful Spring Bayou, downtown antique shops, and area attractions of a small Greek village. Excellent restaurants are nearby, and guests have a short drive to the beach. Well-appointed rooms have antique furnishings and modern

Spring Bayou Inn

---

conveniences, and guests enjoy spacious wrap-around front porch.

Host: Sharon Birk
Rooms: 5 (3 PB; 2 SB) $60-110
Full Breakfast
Credit Cards: None
Notes: 2, 5, 7, 9, 10, 11, 12

## VERO BEACH

### Redstone Manor Bed & Breakfast

806 43rd Avenue, 32960
(561) 562-8082

Enjoy this Florida ranch-style home on two and one-half acres of beautifully landscaped grounds. There are four tastefully decorated bedrooms with four private baths. The common area consists of a great room, library/music room, dining room, large screened porch, a large pool, and hot tub (spa). A full breakfast and afternoon refreshments are served in gracious style. Just minutes from beaches, shopping mall and outlet, many fine restaurants, and other area activities.

Hosts: Butch and Joyce Redstone
Rooms: 4 (PB) $90-120
Full Breakfast
Credit Cards: A, B, F
Notes: 2, 5, 7, 10, 11, 12

## WELLBORN

### 1909 McLeran House

12408 County Road 137, 32094
(904) 963-4603

A beautifully restored two-story Victorian home on five landscaped acres features a lovely garden area with gazebo, garden swing, deck area, goldfish pond, and an abundance of trees and shrubs. Guests enjoy large comfortable rooms with mini-refrigerators and cable TV. The private bath downstairs features a claw-foot tub with shower. Enjoy the many

1909 McLeran House

antiques throughout the house, relax in the garden, stroll the grounds, or visit the "collectibles" shop in the old barn. Additional charge for extra people.

Hosts: Bob and Mary Ryals
Rooms: 2 (PB) $75
Full Breakfast
Credit Cards: None
Notes: 2, 5, 7, 9, 10, 11, 12

## WELLINGTON/WEST PALM BEACH

### Southern Palm Ranch Bed & Breakfast

15130 Southern Palm Way, Loxahatchee, 33470
(561) 790-1413; FAX (561) 790-3035

Completed in 1997. Five spacious guest rooms, with hardwood floors, all with private baths. Most guest suites have balconies overlooking a tropical pond, which hosts a variety of wildlife. The pond has an island on which sits on cheekee hut which guests are welcome to use to enjoy the tranquility and sounds of nature. Guests are just minutes away from the equestrian show ground, Coral Sky Amphitheater, Lion Country Safari, golf, and Palm Beach nightlife.

Rooms: 5 (PB) $125
Continental Breakfast
Credit Cards: A, B, C, D
Notes: 2, 5, 7, 10, 11, 12, 15

---

NOTES: Credit cards accepted: A MasterCard; B Visa; C American Express; D Discover; E Diner's Club; F Other; 2 Personal checks accepted; 3 Lunch available; 4 Dinner available; 5 Open all year; 6 Pets welcome;

## WEST PALM BEACH

### *Tropical Gardens Bed & Breakfast*

419 Thirty-second Street, 33407-4809
(561) 848-4064; (800) 736-4064
FAX (561) 848-2422; e-mail: wpbbed@aol.com
www.tropicalgardensbandb.com

A cozy Key West-style cottage built in the 1930s has all of today's conveniences: private baths, air conditioning, paddle fans, and cable TV. The hosts have retained the charm of Old Florida with white wicker furniture in a colorful Caribbean decor; sun by the lush tropical pool, ride complimentary bicycles, or just relax! In the Old Northwood Historic District, just one block from the waterway, and minutes to the tropical waters of the Atlantic or to Palm Beach. A Continental plus breakfast is served.

Hosts: Robert Rosario and Emil Scipioni
Room: 6 (PB) $55-125
Continental Breakfast
Credit Cards: A, B, C, D
Notes: 2, 5, 7, 9, 10, 11, 12, 14

Tropical Gardens

## ZOLFO SPRINGS

### *Double M Ranch Bed & Breakfast*

4202 Sweetwater Road, 33890
(941) 735-0266 (after 6 P.M.)
e-mail: fsulaw@strato.net
www.innformation.com/fl/doublem

Double M Ranch

The Mathenys welcome guests to this 4,400-acre working cattle, citrus, and timber ranch in the heart of agricultural Florida. There are numerous recreational opportunities nearby, including fishing, canoeing, and a state park. There is a seven-station sporting clays course on the ranch. Accommodations include approximately 1,000 square feet of space including a pool table and a private entrance. A ranch tour is an option most guests enjoy taking. If guests want to see a part of Florida most tourists miss, come out to the ranch! Two-night minimum stay required. A lake home for weekly stays or longer also available. A heavy Continental breakfast is served.

Hosts: Mary Jane and Charles Matheny
Rooms: 2 (1 PB; 1 SB) $65
Continental Breakfast
Credit Cards: None
Notes: 2, 5, 7, 9, 11, 12, 14

7 No smoking; 8 Children welcome; 9 Social drinking allowed. 10 Tennis nearby; 11 Swimming nearby; 12 Golf nearby; 13 Skiing nearby; 14 May be booked through a travel agent; 15 Handicapped accessible.

Georgia

# Georgia

Credit Cards: A, B, C, D
Notes: 2, 4, 5, 7, 8, 9, 10, 11, 12, 14, 15

1906 Pathway Inn

## AMERICUS

### 1906 Pathway Inn Bed & Breakfast

501 South Lee Street, 31709
(912) 928-2078; (800) 889-1466

Parlors, porches, whirlpools, down comforters, fireplaces, friends, muffins, and more await guests at an English Colonial Revival inn. Stained glass, sumptuous candlelight breakfast. Near Civil War Andersonville and Plains, where President Carter teaches Sunday school. Thirty minutes west of I-75 and two hours south of Atlanta. Romantic getaway. "Pampering's our specialty." Pets welcome with prior approval.

Hosts: Angela and Chuck Nolan
Rooms: 5 (PB) $77-137
Full Breakfast

## ATHENS

### Magnolia Terrace Guest House

277 Hill Street, 30601
(706) 548-3860; FAX (706) 369-3439

Enjoy warm and gracious hospitality in an elegantly restored Colonial Revival home in the classic city's oldest neighborhood. Built in 1912, this spacious guest house is close to downtown Athens and the University of Georgia. Distinctive architectural features include Corinthian columns, beveled glass entrance, and original mantels. Tastefully furnished with antiques, each of the seven guest rooms offers a large private bath, many featuring claw-foot tubs or Jacuzzi.

Hosts: Shelia Rabun and Myra Moore
Rooms: 7 (PB) $75-150
Continental Breakfast
Credit Cards: A, B, C
Notes: 2, 5, 6, 7, 8, 9, 10, 11, 12, 14

## ATLANTA

### Ansley Inn

253 Fifteenth Street NorthEast, 30309
(800) 446-5416; FAX (404) 892-2318
e-mail: ansleyinn@aol.com

A stay at Ansley Inn enables guests to experience a charming 1907 English Tudor home

NOTES: Credit cards accepted: A MasterCard; B Visa; C American Express; D Discover; E Diner's Club; F Other; 2 Personal checks accepted; 3 Lunch available; 4 Dinner available; 5 Open all year; 6 Pets welcome; 7 No smoking; 8 Children welcome; 9 Social drinking allowed; 10 Tennis nearby; 11 Swimming nearby; 12 Golf nearby; 13 Skiing nearby; 14 May be booked through a travel agent; 15 Handicapped accessible.

Ansley Inn

with all of the modern conveniences that guests expect. Every room is equipped with cable TV, direct dial telephone, in-room coffee maker, individual climate control, and private bath with Jacuzzi. The full breakfast is included in the room rate.

Rooms: 22 (PB) $109-169
Full Breakfast
Credit Cards: A, B, C
Notes: 2, 5, 7, 8, 9, 10, 12, 14, 15

## Bed & Breakfast Atlanta

1608 Briarcliff Road, Suite 5, 30306
(404) 875-0525; (800) 967-3224
FAX (404) 875-8198
e-mail: bnbinfo@mindspring.com
www.bedandbreakfastatlanta.com

**A-1.** This early 1900s neighborhood of winding streets and beautiful parks is on the historic register. Guest accommodation is a private cottage behind a Dutch Colonial home in the midtown/Ansley Park area. Bright, spacious unit has bedroom alcove, living/dining space with double sleeper-sofa and breakfast table, full bath, and minor kitchen. Provisions set in by host for a self-catered breakfast. Cable TV, desk, attractive private outdoor area, and off-street parking are among the amenities offered at this nonsmoking bed and breakfast. Good access to major transportation arteries and MARTA. $95.

**A-2.** Bed and breakfast is two to three miles to downtown and has excellent public transportation with many points of interest nearby. The private entry guest suite offers a bedroom with twin beds, adjacent sitting room with cable TV (an additional single bed as well), private shower only bath, and special amenities for minor cooking such as a small refrigerator, coffee maker, toaster, and a microwave. Breakfast provisions are stocked for self-catering. A second room with king-size bed, small refrigerator, coffee maker, and full bath is available upstairs; with Continental breakfast provided. Nonsmokers welcome. Resident cat and dog. $68-80.

**A-16.** This 1903 English Tudor mansion built by Atlanta department store magnate George Muse in the beautiful neighborhood of Ansley Park. Walk to Piedmont Park, High Museum, Arts Center Marta station, and midtown business district. Twenty-two rooms available. All rooms feature newly restored private baths with Jacuzzi tubs, cable TV, private line telephone, and individual climate control. Lounge in front of the huge original fireplace in the parlor, and enjoy a large Continental breakfast in the dining room under a beautiful arched ceiling. Evening iced tea and hors d'oeuvres served in the living room. Plenty of off-street parking. Rates from $109-159.

**A-17.** Walk to Georgia Tech, Piedmont Park, and midtown business district; easy walking distance to MARTA. Enjoy a great neighborhood ambiance while visiting this spectacular 1896 mansion. Relax in the large parlors under Palladiam windows and stained glass. Many original fixtures, beautiful tiled fireplaces. Three guest bedrooms are offered. Italian and French are spoken. One cat in residence. Nonsmokers only. $85-95.

**B-2.** Renovated two-story brick traditional home is minutes from Peachtree Road; close-in Buckhead location serves business or pleasure travelers well. Two guest rooms are offered,

NOTES: Credit cards accepted: A MasterCard; B Visa; C American Express; D Discover; E Diner's Club; F Other; 2 Personal checks accepted; 3 Lunch available; 4 Dinner available; 5 Open all year; 6 Pets welcome;

one with small refrigerator and small desk, and one with TV, radio, and built-in closet; they share one full bath on the second floor. Only one room is used unless party is traveling together; there is an additional full bath available for guest use downstairs. Continental breakfast is offered. One cat in residence. Nonsmokers only. $72-90.

**E-1.** Charming traditional two-story house with spectacular swimming pool is on 10 beautifully wooded acres one mile from Emory University. Two guest rooms share one bath. Both rooms have traditional furniture, handmade quilts, and tastefully chosen family collectibles. Gracious Continental breakfast each morning. $68-76.

**I-3.** In Atlanta's only Victorian neighborhood, Inman Park, only two miles east of downtown. Excellent public transit. Upstairs, the Santa Fe Suite is a private living unit with huge bedroom, sitting room, kitchen and breakfast area, office, bath with shower stall and dressing room. Two first-floor guest rooms are also available. Both rooms share one bath. Host speaks French and German. Secured parking is available. Cat in residence. Nonsmokers, please. $68-100.

**I-5.** This 1892 Queen Anne Victorian in Atlanta's first planned suburb, two miles east of downtown, great for meetings downtown, easy access to MARTA and highway. Three guest accommodations are available in main house offering complete privacy—none of the rooms even has adjoining walls. Just behind the main house is a guest cottage with living room, fireplace, kitchen, loft bedroom, full bath with whirlpool tub, and brick patio. Continental breakfast served in the dining room. No smoking. $80-125.

**K-1.** Kosher bed and breakfast in northeast Atlanta, near Toco Hills-Emory area. Downtown convention center reached via public transportation or in 15 minutes by car.

Recently renovated 1960s brick ranch-style home offers two sunny guest rooms, each with private bath. Free parking available at curbside or in driveway. Central air conditioning. Nutritious Continental or full breakfast. Nonsmokers, please. $68-88.

**M-1.** Brick Colonial, built in 1921, in Morningside, one of Atlanta's charming intown neighborhoods. Excellent public transportation, walk to shops, restaurants, and points of interest. Three bed and breakfast accommodations. One third-floor suite has private bath. One second-floor guest room has private bath, and a second guest room can be utilized as an additional room if the party is traveling together. Full breakfast served daily. Off-street parking. Dog in residence. Smoking permitted on outside screened porch only. $80-98.

**M-2.** Large private-entry apartment in a 1920s neighborhood with good access to major transportation arteries and public transportation. This immaculately kept second-floor guest suite offers a bedroom, spacious living/dining room, well-equipped kitchen, and private full bath. A second guest room with an antique sleigh bed is across the hall from the suite, used only for overflow guests in the apartment. This room shares the suite's bath and kitchen. Host sets in ample provisions for self-catered breakfast. Cable TV, separate heat and air conditioning, and private-line telephone. Nonsmokers, please. $68-100.

**M-3.** Walk to shops and restaurants in nearby Virginia-Highland, attend meetings with ease. Private guest cottage is an efficiency unit with double bed, kitchen equipped for minor cooking (microwave, full refrigerator, toaster oven, coffee maker, and dishwasher). Breakfast provisions are set in daily for self-catering. Amenities include washer and dryer, off-street parking, and TV with remote control. Nonsmokers, please. $100.

7 No smoking; 8 Children welcome; 9 Social drinking allowed; 10 Tennis nearby; 11 Swimming nearby; 12 Golf nearby; 13 Skiing nearby; 14 May be booked through a travel agent; 15 Handicapped accessible.

**M-7.** English country home built in the early '80s as charming as older Morningside neighbors. Walk to shops and restaurants in Virginia-Highland and attend meetings with ease using public transit. Guest accommodation is an upstairs bedroom with full bath. Continental plus breakfast. Special amenity is a cable TV and VCR with an extensive tape library. Dog and cat in residence. Non-smokers. $72.

**V-1.** Modest garden cottage behind a large home in Virginia-Highland, a neighborhood with unique shops, diverse entertainment, and wonderful restaurants. Bed and breakfast offers a living room, TV, bedroom with double bed, bath, and well-equipped kitchen. Provisions are set in for a self-served Continental breakfast. Guests also enjoy a rear patio and private-line telephone. Nonsmokers. $75.

**V-3.** Built in 1913 and completely renovated in 1990, this Craftsman-style home is in close proximity to some of the city's most popular restaurants. Good access to expressways and public transportation. Inn offers six guest rooms with private baths. Some with whirlpool tubs, fireplaces, or laundry facilities. Continental breakfast served in the dining room. $95-195.

**V-4.** Caruso Manor is a Georgian-style brick home built in 1910 in the popular in-town Virginia-Highland neighborhood. Easy access to MARTA bus. Two large guest rooms share a bath with shower. Each room has cable TV, clock, and radio. Continental breakfast is served. Please, no smoking. $60-80.

**V-5.** Virginia-Highland private-entry room with kitchen privileges only three to five miles from Emory/Egleston Complex. Blue dormer bedroom with a full bath across the hall. Parquet hardwood floors, good light, ceiling fans, separate upstairs heating and air-conditioning unit, and a well-equipped kitchen make this an exceptional accommoda-

tion for short and long-term stays. Weekly and monthly discount rates available upon request. Rates are based on number of bedrooms used. $125-225.

Beverly Hills Inn

## Beverly Hills Inn

65 Sheridan Drive, 30305
(404) 233-8520; www.beverlyhillsinn.com

A charming city retreat one-half block from public transportation, one and one-half miles from Lenox Square, and five minutes from the Atlanta Historical Society. Full kitchens, library, free parking, color TV, and Continental breakfast.

Host: Mit Amin
Rooms: 18 (PB) $99-160
Continental Breakfast
Credit Cards: A, B, C, E, F
Notes: 2, 5, 6, 8, 14

## Gaslight Inn Bed & Breakfast

1001 St. Charles Avenue, 30306
(404) 875-1001; FAX (404) 876-1001
e-mail: innkeeper@gaslightinn.com
www.gaslightinn.com

Urbane sophistication in one of Atlanta's most popular and historic in-town neighborhoods. Historic inn featured in national and local publications and on international travel TV. Fireplaces, whirlpools, steam showers, multiple verandas, courtyard gardens. Within walking distance are antique shops, galleries, restaurants, museums, theaters. Five minutes to

Gaslight Inn

downtown Atlanta. A-rated and triple crowns by ABBA.

Host: Jim Moss
Rooms: 6 (PB) $95-195
Continental Breakfast
Credit Cards: A, B, C, D, E
Notes: 2, 5, 7, 8, 9, 10, 11, 12, 14, 15

## Inman Park Bed & Breakfast

100 Waverly Way Northeast, 30307
(404) 688-9498; FAX (404) 524-9939

The honeymoon cottage of Robert Woodruff, Atlanta's famous soft-drink magnate, is a totally restored Victorian in historic Inman Park. One block from the subway station, close to dining. Its 12-foot ceilings, heart-pine woodwork, fireplaces, antiques, screened porch, and private garden are to enjoy. Secured parking available on-site. Personal checks accepted for deposit only.

Host: Eleanor Matthews
Rooms: 3 (PB) $90-100
Continental Breakfast
Credit Cards: A, B, C
Notes: 5, 7, 9, 12, 14

## King-Keith House

889 Edgewood Avenue Northeast, 30307
(404) 688-7330; (800) 728-3879
www.kingkeith.com

One of Atlanta's most photographed houses. The 1890 Victorian "painted lady" close to Atlanta's most popular in-town shopping, restaurant, and theater districts. Two miles to downtown Atlanta. Two and a half blocks to MARTA (subway) with direct connections to the airport. Unusually spacious guest rooms, filled with antiques and collectibles. This bed and breakfast has all the bells and whistles one is looking for.

Hosts: Jan and Windell Keith
Rooms: 4 (PB) $80-175
Full Breakfast
Credit Cards: A, B, C, D
Notes: 2, 5, 7, 8, 9, 10, 11, 12, 14

## The Woodruff Bed & Breakfast

223 Ponce de Leon Avenue, 30308
(404) 875-9449; (800) 473-9449 (reservations only)
FAX (404) 875-2882
e-mail: RSVP@mindspring.com

Southern hospitality and charm await guests at this historic, beautifully restored bed and breakfast inn. In midtown Atlanta and convenient to everything. Filled with antiques, oriental rugs, stained glass, and hardwood floors. A full southern breakfast cooked by the on-site owners is a real treat.

Hosts: Douglas and Joan Jones
Rooms: 12 (10 PB; 4 SB) $89-149
Full Breakfast
Credit Cards: A, B, C, D
Notes: 5, 7, 8, 9, 11, 14

## ATLANTA (SENOIA)

## The Veranda

252 Seavy Street, P.O. Box 177, Senoia, 30276-0177
(770) 599-3905; FAX (770) 599-0806

Guests stay in beautifully restored spacious Victorian rooms in a 1907 hotel on the National Register of Historic Places. Just 30 miles south of Atlanta airport. Freshly prepared southern gourmet meals by reservation. Unusual gift shop featuring kaleidoscopes.

7 No smoking; 8 Children welcome; 9 Social drinking allowed; 10 Tennis nearby; 11 Swimming nearby; 12 Golf nearby; 13 Skiing nearby; 14 May be booked through a travel agent; 15 Handicapped accessible.

The Veranda

Memorabilia and 1930 Wurlitzer player piano pipe organ. One room has a whirlpool bath; all have private baths and air conditioning.

Hosts: Jan and Bobby Boal
Rooms: 9 (PB) $99-150
Full Breakfast
Credit Cards: A, B, C, D
Notes: 2, 4, 5, 7, 8, 10, 12, 14, 15

## AUGUSTA

### The Perrin Guest House Inn

208 LaFayette Drive, 30909
(706) 731-0920; (800) 668-8930
FAX (706) 731-9009

The Perrin Place is an old cotton plantation established in 1863. The plantation has long since become the site for the Augusta National, home of the Masters, while the three acres of the homeplace remain a little spot of magnolia heaven surrounded by shopping, golfing, and fine dining. The guest house has bedrooms that feature fireplaces and Jacuzzis. Share the pleasure of a front porch rocker, the comfort of a cozy parlor, or the cool of a scuppernong arbor with other guests. Weddings, receptions, and other social functions, treasured events when held at the Perrin Inn. Available by reservation only.

Hosts: Ed and Audrey Peel
Rooms: 10 (PB) $75-125
Continental Breakfast
Credit Cards: A, B, C
Notes: 2, 5, 7, 8, 9, 10, 11, 12, 13, 14

## BRUNSWICK

### Brunswick Manor

825 Egmont Street, 31520
(912) 265-6889; FAX (912) 265-7879

Nestled in the heart of historic Old Town Brunswick and across the street from a residential square, this grand Victorian inn features original carved oak staircase, high ceilings, Victorian mantels, period lighting, and elegant antiques. Guests may relax on the wraparound veranda furnished with wicker including a porch swing. Views include moss-draped oaks and graceful palms. A stroll through the gardens brings guests to the fish pond with fountain and arbor-covered hot tub. The inn boasts a *Country Inns*/Waverly Fabrics award-winning room. A full complimentary gourmet breakfast is prepared each morning, and afternoon tea is served. Boating nearby.

Hosts: Claudia and Harry Tzucanow
Rooms: 7 (PB) $80-95
Full Breakfast
Credit Cards: A, B
Notes: 2, 5, 8, 9, 10, 11, 12, 14

## CHAMBLEE

### Bed & Breakfast Atlanta

1608 Briarcliff Road, Suite 5, Atlanta, 30306
(404) 875-0525; (800) 967-3224
FAX (404) 875-8198
e-mail: bnbinfo@mindspring.com
www.bedandbreakfastatlanta.com

**C-1.** Ideal apartment for relocating business persons. Contemporary multilevel home. Good expressway access, just outside of the perimeter, is the location of this private-entry bed and breakfast unit. The apartment has full kitchen, dining area, living room with sleeper-sofa, private-line telephone, TV, VCR, stereo, full bath, work space with desk, and washer and dryer.

NOTES: Credit cards accepted: A MasterCard; B Visa; C American Express; D Discover; E Diner's Club; F Other; 2 Personal checks accepted; 3 Lunch available; 4 Dinner available; 5 Open all year; 6 Pets welcome;

Provisions for a self-catered breakfast are set in by the hostess. A large patio with porch swing and chairs overlooking a deep wooded lot and creek is bound to be a favorite spot for guests. Smoking acceptable. Discounted monthly. $88.

## CHICKAMAUGA

### Gordon-Lee Mansion Bed & Breakfast Inn

217 Cove Road, 30707
(706) 375-4728; (800) 487-4728

Circa 1847. Step back in time and enjoy this beautifully restored antebellum plantation house, set on seven acres with formal gardens and furnished with museum-quality period antiques in the atmosphere of early southern aristocracy. Used as a Union headquarters and hospital. Near the Chickamauga Battlefield and 15 miles from Chattanooga, Tennessee. Breakfast served in the elegant dining room. Civil War artifacts museum. Private baths. Cable TV. National Register of Historic Places. Civil War Trust Discovery Trail.

Host: Richard Barclift
Rooms: 5 (PB) $70-125
Full Breakfast
Credit Cards: A, B
Notes: 2, 5, 7, 9, 10, 12, 14

## CLARKESVILLE

### Glen-Ella Springs Inn

1789 Bear Gap Road, 30523
(706) 754-7295; FAX (706) 754-1560
www.glenella.com

Deep in the woods in a peaceful valley lies an inn in the National Register of Historic Places.

Glen-Ella Springs Inn

Relax in heart-pine rooms furnished in antiques and folk art, some with fireplaces. Share gardens and meadows with deer, butterflies, and hummingbirds. Enjoy fine dining and swim in the pool. Find serenity and exceptional service for personal or executive retreats on the edge of the Blue Ridge Mountains. Waterfalls, trails, antiques, folk art, and charming villages nearby.

Hosts: Barrie and Bobby Aycock
Rooms: 16 (PB) $100-185
Full Breakfast
Credit Cards: A, B, C
Notes: 2, 4, 5, 7, 9, 11, 12, 14, 15

## CLAYTON

### English Manor Inns Bed & Breakfast

43 Europe Lane (US 76 East), P.O. Box 1605, 30525
(800) 782-5780
e-mail: englishmanorinn@rabun.net

Seven elegant inns on seven acres provide privacy and romance for two or beautifully spacious accommodations for families, groups, and conferences. All guest rooms and suites have private bath (8 with whirlpool), cable TV, air conditioning, coffee service, and 14 have fireplaces. No telephones in rooms—one in each inn for guests' use. Copier, fax, computer, and internet are all available. White-water rafting, flea markets, antique shops are minutes

---

7 No smoking; 8 Children welcome; 9 Social drinking allowed; 10 Tennis nearby; 11 Swimming nearby; 12 Golf nearby; 13 Skiing nearby; 14 May be booked through a travel agent; 15 Handicapped accessible.

away. Fantastic restaurants nearby. Wine and set-ups available. Continental breakfast served 6:00-7:30 A.M. by request. Full breakfast served 7:30-10:00 A.M. Hors d'oeuvres are served 5:00-6:00 P.M. Two-night minimum for holidays and weekends in October. Lunch and dinner available by special arrangement. Open for groups January through April.

Hosts: Susan and English Thornwell; Diane Justice (manager)
Rooms: 43 (PB) $109-199
Full and Continental Breakfast
Credit Cards: A, B, C, F
Notes: 2, 8, 9, 10, 11, 12, 13, 14, 15

## COLQUITT

## *Tarrer Inn*

155 South Cuthbert Street, 31737
(912) 758-2838; (888) 2-TARRER

Southern hospitality at its finest. A welcome haven to weary travelers since 1905 the inn is in Colquitt in the heart of Georgia's Plantation Trace, the mayhaw berry capital of the world. Refurbished in 1995 in Victorian-style with Spanish antiques, the inn has 12 rooms and a suite. Elegant restaurant, full breakfast every morning, lunch buffet, and evening dining. Hunting, golf, tennis, fishing, and bird watching are available nearby. Lunch available Wednesday, Thursday, Friday, and Sunday.

Tarrer Inn

Dinner available Friday and Saturday. Inquire about accommodations for pets.

Hosts: Mavis and Jerry Phillips
Rooms: 13 (PB) $89-115
Full Breakfast
Credit Cards: A, B, C, D, E, F
Notes: 2, 5, 7, 8, 9, 10, 12, 15

## COLUMBUS

Woodruff House

## *The Woodruff House & the Mansion*

1414 Second Avenue, 31901
(888) 320-9309; FAX (706) 320-9304
e-mail: lbussey@mindspring.com

In the high uptown historic district, the Woodruff House is the birthplace of Robert W. Woodruff. Through his vision and leadership, Coca-Cola became the world's refreshment. Built in 1885, the Woodruff House remains a picture of charm and beauty. With nearby corporate offices, dining establishments, and entertainment, guests' convenience is assured. The Woodruff House is guests' home away from home offering 12 luxury guest suites, each with private bath, fireplace, cable TV, and telephone. A Continental plus breakfast is included.

Host: Larry W. Bussey
Rooms: 13 (PB) $95-160
Continental Breakfast
Credit Cards: A, B, C, D
Notes: 5, 7, 8, 9, 10, 12, 14, 15

NOTES: Credit cards accepted: A MasterCard; B Visa; C American Express; D Discover; E Diner's Club; F Other; 2 Personal checks accepted; 3 Lunch available; 4 Dinner available; 5 Open all year; 6 Pets welcome;

## COMMERCE

### The Pittman House

81 Homer Road, 30529
(706) 335-3823

This house is a grand 1890 Colonial completely furnished with period antiques. Wraparound porch just waiting to be rocked on. In the northeastern Georgia foothills near many interesting places. One hour northeast of Atlanta just off I-85. Tennis, golf, discount shopping mall, fishing, antiquing, and water sports all nearby. Seventy-two-hour cancellation notice required.

Hosts: Tom and Dot Tomberlin
Rooms: 4 (2 PB; 2 SB) $55-75
Full Breakfast
Credit Cards: A, B
Notes: 2, 5, 7, 10, 11, 12, 13, 14

Pittman House

## DAHLONEGA

### Mountain Top Lodge at Dahlonega

447 Mountain Top Lodge Road, 30533
(706) 864-5257; (800) 526-9754

Share the magic of a secluded bed and breakfast inn surrounded by towering trees and spectacular views. Enjoy antique-filled rooms, cathedral ceiling, great room, spacious decks, and heated outdoor spa; some rooms have fireplaces, whirlpool tubs, and porches. Deluxe room accommodations also available. Generous country breakfast with homemade biscuits.

Two-night minimum stay required for holidays and weekends during the fall season. Children over 12 are welcome.

Host: Karen Lewan
Rooms: 13 (PB) $78.40-151.20
Full Breakfast
Credit Cards: A, B, C, F
Notes: 2, 5, 7, 9, 12

## DALTON

### The Holly Tree House

217 West Cuyler Street, 30720
(706) 278-6620; FAX (706) 278-1851

Lovely restored home, circa 1924, in historical district of noteworthy Civil War and Cherokee Indian area. Convenient to many points of interest, the home is furnished in antiques and collectibles from around the world. Each spacious room has a private bath, TV, and VCR. A video library is available for guests' use. A three-course breakfast is served of carefully prepared specialities. Before retiring, cordials are available. The home is 100 miles north of Atlanta and 30 miles south of Chattanooga.

Host: Doris FioRito
Rooms: 4 (PB) $75-85
Full Breakfast
Credit Cards: A, B, C, D
Notes: 2, 5, 7, 9, 12

## DARIEN

### Open Gates Bed & Breakfast

Vernon Square National Historic District, 31305
(912) 437-6985

On a loop connecting exits 9 and 10, and across the Altamaha River delta via a scenic byway one and one-half miles east of I-95. In the old port town of Darien, this 1876 timber baron's home has been featured on the cover of *Southern Homes*, in *Georgia Off the Beaten Path, Fodor's Bed and Breakfasts*, and *Country Inns*. Locally harvested seafood and caviar and a hostess knowledgeable about Georgia's

7 No smoking; 8 Children welcome; 9 Social drinking allowed; 10 Tennis nearby; 11 Swimming nearby; 12 Golf nearby; 13 Skiing nearby; 14 May be booked through a travel agent; 15 Handicapped accessible.

Open Gates

second oldest town enhance guests' stay. Eco-logical and historical tours by boat to barrier islands and the old rice plantations of the delta by the naturalist hostess. Fishing nearby. Excellent library of coastal material and maps. Inquire about accommodations for pets and children.

Host: Carolyn Hodges
Rooms: 4 (2 PB; 2 SB) $63.80-69.30
Full Breakfast
Credit Cards: None
Notes: 2, 5, 7, 9

## DECATUR

### Bed & Breakfast Atlanta

1608 Briarcliff Road, Suite 5, Atlanta, 30306
(404) 875-0525; (800) 967-3224
FAX (404) 875-8198
e-mail: bnbinfo@mindspring.com
www.bedandbreakfastatlanta.com

**D-2.** This 1924 Tudor-style home retains many of its original features. Two guest rooms are offered, each with private bath and cable TV. The queen room has a working fireplace, bath with shower only. Twin room has a private entry, bath with tub only and hand-held shower. Bountiful, Continental breakfast, after-noon tea if desired, and comfortable inviting common rooms add to guest comfort. Walk to the square in Decatur for restaurants, shops, and entertainment. Delightful Irish wolfhound shares this home with host and her two small sons. Nonsmokers, please. $52-80.

**D-3.** This cream-colored Victorian brick house is in an ideal residential setting for downtown meetings (three blocks to MARTA rail), walk-ing to the square in Decatur, and Agnes Scott College. Private- entry suite has large front porch with rocking chairs, library/sitting room with wood burning fireplace, bedroom with antique bed, and adjoining shower-stall bath. Another guest room with private bath is offered upstairs. Full or Continental breakfast served. Resident dogs and cats. Smoking outdoors only, please. $80-120.

**D-20.** This 1940 English cottage-style home, classically and luxuriously decorated. Guest rooms include three large bedrooms. Upstairs rooms share one full bath with Jacuzzi tub (both rooms are used only if party is travelling together). Downstairs bedroom has full private bath. Each room has a beautiful four-poster or sleigh bed appointed with fine linens, sitting areas for reading and relaxation, and oriental rugs. Guests can relax in the living room with working fireplace or the formal dining room. Complete kitchen with eat-in area also avail-able for groups. $125-150.

## EATONTON

### The Crockett House

671 Madison Road, 31024
(706) 485-2248
www.bbonline.com/ga/crocketthouse/

The Crockett House, circa 1895, is nestled among 100-year-old red pecan, oak, pine, and magnolia trees, and beautiful weeping willows. Experience luxurious accommodations, fine dining, and a slower pace at this historic Victo-rian home. "The Crockett House is the perfect place for a romantic rendezvous"—*Atlanta Journal*. Features include 11 fireplaces, large wraparound porch, antique-filled guest rooms, claw-foot tubs beside working fireplaces, refreshments upon arrival, and Christa's mem-orable gourmet breakfast served in elegant

NOTES: Credit cards accepted: A MasterCard; B Visa; C American Express; D Discover; E Diner's Club; F Other; 2 Personal checks accepted; 3 Lunch available; 4 Dinner available; 5 Open all year; 6 Pets welcome;

The Crockett House

style. The Crockett House is on Georgia's historic antebellum trail.

Hosts: Christa and Peter Crockett
Rooms: 6 (PB) $85-95
Full Breakfast
Credit Cards: A, B
Notes: 2, 4, 5, 9, 10, 11, 12, 14, 15

## ETON

### *Ivy Inn*

245 Fifth Avenue, E., P.O. Box 406, 30724
(706) 517-0526; e-mail: ivyinn@ocsonline.com
www.bbonline.com/ga/ivyinn/

This inn reminds its guests of those restful, secure nights at Grandmother's or a favorite aunt's country home. Rooms are furnished in pieces from the '30s and '40s. A casual air with rocking chair porches is waiting for weary travelers. The Ivy Inn has bicycles for guests'

Ivy Inn

use. Horseback riding and stables are next door; white-water rafting is only 25 minutes away. Smoking is limited to front porch and grounds. Twelve miles from carpet capital of the world; three miles from crafts and antique shops.

Hosts: Gene and Juanita Twiggs
Rooms: 3 (PB) $87
Full Breakfast
Credit Cards: None
Notes: 2, 5, 8, 10, 11, 12, 13

## FITZGERALD

Dorminy-Massee House

### *Dorminy-Massee House*

516 West Central Avenue, 31750
(912) 423-3123

Just 20 miles east of I-75, this beautiful family-owned 1915 Colonial home, designed by architect T. F. Lockwood, contains eight charmingly furnished, air-conditioned bedrooms, with TV, telephone, computer modem, and private bath. Guests enjoy the dining, living, and parlor areas. Spacious, beautifully landscaped grounds include fish pool, gazebo, smokehouse, carriage house, and private parking. Walk three blocks to the Blue-Gray museum and learn Fitzgerald's history—the only town colonized by Union and Confederate veterans.

Hosts: Mark and Sherry Massee;
    Marion and Joyce Massee
Rooms: 8 (FB) $75-85
Continental Breakfast
Credit Cards: A, B, C
Notes: 5, 7, 8, 10, 12, 15

7 No smoking; 8 Children welcome; 9 Social drinking allowed; 10 Tennis nearby; 11 Swimming nearby; 12 Golf nearby; 13 Skiing nearby; 14 May be booked through a travel agent; 15 Handicapped accessible.

Whitworth Inn

## FLOWERY BRANCH

### *Whitworth Inn*

6593 McEver Road, 30542
(770) 967-2386; FAX (770) 967-2649
e-mail: visit@whitworthinn.com
www.whitworthinn.com

Contemporary country inn on five wooded acres offers relaxing atmosphere, 11 uniquely decorated guest rooms, and two guest living rooms. Full country breakfast served in large sunlit dining room. Meeting and party space available. Thirty minutes northeast of Atlanta at Lake Lanier. Nearby attractions and activities include boating, golf, beaches, and water parks. Close to Road Atlanta and Chateau Elan Winery and Golf Course. Easily accessible from major interstates. Three-diamond AAA rating.

Hosts: Ken and Chris Jonick
Rooms: 10 (PB) $65-89
Full Breakfast
Credit Cards: A, B, C
Notes: 2, 5, 7, 8, 10, 11, 12, 14, 15

## GREENVILLE

### *Georgian Inn*

566 South Talbotton Street, Hwy. 18 & 27 A, P.O.
   Box 1000, 30222
(706) 672-1600; FAX (706) 672-1666
e-mail: georgianinn@hotmail.com
www.bbonline.com/ga/georgian/

Enjoy true southern elegance and hospitality in this historic home. Refreshments and delicious breakfast served. Great getaway conveniently off I-85, just 45 minutes south of Atlanta's Hartsfield airport, minutes from Warm Springs, Roosevelt's beloved Little White House, and beautiful Callaway Gardens. Imagine refreshing the spirit, awakening the senses, and soothing the soul. A stay at Georgian Inn is a worthy memory for anyone who savors life in the South and wishes to indulge in memories of bygone days.

Host: Angela Hand
Rooms: 5 (PB) $125
Full Breakfast
Credit Cards: A, B, C
Notes: 2, 3, 4, 5, 7, 8, 9, 10, 11, 12, 13, 14

## HAMILTON

### *Magnolia Hall*
### *Bed & Breakfast*

127 Barnes Mill Road, P.O. Box 326, 31811
(706) 628-4566

Magnolia Hall is a beautifully restored 1890 Victorian home furnished with antiques. All five guest quarters have queen-size beds and private baths. Lovely Callaway Gardens is five miles away, and FDR's Little White House at historic Warm Springs is only a short drive.

Hosts: Dale and Kendrick Smith
Rooms: 5 (PB) $95-115
Full Breakfast
Credit Cards: None
Notes: 2, 5, 7, 9, 10, 11, 12, 14

Magnolia Hall

NOTES: Credit cards accepted: A MasterCard; B Visa; C American Express; D Discover; E Diner's Club; F Other; 2 Personal checks accepted; 3 Lunch available; 4 Dinner available; 5 Open all year; 6 Pets welcome;

## HELEN

### Chattahoochee Ridge Lodge & Cottages

P.O. Box 175, 30545
(706) 878-3144; (800) 476-8331
e-mail: rooms@stc.net
www.stc.net/~rooms

Perched on a wooded ridge a mile from Alpine Helen, each new unit has cable TV, air conditioning, refrigerator, coffee maker, free telephone, and large Jacuzzi. Some have a full kitchen, extra bedroom, and fireplace. There is also a gas grill on the back deck. Hosts are "earth friendly" with double insulation and back-up solar heating. Everything guests need is furnished and on the premises, including hosts who can fill guests in on attractions. Cottages in the woods are also available; please inquire.

Hosts: Bob and Mary Swift
Rooms: 5 (PB) $50-85
Credit Cards: A, B, C, D
Notes: 2, 5, 8, 9, 10, 11, 12

### The Lodge at Smithgall Woods

61 Tsalaki Trail, 30545
(706) 878-3087; (800) 318-5248
FAX (706) 878-0301; e-mail: sgwoods@stc.net
www.smithgallwoods.com

A 5,555-acre mountain retreat and conservation area, the Lodge at Smithgall Woods combines a unique natural setting with the seclusion and rustic charm of a private mountain estate. The Lodge offers elegantly rustic accommodations for just 28 overnight guests, countless outdoor recreational activities, one of the southeast's finest trout streams and gourmet cuisine. Peaceful and secluded, the Lodge at Smithgall Woods is ideal for weekend getaways, corporate retreats, small meetings, and special occasions.

Host: John Erbele
Rooms: 14 (PB) $235-490
Full Breakfast
Credit Cards: A, B, C, D, E
Notes: 2, 3, 4, 5, 9, 12, 14, 15

The Lake Rabun Hotel

## LAKEMONT

### The Lake Rabun Hotel

P.O. Box 10, 30552-0010
(706) 782-4946

Circa 1922 original mountain inn/bed and breakfast overlooking pristine Lake Rabun, one of the 10 prettiest spots in the eastern U.S. Near Tallulah Gorge. Northeast Georgia mountains. Featuring 16 rustic, charming guest rooms and suites, a loft apartment, and saloon and sports grille open Friday and Saturday nights. Featured in numerous magazines, books, newspaper articles, and on TV programs.

Hosts: Roberta and Bill Pettys
Rooms: 16 (4 PB; 5 SB) $65-125
Full Breakfast
Credit Cards: A, B, D
Notes: 2, 4, 5, 7, 8, 9, 10, 11, 12, 13, 14

## LITTLE ST. SIMONS ISLAND

### The Lodge on Little St. Simons Island

P.O. Box 21078ABB, 31522-0578
(912) 638-7472; (888) 733-5774
FAX (912) 634-1811
e-mail:issi@mindspring.com
www.littlestsimonsisland.com

Privately owned, 10,000-acre barrier island retreat has seven miles of pristine beaches. Comfortable accommodations, bountiful

7 No smoking; 8 Children welcome; 9 Social drinking allowed; 10 Tennis nearby; 11 Swimming nearby; 12 Golf nearby; 13 Skiing nearby; 14 May be booked through a travel agent; 15 Handicapped accessible.

family-style meals with hors d'oeuvres and wine. Endless recreational activities include horseback riding, fishing, boating, canoeing, bird watching, and naturalist expeditions. Fly-fishing instruction and excursions available. Limited boat docking also available. A unique experience in an unspoiled, natural environment. Day trips and full island rentals available. Smoking permitted in designated areas only. Inquire about accommodations for children. Full American Plan.

Host: Debbie McIntyre
Rooms: 13 (PB) $325-550 FAP
Full Breakfast
Credit Cards: A, B, C, D
Notes: 2, 3, 4, 5, 9, 11, 14, 15

## MADISON

### The Brady Inn

250 North Second Street, 30650
(706) 342-4400

Two Victorian cottages linked together by an extended porch filled with rockers welcome guests to this bed and breakfast. All rooms have private baths, heart-pine floors, and antiques. Come enjoy southern hospitality and see "the town Sherman refused to burn."

Hosts: C. G. and L. J. Rasch
Rooms: 7 (PB) $55-75
Full Breakfast
Credit Cards: A, B, C, D, F
Notes: 2, 3, 4, 5, 8, 9, 10, 11, 12, 14

## PALMETTO

### Serenbe

10950 Hutcheson Ferry Road, 30268
(770) 463-2610; FAX (770) 463-4472
e-mail: serenbe.com

A turn-of-the-century farm in the rolling hills 32 miles southwest of Atlanta. Rooms are furnished with antiques accented with traditional, modern, and folk art. Flower and vegetable gardens, a large pool and hot tub, three streams,

two waterfalls, a well-stocked lake with canoes, many trails, and over 100 farm animals are some of the attractions to explore. Afternoon tea, evening sweets, and a full country breakfast included. See web site for pictures.

Hosts: Marie and Steve Nygren
Rooms: 8 (PB) $140-175
Full Breakfast
Credit Cards: None
Notes: 2, 5, 7, 8, 9, 11, 12, 14

## PERRY

### Swift Street Inn

1204 Swift Street, 31069
(912) 988-9148

A friendly and relaxing stay for business and leisure travelers alike, the inn is convenient to I-75 and the Georgia National Fairgrounds and Agricenter. This 1857 coastal plantation-style cottage features high ceilings, fireplaces, antiques, private baths, and a double whirlpool tub in the honeymoon room. Guests are invited to browse through their hosts' library containing more than 1,000 books, videos, games, and musical selections. A hearty breakfast is served in the dining room, and afternoon refreshments are enjoyed in the gardens or on the front porch. Closed Christmas Day. Children over eight welcome with prior arrangements.

Hosts: Joy and Mike Skeen
Rooms: 4 (PB) $65-90
Full Breakfast
Credit Cards: A, B
Notes: 2, 7, 9

## ST. MARYS

### Goodbread House Bed & Breakfast

209 Osborne Street, 31558
(912) 882-7490; (888) 236-6482

Circa 1870. In the heart of St. Marys historic district, this Victorian inn offers spacious and private guest rooms with baths, three with fire-

NOTES: Credit cards accepted: A MasterCard; B Visa; C American Express; D Discover; E Diner's Club; F Other; 2 Personal checks accepted; 3 Lunch available; 4 Dinner available; 5 Open all year; 6 Pets welcome;

Goodbread House

places and two with claw-foot tubs. Visitors will enjoy the original wood trim, high ceilings, wide-plank floors, and two-story veranda with swings. Near Intracoastal Waterway and a short three-minute walk from Cumberland Island Ferry, marina, and shopping. Okefenokee Swamp is 30 minutes away. Airport in Jacksonville, Florida, is 30 minutes south. Near Kings Bay Sub Base and Crooker River State Park.

Rooms: 5 (PB) $65-85
Full Breakfast
Credit Cards: A, B, C, D, E
Notes: 2, 5, 7, 8, 9, 10, 12, 14

## Riverview Hotel

105 Osborne Street, 31558
(912) 882-3242; (888) 882-1807

Circa 1916. The hotel rests on the banks of the St. Marys River, across from the ferry to Cumberland Island. It has been owned by the Brandon family since the 1920s. One block from recreation areas, marina, and boat ramp. Easy walking distance to shops, museums, and eateries. Charming guest rooms with private baths, veranda, saloon, and Seagle's Seafood Restaurant, featuring their famous rock shrimp. Within an hour's drive are the Okefenokee Swamp and Georgia's Golden Isles. Within

two hours are Savannah to the north and St. Augustine to the south. Jacksonville International Airport is 30 minutes south on I-95.

Rooms: 18 (PB) $45-70
Continental Breakfast
Credit Cards: A, B, C, D
Notes: 2, 4, 5, 6, 7, 8, 10, 12, 14

## SAUTEE

## The Stovall House

1526 Highway 255 North, 30571
(706) 878-3355

This 1837 Victorian farmhouse, restored in 1983, is listed in the National Register of Historic Places. The inn has views of the mountains from all directions on the 26 acres in the historic Sautee Valley. The recipient of several awards for its attentive restoration, the inn is furnished with family antiques and decorated with hand stenciling. The restaurant, open to the public, features regional cuisine prepared with a fresh difference served in an intimate yet informal setting. It's a country experience.

Host: Ham Schwartz
Rooms: 5 (PB) $72-85
Continental Breakfast
Credit Cards: A, B
Notes: 2, 4, 5, 7, 8, 10, 11, 12

## SAVANNAH

## East Bay Inn

225 East Bay Street, 31401
(912) 238-1225; (800) 500-1225
FAX (912) 232-2709

The East Bay Inn has 28 charming guest rooms that invite guests to relax and enjoy Savannah. Walk to historic house museums and through the beautiful city squares. Return for evening wine and cheese reception. All rooms are furnished in a 19th-century style; with private baths and coffee makers in each room. Enjoy Continental plus breakfast each morning, a wine and cheese social each

---

7 No smoking; 8 Children welcome; 9 Social drinking allowed; 10 Tennis nearby; 11 Swimming nearby; 12 Golf nearby; 13 Skiing nearby; 14 May be booked through a travel agent; 15 Handicapped accessible.

evening, and turndown service with chocolates at night. Higher rates apply for special events. Nonsmoking rooms available.

Innkeeper: Glenn Anderson
Rooms: 28 (PB) $119-169
Continental Breakfast
Credit Cards: A, B, C, D, E
Notes: 3, 4, 5, 8, 9, 10, 11, 12, 14, 15

## Eliza Thompson House

5 West Jones Street, 31401
(912) 236-3620; (800) 348-9378

An 1847 three-story mansion on Savannah's finest street in the historic district. Twenty-three rooms, all with private baths, antiques, color TVs, and telephones. A lovely carriage house connected by a brick courtyard with three fountains. Complimentary wine and cheese served each evening and cheesecake and coffee served after dinner hour every night. Continental plus breakfast. All rooms renovated in 1996 by new owners.

Hosts: Carol and Steve Day
Rooms: 25 (PB) $99-210
Full Breakfast
Credit Cards: A, B
Notes: 2, 5, 7, 8, 9, 10, 11, 12, 14

Eliza Thompson House

## The Forsyth Park Inn

102 West Hall Street, 31401
(912) 233-6800

Circa 1893 Queen Anne Victorian mansion with 16-foot ceilings and 14-foot doors.

The Forsyth Park Inn

Ornate woodwork, floors, stairways, some fireplaces, antiques, some whirlpool baths, and courtyard cottage. Faces a 25-acre park in large historic district. Complimentary wine. Fine dining, tours, museum homes, river cruises, and beaches nearby. Personal checks accepted in advance.

Hosts: Virginia and Hal Sullivan
Rooms: 10 (PB) $135-200
Continental Breakfast
Credit Cards: A, B, C, D
Notes: 5, 8, 9, 10, 11, 12

## Joan's on Jones Bed & Breakfast

17 West Jones Street, 31401
(912) 234-3863; (800) 407-3863

In the heart of the historic district, two charming bed and breakfast suites distinguish the garden level of this three-story Victorian private home. Each suite has private entry, off-street parking, sitting room, kitchen, private telephone, cable TV. Note the original heart-pine floors, period furnishings, and Savannah gray brick walls. The innkeepers live upstairs and invite guests on a tour of their home if they are staying two nights or more. Inquire about accommodations for pets.

Hosts: Joan and Gary Levy
Suites: 2 (PB) $125-140

---

NOTES: Credit cards accepted: A MasterCard; B Visa; C American Express; D Discover; E Diner's Club; F Other; 2 Personal checks accepted; 3 Lunch available; 4 Dinner available; 5 Open all year; 6 Pets welcome;

Joan's on Jones

Continental Breakfast
Credit Cards: None
Notes: 2, 5, 7, 8, 9, 10, 11, 12, 14

## Lion's Head Inn

120 East Gaston Street, 31401
(912) 232-4580; (800) 355-LION

A stately 19th-century home is in a quiet neighborhood just north of picturesque Forsyth Park. This lovely 9,200-square-foot mansion is filled with fine Empire antiques. Each guest room is exquisitely appointed with four-poster

Lion's Head Inn

beds, private baths, period furnishings, fireplaces, TVs, VCRs, and telephones. Each morning enjoy a Continental plus breakfast, and in the evening enjoy wine and cheese served on the sweeping veranda overlooking the marbled courtyard.

Host: Christy Dell'Orco
Rooms: 7 (PB) $125-180
Continental Breakfast
Credit Cards: A, B, C, D
Notes: 2, 5, 7, 8, 9, 10, 11, 12, 14, 15

Magnolia Place Inn

## Magnolia Place Inn

503 Whitaker Street, 31401
(912) 236-7674; (800) 238-7674
FAX (912) 236-1145
e-mail: b.b.magnolia@mci2000.com
www.magnoliaplaceinn.com

This 1878 steamboat Gothic overlooks Forsyth Park. Birthplace of Pulitzer Prize-winning poet Conrad Aiken. In the main house, 13 bedrooms with private baths. Eleven of the rooms have fireplaces and six have double whirlpool tubs, plus two suites in the adjoining historic property, both with fireplaces and one with a jumbo whirlpool tub. Limited handicapped accessibility.

Hosts: Kathy Medlock; Jane and Rob Sales
Rooms: 15 (PB) $145-250
Continental Breakfast
Credit Cards: A, B, C, D
Notes: 2, 5, 7, 9, 10, 11, 12, 14

7 No smoking; 8 Children welcome; 9 Social drinking allowed; 10 Tennis nearby; 11 Swimming nearby; 12 Golf nearby; 13 Skiing nearby; 14 May be booked through a travel agent; 15 Handicapped accessible.

## Olde Harbour Inn

508 East Factor's Walk, 31401
(912) 234-4100; (800) 553-6533
FAX (912) 233-5979
www.oldeharbourinn.com

Overlooking the Savannah River, the Olde Harbour Inn offers 24 guest suites. All suites have a full kitchen. Rooms are decorated in 19th-century style, and range from studio suites to two bedrooms with loft. Within walking distance to Savannah's beautiful city squares and historic homes. Return to the Grand Salon for wine and cheese reception in the evening, and retire to find the guest room "turned down" and a special treat. Higher rates apply for special events. Evening cordials included in rates. Lunch and dinner are available nearby.

Innkeeper: Glenn Anderson
Rooms: 24 (PB) $130-195
Continental Breakfast
Credit Cards: A, B, C, D, E
Notes: 5, 7, 8, 9, 10, 11, 12, 13, 14

## The President's Quarters Inn & Guesthouse (A Premier Historic Inn on Oglethorpe Square)

225 East President Street, 31401
(912) 233-1600; (800) 233-1776
FAX (912) 238-0849

Four-diamond award-winning inn in the heart of historic district. Spacious rooms and suites with antiques, four-poster and canopied beds, Jacuzzis, working fireplaces, some with balconies overlooking beautiful courtyard. Complimentary amenities include fruit and wine on arrival, afternoon hors d'oeuvres, nightly turndown with sweet and cordial, and Continental plus breakfast. Private parking and elevator accessible with 24-hour concierge and bellman.

Hosts: Stacy Stephens and Hank Smalling
Rooms: 19 (PB) $137-225

Continental Breakfast
Credit Cards: A, B, D
Notes: 2, 3, 5, 7, 8, 9, 10, 11, 12, 14, 15

## Sonja's R.S.V.P. Savannah: Bed & Breakfast Reservation Service

611 East 56th Street, 31401
(912) 232-7787; (800) 729-7787
FAX (912) 353-8060

All accommodations are in historic homes or inns. All are within walking distance to major museums, parks, shops, churches, restaurants, and waterfront areas in historic Savannah, Charleston, and Beaufort, South Carolina. Sonja, the agent, has been in every room in each inn and will help with accommodations, send a map leading guests to the door of the inn, and provide information on tours, restaurants, etc. Forty inns are available, including hosted private homes, bed and breakfast inns, and unhosted accommodations. Many provide sleeper-sofa or cots, and some have kitchens. All are air-conditioned. Discount for seven days or more. Agent: Sonja Lazzaro. $90-400.

## STONE MOUNTAIN

## Bed & Breakfast Atlanta

1608 Briarcliff Road, Suite 5, Atlanta, 30306
(404) 875-0525; (800) 967-3224
FAX (404) 875-8198
e-mail: bnbinfo@mindspring.com
www.bedandbreakfastatlanta.com

**S-3.** This inn is a reproduction of a southern plantation one mile outside of Stone Mountain National Park, in the village of Stone Mountain. Five guest rooms with private baths and three rooms with Jacuzzi baths. Also available is a guest cottage with two bedrooms, living room with fireplace, and kitchen. The inn is family owned and operated. Southern hospital-

---

NOTES: Credit cards accepted: A MasterCard; B Visa; C American Express; D Discover; E Diner's Club; F Other; 2 **Personal checks accepted**; 3 Lunch **available**; 4 Dinner available; 5 Open all year; 6 Pets welcome;

ity abounds. Full breakfast. Nonsmoking. Wheelchair accessible. $98-175.

## The Village Inn Bed & Breakfast

992 Ridge Avenue, 30083
(770) 469-3459; (800) 214-8385
FAX (770) 469-1051
e-mail: villageinn@mindspring.com

Come experience southern hospitality and classic antebellum charm...Built in the 1820s, restored in 1995, the Village Inn is Stone Mountain's only historic bed and breakfast. Walk to more than 60 unique shops and restaurants. Less than one mile from Georgia's Stone Mountain Park. Cozy, charming rooms with TV/VCR and telephone. Private oversized whirlpool baths, gas fireplaces, air conditioned, great views. Just 15 miles east of Atlanta. Full

The Village Inn

southern breakfast and complimentary snacks and beverages. Honeymoons, weddings, anniversaries, showers.

Hosts: Earl and Christy Collins
Rooms: 6 (PB) $105-140
Full Breakfast
Credit Cards: A, B, C, D
Notes: 5, 7, 8, 9, 10, 12, 14, 15

## THOMSON

## Four Chimneys

2316 Wire Road Southeast, 30824
(706) 597-0220

Early 1800s plantation-plain country house has original hand-planed pine-board floors, walls, and ceilings. Furnished with antiques and reproductions; all guest rooms have fireplaces and four-posters. Beautiful grounds with colonial-style herb and flower garden, and certified "Backyard Wildlife Habitat." Restaurants, historic sites, golf, and antique shops are nearby. Easy access to I-20 and the Masters Golf Tournament in Augusta. Two miles to town and restaurants. Higher rates for special events. Inquire about picnics or suppers. No smoking in guest rooms.

Hosts: Maggie and Ralph Zieger
Rooms: 4 (2 PB  2 SB) $35-75
Full Breakfast
Credit Cards: A, B
Notes: 2, 5, 9, 12

7 No smoking; 8 Children welcome; 9 Social drinking allowed; 10 Tennis nearby; 11 Swimming nearby; 12 Golf nearby; 13 Skiing nearby; 14 May be booked through a travel agent; 15 Handicapped accessible.

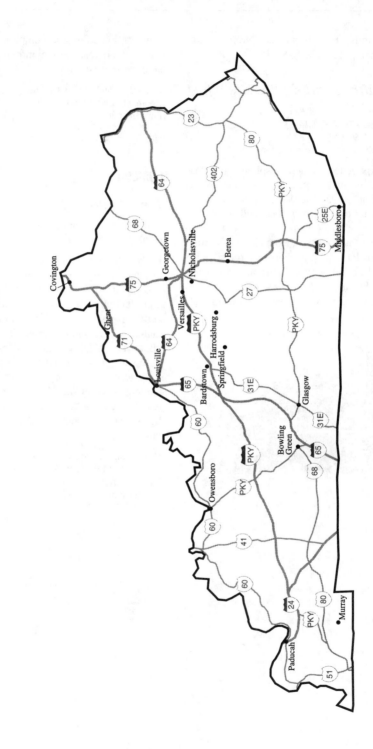

Kentucky

# Kentucky

## Arbor Rose

209 East Stephen Foster, 40004
(502) 349-0014; (888) 828-3330

This 1820 home was totally renovated to late Victorian style and is in the historic district of Bardstown, the town associated with Stephen Foster. It has king-size beds and a garden terrace with pond, fountain, and gardens. Minutes from shopping for antiques, tours of mansions, four distilleries, golfing, Civil War history, and much more. Partially handicapped accessible.

Hosts: Derrick and Judy Melzer
Rooms: 5 (PB) $79-99
Full Breakfast
Credit Cards: A, B, C, D
Notes: 2, 5, 7, 8, 9, 10, 11, 12, 14

## Beautiful Dreamer Bed & Breakfast

440 East Stephen Foster Avenue, 40004
(502) 348-4004; (800) 811-8312

Antiques and cherry furniture complement this Federal-design home that overlooks historic My Old Kentucky Home. The Beautiful Dreamer Room has a double Jacuzzi. The Captain's Room has a single Jacuzzi and fireplace. The Stephen Foster Room is conveniently on the first floor. All rooms are air conditioned, have queen-size beds, and color TVs. Hearty breakfast included. Within walking distance of *The Stephen Foster Story*.

Host: Lynell Ginter
Rooms: 3 (PB) $99-119
Full Breakfast
Credit Cards: A, B, C, D
Notes: 2, 5, 7, 10, 11, 12

## Bruntwood Inn

714 North Third Street, 40004
(502) 348-8218

This gracious antebellum mansion built in 1830, complete with spiraling staircase, grand entry foyer, elegant chandeliers, antique furnishings, and decorative original fireplaces in every room, may have been the type of setting that moved Stephen Foster to write about his "Old Kentucky Home." The poplar and ash floors with oriental rugs and the 12- and 13-foot-high ceilings add to the charm and spaciousness of the house. A full plantation breakfast is served daily at 9 A.M. Bruntwood Inn is within five minutes of many historic sites for touring. A formal high tea, at additional cost, is available.

Host: Susan Danielak
Rooms: 7 (5 PB; 2 SB) $90-125
Full Breakfast
Credit Cards: A, B
Notes: 2, 5, 7, 8, 9, 10, 11, 14

NOTES: Credit cards accepted: A MasterCard; B Visa; C American Express; D Discover; E Diner's Club; F Other; 2 Personal checks accepted; 3 Lunch available; 4 Dinner available; 5 Open all year; 6 Pets welcome; 7 No smoking; 8 Children welcome; 9 Social drinking allowed; 10 Tennis nearby; 11 Swimming nearby; 12 Golf nearby; 13 Skiing nearby; 14 May be booked through a travel agent; 15 Handicapped accessible.

Jailer's Inn

## Jailer's Inn

111 West Stephen Foster Avenue, 40004
(502) 348-5551; (800) 948-5551
FAX (502) 349-1837; e-mail: cpaul@jailersinn.com
www.jailersinn.com

Iron bars on windows, 30-inch thick stone walls, and a heavy steel door slamming behind one may not sound like the typical tourist accommodation, and Jailer's Inn is anything but typical. The historic Jailer's Inn, circa 1819, offers a unique and luxurious way to "do time." Jailer's Inn is a place of wonderful, thought-provoking contrasts. Each of the six guest rooms is beautifully decorated with antiques and heirlooms, all in the renovated front jail. The back jail, built in 1874, is basically unchanged; guests will get a chilling and sobering look at what conditions were like in the old Nelson County jail that was in full operation as recently as 1987. Call for rates.

Host: Paul McCoy
Rooms: 6 (PB)
Full Breakfast
Credit Cards: A, B, C, D
Notes: 2, 7, 8, 9, 10, 11, 12, 14

## The Mansion Bed & Breakfast

1003 North 3rd Street, 40004
(502) 348-2586; (800) 399-2586

This beautiful Greek Revival mansion, built in 1851, is in the National Register of Historic Places. On more than three acres of land with magnificent trees and plantings, it reminds one of more genteel times. The Mansion is on the site where the Confederate flag, the Stars and Bars, was raised in Kentucky for the first time. The rooms feature period antiques, hand-crocheted bedspreads, dust ruffles, shams, king-size beds, and private baths. Gourmet breakfast. Smoking permitted in designated areas only. Children over 10 welcome.

Host: Joseph D. Downs
Rooms: 8 (PB) $85-125
Continental Breakfast
Credit Cards: C, D
Notes: 2, 5, 9, 10, 11, 12, 14

## BEREA

## The Doctor's Inn of Berea

617 Chestnut Street, 40403-1550
(606) 986-3042 (phone/FAX)
e-mail: docsinn@mis.net

The Doctor's Inn is Berea's premier bed and breakfast, nestled in the foothills of the Appalachians just off I-75 in the heart of Kentucky's designated capital of folk arts and crafts. The hosts offer a warm welcome along with the "hound of the inn," Coco. For leisure time there is satellite TV, a baby grand piano, library of books, or lively conversation during

The Doctor's Inn

---

NOTES: Credit cards accepted: A MasterCard; B Visa; C American Express; D Discover; E Diner's Club; F Other; 2 Personal checks accepted; 3 Lunch available; 4 Dinner available; 5 Open all year; 6 Pets welcome;

evening social hour before leaving for dinner. Shopping for crafts, jewelry, pottery, fine furniture, hand-woven items, antiques, tours of Berea College are all within walking distance.

Hosts: Dr. Bill and Biji Baker
Rooms: 3 (PB) $125
Full Breakfast
Credit Cards: None
Notes: 2, 5, 9, 10, 11, 12

## BOWLING GREEN

### Alpine Lodge

5310 Morgantown Road, 42101-8201
(502) 843-4846

Alpine Lodge is a spacious Swiss chalet-style home that has more than 6,000 square feet and is built on a little more than 11 acres. The furnishings are mostly antiques. A typical breakfast, southern style, of eggs, sausage, biscuits, gravy, fried apples, grits, coffee, and orange juice starts the guests' day. Swimming pool, gazebo, outdoor spa, and lots of trails to stroll through. All rooms have telephones and cable TVs. Inquire about accommodations for pets.

Hosts: Dr. and Mrs. David Livingston
Rooms: 5 (3 PB; 2 SB) $45-85
Full Breakfast
Credit Cards: None
Notes: 2, 7, 8, 9, 10, 11, 12, 14

### Walnut Lawn Bed & Breakfast

1800 Morgantown Road, 42101
(270) 781-7255

This is a restored Victorian house, part of which was built in 1805. It is furnished with family antiques of the period. On a farm three miles from the center of Bowling Green and just off Natchez Parkway and I-65. The place has been in the family for more than 125 years. Walnut Lawn requires reservations and serves a Continental breakfast.

Host: George Anna McKenzie
Rooms: 4 (3 PB; 1 SB) $65
Continental Breakfast

Credit Cards: None
Notes: 2 5, 7, 9

## COVINGTON

### Amos Shinkle Townhouse Bed & Breakfast

215 Garrard Street, 41011-1715
(606) 431-2118; (800) 972-7012
FAX (606) 491-4551; e-mail: ashinkle@one.net
www.amosshinkle.net

This superb, two-story brick townhouse was built in 1854 and utilized the talents of dedicated artisans of that era, the Amos Shinkle home was built in a Greco-Italianate style. Every room has antique furniture and its own private bath. One room has a whirlpool tub and a crystal chandelier in the opulent bathroom. A variety of accommodations are available. Partially handicapped accessible.

Hosts: Don Nash and Bernie Moorman
Rooms: 7 (PB) $79-140
Full Breakfast
Credit Cards: A, B, C, D, E
Notes: 2, 5, 8, 9, 14

## GEORGETOWN

### Blackridge Hall

4055 Paris Pike, 40324
(502) 863-2069; (800) 768-9308

Blackridge Hall is an upscale, luxurious southern Georgian-style mansion on five acres in Bluegrass horse country. There are six guest suites/rooms containing antique and

Blackridge Hall

7 No smoking; 8 Children welcome; 9 Social drinking allowed; 10 Tennis nearby; 11 Swimming nearby; 12 Golf nearby; 13 Skiing nearby; 14 May be booked through a travel agent; 15 Handicapped accessible.

reproduction furnishings. Two master suites have marble Jacuzzi tubs, while all baths are private. A full gourmet candlelight breakfast is served in the dining room or on the veranda. A cozy guest kitchenette is available with snacks and soft drinks. Minutes to Lexington, Kentucky Horse Park, Keeneland and Red Mile racetracks, University of Kentucky, Toyota Motor Corporation tours, and historic Georgetown antique shops. Near I-64 and I-75.

Host: Jim D. Black, proprietor
Rooms: 6 (PB) $89-179
Full Breakfast
Credit Cards: A, B, C, D
Notes: 2, 5, 7, 9, 10, 11, 12, 14

## GHENT

### Ghent House Bed & Breakfast

411 Main Street (US 42), P.O. Box 478, 41045
(502) 347-5807; www.bbonline.com/ky/ghent/

Ghent House is a gracious reminder of the antebellum days of the Old South. Federal style with a beautiful fantail window, two slave walls, rose and English gardens, gazebo, crystal chandeliers, fireplaces, outdoor hot tub, and whirlpool. Ghent House has a spectacular view of the Ohio River halfway between Cincinnati and Louisville, and one can almost visualize the steamboats. Go back in time and stay at the Ghent House. Come as a guest—leave as a friend.

Hosts: Wayne and Diane Young
Rooms: 3 (PB) $60-120
Full Breakfast
Credit Cards: A, B, C, D
Notes: 2, 5, 7, 8, 9, 10, 11, 12, 14

## GLASGOW

### Four Seasons Country Inn

4107 Scottsville Road, 42141
(502) 678-1000

Charming Victorian-style inn built in 1989. Most rooms have queen-size, four-poster beds,

Four Seasons Country Inn

private baths, remote-equipped TVs with cable. Continental breakfast served in inviting lobby with wood-burning fireplace. Some rooms open out to spacious deck or large front porch. Swimming pool. Honeymoon suite. Near the caves, lakes, and Corvettes.

Host: Charles Smith
Rooms: 21 (PB) $60-99
Continental Breakfast
Credit Cards: A, B, C, D, E
Notes: 5, 9, 10, 11, 12, 14, 15

## HARRODSBURG

### Bauer Haus Bed & Breakfast

362 North College Street, 40330
(606) 734-6289; (877) 734-6289

Savor the craftsmanship of the past in this 1880s Victorian home listed in the National Register of Historic Places and designated a Kentucky landmark. Nestle in the sitting room, sip tea or coffee in the dining room, repose in the parlor, or ascend the staircase to a private room for a relaxing visit. In Kentucky's oldest settlement, Bauer Haus is within walking distance of Old Fort Harrod State Park and historic Harrodsburg.

Hosts: Dick and Marian Bauer
Rooms: 5 (3 PB; 2 SB) $65-125
Full Breakfast
Credit Cards: A, B, C
Notes: 2, 5, 7, 9, 10, 12, 14

NOTES: Credit cards accepted: A MasterCard; B Visa; C American Express; D Discover; E Diner's Club; F Other; 2 Personal checks accepted; 3 Lunch available; 4 Dinner available; 5 Open all year; 6 Pets welcome;

## Inn at Shaker Village of Pleasant Hill

3501 Lexington Road, 40330
(606) 734-5411

The Shaker Village of Pleasant Hill offers a one-of-a-kind guest experience. Its 80 guest rooms in buildings where Shakers once lived and worked are simply and beautifully furnished with Shaker-crafted furniture. This national historic landmark sits on 2,700 acres of rolling bluegrass farmland. The village offers tours, daily exhibitions of Shaker crafts, and hearty country dining. Riverboat excursions from April through October.

Host: James Thomas
Rooms: 80 (PB) $55-100
Full and Continental Breakfast
Credit Cards: A, B
Notes: 2, 3, 4, 5, 8, 9, 11, 12, 14

## LOUISVILLE

## Aleksander House Bed & Breakfast

1213 South First Street, 40203
(502) 637-4985; FAX (502) 635-1398

The Aleksander House is a gracious 1882 Victorian Italianate home in historical Old Louisville. Tastefully decorated in antiques, the home features original fireplaces, wood floors, light fixtures, stained glass, and staircases. The three guest rooms and one suite are spacious with TVs, VCRs, fireplaces, telephones, air conditioning, and heat control. Aleksander House is near downtown, the airport, the university, I-65, and Kentucky Expo Center. A full gourmet breakfast is served each morning. Discount rates are available. Children welcome.

Host: Nancy Hinchliff
Rooms: 4 (2 PB; 2 SB) $75-119
Full Breakfast
Credit Cards: A, B, C, D
Notes: 2, 5, 6, 7, 8, 9, 10, 11, 12, 14

## Ashton's Victorian Secret Bed & Breakfast

1132 South First Street, 40203
(502) 581-1914; (800) 449-4691 (#0604)

In historic Old Louisville, guests will find a three-story brick mansion appropriately named the Victorian Secret Bed and Breakfast. Its 14 rooms offer spacious accommodations, high ceilings, 11 fireplaces, and original woodwork. Recently restored to its former elegance, the 110-year-old structure provides a peaceful setting for enjoying period furnishings and antiques.

Hosts: Nan and Steve Roosa
Rooms: 3 (1 PB; 2 SB) $53-89
Continental Breakfast
Credit Cards: B
Notes: 2, 5, 10, 12, 14

## Inn at the Park

1332 South Fourth Street, 40208
(502) 637-6930; FAX (502) 637-2796
e-mail: innatpark@aol.com
www.bbonline.com/ky/innatpark/

This Victorian mansion was built in 1886 as a premier example of Richardsonian Romanesque architecture. The inn is elegantly furnished in Victorian antiques and antique reproductions. Very spacious with 14-foot ceilings, eight fireplaces, picturesque porches overlooking Central Park, and rich hardwood floors. The grand, sweeping staircase is magnificent! Appropriate for special occasions and the very particular guest. Enjoy an evening stroll in the park, personal attention from the innkeepers, and an excellent full breakfast.

Hosts: John and Sandra Mullins
Rooms: 7 (PB) $79-149
Full Breakfast
Credit Cards: A, B, C, D
Notes: 2, 5, 7, 9, 10, 11, 12, 14

7 No smoking; 8 Children welcome; 9 Social drinking allowed; 10 Tennis nearby; 11 Swimming nearby; 12 Golf nearby; 13 Skiing nearby; 14 May be booked through a travel agent; 15 Handicapped accessible.

Old Louisville Inn

## Old Louisville Inn

1359 South Third Street, 40208
(502) 635-1574; FAX (502) 637-5892
e-mail oldlouin@aol.com
www.oldlouinn.com

Wake up to the aroma of freshly baked popovers and muffins when staying in one of the 10 guest rooms or suites. Conveniently between downtown and the airport. Stay for a romantic getaway or relax on a business trip and consider this inn home away from home.

Host: Marianne Lesher
Rooms: 10 (PB) $75-195
Full Breakfast
Credit Cards: A, B, C, D
Notes: 2, 5, 8, 9, 10, 12, 14

## Rocking Horse Manor Bed & Breakfast

1002 South Third Street, 40203
(502) 583-0408; (888) HORSE BB
FAX (502) 583-6077 ext#129
www.bbonline.com/ky/rockinghorse/

Stay in an 1888 Victorian mansion. Five guest rooms each with en suite private bath, cable TV, telephone, and heat/air-condition control. Conveniently in Old Louisville. A gourmet breakfast and complimentary evening snacks provided. Relax in the Victorian parlor or library with wet bar, or choose the third-floor sitting area that has a mini-office for those who can't

leave work behind. Jacuzzi suite. Corporate rates. AAA-rated. Gift certificates available.

Hosts: Diana Jachimiak and Brad Vossberg
Rooms: 5 (PB) $60-120
Full Breakfast
Credit Cards: A, B, C, D
Notes: 2, 5, 7, 9, 10, 11, 12, 14

## Welcome House Bed & Breakfast

1613 Forest Hill Drive, 40205
(502) 452-6629

Gracious Colonial home in a lovely suburban neighborhood offers two queen-size, two double, and two single bedrooms with three baths. Off the beaten path, but convenient to antique shops, shopping malls, and the expressways. Great for reunions and conventions. Close to fairgrounds.

Host: Jo DuBose Boone
Rooms: 5 (3 PB; 2 SB) $50-65
Full Breakfast
Credit Cards: None
Notes: 2, 5, 8, 9, 10, 11, 12, 14

## Woodhaven Bed & Breakfast

401 South Hubbards Lane, 40207
(502) 895-1011; (888) 895-1011
www.bbonline.com/ky/woodhaven/

Beautiful Gothic Revival mansion, built in 1853, features elaborately carved woodwork, winding staircases, and spacious rooms taste-

Woodhaven

fully decorated with antiques. The seven bedrooms and one cottage suite offer private baths (some with whirlpools), TVs, telephones, clock radios, and complimentary coffee and tea stations. Guests enjoy a welcoming snack and a full gourmet breakfast in the formal dining room. Common areas have 14-foot ceilings and floor-to-ceiling windows. Three porches and perennial gardens circle the property.

Host: Marsha Burton
Rooms: 7 (PB) $75-175
Full Breakfast
Credit Cards: A, B, C
Notes: 2, 4, 5, 6, 7, 8, 9, 10, 11, 12, 14, 15

## MIDDLESBORO

### The RidgeRunner Bed & Breakfast

208 Arthur Heights, 40965
(606) 248-4299
www.bbonline.com/ky/ridgerunner/

This 1891 Victorian home is furnished with authentic antiques and is nestled in the Cumberland Mountains. A picturesque view is enjoyed from the 60-foot front porch, welcoming guests with rocking chairs, swings, and hammocks. Guests are treated like special people, in a relaxed, peaceful atmosphere. Five minutes from Cumberland Gap National Park, the newly opened Twin Tunnels through historical Cumberland Gap, 12 minutes from Pine Mountain State Park, 50 miles from Knoxville, Tennessee, 2 miles from the P-38 Restoration Project Museum.

The RidgeRunner

Hosts: Sue Richards and Irma Gall
Rooms: 4 (2PB; 2SB) $65-75
Full Breakfast
Credit Cards: None
Notes: 2, 5, 7, 9, 10, 12, 14

## MURRAY

### Diuguid House Bed & Breakfast

603 Main Street, 42071
(502) 753-5470; (888) 261-3028

This beautiful home, listed in the National Register of Historic Places, features a sweeping oak staircase, comfortable and spacious rooms, and a generous guest lounge area. This bed and breakfast is in town near the university, lake area, and many antique shops. Full breakfast is included in the reasonable rates, and the area has the reputation for being a top-rated retirement area.

Hosts: Karen and George Chapman
Rooms: 3 (SB) $40
Full Breakfast
Credit Cards: A, B, D, E
Notes: 2, 5, 7, 8, 10, 12, 14

## NICHOLASVILLE

### Sandusky House and O'Neal Log Cabin

1626 Delaney Ferry Road, 40356
(606) 223-4730; e-mail: humphlin@aol.com

A tree-lined drive to the Sandusky House is just a prelude to the handsome Greek Revival residence built about 1850 with bricks fired on the premises. Today the bed and breakfast sits on a 10-acre estate amid horse farms, yet close to downtown Lexington, Keeneland Race Track, Kentucky Horse Park, and many other attractions. The 180-year-old authentic log cabin has been reconstructed and has two bedrooms, kitchen, living room with a fireplace, whirlpool tub, and air conditioning. Full breakfast for house guests and Continental plus breakfast for cabin guests. Children over 12

7 No smoking; 8 Children welcome; 9 Social drinking allowed; 10 Tennis nearby; 11 Swimming nearby; 12 Golf nearby; 13 Skiing nearby; 14 May be booked through a travel agent; 15 Handicapped accessible.

Sandusky House

welcome in house. Children of all ages welcome in cabin.

Hosts: Jim and Linda Humphrey
House: 3 (PB) $85
Cabin: $119
Full or Continental Breakfast
Credit Cards: A, B, C
Notes: 2, 5, 7, 9, 12

## OWENSBORO _____

# Trail's End

5931 Highway 56, 42301
(502) 771-5590; FAX (502) 771-4723
e-mail: jramey@mindspring.com
www.mindspring.com/~jramey

A condo cottage, in Indiana, furnished with antiques and gas-log fireplace, has three bedrooms, fully equipped kitchen with stocked refrigerator of breakfast fixings, laundry facilities, patio, and stables for lessons or trail riding on the property. A second condo cottage, in Kentucky, has three bedrooms. Guests may enjoy indoor/outdoor tennis, Nautilus fitness, and a sauna. Country-style breakfast served at the tennis club on property. Pool and a fireplace. Cottages are air conditioned. Also available is a two-bedroom trailer with two baths. Weekly rates available. Ten dollars for additional persons over two.

Host: Joan G. Ramey
Condo: 2 (PB) $50-75

Trailer: 2 (PB) $35
Full Breakfast
Credit Cards: A, B, D
Notes: 2, 5, 7, 8, 9, 10, 11, 12, 14, 15

## PADUCAH _____

# Ehrhardt's Bed & Breakfast

285 Springwell Lane, 42001
(270) 554-0644; e-mail: ziazio@vci.net

This brick Colonial home is just one mile off I-24. The hosts strive to make their guests feel at home with antique-filled bedrooms and a cozy den. The home is all on one level and is easily accessible to most seniors. A nice discount is available to seniors. A country breakfast is served. "Come visit with us."

Rooms: 2 (2 SB) $65
Full Breakfast
Credit Cards: None
Notes: 2, 5, 7, 10, 11, 12

# Trinity Hills Farm
# Bed & Breakfast Home and
# Stained Glass Studio

10455 Old Lovelaceville Road, 42001
(502) 488-3999; (800) 488-3998
e-mail: trinity8@apex.net
www.bbonline.com/ky/trinityhills/

Share the serenity of this 17-acre country retreat, ideal for romantic getaways or family gatherings. Enjoy bird watching, hiking, boating, fishing, farm animals, peacocks, or simply relaxing in the spa near water gardens. New three-story home features romantic third-floor suites with private whirlpool or spa and first-floor guest rooms with private entrances; unique stained glass, fireplaces, vaulted ceilings, exercise room, copier, fax, and computer access. TV/VCRs, remote control CD/tape/radio, large rooms with comfortable furnishings. Amenities include bathrobes, candles, clock radio, and evening refreshments. Well behaved children and small pets welcome with prior notice.

---

NOTES: Credit cards accepted: A MasterCard; B Visa; C American Express; D Discover; E Diner's Club; F Other; 2 Personal checks accepted; 3 Lunch available; 4 Dinner available; 5 Open all year; 6 Pets welcome;

Trinity Hills Farm

Hosts: Mike and Ann Driver; Jim and Nancy Driver
(Mike's parents)
Rooms: 5 (PB) $80-120
Full Breakfast
Credit Cards: A, B, D
Notes: 2, 5, 7, 9, 10, 11, 12, 15

## SPRINGFIELD

## Maple Hill Manor

2941 Perryville Road, 40069
(606) 336-3075; (800) 886-7546
www.bbonline.com/ky/maplehill/

Under construction for three years, this 14-room antebellum mansion, circa 1851, is listed in the National Register of Historic Places. On

Maple Hill Manor

14 tranquil acres in the bluegrass region. The honeymoon hideaway has a canopy bed and Jacuzzi. One hour from Louisville and Lexington, close to the Stephen Foster home and Perryville Battlefield. Complimentary dessert and beverages served in the evenings. Brochure available. Gift certificate; murder mystery packages.

Hosts: Kay and Bob Carroll
Rooms: 7 (PB) $65-90
Full Breakfast
Credit Cards: A, B
Notes: 2, 5 7, 8, 9, 10, 11, 12, 14

## VERSAILLES

## Bed & Breakfast at Sills Inn

270 Montgomery Avenue, 40383
(606) 873-4478; (800) 526-9801
fax (606) 873-7099; e-mail: sillsinn@aol.com

Enjoy the ambiance of Southern hospitality while stepping into the 1911 three-storied restored Victorian inn. The nearly 10,000 square feet are highly decorated and filled with Kentucky antiques. Guests can relax on the wraparound porch in a swing or rocking chair, or step inside to enjoy a book from the library. The staff will be at your beck and call to help with travel plans, restaurants, reservations, and any other needs. So make reservations today with the Sills Inn for a memory cherished tomorrow. AAA four-diamond-rated.

Rooms: 12 (PB) $69-159
Full Breakfast
Credit Cards: A, B, C, D, E, F
Notes: 5, 7, 9, 10, 12, 14

7 No smoking; 8 Children welcome; 9 Social drinking allowed; 10 Tennis nearby; 11 Swimming nearby; 12 Golf nearby; 13 Skiing nearby; 14 May be booked through a travel agent; 15 Handicapped accessible.

Louisiana

# Louisiana

Tyrone Plantation

## ALEXANDRIA

### Tyrone Plantation on Bayou Rapides

6576 Bayou Rapides, 71303
(318) 442-8528; FAX (318) 449-3972

Historic three-story plantation house: country setting, overlooking scenic bayou. Each room furnished with antiques. Convenient to airport, interstate, highway, and restaurants. State parks, area zoo, and museums nearby.

Hosts: Marion Donaldson and daughter, Rae Swent
Rooms: 4 (PB) $65-90
Full Breakfast
Credit Cards: A, B
Notes: 2, 5, 7, 8, 9, 10, 11, 12, 15

## CARENCRO

### La Maison de Campagne

825 Kidder Road, 70520
(318) 896-6529; (800) 895-0235
e-mail: fmclemore@the-fish.net

Circa 1871. This beautiful Victorian is on nine acres in the country only minutes from Lafayette—the "gateway to Acadiana." Nestled among century old live oaks and pecan trees, come watch the grass grow from one of the many porches and enjoy life the way it was meant to be. Each room is appointed with antiques, wallpaper, and private baths to surround guests with a step back in time. The best full gourmet Cajun country breakfast and Community coffee (the state coffee) starts guests' day to adventure and discovery guided by the hosts. Home of "Enchanting Evenings."

Hosts: Joeann and Fred McLemore
Rooms: 4 (PB) $105-135
Full Breakfast
Credit Cards: A, B, D
Notes: 2, 5, 7, 11, 12, 14

## HUSSER

### Grand Estate Mansion Bed & Breakfast

55314 Highway 445, 70442
(504) 748-2915; (888) 792-2915
e-mail: gme@i-ss.com
www.grandestatemansion.com

An elegant three-story southern mansion that is the perfect setting for a romantic getaway. Private majestic bedrooms and baths. Queen-size beds, fireplaces, period antiques, library, sunroom, formal parlor, great room with big screen TV/VCR. Honeymoon suite with double oversized pink marble Jacuzzi tub with columns. Three porches with rocking chairs. Large wraparound balcony overlooking built-in swimming

---

NOTES: Credit cards accepted: A MasterCard; B Visa; C American Express; D Discover; E Diner's Club; F Other; 2 Personal checks accepted; 3 Lunch available; 4 Dinner available; 5 Open all year; 6 Pets welcome; 7 No smoking; 8 Children welcome; 9 Social drinking allowed; 10 Tennis nearby; 11 Swimming nearby; 12 Golf nearby; 13 Skiing nearby; 14 May be booked through a travel agent; 15 Handicapped accessible.

pool and fishing pond. Ballroom suitable for weddings, receptions, business meetings, and special events. One-hour drive from New Orleans, Baton Rouge, or MSY airport.

Host: Mary Ann Brauninger
Rooms: 5 (3 PB; 2 SB) $75-200
Full Breakfast
Credit Cards: A, B
Notes: 2, 5, 7, 8, 9, 10, 11, 12, 14

## JACKSON

Milbank

## Milbank

3045 Bank Street, 70748
(504) 634-5901

Built in 1836, Milbank is a romantic antebellum mansion with irresistible charm. Sleep in a queen-size canopied Mallard bed. Historic walking tour includes homes, churches, cemeteries, commemorative area, museum, winery, and antique shops. Bear Corners restaurant is next door with lunch served Monday through Saturday and evening dining Friday and Saturday. Children over 12 welcome.

Hostess: Marjorie Collamer
Rooms: 3 (PB) $75
Suite: 1 (SB) $125
Full Breakfast
Credit Cards: A, B, D
Notes: 2, 5, 7, 9, 12, 14

## KENNER (NEW ORLEANS)

## Seven Oaks Plantation

2600 Gay Lynn Drive, 70065
(504) 888-8649

This 10,000-square-foot West Indies-style home overlooking the lake is convenient to the airport and is 20 minutes from the New Orleans French Quarter. Guest rooms open into a large living room and onto 12-foot galleries. A full plantation breakfast is served and the entire home can be toured. Antiques and Mardi Gras memorabilia are found throughout. Seven Oaks offers southern hospitality and makes guests' visits full of warm, pleasant memories.

Hosts: Kay and Henry Andressen
Rooms: 2 (PB) $95-115
Full and Continental Breakfast
Credit Cards: A, B, C
Notes: 2, 5, 7, 8, 9, 12, 14

## LAFAYETTE

## Alida's: A Bed & Breakfast

2631 SE Evangeline Throughway, 70508-2168
(318) 264-1191; (800) 9 CAJUN 7 (922-5867)
e-mail:info@alidas.com
www.alidas.com

In the heart of Cajun Country, Alida's is characterized by the gracious hospitality that its

Alida's

---

NOTES: Credit cards accepted: A MasterCard; B Visa; C American Express; D Discover; E Diner's Club; F Other; 2 Personal checks accepted; 3 Lunch available; 4 Dinner available; 5 Open all year; 6 Pets welcome;

innkeepers provide. They give generously of themselves, making every guest feel comfortable, at ease, and at home. At the end of the day, guests can slip into one of the huge antique claw-foot tubs, sip a glass of wine in the parlor, or just relax on one of the swings on the front porch or rear patio. Smoking outside only.

Hosts: Tanya and Douglas Greenwald
Rooms: 4 (PB) $75-150
Full Breakfast
Credit Cards: A, B, C, D
Notes: 2, 5, 7, 9, 10, 11, 12, 14

Fleur de Lis

## NATCHITOCHES

### Breazeale House Bed & Breakfast

926 Washington Street, 71457
(318) 352-5630; (800) 352-5631

Built for Congressman Phanor Breazeale in the late 1800s, Breazeale House is within walking distance of the historic downtown district. This Victorian home features 11 fireplaces, 12-foot ceilings, 9 stained-glass windows, a set of servants' stairs, 3 balconies, 8 bedrooms, and 3 floors with over 6,000 square feet of living space. President Taft slept here, and this house can be seen in *Steel Magnolias*.

Hosts: Willa and Jack Freeman
Rooms: 4 (PB) $70-85
Full Breakfast
Credit Cards: A, B, C
Notes: 2, 5, 7, 8, 9, 10, 11, 12, 14

### Fleur de Lis Bed & Breakfast Inn

336 Second Street, 71457
(318) 352-6621; (800) 489-6621

This grand old Victorian house is in the oldest settlement in the Louisiana Purchase and is listed in the National Register of Historic Places. Guests at the inn may expect a warm welcome, a room tastefully decorated with king- or queen-size bed, private bath, makeup

vanity, sitting area, as well as the many amenities one expects in a friend's home. Delicious full breakfast with rich Louisiana coffee and orange juice. Guest house also available.

Hosts: Tom and Harriette Palmer
Rooms: 5 (PB) $75-100
Full Breakfast
Credit Cards: A, B, C, D, E, F
Notes: 2, 5, 7, 8, 9, 10, 11, 12, 14

### The Levy-East House Bed & Breakfast Inn

358 Jefferson Street, 71457
(318) 352-0662 (800) 840-0662

A most luxurious bed and breakfast in the heart of the historic district. The beautiful Greek Revival house circa 1838, has been recently restored and tastefully renovated to capture the spirit of an earlier time. Furnished with fine antiques that have been in the house for over 100 years. The Levy-East House offers a gourmet breakfast, queen-size bed, private whirlpool bath, telephone, and TV and VCR in each room. Private parking. Enjoy elegant rooms and luxurious leisure.

Hosts: Judy and Avery East
Rooms: 4 (PB) $105-200
Full Breakfast
Credit Cards: A, B
Notes: 2, 5, 7, 9, 10, 11, 12

7 No smoking; 8 Children welcome; 9 Social drinking allowed; 10 Tennis nearby; 11 Swimming nearby; 12 Golf nearby; 13 Skiing nearby; 14 May be booked through a travel agent; 15 Handicapped accessible.

## NEW ORLEANS

### Bougainvillea House

841 Bourbon Street, 70116
(504) 522-3983

Antique ambiance with all of the modern conveniences in the heart of the French Quarter. Off-street parking, cable TV, balconies, patios, elegant decor, central air and heat, private telephones, walk to riverboats, bars, restaurants, aquarium, and the convention center.

Host: Flo Cairo
Rooms: 3 (PB) $90-200
Continental Breakfast
Credit Cards: B, C
Notes: 5, 7, 9, 12

The Cotton Brokers

### The Cotton Brokers Houses of Esplanade Avenue "Benachi House" and "Esplanade Villa"

2257 Bayou Road, 70119
(504) 525-7040; (800) 308-7040
FAX (504) 525-9760; e-mail: cotton@nolabb.com
www.nolabb.com

Choose from the distinctive bed and breakfasts of Esplanade Avenue. Sensitive restorations of classic New Orleans homes. Rooms and suites. Private baths. Gardens, patios, and porches. Delightful gourmet breakfast. Secure, free parking. Convenient to French Quarter and central business district. Triples and small groups welcome.

Host: James G. Derbes
Rooms: 9 (7 PB; 2 SB) $105-175
Full Breakfast
Credit Cards: A, B, C, D
Notes: 2, 5, 7, 8, 9, 10, 12, 14

### The Dusty Mansion

2231 General Pershing, 70115
(504) 895-4576; FAX (504) 891-0049

Rooms in this turn-of-the-century home have hardwood floors and are uniquely decorated with a New Orleans flavor. Amenities include ceiling fans and air conditioning. Sun deck on third floor. Pool table. Enclosed hot tub. Close to historic St. Charles streetcar, which provides easy access to French Quarter, aquarium, Garden District, zoo, and more. Excellent restaurants nearby.

Host: Cynthia Riggs
Rooms: 4 (2 PB; 2 SB) $50-80
Continental Breakfast
Credit Cards: A, B, C, D
Notes: 2, 5, 8, 9, 10, 12, 14

### The Glimmer Inn

1631 Seventh Street, 70115
(504) 897-1895
www.bbonline.com/la/glimmer/

This restored 1891 Victorian home features 12-foot cove ceilings, cypress woodwork,

The Glimmer Inn

NOTES: Credit cards accepted: A MasterCard; B Visa; C American Express; D Discover; E Diner's Club; F Other; 2 Personal checks accepted; 3 Lunch available; 4 Dinner available; 5 Open all year; 6 Pets welcome;

side and front galleries, wraparound porch, and enclosed brick patio. Across the street from the Garden District, just a half-block to St. Charles streetcar, and easy access to French Quarter and Audubon Park and Zoo. A private carriage house is also available. All rooms are air conditioned. Continental plus breakfast served.

Hosts: Sharon Agiewich and Cathy Andros
Rooms: 6 (1 PB; 5 SB) $70-85
Continental Breakfast
Credit Cards: None
Notes: 2, 5, 6, 8, 9, 10, 12, 14

## Hotel St. Pierre

911 Burgundy Street, 70116
(504) 524-4401; (800) 535-7785

Hotel St. Pierre embodies the architecture and ambiance of the 18th-century French Quarter. The 75 guest rooms and suites are set among courtyards and swimming pools. Each morning, complimentary coffee and doughnuts await guests in the Louis Armstrong Breakfast Room. Two blocks off Bourbon Street and all that jazz!

Host: James Lentz
Rooms: 75 (PB) $109-159
Continental Breakfast
Credit Cards: A, B, C, D, E
Notes: 5, 8, 9, 10, 11, 12, 14

## Lafitte Guest House

1003 Bourbon Street, 70116
(504) 581-2678; (800) 331-7971
www.lafitteguesthouse.com

This elegant French manor house, in the heart of the French Quarter, is meticulously restored to its original splendor and furnished in fine antiques and reproductions. Every modern convenience, including air conditioning, is provided for guests' comfort. Complimentary Continental breakfast; wine and hors d'oeuvres at cocktail hour. On-site parking at $9.00 per night.

Lafitte Guest House

Hosts: Andrew J. Crocchiolo and Edward G. Doré
Rooms: 14 (PB) $109-199
Continental Breakfast
Credit Cards: A, B, C, D, E, F
Notes: 5, 7, 8, 9, 11, 12, 14

## La Maison Faubourg

608-10 Kerlerec Street, 70116
(504) 271-0228 (phone/FAX); (800) 307-7179

Built in 1805 by Bernard De Marigny in the historical area called Faubourg Marigny, an area of architectural significance with the Creole cottage as the predominant form of early

La Maison Faubourg

7 No smoking; 8 Children welcome; 9 Social drinking allowed; 10 Tennis nearby; 11 Swimming nearby; 12 Golf nearby; 13 Skiing nearby; 14 May be booked through a travel agent; 15 Handicapped accessible.

development. All suites include private baths, parlor with color cable TV and telephone, and bedroom. Special events rates are given upon request. Cancellation policy is seven days' advance notice.

Host: Alma F. Hulin
Suites: 8 (PB) $85-165
Continental Breakfast
Credit Cards: A, B, C, D
Notes: 2, 5, 7, 9, 14

## Macarty Park Guest House/Historic Homes

3820 Burgundy Street, 70117-5708
(504) 943-4994; (800) 521-2790
e-mail: macpar@aol.com
www.macartypark.com

Feel right at home in a century-old classic Victorian guest house and cottages just five minutes from the French Quarter. Step out of your room into lush tropical gardens and jump into the sparkling heated swimming pool. Rooms are tastefully decorated in antique, reproduction, or contemporary furnishings, each with private bath, color cable TV, telephone, and air conditioning. Free parking. Continental plus breakfast.

Host: John Maher
Rooms: 8 (PB) $45-160
Continental Breakfast
Credit Cards: A, B, C, D
Notes: 5, 9, 11, 14

## Melrose Mansion

937 Esplanade Avenue, 70116
(504) 944-2255

The Melrose is an 1884 Victorian mansion that has been completely restored to perfection. This opulent, galleried mansion features nine antique-filled guest rooms with luxurious private baths, spacious heated pool and tropical patio, whirlpools, and wet bars with refrigerators in the rooms. Cocktail hour and Continental breakfast. New Orleans grandeur at its very finest. Limited smoking.

Melrose Mansion

Hosts: The Torres Family
Rooms: 9 (PB) $225-425
Continental Breakfast
Credit Cards: A, B, C, D
Notes: 2, 5, 9, 11, 14

## New Orleans Bed & Breakfast and Accommodations: A Reservation Service

P.O. Box 8163, 70182
(504) 838-0071; FAX (504) 838-0140
e-mail: info@nworleansbandb.com
www.neworleansbandb.com

**BSJ 1.** In the rear of this main house is an 1890 Victorian Creole cottage with kitchenette, bedroom, full bathroom, sofa bed in living room. Continental breakfast is served in the dining room of the main house. Walking distance to city park and New Orleans Museum of Art. $75.

**FM 1.** Stroll the streets of this unique neighborhood to admire the many distinctive home styles. This Greek Revival home built in 1845 is one to remember. Just four blocks to the French Quarter, this home has a bedroom, private bath, and private entrance. It includes TV,

NOTES: Credit cards accepted: A MasterCard; B Visa; C American Express; D Discover; E Diner's Club; F Other; 2 Personal checks accepted; 3 Lunch available; 4 Dinner available; 5 Open all year; 6 Pets welcome;

refrigerator, and microwave. Continental breakfast is left for guests in the refrigerator each morning. Guests can relax on the deck which overlooks tropical garden and ponds in the rear of the house. $75.

**FM 2, 3.** Built in 1832, this home was purchased by the Clairborne family in 1894. The owners are direct descendants of Governor Clairborne. This home has many antiques and Civil War treasures. On the upper level, guests may discover some Robert E. Lee's letters and heirlooms dating back to pre-war. On the ground floor, the guests enjoy two apartments. Each has a kitchen, living area, full bathroom. A Continental breakfast is left in the refrigerator for guests. $75.

**FM 8, 9.** This house built in early 1900s has been renovated with all modern conveniences into apartments. Each has living area, bedrooms with queen- and king-size beds. Lush gardens overlook each room. Kitchen, courtyards, and pool facilities available. Steps away from French Quarter. $75.

**FQ 8.** This two-level apartment on the first level has a living room, dining area, and fully furnished kitchen. TV and telephone; on the second level is a queen-size bed and a private bathroom with a balcony which overlooks a lovely courtyard and a heated swimming pool. $125.

**FQ 18, 19.** This one-bedroom apartment features a living room with entertainment center, sofa bed, fully furnished kitchen, private bath with Jacuzzi, and queen-size bed in bedroom. Furnished in antiques. $125.

**FQ 32.** This one-bedroom apartment is on the second floor. This has a living area with nonworking fireplace, oversized furniture, cable TV, telephone, and a balcony that faces a courtyard; fully furnished kitchen, dining area with bar-style table. A king-size bed in bedroom,

full bath, nonworking fireplace, and second balcony faces the courtyard. $125.

**GD 1.** Guests in this historic 1840 home enjoy a suite that has a sitting room overlooking the pool, a spacious bedroom with king-size bed, two marble bathrooms, and a wet bar. The sitting area is furnished with a day bed that accommodates two singles and another couple. $95.

**GD 3, 8.** Adjoining GD 1 is another restored home. One bedroom has private bathroom, and two bedrooms have a shared bathroom, a common sitting room is suitable for three congenial couples or a family. A Continental breakfast is served in the dining room of GD 1 or on the veranda. $65-75.

**GD 4.** In an 1850 Greek Revival home. On the second floor is a cozy bedroom with a raised four-poster bed, bleached hardwood floors, nonworking fireplace and mantle with beautiful decorative pieces, windows surround the room which overlooks trees and garden. A private full bath in hall. Breakfast is served in the dining room or on the patio if requested in advance. Hostess shares living and dining room with guests. It is close to restaurants. $75.

**GD 17.** In an area of New Orleans great historic homes and spacious gardens is a Greek Revival home built in 1856. This home has a two-story apartment furnished with English and French antiques, game table, cable TV, and VCR. Kitchen accesses balcony through a New Orleans floor-to-ceiling window. Hardwood floors are throughout the house. In bedroom is a four-poster raised bed, a crystal chandelier, a nonworking fireplace, a fainting couch, and private bath. The third floor has two antique French beds, sitting area, and private bathroom. $125-200.

**MC 2.** A private home close to New Orleans cemeteries—features one room with a full bed and independent full bath, a living room, dining

7 No smoking; 8 Children welcome; 9 Social drinking allowed; 10 Tennis nearby; 11 Swimming nearby; 12 Golf nearby; 13 Skiing nearby; 14 May be booked through a travel agent; 15 Handicapped accessible.

room, where heirlooms can be enjoyed; fully furnished kitchen and hardwood floors. A Continental breakfast is left in refrigerator for guests each morning. It has patio in rear of home where guests sit and enjoy the view. $85.

**UP 2.** A 1940 stucco cottage has a living room with art deco, a bedroom with queen-size bed, TV, private bath, furnished kitchen, and a bricked courtyard. This cottage is the rear of a 1902 Colonial Revival home. This cottage is on the St. Charles Avenue's historic streetcar line. Minutes away from the French Quarter. $95.

**UP 3.** This renovated historic uptown residence was once a plantation home. It consists of five bedrooms, each with a private bathroom. Built in 1846, the house is furnished with antiques. One and one-half blocks to the St. Charles Avenue streetcar line. Near many cafés and small restaurants. Continental breakfast is served in the formal dining room. $95-125.

**UP 24.** One bedroom apartment, close to universities, has a fully furnished kitchen, living area with hardwood floors, dining area, balcony, king-size bed in the bedroom and a full bathroom. A Continental breakfast is left in the refrigerator. It is two blocks away from historic Streetcar line. $95.

## Nine-O-Five Royal Hotel

905 Royal Street, 70116
(504) 523-0219

This quaint European-style hotel is in the heart of the French Quarter. One of the first smaller hotels in the French Quarter. Built in the 1890s, the Nine-O-Five has a courtyard and balconies overlooking the southern charm and hospitality of Royal Street. Period furnishings, high ceilings, and kitchenettes in all rooms.

Rooms and Suites: 10 (PB) $75-125 and up
Credit Cards: A, B
Notes: 5, 8

## The Prytania Inn

1415 Prytania Street, 70130
(504) 566-1515; FAX (504) 566-1518
www.prytaniainns.com

Restored to its pre-Civil War glory, this inn in the historic district received the 1984 Commission Award. Tender care; full gourmet breakfast. Patio, slave quarters, 18 rooms with private baths, and most with kitchen facilities or microwave and refrigerator. Five minutes to the French Quarter and one-block walk to St. Charles Avenue and the streetcar. Free parking. Hosts speak German. Nonsmoking rooms available.

Hosts: Sally and Peter Schreiber
Rooms: 18 (PB) $35-55
Full Breakfast
Credit Cards: A, B, C, D, E, F
Notes: 2, 5, 6, 8, 9, 10, 11, 12, 15

## ST. FRANCISVILLE

## Barrow House Inn

9779 Royal Street, Box 700, 70775-0700
(504) 635-4791

Sip wine and relax in a wicker rocker on the front porch while enjoying the ambiance of a quiet neighborhood of antebellum homes. Guest rooms are all furnished in beautiful

Barrow House Inn

antiques from 1840 to 1870. Delicious gourmet candlelight dinners are available upon request, and a cassette walking tour of the historic district is included for guests.

Hosts: Shirley Dittloff and Chris Dennis
Rooms: 5 (PB) $85-105
Suites: 3 (PB) $130-150
Full or Continental Breakfast
Credit Cards: A, B, D
Notes: 2, 4, 5, 7, 8, 9, 12, 14

Lake Rosemound Inn

## Butler Greenwood Plantation

8345 U.S. Highway 61, 70775
(504) 635-6312; FAX (504) 635-6370
e-mail: ButlerGree@aol.com
www.butlergreenwood.com

The 1790s plantation in English Louisiana is still owned and occupied by original family. Full of priceless antiques. Listed in National Register of Historic Places. Overnight accommodations in six private cottages on peaceful grounds. Pool, pond, plenty of live oaks, and gardens. Cottages all have baths, kitchens, porches or decks, cable TV, ceiling fans, Jacuzzis. Some have fireplaces. Rates include breakfast and tour of main antebellum home.

Host: Anne Butler
Rooms: 6 (PB) $100-110
Continental Breakfast
Credit Cards: A, B, C
Notes: 2, 5, 6, 8, 9, 11, 12, 14

## Lake Rosemound Inn

10473 Lindsey Lane, 70775
(225) 635-3176; FAX (225) 635-2224
www.lakerosemoundinn.com

Amid towering trees and rolling hills Lake Rosemound Inn, on picturesque Lake Rosemound, is midway between Baton Rouge and Natchez, Mississippi, in the heart of plantation country. All four beautifully decorated rooms have lake views. For guests' enjoyment amenities include: king- and queen-size beds, fireplace, Jacuzzis for two, air conditioning, TV, canoe, paddleboat, fishing gear, hammocks, porch swings, and famous "help your-

self" ice cream parlor with Brunswick pool table. Full country breakfast. Smoking permitted outside only.

Host: Jeane Peters
Rooms: 4 (PB) $75-105
Full Breakfast
Credit Cards: A, B, C, D
Notes: 2, 5, 6, 7, 8, 9, 11, 12, 15

## The Myrtles Plantation Bed & Breakfast

7747 U.S. Highway 61, P.O. Box 1100, 70775
(225) 635-6277; FAX (225) 635-5837

The Myrtles Plantation, circa 1796, invites guests to step into the past for a guided tour of antebellum splendor. Guests will see fine antiques and architectural treasures of the south and discover why the CBS *Morning News* and *The Wall Street Journal* call the Myrtles Plantation "America's Most Haunted House." Inquire about accommodations for children.

Hosts: John and Teeta Moss
Rooms: 10 (PB) $95-195
Continental Breakfast
Credit Cards: A, B, C
Notes: 2, 3, 4, 5, 12, 15

## ST. MARTINVILLE

## Old Castillo Bed & Breakfast

220 Evangeline Boulevard, 70582
(318) 394-4010; (800) 621-3017
FAX (318) 394-7983; e-mail: phylin@worldnet.net

Beneath the moss-draped branches of the legendary Evangeline Oak, the Greek Revival

---

7 No smoking; 8 Children welcome; 9 Social drinking allowed; 10 Tennis nearby; 11 Swimming nearby; 12 Golf nearby; 13 Skiing nearby; 14 May be booked through a travel agent; 15 Handicapped accessible.

Old Castillo

structure of the Old Castillo Bed and Breakfast, circa 1825, rises from the banks of the historic Bayou Teche. Now both tourists and area residents can step back in time to share the warmth of Acadian culture and cuisine. Cherish time spent leisurely beside the slow-moving waters of Bayou Teche. Listed in the National Register of Historic Places since 1978.

Host: Peggy Hulin
Rooms: 5 (PB) $50-80
Full Breakfast
Credit Cards: A, B, C
Notes: 3, 4, 5, 8, 9, 10, 11, 12, 13, 14, 15

## SLIDELL

Salmen-Fritchie House

## *Salmen-Fritchie House Bed & Breakfast*

127 Cleveland Avenue, 70458
(504) 643-1405; (800) 235-4168
www.salmen-fritchie.com

This beautiful 1895 mansion is featured on *Taste of Louisiana* TV series with Chef John Folse on PBS. It's listed in the National Register of Historic Places and is just 30 minutes from New Orleans French Quarter and the Mississippi Gulf Coast. Elegant large bedrooms with private baths and period antiques include TVs and telephones. Some have fireplaces. A private cottage that sleeps two to four people has a courtyard and screened porch; living room/kitchen; bedroom; bath with large Jacuzzi, and laundry. Smoking permitted on porches only. Children over 10 welcome. Twenty-five dollars for each additional person.

Hosts: Sharon and Homer Fritchie
Rooms: 5 (PB) $85-95
Suites: $115-125
Cottage: $150
Full Breakfast
Credit Cards: A, B, C, D
Notes: 2, 5, 9, 10, 12

## VACHERIE

## *Oak Alley Plantation, Restaurant, and Inn*

3645 Highway 18 (Great River Road), 70090
(800) 44 ALLEY
e-mail: oakalleyplantation@worldnet.att.net
www.oakalleyplantation.com

Nowhere in the Mississippi Valley is there a more spectacular setting! Turn-of-the-century Creole cottages, decorated in a quaint country style, are on the grounds of Oak Alley Plantation, a national historic landmark. A full country breakfast is served in the restaurant from 8:30 to 10:00 A.M. Just one hour from New Orleans and Baton Rouge. Tours of the mansion are not included in rate.

Owner: Zeb Mayhew Jr.
Rooms: 5 (PB) $95-125
Full Breakfast
Credit Cards: A, B, C, D
Notes: 3, 5, 7, 8, 9, 14

NOTES: Credit cards accepted: A MasterCard; B Visa; C American Express; D Discover; E Diner's Club; F Other; 2 Personal checks accepted; 3 Lunch available; 4 Dinner available; 5 Open all year; 6 Pets welcome;

## WHITE CASTLE

### *Nottoway Plantation Restaurant and Inn*

30970 Highway 405, 70788-0160
(225) 545-2730; FAX (225) 545-8632
e-mail: nottoway@worldnet.att.net

Experience the grandeur and elegance of 19th century southern living in the largest antebellum plantation home in the south, circa 1859. Overnight accommodations available in the mansion and overseers cottage, all with private baths. Rates include a guided tour, wake-up breakfast, and full plantation breakfast. Daily guided tours 9:00 A.M.-5:00 P.M. Restaurant serves Cajun and Creole cuisine 11:00 A.M.-3:00 P.M. and 6:00-9:00 P.M. daily. Gift shop. Pool.

Host: Cincy A. Hidalgo
Rooms: 13 (PB) $125-250
Full Breakfast
Credit Cards: A, B, C, D
Notes: 2, 3, 4, 5, 7, 8, 9, 10, 11, 12, 14

7 No smoking; 8 Children welcome; 9 Social drinking allowed; 10 Tennis nearby; 11 Swimming nearby; 12 Golf nearby; 13 Skiing nearby; 14 May be booked through a travel agent; 15 Handicapped accessible.

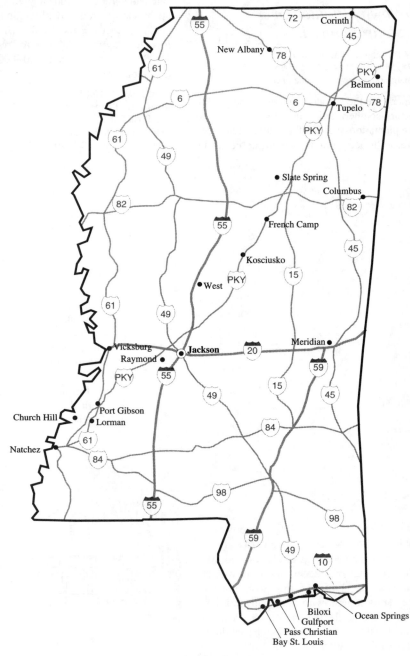

Mississippi

# Mississippi

## Lincoln, Ltd.;
## Bed & Breakfast Mississippi

P.O. Box 3479, Meridian, 39303
(601) 482-5483 (information)
(800) 633-MISS (reservations)
FAX (601) 693-7447
e-mail: blincolnh@aol.com

**79.** Overlooking the Mississippi Sound Bay, this turn-of-the-century home welcomes guests to the ambiance and quaintness of Bay St. Louis. Enjoy the view from bay windows in the room or rock on the front porch and watch for dolphins playing in the water. All rooms decorated in the taste of their former owners. Seven rooms. Continental breakfast. Children accepted by arrangement. $75-85.

## Natchez Trace Bed & Breakfast Reservation Service

P.O. Box 193, Hampshire, TN 38461
(931) 285-2777; (800) 377-2770
e-mail: natcheztrace@worldnet.att.net
www.bbonline.com/natcheztrace

**Belmont Hotel.** This Georgian-style hotel in downtown Belmont was built in 1924 and is six miles from the trace. It is newly restored, with all the comforts of a modern hotel, but with the charm and decor of an earlier, more gracious time. Truly a gem, with wide hallways, high ceilings, and a relaxing atmosphere. A Continental breakfast is served in the elegant dining room. Children welcome. $55-60.

## The Old Santini House
## Bed & Breakfast

964 Beach Boulevard, 39530
(228) 436-4078; (800) 686-1146
www.waidsoft.com/santinibnb

The Old Santini House, listed in the National Register of Historic Places, was built in 1837. The hosts offer the perfect romantic getaway for newlyweds or just a special occasion. The exquisite furnishings feature a brass wet bar, lush leather furniture, king-size bed, and Jacuzzi tub. Wake up to the smell of freshly brewed coffee and sit down to a full breakfast on fine china. Guests will take home fond memories of their moonlight stroll on the beach with their loved one. Newly added to bed and breakfast is a new dining room, a separate game area for playing table games, outside hot tub with decks and lounge chairs. Effective July 1, each guest room will have a

The Old Santini House

telephone and computer data ports. Children over 12 welcome.

Hosts: James and Patricia Dunay
Rooms: 4 (PB) $115-175
Full Breakfast
Credit Cards: A, B, C, D
Notes: 5, 7, 9, 11, 12, 14

## BILOXI (LONG BEACH)

### Red Creek Inn, Vineyard & Racing Stable

7416 Red Creek Road, Long Beach, 39560
(228) 452-3080 (information)
(800) 729-9670 (reservations)
e-mail: info@redcreekinn.com
www.redcreekinn.com

This three-story raised French cottage is on 11 acres of live oaks and magnolias. The 64-foot porch and six fireplaces add to the relaxing, country atmosphere of this circa 1899 brick-and-cypress home. English, French, and Victorian antiques, wooden radios, and a Victrola are for guests' use. Casinos are nearby. Vineyard and racing stable are under development. The inn is one and one-half miles south of I-10 off exit 28, or from Beach Highway 90, via Espy Avenue in Long Beach or Menge Avenue in Pass Christian, then north on Red Creek Road. Biloxi is 20 minutes away and New Orleans an hour. Come bed and breakfast awhile! Continental plus breakfast served.

Hosts: Karl and "Toni" Mertz
Rooms: 7 (5 PB; 2 SB) $49-99

Red Creek Inn

Continental Breakfast
Credit Cards: None
Notes: 2, 5, 7, 8, 9, 10, 11, 12, 14

## CHURCH HILL

### Natchez Trace Bed & Breakfast Reservation Service

P.O. Box 193, Hampshire, TN 38461
(931) 285-2777; (800) 377-2770
e-mail: natcheztrace@worldnet.att.net
www.bbonline.com/natcheztrace

**The Cedars.** Just north of Mount Locust, only six miles from the trace, overlooking 176 acres of wooded landscape, accented with beautiful moss-draped trees and ponds, this magnificent plantation home was previously owned by actor George Hamilton. There's a classic Greek Revival front section with a double gallery and white columns. A gracious southern plantation breakfast is served. Large bedrooms, one with a fireplace, and a third-floor suite with fireplace and Jacuzzi are available. $150-200.

**Jim's Cabin.** In Church Hill, six miles from the trace and near Natchez, this rustic cabin has brick floors, two bedrooms, a bath, and a furnished kitchen. It is in a lovely setting, with stately trees, and the state road on which it fronts is a scenic byway with a number of antebellum homes along the way. $75-130.

## COLUMBUS

### Lincoln, Ltd.; Bed & Breakfast Mississippi

P.O. Box 3479, Meridian, 39303
(601) 482-5483 (information)
(800) 633-MISS (reservations)
FAX (601) 693-7447
e-mail: blincolnh@aol.com

**5.** This is a Federal-style house and the oldest brick house in Columbus. It was built in 1828,

---

NOTES: Credit cards accepted: A MasterCard; B Visa; C American Express; D Discover; E Diner's Club; F Other; 2 Personal checks accepted; 3 Lunch available; 4 Dinner available; 5 Open all year; 6 Pets welcome;

the same year Andrew Jackson was elected president. The house has been completely restored and is furnished with antiques of the period. Three bedrooms, each with private bath. Full breakfast is included. $100.

**71.** Enjoy this Italian villa-style home built in 1848 and owned by the family of the original builders. Furnished in period antiques and in the National Register of Historic Places. A full southern breakfast is served. Four guest rooms with private baths. $100.

## CORINTH

### The Generals' Quarters Bed & Breakfast Inn

924 Fillmore Street, 38834
(601) 286-3325; FAX (601) 287-8118

Circa 1870, this fabulous Victorian has many original features such as leaded-glass windows, staircase, and fireplaces in every room. Eighty-four miles east of Memphis in the historic district of an old Civil War town, this fully restored inn is surrounded by quiet tree-lined streets. Guest rooms are furnished with antiques, contemporary pieces, cable TVs, and telephones. Walk to museums, antique shops, restaurants, hiking/biking trails. Shiloh Military Park and Natchez Trace are minutes away. AAA-rated three diamonds. ABBA-rated three crowns. Full gourmet breakfast served.

Hosts: Charlotte and Luke Doehner; Scott Stephenson
Rooms: 3 (PB) $75
Suites: 2 (PB) $80-90
Full Breakfast
Credit Cards: A, B, D
Notes: 2, 4, 5, 7, 9, 10, 12, 14

### Lincoln, Ltd.; Bed & Breakfast Mississippi

P.O. Box 3479, Meridian, 39303
(601) 482-5483 (information)
(800) 633-MISS (reservations)
FAX (601) 693-7447
e-mail: blincolnh@aol.com

**37.** A beautiful Victorian home, completely furnished with antiques. Convenient to Memphis, Tennessee, and Shiloh National Military Park, a Civil War battlefield. A full southern breakfast is served to guests. Lunch and dinner are also available. Four guest rooms. $75-90.

**75.** Circa 1869, this southern-style Colonial house is on two acres of oak and dogwood in the city of Corinth. The host is a native of Oxford, England, and he and his wife are very knowledgeable about the area. Enjoy the original pine floors and walls of two-inch-thick planks. A full breakfast is served on the back veranda as guests relax in antique wicker furniture. Three guest rooms available. $85-90.

**103.** The aroma of freshly baked bread and cozy fireside chairs serve as a warm welcome at one of Corinth's finest homes. Built in 1892, this restored home is furnished with exquisite Victorian antiques. Outdoors, guests can enjoy the formal gardens, lawn games, and four verandas with fans, rockers, and swings. $75.

### Natchez Trace Bed & Breakfast Reservation Service

P.O. Box 193, Hampshire, TN 38461
(931) 285-2777; (800) 377-2770
e-mail: natcheztrace@worldnet.att.net
www.bbonline.com/natcheztrace

**The General's Quarters.** Milepost 320. Built circa 1870s. In the historic district of the old Civil War village of Corinth, near Battery Robinett and the site of Fort Williams. Only 22 miles from Shiloh National Military Park; host will be happy to tell guests all about the history of the area. Five rooms with private baths. Full southern breakfast is served. $75-95.

**Robbins' Nest Bed and Breakfast.** Milepost 270, 320, or 320-A. This southern Colonial-style home, circa 1870, is on two acres of oak trees, dogwoods, boxwoods, and azaleas in historic Corinth. Guests can enjoy a delicious breakfast on the back porch, relaxing in antique wicker furniture with veranda ceiling fans. Complimentary afternoon tea and refreshments are served on arrival. Convenient to Shiloh and Pickwick Lake and state park. $90.

**Samuel D. Bramlitt House.** Built in 1892 and just opened as a bed and breakfast, this home sits atop a hill, deserving of its reputation as a small town mansion. Wrapped in upper and lower verandas, perfect places for sipping homemade lemonade or iced tea. Guests will enjoy the rose gardens, fountain, and an old magnolia tree with a bench for resting in its shade. Original walnut staircase, beautifully decorated. $85.

## Ravenswood Bed & Breakfast

1002 Douglas Street (at Linden), 38834-4227
(601) 665-0044

A 1929 Arts and Crafts-style home with spacious public areas featuring a fireplace, library, TV/VCR, and two porches with swings. Sited on one and one-half acres, the grounds contain Civil War earthworks and abundant wildlife. Antebellum and Victorian homes, Civil War walking tours, an information and visitor center, and museum are all within walking distance in historic downtown. Continental breakfast buffet in the breakfast room. Private guest rooms on second floor. Twenty-three miles to Shiloh National Military Park. Seasonal watersports and fishing at Pickwick Landing State Park, about 20 miles. Near the Natchez Trace. Inquire about accommodations for pets.

Hosts: Ron Wayne Smith and Timothy Hodges
Rooms: 3 (PB) $75-125
Continental Breakfast

Credit Cards: A, B
Notes: 2, 8, 9, 10, 11, 12

## FRENCH CAMP

## Natchez Trace Bed & Breakfast Reservation Service

P.O. Box 193, Hampshire, TN 38461
(931) 285-2777; (800) 377-2770
e-mail: natcheztrace@worldnet.att.net
www.bbonline.com/natcheztrace

**French Camp Bed and Breakfast.** Milepost 181. Two blocks from the trace, a rustic inn constructed from two century-old log cabins. Known as French Camp, this area is steeped in early trace history. Enjoy a breakfast of sorghum-soaked biscuits, creamy grits, fresh eggs, crispy bacon, and homemade jams and jellies. Hosts will share the tale of the origin of this historic two-story log cabin and their collection of quilts, antique books, and linens. $60.

## GULFPORT

## Magnolia Plantation

16391 Robinson Road, 39503-4817
(800) 700-7858; FAX (228) 832-3010

Thirty-two luxurious king- and queen-size rooms and suites that are on ground level and self-contained. Guests enjoy a tranquil backdrop of lakes and waterfalls. Just minutes from white-sand beaches, golf courses, casinos, and many other exciting attractions. Complimentary in-room coffee, breakfast buffet, afternoon tea, and evening social hour. Corporate meetings, retreats, and receptions. Lunch and receptions available for groups. Heated pool and Jacuzzi. Complimentary local airport transportation. Arrange in advance.

Host: Ralph Burton
Rooms: 32 (PB) $69-85
Suites: $125-250
Full Breakfast
Credit Cards: A, B, C
Notes: 5, 7, 8, 9, 10, 11, 12, 13, 14, 15

NOTES: Credit cards accepted: A MasterCard; B Visa; C American Express; D Discover; E Diner's Club; F Other; 2 Personal checks accepted; 3 Lunch available; 4 Dinner available; 5 Open all year; 6 Pets welcome;

## JACKSON

### Fairview Inn

734 Fairview Street, 39202
(601) 948-3429; (888) 948-1908
FAX (601) 948-1203
e-mail: fairview@fairviewinn.com
www.fairviewinn.com

A grand Colonial Revival mansion in national historic register offers luxury accommodations and fine dining for groups along with data ports and voice mail. Fairview Inn was named a Top Inn of 1994 by *Country Inns* magazine. AAA four-diamond-rated. "The Fairview Inn is southern hospitality at its best."—*Travel & Leisure*. Dinner available for groups.

Hosts: Carol and William Simmons
Rooms: 8 (PB) $115-165
Full Breakfast
Credit Cards: A, B, C, D
Notes: 2, 5, 7, 8, 9, 10, 12, 14, 15

### Lincoln, Ltd.; Bed & Breakfast Mississippi

P.O. Box 3479, Meridian, 39303
(601) 482-5483 (information)
(800) 633-MISS (reservations)
FAX (601) 693-7447
e-mail: blincolnh@aol.com

**50.** Circa 1888. Step through the door and step back across 100 years into a graceful world of sparkling chandeliers and finely crafted furnishings in this 19th-century home. Mere moments away from the city's central business and government districts. Convenient to many of Jackson's finest shopping, dining, and entertainment opportunities. The bedrooms are individually decorated, each accompanied by a fully modern private bath. Eleven guest rooms. Single rates available. $85-180.

## KOSCIUSKO

### Lincoln, Ltd.; Bed & Breakfast Mississippi

P.O. Box 3479, Meridian, 39303
(601) 482-5483 (information)
(800) 633-MISS (reservations)
FAX (601) 693-7447
e-mail: blincolnh@aol.com

**63.** One of the finest examples of Queen Anne architecture, this historic inn stands as a visual example of the lifestyle and culture of 1884. Four lovely bedrooms, furnished with antiques. Lunch and dinner are available by reservation. Breakfast included. $85-125.

### Natchez Trace Bed & Breakfast Reservation Service

P.O. Box 193, Hampshire, TN 38461
(931) 285-2777; (800) 377-2770
e-mail: natcheztrace@worldnet.att.net
www.bbonline.com/natcheztrace

**Redbud Inn.** Milepost 160. Stately two-story structure built in 1884, one of Kosciusko's finest examples of Queen Anne architecture, with a distinctive Victorian multicolor scheme, a three-story octagonal corner tower, and fish-scale shingles. Houses a tea room as well, which serves lunch Monday through Friday, dinner by prior arrangement for guests. Only two miles from the trace. $85-150.

## LORMAN

### Lincoln, Ltd.; Bed & Breakfast Mississippi

P.O. Box 3479, Meridian, 39303
(601) 482-5483 (information)
(800) 633-MISS (reservations)
FAX (601) 693-7447
e-mail: blincolnh@aol.com

**84.** Circa 1855, this Italianate Revival home is on a working plantation. It is a wildlife preserve

---

7 No smoking; 8 Children welcome; 9 Social drinking allowed; 10 Tennis nearby; 11 Swimming nearby; 12 Golf nearby; 13 Skiing nearby; 14 May be booked through a travel agent; 15 Handicapped accessible.

with guided jeep tours of the area, nature trails, and a heated swimming pool. Enjoy a wood-burning fireplace or stove and see wild deer or turkey on a tour or walking the nature trails. A full, seated breakfast and dinner are included in the price. $165-195.

## Natchez Trace Bed & Breakfast Reservation Service

P.O. Box 193, Hampshire, TN 38461
(931) 285-2777; (800) 377-2770
e-mail: natcheztrace@worldnet.att.net
www.bbonline.com/natcheztrace

**Rosswood.** Milepost 30. Completed in 1857 by an architect of Windsor, whose awesome ruins stand nearby. Classic Greek Revival with 14 rooms, 14-foot ceilings, columned galleries, winding stairway, and original slave quarters. Visitors may read in the diary of an early owner of the house about plantation life before and during the Civil War. Even a resident ghost! Rooms are upstairs; canopied beds, private baths, TV, movies, and telephones. Refreshments on arrival, full breakfast, heated pool, and spa. AAA-approved. $115-135.

## MERIDIAN

## Lincoln, Ltd.; Bed & Breakfast Mississippi

P.O. Box 3479, Meridian, 39303
(601) 482-5483 (information)
(800) 633-MISS (reservations)
FAX (601) 693-7447
e-mail: blincolnh@aol.com

**16.** A charming guest suite in a home in one of Meridian's historic neighborhoods. Bedroom, bath, and a living area decorated in antiques. Kitchen privileges. Private entrance. Continental breakfast. Weekly and monthly rates available. $75-85.

**18.** In one of Meridian's loveliest neighborhoods, this home is set among flowering shrubs and dogwood trees. The host and hostess have always been active in civic and cultural activities, both locally and throughout the state. Attractively furnished, two bedrooms with shared bath (for family or four people traveling together, only) or a double room with private bath. Full Mississippi breakfast. $75-100.

**58.** A contemporary inn convenient to I-59 and I-20 with 100 beautiful, spacious guest rooms. Meeting space for up to 60 people. Swimming pool and whirlpool on premises. Weekly and monthly rates available. Continental breakfast. $45-55.

## NATCHEZ

## Dunleith

84 Homochitto Street, 39120
(601) 446-8500; (800) 433-2445

A national historic landmark, circa 1856, this picturesque Greek Revival mansion is on a 40-acre landscaped park near downtown Natchez. There are 11 guest rooms: three in the main house, eight in the courtyard wing. All rooms have working fireplaces. Full southern breakfast is served in the Poultry House. No children under 18.

Host: Nancy Gibbs
Rooms: 11 (PB) $95-140
Full Breakfast
Credit Cards: A, B, D
Notes: 7

Dunleith

---

NOTES: Credit cards accepted: A MasterCard; B Visa; C American Express; D Discover; E Diner's Club; F Other; 2 Personal checks accepted; 3 Lunch available; 4 Dinner available; 5 Open all year; 6 Pets welcome;

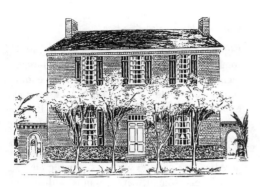

The Governor Holmes House

## The Governor Holmes House

207 South Wall Street, 39120
(601) 442-2366; (888) 442-0166
FAX (601) 442-0166

The Governor Holmes House was built in 1794, one of the oldest and most historic homes in the Old Spanish Quarter. It was the home of the last governor of the Mississippi Territory and the first governor of the state of Mississippi when it became a state in 1817. The home was also in the painting of Natchez that Audubon painted in 1823 and is in the National Register of Historic Places. Rates are subject to change without notice. No smoking permitted in rooms.

Host: Robert Pully, owner/manager
Rooms: 4 (PB) $105-140
Full Breakfast
Credit Cards: A, B, C, D
Notes: 2, 5, 9, 10, 11, 12, 14

## Lincoln, Ltd.; Bed & Breakfast Mississippi

P.O. Box 3479, Meridian, 39303
(601) 482-5483 (information)
(800) 633-MISS (reservations)
FAX (601) 693-7447
e-mail: blincolnh@aol.com

**19.** Circa 1832. This three-story mansion's outstanding architectural feature is the semi-elliptical stairway. Horses once trod where a collection of priceless furnishings and fine paintings now reside. Listed in the National Register of Historic Places. Swimming pool on premises. Ten guest rooms. Full breakfast served. $120-200.

**20.** Dating from 1774 to 1789 and surrounded by old-fashioned gardens, this home was once the home of a Spanish governor. In keeping with the period of the house, it is charmingly furnished with family heirlooms and other rare antiques. Formerly the home of Mr. and Mrs. J. Balfour Miller. The late Mrs. Miller was the originator of the Natchez Pilgrimage. Listed in the National Register of Historic Places. Four guest rooms. Full breakfast served. $100.

**21.** Circa 1790. Once the home of Thomas B. Reed, first elected U.S. senator from Mississippi, this architectural gem of the Federal period has been occupied since 1849 by the Conner family. Listed in the National Register of Historic Places. Seven guest rooms. Full breakfast served. $95 and up.

**22.** Circa 1818. The former home of Gen. John A. Quitman, an early Mississippi governor of Mexican War fame. This antebellum home contains many original Quitman pieces. Listed in the national register. Fourteen guest rooms; suite available. $110-210.

**30.** An outstanding historical home with a panoramic view of the Mississippi River. Furnished with an impressive collection of antiques, including the works of John Belter and P. Mallard. Welcoming beverage, tour of the home, and a large plantation-style breakfast are included. Five guest rooms. $95 and up.

**69.** Once owned by the last territorial governor and the first U.S. governor of Mississippi, this home was built in 1794 in the heart of Natchez. Many of the rooms have original 18th-century paneling and are furnished in period antiques. Enjoy the formal drawing room and eat a full plantation breakfast in the elegant dining room

---

7 No smoking; 8 Children welcome; 9 Social drinking allowed; 10 Tennis nearby; 11 Swimming nearby; 12 Golf nearby; 13 Skiing nearby; 14 May be booked through a travel agent; 15 Handicapped accessible.

or cozy breakfast room. Five guest rooms and one suite available. $105 and up.

**98.** Circa 1883-1889. This beautifully ornate home was once the gathering place of famous writers, publishers, politicians, and the elite of Natchez. In it guests will find treasures such as the parquet floor in the Gold Room, a bas relief design around the ceiling in the dining room, and a beautiful sweeping staircase in the grand entrance hall. With the price of a guest room, guests will enjoy a tour of the home, carriage ride around Natchez, and cocktails. $100-115.

**102.** Circa 1894. On the bluff, guests will get a panoramic view of the Mississippi River from this home. Mornings, guests will enjoy a full southern breakfast brought right to their room. An excellent home for families. Only blocks away from shops, historic homes, and restaurants. $110.

## Linden

1 Linden Place, 39120
(601) 445-5472; (800) 2-LINDEN
FAX (601) 492-7548; www.natchezms.com/linden

Linden sits on seven landscaped acres and has been in the present owner's family for six generations. All seven bedrooms, each with private bath, have four-poster beds and other antiques of the Federal period. The front doorway was copied in *Gone With the Wind*. Rate includes early morning coffee, a full southern plantation breakfast, and a tour of the house. Limited smoking allowed. Children over 10 welcome.

Host: Jeanette S. Feltus
Rooms: 7 (PB) $90-120
Full Breakfast
Credit Cards: None
Notes: 2, 5, 9, 10, 11, 12, 14, 15

## Natchez Trace Bed & Breakfast Reservation Service

P.O. Box 193, Hampshire, TN 38461
(931) 285-2777; (800) 377-2770

e-mail: natcheztrace@worldnet.att.net
www.bbonline.com/natcheztrace

**Elgin Plantation.** Set on 25 acres, four miles south of Natchez, built in 1772; in the national register and featured in *Country Inns*. Splendid columned two-story 1840 wing is set aside for guests, with three bedrooms upstairs and living room, dining room (where a full southern breakfast is served), and kitchen downstairs. Two-bedroom suite also available. Double-tiered gallery with jib windows opening out to both levels. Magnificent grounds with huge moss-draped oaks, beautiful antiques. A tour of the main house, including antebellum costumes for photographs, is available to guests. $90-130.

**Linden—In Natchez.** Linden's front door was copied for "Tara" in *Gone With the Wind*, so guests can imagine how beautiful the rest of the house is. The home has been in the owner's family for six generations and it is the epitome of dignity, comfort, and hospitality. Most of the bedrooms open onto the galleries, where old-fashioned rocking chairs welcome their guests to relax. Featured in *Southern Living*, *Colonial Homes*, and other magazines. Full breakfast served in the dining room or the back gallery. $90-120.

**Governor Holmes House.** Milepost 8. Built in 1794, this is one of the oldest and most historic homes in Natchez, having been the home of the last governor of the Mississippi Territory and first governor of Mississippi. Listed in the National Register of Historic Places, it is beautifully decorated with period furnishings, porcelain, paintings, and oriental carpets. It features suites with private, modern baths. A delicious plantation breakfast is served in the formal dining room or the quaint breakfast room. $105.

**Hope Farm.** Milepost 8. This Natchez home, built between 1774 and 1789, is listed in the National Register of Historic Places and was owned by the first Spanish governor of the territory. It features exquisite antique furniture from the early 18th century. Each guest room is furnished with a distinctive four-poster bed with draped testers. Private baths. No small children. A large southern-style breakfast and tour of the home are included. Twenty dollars for each additional person. $90-100.

**Main Street Balcony Bed and Breakfast.** Milepost 11. In a building built in 1887, these luxurious one- and two-bedroom apartments are just across from a trolley stop. The building façade has cast-iron posts and a balcony overlooking the street and is central to antique shops, restaurants, and all the Natchez attractions. Bedrooms, private baths, kitchen, and living room. Guests can choose either a Continental breakfast or a coupon for a buffet at the hotel across the street. Twenty-five dollars for each additional person. $140.

**The Victorian.** Sitting on a hill above Pearl Street in the historic district, this classic Victorian home was one of twin houses built around 1900; the mirror image of the house sits just next door. Stroll to downtown restaurants and antique shops. There is a guest kitchen with wet bar and refrigerator, a sunroom decorated with the owner's American pottery collection, and cable TV in every room. Rates $10 higher during the Pilgrimage. $59-89.

**Wensel House.** This 1888 Victorian townhouse completely renovated and beautifully furnished with antiques. In the heart of the historic district across from Natchez Pilgrimage headquarters, shopping, touring, and dining. Guests enjoy the parlor and dining room where complimentary fresh fruit and drinks are available. Generous plantation breakfast served in the dining room. Three large bedrooms, private bath, cable TV, telephone, iron and ironing board, and hair dryer. Fifteen dollars for additional persons. Two-bedroom cottage also available. $85.

## Oakland Plantation

1124 Lower Woodville Road, 39120
(601) 445-5101; (800) 824-0355

This charming retreat is about eight miles south of Natchez, with 360 acres of pastures, nature trails, fishing ponds, and a tennis court. The guest house dates back to 1785, and guests to the estate include Andrew Jackson and his wife, Rachel. Come for the peace and quiet and relax in an 18th-century atmosphere. Smoking outside only.

Hosts: Andy and Jeanie Peabody
Rooms: 3 (2 PB; 1 SB) $65-75
Full Breakfast
Credit Cards: A, B, C
Notes: 2, 5, 8, 9, 10, 11, 12, 14

## NEW ALBANY

## Natchez Trace Bed & Breakfast Reservation Service

P.O. Box 193, Hampshire, TN 38461
(931) 285-2777; (800) 377-2770
e-mail: natcheztrace@worldnet.att.net
www.bbonline.com/natcheztrace

**Heritage House.** Twenty miles from the trace and in a quiet neighborhood, this historic home was built in 1906 and has six guest rooms. There is a shaded front porch for reading the morning paper, and inside are rooms with 12-foot ceilings and antique furnishings. Suite with two bedrooms, sitting room with TV, and bathroom available. Children welcome. $65-75.

## OCEAN SPRING

## Lincoln, Ltd.; Bed & Breakfast Mississippi

P.O. Box 3479, Meridian, 39303
(601) 482-5483 (information)
(800) 633-MISS (reservations)
FAX (601) 693-7447
e-mail: blincolnh@aol.com

7 No smoking; 8 Children welcome; 9 Social drinking allowed; 10 Tennis nearby; 11 Swimming nearby; 12 Golf nearby; 13 Skiing nearby; 14 May be booked through a travel agent; 15 Handicapped accessible.

**The Wilson House**, circa 1922, rustic log construction, pine floors, large wraparound porch for enjoying warm, friendly breezes and the fresh southern air. Six guest rooms, two of which contain fireplaces with gas logs. Enjoy a hearty southern breakfast, welcoming beverage, and a cozy atmosphere. Children over 12 welcome. $55-110.

## PASS CHRISTIAN

### Lincoln, Ltd.; Bed & Breakfast Mississippi

P.O. Box 3479, Meridian, 39303
(601) 482-5483 (information)
(800) 633-MISS (reservations)
FAX (601) 693-7447
e-mail: blincolnh@aol.com

**77.** Across from Pass Christian Yacht Harbor, this three-story home allows guests to enjoy a harbor view from the front porches, with French doors opening onto the porches from all rooms facing the gulf. As guests stay among the family antiques and art, they may enjoy the reception and dining parlors, play cards or billiards in the kitchen or den, or simply enjoy the peaceful harbor view. Five rooms. Children over 14 are welcome. $88 and up.

## PORT GIBSON

### Lincoln, Ltd.; Bed & Breakfast Mississippi

P.O. Box 3479, Meridian, 39303
(601) 482-5483 (information)
(800) 633-MISS (reservations)
FAX (601) 693-7447
e-mail: blincolnh@aol.com

**26.** Enjoy a night in one of the South's most beautiful antebellum mansions. In the National Register of Historic Places, this home is furnished with family heirlooms. Visitors will step back in history to an era of gracious living. Includes a full southern-style

breakfast and a tour of the home. Eleven guest rooms. $95 and up.

### Natchez Trace Bed & Breakfast Reservation Service

P.O. Box 193, Hampshire, TN 38461
(931) 285-2777; (800) 377-2770
e-mail: natcheztrace@worldnet.att.net
www.bbonline.com/natcheztrace

**Oak Square.** This home in Port Gibson is two miles from the trace. The grounds of this 1850 mansion contain three guest houses with 12 rooms for guests, each with a massive four-poster canopied bed and other antique furnishings. A tour of the full house and grounds is conducted every evening. A full southern breakfast, complete with grits and biscuits, is served each morning. $95.

### Oak Square Plantation

1207 Church Street, 39150
(601) 437-4350; (800) 729-0240

Oak Square, circa 1850, is Port Gibson's largest and most palatial Greek Revival antebellum mansion. Visitors experience a quiet retreat into the past. Family heirloom antiques, canopied beds, full southern breakfast, and a tour of the mansion and grounds. In the National Register of Historic Places. Port Gibson is the third oldest town in Mississippi, referred to by Gen. U. S. Grant as "the town

Oak Square Plantation

too beautiful to burn." Area attractions include antebellum homes, churches, a military state park, Civil War battlefields, and museums. Inquire about accommodations for children. Limited social drinking permitted. Limited handicapped accessible.

Hosts: Mr. and Mrs. William D. Lum
Rooms: 12 (PB) $85-95
Full Breakfast
Credit Cards: A, B, C, D
Notes: 2, 5, 7, 9, 12

# RAYMOND

## Natchez Trace Bed & Breakfast Reservation Service

P.O. Box 193, Hampshire, TN 38461
(931) 285-2777; (800) 377-2770
e-mail: natcheztrace@worldnet.att.net
www.bbonline.com/natcheztrace

**Mamie's Cottage.** Just a few miles from the trace, near Raymond, this beautifully restored, quaint 1840s cottage has two suites, each with an outside entrance. The larger suite has a queen-size bed and adjoining small bedroom with a double bed; the other has a double bed and adjoining small bedroom with a twin bed. There is a porch, a deck, TVs and VCRs, and a small refrigerator in each. A full breakfast is served in the main house, and on request, the hosts may be able to serve guests' dinner as well. Fifteen dollars for each additional person. $85-95.

# SLATE SPRING

## Lincoln, Ltd.; Bed & Breakfast Mississippi

P.O. Box 3479, Meridian, 39303
(601) 482-5483 (information)
(800) 633-MISS (reservations)
FAX (601) 693-7447
e-mail: blincolnh@aol.com

**65.** Circa 1890. This lovely old farmhouse with curved staircase has been lovingly restored to its present beauty with half-tester Victorian beds and heirloom antiques. Walk the 150-acre farm with its beautiful wildflowers, colorful birds, and trees. Enjoy a full southern breakfast and a full-course dinner included in the price. Three guest rooms with private baths. $75-105.

# TUPELO

## The Mockingbird Inn Bed & Breakfast

305 North Gloster, 38801
(601) 841-0286
e-mail: sandbird@netdoor.com
www.bbonline.com/ms/mockingbird/

Discover the romance of a different place and time in an award-winning enchanting getaway in the heart of Tupelo. Guest rooms have international decor, private baths, telephones, modem hookup, cable TVs, and alarm clocks. One guest room has a double Jacuzzi, another a fireplace, and another a sitting area. Light evening snack and beverages are complimentary. Two Civil War battlefields are nearby; five minutes to Elvis's birthplace. Just off the Natchez Trace Parkway. Near the coliseum and popular restaurants. Rated in the Top Ten Best Bed and Breakfasts in Mississippi. Children over 10 welcome. Inquire about accommodations for pets.

Hosts: Jim and Sandy Gilmer
Rooms: 7 (PB) $65-125
Full Breakfast
Credit Cards: A, B, C, D
Note: 5, 7, 9, 10 11, 12, 14, 15

Mockingbird Inn

7 No smoking; 8 Children welcome; 9 Social drinking allowed; 10 Tennis nearby; 11 Swimming nearby; 12 Golf nearby; 13 Skiing nearby; 14 May be booked through a travel agent; 15 Handicapped accessible.

## Natchez Trace Bed & Breakfast Reservation Service

P.O. Box 193, Hampshire, TN 38461
(931) 285-2777; (800) 377-2770
e-mail: natcheztrace@worldnet.att.net
www.bbonline.com/natcheztrace

**Mockingbird Inn.** In downtown Tupelo—across the street from Elvis's school—and about two miles from the trace, each room in this home is of a different theme, each reflecting the style and charm of a different part of the world. Private telephones, internet connection, evening snacks, handicapped accessible. Special romance package available. Rated in the Top Ten Best Bed and Breakfasts in Mississippi. $75-125.

## VICKSBURG

## Anchuca

1010 East First Street, 39180
Vicksburg, MS 39180
(601) 661-0111; (888) 686-0111
FAX (601) 661-0420

This early Greek Revival mansion rises splendidly above the brick-paved streets of Vicksburg. Confederate President Jefferson Davis once addressed the townspeople from the balcony while his brother was living in the home after the Civil War. Magnificently furnished in period antiques. Overnight guests accommodated in the main house and a turn-of-the-century guest cottage. Seated plantation breakfast served, swimming pool, Jacuzzi, tours, and dinner parties all available.

Host: Loveta Byrne
Rooms: 6 (PB) $85-140
Full Breakfast
Credit Cards: A, B
Notes: 2, 5, 7, 9, 10, 11, 12, 14

Annabelle

## Annabelle

501 Speed Street, 39180
(601) 638-2000; (800) 791-2000
FAX (601) 636-5054
e-mail: annabelle@vicksburg.com
www.missbab.com/annabelle

Overnight memories are taken from this historic 1868 two-story Victorian home in Vicksburg's historic garden district. Elegantly, but comfortably, furnished in beautiful antiques, Annabelle offers king- and queen-size beds, 12-foot-high ceilings, in-room cable TV, whirlpool tubs, air conditioning, a beautiful Vieux Carré courtyard, and sparkling swimming pool surrounded by crepe myrtle, pecan, and magnolia trees. A delicious southern breakfast is served in the formal dining room. AAA three-diamond rating. Mobil Travel Guide three-star rating. German spoken.

Hosts: Carolyn and George Mayer
Rooms: 5 (PB) $95-125
Suites: 2 (PB) $125-145
Full Breakfast
Credit Cards: A, B, C, D
Notes: 2, 5, 7, 9, 10, 11, 12, 14

## Belle of the Bends

508 Klein Street, 39180
(800) 844-2308

The Belle of the Bends is a Victorian mansion, built in 1876 in classic Italianate architecture.

NOTES: Credit cards accepted: A MasterCard; B Visa; C American Express; D Discover; E Diner's Club; F Other; 2 Personal checks accepted; 3 Lunch available; 4 Dinner available; 5 Open all year; 6 Pets welcome;

Belle of the Bends

It is nestled on a bluff providing a view of the Mississippi River from the verandas that wrap around three sides of this charming southern mansion. The home is elegantly decorated in period family antiques. In-residence owners, Wally and Jo Pratt, will conduct a personal tour of the home and gardens.

Host: Jo Pratt
Rooms: 5 (PB) $95-135
Full Breakfast
Credit Cards: A, B, C, D
Notes: 2, 5, 7, 8, 9, 12, 14

## Cedar Grove Mansion Inn & Restaurant

2300 Washington Street, 39180
(800) 862-1300; FAX (601) 634-6126

Make Cedar Grove the next romantic escape. Capture *Gone With the Wind* elegance and romance in exquisite guest rooms/suites. Each room is lavishly decorated and furnished with period antiques combined with the conveniences of private bath, cable TV, telephone, and air conditioning. Relax with a mint julep in the piano bar—the perfect prelude to a romantic gourmet candlelight dinner in the Garden Room Restaurant. Awake to a full southern breakfast followed by a historic tour.

Host: Rhonda Abraham
Rooms: 29 (PB) $85-165
Full Breakfast
Credit Cards: A, B, C, D, E
Notes: 4, 5, 9, 10, 11, 12, 15

## Lincoln, Ltd.; Bed & Breakfast Mississippi

P.O. Box 3479, Meridian, 39303
(601) 482-5483 (information)
(800) 633-MISS (reservations)
FAX (601) 693-7447
e-mail: blincolnh@aol.com

**35.** This home, circa 1873, was built as a wedding present from father to daughter. It is an interesting mixture of Victorian and Greek Revival architectural styles. All bedrooms are furnished with antiques and have private baths. Some rooms are available with fireplaces and TVs. Enjoy a spectacular view of the Mississippi River and valley from a rocking chair on the front gallery. Full plantation breakfast is included. Listed in the National Register of Historic Places. Six guest rooms. $110 and up.

**36.** Lavish antebellum mansion built between 1840 and 1858 as a wedding present from a wealthy businessman to his bride. *Gone With the Wind* elegance that guests won't soon forget. Exquisitely furnished with many original antiques. Enjoy the beautiful formal gardens, gazebos, and fountains. Relax in the courtyard. Pool and spa available. Listed in the National Register of Historic Places. Its 17 guest rooms have private baths. $85-160.

**41.** Elegant antebellum mansion, circa 1856, in Vicksburg's historic district. It is the best example of Palladian architecture found in Mississippi. Used as a hospital during the Civil War, it was shelled during the siege of Vicksburg. Listed in the National Register of Historic Places. A welcoming beverage, tour of the home, and full breakfast are included. Eight guest rooms. $95 and up.

**73.** This historic home, circa 1876, was named after an excursion riverboat and overlooks the Mississippi River. Sit on the porch and watch riverboats pass by, or stroll in the informal gardens. The home is an easy walk to other historic homes, restaurants, and attractions. Enjoy

7 No smoking; 8 Children welcome; 9 Social drinking allowed; 10 Tennis nearby; 11 Swimming nearby; 12 Golf nearby; 13 Skiing nearby; 14 May be booked through a travel agent; 15 Handicapped accessible.

one of the three guest rooms filled with family antiques. $95 and up.

**96.** Circa 1835, frequented by notable military leaders such as General Stephen D. Lee. Complemented by its enchanting three-story elliptical spiral staircase, Balfour House is considered to be one of the first Greek Revival structures in Mississippi. Listed in the National Register of Historic Places. Arrangements for groups include candlelight tours, basket lunches, refreshments on the galleries, and southern breakfasts. Welcoming beverage and plantation breakfast included. Telephone and cable TV. Four guest rooms. $95 and up.

## Natchez Trace Bed & Breakfast Reservation Service

P.O. Box 193, Hampshire, TN 38461
(931) 285-2777; (800) 377-2770
e-mail: natcheztrace@worldnet.att.net
www.bbonline.com/natcheztrace

**Cedar Grove Mansion.** Fifteen miles from the trace, in Vicksburg. Stay in one of the lavishly decorated 14 rooms in the main mansion, completed in 1852, the carriage house, or one of the cottages, some with fireplaces and Jacuzzis. There are five acres of formal gardens, croquet, a swimming pool, and a terraced room garden. Guests can relax in the piano bar—the perfect prelude to a romantic gourmet candlelight dinner in their on-site Garden Room Restaurant. $90-145.

**The Corners.** Milepost 60 or 67. In historic Vicksburg, 15 miles from the trace, this circa 1873 mansion, built as a wedding present to a daughter, is listed in the National Register of Historic Places. All rooms are furnished with antiques and include TV; some have working fireplaces. There is a 68-foot gallery with a spectacular view of the Mississippi River. Full plantation breakfast is included. $85-125.

**Stained Glass Manor.** "One of the most lavish residential displays of leaded & stained glass,"

according to the National Register of Historic Places. A fine example of Mission-style architecture, built by a descendant of the founder of Vicksburg. Beautiful furnishings—working fireplaces in many rooms. One room very suitable for families, with children welcome. Smoking permitted in some areas. $99-124.

## WEST

## The Alexander House

210 Green Street, P.O. Box 187, 39192
(601) 967-2266; (800) 350-8034

Step inside the front door of the Alexander House bed and breakfast and return to a more leisurely and gracious way of life. The Alexander House represents Victorian decor at its prettiest and country hospitality at its best. Captain Alexander, Dr. Joe, Ulrich, Annie, and Miss Bealle are the names of the rooms waiting to cast a spell over those who visit. Day trips to historic or recreational areas may be charted or chartered.

Hosts: Ruth Ray and Woody Dinstel
Rooms: 5 (3 PB; 2 SB) $65
Full Breakfast
Credit Cards: A, B, C, D
Notes: 2, 3, 4, 5, 7, 9, 14

The Alexander House

# North Carolina

## The Doctor's Inn

716 South Park Street, 27203
(336) 625-4916; (336) 625-4822

The Doctor's Inn is a home filled with antiques. It offers its guests the utmost in personal accommodations. Amenities include a gourmet breakfast served on fine china and silver, fresh flowers, terry-cloth robes and slippers, homemade goodies, and a refrigerator stocked with soft drinks, juices, and ice cream parfaits. Nearby are 60 potteries and the North Carolina Zoo.

Hosts: Marion and Beth Griffin
Rooms: 2 (1 PB; 1 SB) $95
Full Breakfast
Credit Cards: None
Notes: 2, 5, 7, 9, 10, 12

## Acorn Cottage

25 St. Dunstans Circle, 28803
(828) 253-0609; (800) 699-0609
FAX (828) 258-2129

An Art and Crafts bungalow country cottage in the heart of Asheville. The four individually decorated guest rooms feature queen-size beds, fine linens, air conditioning, TVs, and private baths. Come relax in this 1925 architecturally designed home built of North Carolina granite, maple hardwood floors, and a beautiful stone fireplace. Acorn Cottage is in a natural woodland setting only one-quarter mile from the

Acorn Cottage

Biltmore Estate. Inquire about accommodations for children.

Host: Sharon Tabor
Rooms: 4 (PB) $80-100
Full Breakfast
Credit Cards: A, B, C, D
Notes: 2, 5, 7, 9, 10, 11, 12, 13, 14

## Albemarle Inn

86 Edgemont Road, 28801
(828) 255-0027; (800) 621-7435
FAX (828) 236-3397
e-mail: info@albemarleinn.com
www.albemarleinn.com

This elegant Greek Revival mansion listed in the National Register of Historic Places is located in the residential Grove Park section of Asheville. The inn features an exquisite carved oak staircase with unique circular balcony and a stone veranda overlooking three-fourths of an acre of landscaped grounds and gardens. Exceptionally spacious period guest rooms offer private baths with claw-foot tubs, fine European linens, and queen- or king-size beds. Full gourmet breakfasts.

7 No smoking; 8 Children welcome; 9 Social drinking allowed; 10 Tennis nearby; 11 Swimming nearby; 12 Golf nearby; 13 Skiing nearby; 14 May be booked through a travel agent; 15 Handicapped accessible.

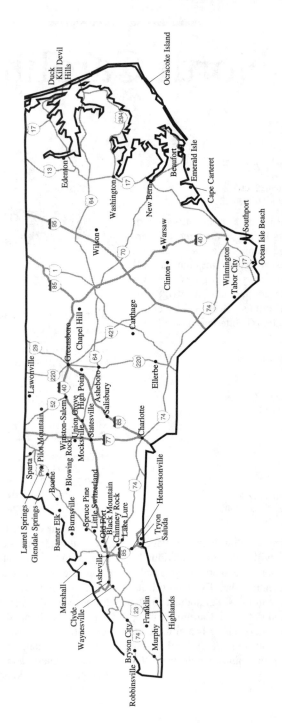

North Carolina

Albemarle Inn

Hosts: Cathy and Larry Sklar
Rooms: 11 (PB) $110-235
Full Breakfast
Credit Cards: A, B, D
Notes: 2, 5, 7, 9, 10, 12

## Applewood Manor Inn

62 Cumberland Circle, 28801-1718
(828) 254-2244; (800) 442-2197
FAX (828) 254-0899
http: //comscape.com/apple

A fine turn-of-the-century Colonial Revival
manor set on one and one-half acres of rolling
lawn and woods in Asheville's historic Montford district. Within 15 minutes of the finest
restaurants, antique shops, and area attractions,
including the Biltmore Estate. Amenities
include private baths, queen-size beds, fireplaces, balconies, full gourmet breakfasts, and
complimentary beverages. Bikes, badminton,
and croquet are available.

Applewood Manor Inn

Hosts: Coby and John Verhey
Rooms: ⊂ (PB) $95-115
Cottage: 1
Full Breakfast
Credit Cards: A, B
Notes: 2, 5, 7, 10, 12, 14

## Asheville Accommodations/ Carolina Mornings, Inc.

109 Circadian Way, Chapel Hill, 27516
(800) 770-9055; (888) MORNINGS (667-6467)
FAX (919) 929-5061
e-mail: carolinamornings@mindspring.com
www.carolinamornings.com

A reservation service for bed and breakfasts
and country inns in Asheville and throughout
western North Carolina. The service is able to
assist travelers wishing to visit the Biltmore
Estate with comfortable accommodations at in-
town sites. Many of the bed and breakfasts are
in historic homes elegantly furnished with
antiques. The service is also able to find lodging for those who want to explore the mountains, visit the Piedmont, and enjoy the sandy
beaches. Offering lakeside lodges or hilltop
retreats close to the Blue Ridge Parkway. Also
the service offers secluded cabins and guest
houses throughout the area.

Rates: $70-385
Full Breakfast
Credit Cards: A, B, C, D
Notes: 2, 3, 4, 5, 7, 8, 9, 10, 11, 12, 13

**01.** This 1925 home is built of North Carolina
granite, with maple floors and a beautiful stone
fireplace. In the heart of Asheville, in a lovely
wooded setting, the bed and breakfast is only
one-fourth mile from the entrance to the Biltmore Estate. Children welcome. TV available.
$85-100.

**03.** In the National Register of Historic Places,
this 1883 house is a comfortable blend of Victorian elegance and southern charm. A full breakfast is served in the dining room or opt for a
Continental basket in guests' room. Tandem

NOTES: Credit cards accepted: A MasterCard; B Visa; C American Express; D Discover; E Diner's Club;
F Other; 2 Personal checks accepted; 3 Lunch available; 4 Dinner available; 5 Open all year; 6 Pets welcome;
7 No smoking; 8 Children welcome; 9 Social drinking allowed; 10 Tennis nearby; 11 Swimming nearby;
12 Golf nearby; 13 Skiing nearby; 14 May be booked through a travel agent; 15 Handicapped accessible.

biking packages and weekend workshops available. $105-125.

**05.** Sitting in a quiet neighborhood and minutes from the Biltmore Estate, this quaint one-room cottage offers convenience and flexibility. Prepare own breakfast from the stocked refrigerator and relax in the loft in the queen-size bed. $85.

**08.** Fine Old World charm in the secluded gardens surrounding a heated swimming pool on the grounds of this estate. Rooms feature Jacuzzi baths, four-poster beds, and fireplaces. Delightful British innkeepers serve tea every afternoon at four. TV and telephone on request. $105-150.

**18.** Enjoy a gourmet breakfast at this wonderful, restored 100-year-old stone and shingle home just one mile from the Biltmore Estate entrance. Amenities include antique mahogany furniture, as well as other English antiques and wrought-iron canopied beds. TV in the rooms. $85-110.

**22.** The original tin roof still graces this grand Victorian "painted lady." Two- and three-room suites, many with Jacuzzi baths, all with TV, VCR, telephone, and full kitchen make guests' stay comfortable, convenient, and memorable. Guest cottage available. Children welcome. From $115.09.

**24.** An elegant mansion in the National Register of Historic Places featuring lovely tea gardens and a wraparound porch. Some rooms have one- or two-person Jacuzzis and fireplaces. TV, VCR, and telephone in rooms, as well as a fitness facility and bicycles. $115-250.

**32.** Experience the elegance of this distinguished guest house on 80 rolling acres. Magnificent mountain views and fireplaces in each of the five beautifully appointed rooms. Indulge in the romantic and luxurious suite and spa complete with Jacuzzi. Gourmet

breakfast and champagne reception each evening. $190-385.

**54.** Breathtaking views await this cedar and stone 12-room inn at an impressive 3,200 feet elevation. Enjoy a crackling fireplace in the guest room or relax on own private balcony. The views from the two-person tubs are an added delight. $130-185.

Beaufort House

## *Beaufort House Victorian Bed & Breakfast*

61 North Liberty Street, 28801
(828) 254-8334: www.beauforthouse.com

Built in 1894, Beaufort House stands today as an eloquent testimony to the gentle style of living prevalent at the turn of the century. Encompassing romance, history, and elegance, Beaufort House offers guests the comforts of modern luxuries such as central air conditioning, TVs, VCRs, telephones, Jacuzzis, fireplaces. Enjoy bicycles and mountain views. The Beaufort House is listed in the National Register of Historic Places and was previously featured in *National Geographic Traveler* magazine. AARP, corporate, and government rates. Inquire about accommodations for children.

Hosts: Robert and Jacqueline Glasgow
Rooms: 11 (PB) $65-225
Full Breakfast
Credit Cards: A, B
Notes: 2, 5, 7, 9, 10, 11, 12, 13, 14, 15

---

NOTES: Credit cards accepted: A MasterCard; B Visa; C American Express; D Discover; E Diner's Club; F Other; 2 Personal checks accepted; 3 Lunch available; 4 Dinner available; 5 Open all year; 6 Pets welcome;

## The Black Walnut Bed & Breakfast Inn

288 Montford Avenue, 28801
(828) 254-3878; (800) 381-3878
e-mail: info@blackwalnut.com
www.blackwalnut.com

The Black Walnut is a turn-of-the-century Shingle-style home in the heart of the Montford historic district just minutes from downtown and the Biltmore Estate. Amenities include large guest rooms with air conditioning, working fireplaces, TVs, VCRs, and private baths. Jacuzzi suites are also available. Full breakfast served by candlelight includes a special blend coffee, homemade coffee cakes, muffins, and preserves. Private cottage and loft suite available with kitchenette.

Hosts: Randy and Sandra Glasgow
Rooms: 7 (PB) $95-185
Full Breakfast
Credit Cards: A, B, C, D
Notes: 2, 5, 7, 8, 10, 11, 12, 13, 14

The Black Walnut

## Blake House Inn

150 Royal Pines Drive, 28704
(828) 681-5227; (888) 353-5227
FAX (828) 681-0420; e-mail: blakeinn@aol.com
www.blakehouse.com

Blake House Inn was built circa 1847. Surrounded by 150-year-old pine and sycamore trees, this fine example of Italianate architec-

Blake House Inn

ture with Gothic influence will bring guests back in time to the more relaxed atmosphere of the 1800s. Blake House Inn boasts of 22-inch thick granite walls, 12-foot high ceilings, and 5 spacious guest rooms all with private baths. The newly remodeled Carriage House has a lovely king-size suite. Gourmet breakfasts and afternoon hors d'oeuvres are served daily. Six miles from Biltmore Estate.

Hosts: Nancy and Terry Rice
Rooms: 6 (PB) $95-195
Full Breakfast
Credit Cards: A, B, C, D
Notes: 2, 3, 4, 5, 6, 7, 8, 9, 11, 12, 14

## Cairn Brae

217 Patton Mountain Road, 28804
(828) 252-9219
http://ourworld.compuserve.com/homepages/
    mrichardson/

Cairn Brae is in the mountains above Asheville. Very private, on three acres of woods, but only 12 minutes from downtown. Private guest entrance to living room with fireplace. Full country breakfast. Afternoon refreshments served on the terrace overlooking Beaverdam Valley. Beautiful views. Woodsy trails. Air conditioned. All rooms have private baths. Quiet and secluded. Closed December through March. Children over 10 welcome.

Hosts: Milli and Ed Adams
Rooms: 3 (PB) $95-110

7 No smoking; 8 Children welcome; 9 Social drinking allowed; 10 Tennis nearby; 11 Swimming nearby; 12 Golf nearby; 13 Skiing nearby; 14 May be booked through a travel agent; 15 Handicapped accessible.

Full Breakfast
Credit Cards: A, B, D
Notes: 2, 7, 9, 10, 11, 12, 14

## *Cedar Crest Victorian Inn*

674 Biltmore Avenue, 28803
(828) 252-1389

An 1890 Queen Anne mansion listed in the National Register of Historic Places features carved oak paneling, ornate glasswork, authentic Victorian decor with period antiques, and romantic guest rooms. Croquet court, fireplaces, and English gardens. A full breakfast is served buffet style. One-quarter mile from the entrance to the Biltmore Estate and four miles from the Blue Ridge Parkway. AAA four-diamond-rated. Children over 10 welcome.

Hosts: Jack and Barbara McEwan
Rooms: 9 (PB) $140-200
Suites: 2
Full Breakfast
Credit Cards: A, B, C, D, E
Notes: 2, 5, 7, 9, 10, 11, 12, 14

## *The Colby House*

230 Pearson Drive, 28801
(828) 253-5644; (800) 982-2118

Elegance with comfort is the theme of this Dutch Colonial home in the Montford historic district. Amenities include beautiful gardens, an outdoor sitting porch and fireplaces. Four

The Colby House

individually decorated guest rooms have queen-size beds and private baths. Bountiful breakfasts, evening social hours, and beverages and cookies around-the-clock complete this hospitable setting.

Hosts: Bonnie and Peter Marsh
Rooms: 4 (PB) $115-150
Full Breakfast
Credit Cards: A, B, C, D
Notes: 2, 5, 7, 9, 10, 12, 13, 14

Corner Oak Manor

## *Corner Oak Manor*

53 St. Dunstans Road, 28803
(828) 253-3525

This lovely English Tudor home is just minutes away from the famed Biltmore Estate and Gardens. Antiques, handmade wreaths, weavings, and stitchery complement the restored elegance of this home. Breakfast specialties include orange French toast, blueberry-ricotta pancakes, or four-cheese herb quiche. A living room with fireplace and baby grand piano and outdoor deck with Jacuzzi are among the gracious amenities.

Hosts: Karen and Andy Spradley
Rooms: 4 (PB) $110-165
Full Breakfast
Credit Cards: A, B, C, D
Notes: 2, 5, 7, 9, 10, 11, 12

NOTES: Credit cards accepted: A MasterCard; B Visa; C American Express; D Discover; E Diner's Club; F Other; 2 Personal checks accepted; 3 Lunch available; 4 Dinner available; 5 Open all year; 6 Pets welcome;

## Dry Ridge Inn

26 Brown Street, Weaverville, 28787
(828) 658-3899; e-mail: dryridgeinn@msn.com

This casually elegant bed and breakfast is quietly removed 10 minutes north of Asheville's many attractions. Country-style antiques and contemporary art enhance this unique 1800s village farmhouse. A full breakfast is served with individual seating. Relax in the outdoor spa or with quality spiritual reading after enjoying a day of mountain adventure. Nearby white-water rafting, horseback riding, and Biltmore Estate. Artist-owned; studio and gallery on premises. Art and antiques for sale.

Hosts: Paul and Mary Lou Gibson
Rooms: 7 (PB) $95-135
Full Breakfast
Credit Cards: A, B, C, D
Notes: 2, 5, 7, 8, 9, 12, 13, 14

## Flint Street Inns

116 Flint Street, 28801
(828) 253-6723

Two lovely old homes on an acre lot with century-old trees. Comfortable walking distance to town. Guest rooms, furnished with antiques and collectibles, have air conditioning and queen-size beds, and some have fireplaces. The inns provide complimentary beverages and restaurant menus. Breakfast is full southern style, featuring home-baked breads and iron-skillet biscuits. Smoking in designated areas only.

Hosts: Rick, Lynne, and Marion Vogel
Rooms: 8 (PB) $100
Full Breakfast
Credit Cards: A, B, C, D
Notes: 2, 5, 9, 10, 11, 12, 14

## The Inn on Montford

296 Montford Avenue, 28801
(800) 254-9569; www.innonmontford.com

A turn-of-the-century Arts and Craft home by Asheville's most famous architect. Filled with light, it is a perfect setting for the owners' eclectic collection of antiques, Victorian silver napkin rings, tea caddies, Staffordshire pottery, maps, Baxter prints, period cut glass, and Persian rugs. Fireplaces in all rooms, whirlpools in three rooms, a wide front porch with antique wicker furniture. The inn is in the Montford historic district, close to downtown and a 10-minute drive from the Biltmore Estate.

Hosts: Lynn and Ron Carlson
Rooms: 4 (FB) $145-195
Full Breakfast
Credit Cards: A, B, C, D
Notes: 2, 5, 7, 9, 10, 12, 13, 14

Flint Street Inns

7 No smoking; 8 Children welcome; 9 Social drinking allowed; 10 Tennis nearby; 11 Swimming nearby; 12 Golf nearby; 13 Skiing nearby; 14 May be booked through a travel agent; 15 Handicapped accessible.

## The Old Reynolds Mansion

100 Reynolds Heights, 28804
(828) 254-0496; (800) 709-0496
www.oldreynoldsmansionhistoricinn.com

Bed and breakfast in an antebellum mansion listed in the National Register of Historic Places. Beautifully restored with furnishings from a bygone era. Country setting with acres of trees and mountain views from all rooms. Wood-burning fireplaces, two-story verandas, and pool. Two-night minimum weekends and holidays. Open weekends only January through May.

Hosts: Fred and Helen Faber
Rooms: 10 (8 PB; 2 SB) $60-120
Cottage: $130
Continental Breakfast
Credit Cards: None
Notes: 2, 7, 9, 10, 11, 12, 13

The Old Reynolds Mansion

## Richmond Hill Inn

87 Richmond Hill Drive, 28806
(800) 545-9238; FAX (828) 252-8726

This premier inn of the South features 36 well-appointed rooms with private baths in three distinctive areas: the 1889 Victorian mansion, charming cottages surrounding a croquet court, and the Garden Pavilion with beautiful views of the Parterre Garden and waterfall. Six acres of Victorian gardens. Exquisite dining in Gabrielle's restaurant. AAA four-diamond-rated. Surrounded by the Blue Ridge Mountains and close to Biltmore Estate.

Host: Susan Michel
Rooms: 36 (PB) $145-450

Richmond Hill Inn

Full Breakfast
Credit Cards: A, B, C
Notes: 2, 4, 5, 7, 9, 10, 11, 12, 14, 15

## The Wright Inn and Carriage House

235 Pearson Drive, 28801
(828) 251-0789; (800) 552-5724
FAX (828) 251-0929; www.wrightinn.com

Elegantly restored, circa 1898-1899, a fine example of Queen Anne architecture. Listed in the National Register of Historic Places, centrally air conditioned, with eight distinctive bedrooms (one with fireplace), and a luxurious suite with a fireplace; all with private baths, cable TVs, and telephones. Full scrumptious breakfast, afternoon tea (inn only), and refresh-

The Wright Inn

NOTES: Credit cards accepted: A MasterCard; B Visa; C American Express; D Discover; E Diner's Club; F Other; 2 Personal checks accepted; 3 Lunch available; 4 Dinner available; 5 Open all year; 6 Pets welcome;

ments. Children 12 and older welcome. The three-bedroom carriage house is ideal for groups/families and children of all ages. AAA three-diamond-rated; ABBA-rated "Excellent."

Hosts: Carol and Art Wenczel
Rooms: 8 (PB) $110-135
Suite: 1 (PB) $155
Carriage House: 3 (S2B) $235
Full Breakfast
Credit Cards: A, B, D
Notes: 2, 5, 7, 9, 10, 11, 12, 13

## BANNER ELK

### Archer's Mountain Inn

Route 2, Box 56 A, 28604
(828) 898-9004; www.archersinn.com

Archers Mountain is nestled on Beech Mountain at nearly 5,000 feet above sea level, where activities abound for each season. The inn features 15 rooms, all of which have fireplaces, private baths, and porches overlooking outstanding mountainside views. Room amenities vary from suites which offer private balconies, hot tubs, Jacuzzis, and first-class appointments to smaller more traditional bed and breakfast-style rooms to efficiency-style rooms perfect for families. All rooms include a full gourmet breakfast that is served in the mountain-view dining room. Evening meals are prepared nightly by chef Brian Seeley. The dining room is handicapped accessible.

Hosts: Candi and Tony Catoe
Rooms: 15 (PB) $70-200
Full Breakfast
Credit Cards: A, B, D
Notes: 2, 4, 5, 7, 8, 9, 10, 11, 12, 13

### The Inn at Elk River

875 Main Street West, P.O. Box 2406, 28604
(828) 898-9669; FAX (828) 898-9678

The inn is in the heart of the Blue Ridge Mountains in the village of Banner Elk. This Colonial Williamsburg inn built in 1989 features eight spacious rooms—four with fireplaces, all with private baths and entrances onto the expansive decks which overlook the Blue Ridge Mountains. Boasting the highest peaks in the East, this area is often called the ski capital of the East. During the summer, Banner Elk is a golfer's dream and a hiker's playground.

Hosts: Wayne and Katherine Cumberland
Rooms: 8 (PB) $95-135
Full and Continental Breakfast
Credit Cards: A, B, D
Notes: 4, 5 7, 9, 10, 11, 12, 13, 14

## BEAUFORT

### The Langdon House Bed & Breakfast

135 Craven Street, 28516
(252) 728-5499; e-mail: innkeeper@coastalnet.com

A step into history; a residence for discerning guests, and an experience akin to visiting friends. The art of innkeeping is practiced in this restored Colonial home. Good food, comfort, cleanliness and accommodation of the guests' needs are the innkeeper's priorities. Special diets accommodated with advance notice. Mood is tempered by Vivaldi, Mozart, Windham Hill, Kottke. "After 14 plus years, I still enjoy generally taking care of my guests," proclaims owner/innkeeper Jimm Prest.

Host: Jimm Prest
Rooms: 4 (PB) $115-130
Full Breakfast
Credit Cards: None
Notes: 2, 5, 7, 9, 10, 11, 12

The Langdon House

7 No smoking; 8 Children welcome; 9 Social drinking allowed; 10 Tennis nearby; 11 Swimming nearby; 12 Golf nearby; 13 Skiing nearby; 14 May be booked through a travel agent; 15 Handicapped accessible.

## Pecan Tree Inn

116 Queen Street, 28516
(919) 728-6733

A gracious 1866 Victorian home filled with antiques, one-half block from the waterfront in Beaufort's historic district. Relax on one of the three porches or stroll through the large English garden. There are seven air-conditioned rooms, all with private baths. Two bridal suites feature a Jacuzzi for two and a king-size canopied bed. Guests will enjoy the delicious breakfast with freshly baked homemade muffins, breakfast cakes, and breads, along with a choice of fruit, cereal, and beverages for breakfast. Only a few blocks from wonderful restaurants and quaint shops.

Hosts: Susan and Joe Johnson
Rooms: 7 (PB) $70-135
Continental Breakfast
Credit Cards: A, B, C, D
Notes: 2, 5, 7, 9, 10, 11, 12, 14

## BLACK MOUNTAIN

## Friendship Lodge Bed & Breakfast

P.O. Box 877, 28707
(828) 669-9294

A cozy 10-bedroom bed and breakfast at the edge of Black Mountain and dedicated to the task of helping guests enjoy the natural beauty and the abundant attractions the area has to offer. Start the day with a sumptuous breakfast and follow one's heart to whatever one desires. The cozy bedrooms have two double beds and private baths; each room is delightfully different.

Hosts: Bob and Sarah LaBrant
Rooms: 10 (8 PB: 2 SB) $52-58
Full Breakfast
Credit Cards: None
Notes: 2, 7, 8, 9, 10, 11, 12

The Red Rocker Country Inn

## The Red Rocker Country Inn

136 North Dougherty Street, 28711
(828) 669-5991; (888) 669-5991

The Red Rocker Inn is a meticulously restored 17-room inn, on a quiet tree-lined street in beautiful Black Mountain. Each of the rooms has a private bath, some have fireplaces, all have the comforts of home. The inn is famous for friendly southern hospitality. Enjoy a peaceful afternoon rocking on the covered front porch, or take a quiet stroll through the wonderful antique and furniture shops of Black Mountain. And in the evening, save time to feast on famous mountain dinners, four courses served family style in one of the three lovely dining rooms. Open year-round, offering a perfect setting for group meetings and family reunions. Special rates available during the off-season.

Hosts: Craig and Margie Lindberg
Rooms: 17 (PB) $80-145
Full Breakfast
Credit Cards: A, B
Notes: 2, 3, 4, 5, 7, 8, 10, 11, 12, 13

## BLOWING ROCK

## The Inn at Ragged Gardens

203 Sunset Drive, P.O. Box 1927, 28605
(828) 295-9703
e-mail: ragged-gardens@boone.net
www.ragged-gardens.com

Built at the turn of the century, nestled in the village amidst an acre of gardens. Enter the

NOTES: Credit cards accepted: A MasterCard; B Visa; C American Express; D Discover; E Diner's Club; F Other; 2 Personal checks accepted; 3 Lunch available; 4 Dinner available; 5 Open all year; 6 Pets welcome;

gracious inn with rich hardwood-paneled walls, antique furnishings, covered porches, fireplaces, and a unique stone staircase. Stroll the lovely lawn and gardens. Retire to one of the splendid guest rooms, each with private bath and fireplace complemented by a delicious breakfast. Discover the quiet corner in the heart of the village of Blowing Rock. Children 12 and older welcome.

Hosts: Lee and Jama Hyett
Rooms: 12 (PB) $140-245
Full Breakfast
Credit Cards: A, B
Notes: 2, 5, 7, 9, 10, 11, 12, 13, 14

## Maple Lodge

Box 1236, Sunset Drive, 28605
(828) 295-3331

Elegant furnishings reflect the simplicity and charm of an earlier time. Guest rooms, filled with antiques, goose down comforters, lace, and handmade quilts, have private baths and king- or queen-size beds; some are canopied. A short stroll to craft shops, art galleries, professional summer theater, and fine restaurants. Grandfather Mountain, Linville Falls, the Blue Ridge Parkway, hiking, golf, and white-water rafting nearby.

Hosts: Marilyn and David Bateman
Rooms: 11 (PB) $85-140
Full Breakfast
Credit Cards: A, B, C, D, E
Notes: 2, 7, 9, 10, 11, 12, 13, 14

## BOONE

## Asheville Accommodations/ Carolina Mornings, Inc.

109 Circadian Way, Chapel Hill, 27516
(800) 770-9055; (888) MORNINGS (667-6467)
FAX (919) 929-5061
e-mail: carolinamornings@mindspring.com
www.carolinamornings.com

**62.** This historic home sits on 16 acres at 3,300 feet, complete with trout streams and hiking trails. Enjoy this charming antique-furnished home from guests' own porch or by one of six fireplaces. This home is truly a step back into history and nostalgia. $95-120.

## BREVARD

## The Red House Inn Bed & Breakfast

412 Probart Street, 28712
(828) 884-9349

The Red House on Probart Street was built in 1851 to be a trading post. Through the years it has been a railroad station, a court house, a post office, a private school, and a college. The Red House has been lovingly restored and is now a bed and breakfast. It is charmingly furnished with turn-of-the-century period antiques. Convenient to many area sites of interest and recreational activities. In the evening the famous Flat Rock Playhouse is nearby and, of course, the wonderful music of Brevard's very own nationally acclaimed Music Center. Open year-round.

Host: Lynne Ong
Rooms: 6 (4 PB; 2 SB) $59-99
Full Breakfast
Credit Cards: A, B
Notes: 2, 5, 7, 9, 10, 11, 12, 14, 15

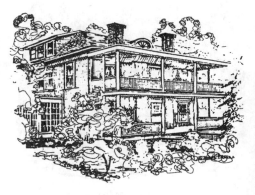

The Red House Inn

7 No smoking; 8 Children welcome; 9 Social drinking allowed; 10 Tennis nearby; 11 Swimming nearby; 12 Golf nearby; 13 Skiing nearby; 14 May be booked through a travel agent; 15 Handicapped accessible.

## Womble Inn

301 West Main, P.O. Box 1441, 28712
(828) 884-4770

Two blocks from the center of Brevard, the Womble Inn invites guests to relax in a welcoming, comfortable atmosphere. Each of the six guest rooms is specially furnished in antiques. All of the guest rooms have private baths and air conditioning. After a sound sleep, guests will be served breakfast on a silver tray, or guests may prefer to be seated in the dining room. Full breakfast is an option.

Hosts: Steve and Beth Womble
Rooms: 6 (PB) $62-72
Continental Breakfast
Credit Cards: A, B, D
Notes: 2, 3, 7, 8, 9, 10, 11

## BRYSON CITY

## Folkestone Inn

101 Folkestone Road, 28713
(828) 488-2730; (888) 812-3385
FAX (828) 488-0722
e-mail: innkeeper@folkestone.com
www.folkestone.com

The Folkestone Inn is a charming 1920s farmhouse nestled among Norway spruces, across a mountain brook, in a valley just a quarter-mile

Folkestone Inn

from the Deep Creek entrance to the Great Smoky Mountains National Park. Take a short walk to three sparkling waterfalls, or hike the park's trails. Enjoy nearby white-water rafting, fishing, horseback riding, and a scenic railway. Or just stay "home" at the inn and enjoy the view from a front porch rocker.

Hosts: Ellen and Charles Snodgrass
Rooms: 10 (PB) $69-98
Full Breakfast
Credit Cards: A, B, C, D
Notes: 2, 5, 7, 9, 12, 14

## Fryemont Inn

1 Fryemont Street, P.O. Box 459, 28713
(828) 488-2159; (800) 845-4879
e-mail: fryemont@dnet.net

Built in 1923, the Fryemont Inn is a unique vantage point from which to enjoy the Smoky Mountains. Enormous stone fireplaces and gleaming hardwood floors enhance this time-honored inn. Relax in rustic elegance, refresh in the mountainside pool, and enjoy favorite beverages in the fireside bar. Excellent dinners and breakfasts cooked to order make a stay at the Fryemont truly memorable. Rates quoted include dinner and breakfast for two.

Hosts: George and Sue Brown; Monica and George Brown, Jr.
Rooms: 45 (PB) $95-165
Full Breakfast
Credit Cards: A, B, D
Notes: 2, 3, 4, 5, 7, 8, 9, 10, 11, 12, 14

## BURNSVILLE

## Hamrick Inn Bed & Breakfast

7787 Highway 80 South, 28714
(704) 675-5251

This charming three-story Colonial-style stone inn is nestled at the foot of Mount Mitchell, highest mountain east of the Mississippi. Much of the lovely furniture was built by the hosts. There is a private porch off each guest room,

Hamrick Inn

where the view and cool mountain breezes may be enjoyed. Golf, hiking, fishing, rock hounding, and craft shopping are local activities. Near the Blue Ridge Parkway. Open April 1 through October 31.

Hosts: Neal and June Jerome
Rooms: 4 (PB) $70-80
Full Breakfast
Credit Cards: A, B
Notes: 2, 7, 9, 10, 11, 12

## CAPE CARTERET

### Harborlight Guest House Bed & Breakfast

332 Live Oak Drive, 28584
(800) 624-VIEW

The Harborlight, on the central North Carolina coast, is on a peninsula; thus, all suites offer panoramic water views. All suites offer private entrances, private baths, individual climate controls. Luxury suites offer two-person Jacuzzis, fireplaces, and in-room breakfasts. The inn is minutes from secluded island excursions, Cape Lookout Lighthouse, and waterfront shopping villages. A gourmet breakfast is served outdoors overlooking the water each morning.

Hosts: Bobby and Anita Gill
Rooms: 9 (PB) $75-200
Full Breakfast
Credit Cards: A, B, C
Notes: 5, 7, 9, 10, 11, 12, 15

## CARTHAGE

### The Blacksmith Inn

703 McReynolds Street, P.O. Box 1480, 28327
(910) 947-1692; (800) 284-4515

Pinehurst (the golf capital of the world) is just 12 minutes away. This beautiful example of 1870 southern architecture has been lovingly restored and is the former home of the blacksmith for the Tyson and Jones Buggy Factory. Four spacious, tastefully decorated rooms are available, with a fireplace in each room. Just 20 minutes from Seagrove (the pottery center of North Carolina), and Cameron and Aberdeen's antique shops and historic districts. In the National Register of Historic Places. In a historic district. No smoking inside.

Hosts: Gary and Shawna Smith
Rooms: 5 (3 PB; 2 SB) $50
Full Breakfast
Credit Cards: A, B
Notes: 2, 5, 8, 12, 14

## CHAPEL HILL

### The Fearrington House Inn

2000 Fearrington Village Center, Pittsboro, 27312
(919) 542-2121; www.fearrington.com

In a cluster of low, attractive buildings grouped around a courtyard and surrounded by gardens and rolling countryside, this elegant inn offers

The Fearrington House Inn

luxurious quarters in a country setting. The restaurant's sophisticated regional cuisine has received national acclaim, including AAA's five-diamond award.

Hosts: The Fitch Family
Rooms: 31 (PB) $175-350
Full Breakfast
Credit Cards: A, B, C
Notes: 3, 4, 5, 7, 9, 10, 11, 12, 14, 15

## The Inn at Bingham School

P.O. Box 267, 27514
(919) 563-5583; (800) 566-5583
FAX (919) 563-9826; e-mail: fdeprez@aol.com
www.bbhost.com/binghamschool
www.chapel-hill-inn.com

The Inn is an award-winning restoration of a National Trust Property. A unique combination of Greek Revival and Federal styles. Listed in the historic registry. Stroll the surrounding woodlands or curl up by the fire. Welcome the day over an elaborate southern breakfast. Just 11 miles west of Chapel Hill, offering a charming combination of peace and history close to gourmet dining, shopping, and UNC. Smoking permitted outside only.

Hosts: François and Christina Deprez
Rooms: 5 (PB) $75-120
Full Breakfast
Credit Cards: A, B, C, D, F
Notes: 2, 5, 8

## CHARLOTTE

### The Elizabeth Bed & Breakfast

2145 East Fifth Street, 28204
(704) 358-1368

This 1923 lavender "lady" is in historic Elizabeth, Charlotte's second-oldest neighborhood. European country-style rooms are beautifully appointed with antiques, ceiling fans, decorator

The Elizabeth

linens, and unique collections. All rooms have central air and private baths; some have TVs and telephones. Enjoy a generous breakfast, then relax in the garden courtyard, complete with charming gazebo, or stroll beneath giant oak trees to convenient restaurants and shopping.

Host: Joan Mastny
Rooms: 4 (PB) $79-109
Full Breakfast
Credit Cards: A, B, D
Notes: 2, 5, 7, 9, 11

### The Homeplace

5901 Sardis Road, 28270
(704) 365-1936
www.bbonline.com/nc/homeplace

Restored 1902 country Victorian with wraparound porch and tin roof, nestled amid two and one-half wooded acres. Secluded "cot-

The Homeplace

tage-style" gardens with a gazebo, brick walkways, and a 1930s log barn further enhance this nostalgic oasis in southeast Charlotte. Experienced innkeepers offer two guest rooms and one suite and a full breakfast. Opened in 1984, the Homeplace is "a reflection of the true bed and breakfast experience." Children over 12 welcome.

Hosts: Peggy and Frank Dearien
Rooms: 2 (2 PB) $120
Suite: 1 (PB) $140
Full Breakfast
Credit Cards: A, B, C
Notes: 2, 5, 7, 14

The Inn Uptown

## The Inn Uptown

129 North Poplar Street, 28202
(704) 342-2800; (800) 959-1990

Constructed in 1890 and historically listed as the Bagley-Mullen House, this chateau-esque home has been restored into "an elegant alternative in uptown hospitality." Convenient for corporate and leisure travelers. Six beautifully appointed rooms feature private baths, complimentary wine, remote control cable TVs, and telephones. A complimentary full breakfast features specialties from the inn's kitchen and is served in the dining room. Three-diamond AAA rating. Corporate rates are available.

Host: Elizabeth J. Rich
Rooms: 6 (PB) $119-169
Full Breakfast
Credit Cards: A, B, C, D, E
Notes: 2, 5, 7, 9, 14

## The Morehead Inn

1122 East Morehead Street, 28204
(704) 376-3357; (888) MOREHEAD
FAX (704) 335-1110

A historic property nestled in the heart of Dilworth, Charlotte's oldest neighborhood. The "Old Coddington House," as locals refer to it, has served as host to North Carolina's most prominent families and public servants. Built in 1917, the estate was the home of Charles and Marjorie Coddington, owners of all the Buick dealerships south of the Mason-Dixon line. The inn now serves as "the single most unique experience in Charlotte." The Georgian Revival mansion boasts all period and European antiques. Continental plus breakfast served.

Hosts: Billy Maddalon and Helen Price
Rooms: 12 (PB) $110-230
Continental Breakfast
Credit Cards: A, B, C, D, E
Notes: 2, 5, 7, 8, 9, 10, 11, 12, 14

## Still Waters

6221 Amos Smith Road, 28214
(704) 399-6299

A log resort home on two wooded acres overlooking the Catawba River at the upper end of Lake Wylie; within 15 minutes of downtown Charlotte. Full breakfast is served on glassed-in porch overlooking the lake. Enjoy the sport court, the garden, swimming, boating, fishing, or sitting in the lakeside gazebo. Convenient to I-85, airport, and Billy Graham Parkway.

Hosts: Janet and Rob Dyer
Rooms: 4 (PB) $55-85
Full Breakfast
Credit Cards: A, B, E
Notes: 2, 5, 7, 8, 9, 10, 11, 12, 14

## CHIMNEY ROCK

## Esmeralda Inn & Restaurant

Highway 74 A, P. O. Box 57, 28720
(828) 625-9105; FAX (828) 625-1915
www.esmeraldainn com

7 No smoking; 8 Children welcome; 9 Social drinking allowed; 10 Tennis nearby; 11 Swimming nearby; 12 Golf nearby; 13 Skiing nearby; 14 May be booked through a travel agent; 15 Handicapped accessible.

Esmeralda Inn

The Esmeralda Inn and Restaurant is a country inn in the beautiful Hickory Nut Gorge of western North Carolina, 27 miles east of Asheville. The lobby of the inn is constructed of locally grown locust trees with mountain laurel railings to the second floor. Glassed dining areas are available for lunch and dinner or meetings, weddings, conferences, and retreats. Dining areas have large windows allowing guests a great view of the wonderful gardens, waterfall, fountains, and Chimney Rock Park. The restaurant is a full-service restaurant serving American regional cuisine. Fourteen guest rooms are available for guests' comfort, all have climate control, TVs, and telephones with plug-ins for computers. "We hope you will plan a trip to Chimney Rock—Lake Lure area and enjoy the mountains, river, lake, and the small town friendliness of our area. We have it all!"

Hosts: Ackie and JoAnne Okpych
Rooms: 14 (PB) $85-110
Continental Breakfast
Credit Cards: A, B
Notes: 2, 3, 4, 5, 7, 8, 9, 10, 11, 12, 15

## CHIMNEY ROCK VILLAGE

### The Dogwood Inn

P.O. Box 159, Highway 64-74, 28720
(828) 625-4403; FAX (828) 625-8825
e-mail: dogwoodinn@blueridge.com
www.blueridge.net/~dogwoodinn

Stay in one of western North Carolina's finest bed and breakfast inns, riverside on the Rocky Broad River with dramatic views. Massive Chimney Rock Mountain can be seen from the porches. A full gourmet breakfast is served each morning. Jacuzzis available. Hiking, canoeing, horseback riding, antiquing all nearby. Packages are also available.

Host: Marsha Reynolds
Rooms: 11 (7 PB; 4 SB) $79-129
Full Breakfast
Credit Cards: A, B, C, D
Notes: 2, 7, 9, 10, 11, 12, 14

## DUCK

### Advice 5¢: a bed & breakfast

111 Scarborough Lane, P.O. Box 8278, 27949
(252) 255-1050; (800) ADVICE5 (238-4235)

Advice 5¢ may very well be "one of the best kept secrets" on the northern beaches of the Outer Banks. In the heart of Duck, this refreshing seaside haven exudes an air of casual simplicity. For special occasions, reserve the Daybreak Room, which includes a sitting area, cable TV, and Jacuzzi-style bathtub. Enjoy refreshing outdoor showers, beach chairs, books galore, and home-baked treats during daily afternoon tea.

Hosts: Nancy Caviness and Donna Black
Rooms: 5 (PB) $95-175
Continental Breakfast
Credit Cards: A, B
Notes: 2, 7, 9, 10, 11, 12

## EDENTON

### The Lords Proprietors' Inn

300 North Broad Street, 27932
(919) 482-3641

Establishing a reputation for the finest accommodations in North Carolina, the inn offers 20 elegantly appointed rooms with private baths and spacious parlors for gathering for after-

---

NOTES: Credit cards accepted: A MasterCard; B Visa; C American Express; D Discover; E Diner's Club; F Other; 2 Personal checks accepted; 3 Lunch available; 4 Dinner available; 5 Open all year; 6 Pets welcome;

The Lords Proprietors' Inn

noon tea by the fire. A four-course dinner is served Tuesday through Saturday by reservation. MAP rates Tuesday through Saturday. One room is handicapped accessible.

Hosts: Arch and Jane Edwards
Rooms: 20 (PB) $225-275
Full Breakfast
Credit Cards: None
Notes: 2, 5, 8, 9, 10, 11, 12, 14, 15

## Trestle House Inn

632 Soundside Road, 27932
(919) 482-2282; (800) 645-8466
e-mail: thinn@coastalnet.com
www.edenton.com/trestlehouse

Inn overlooks wildlife preserve surrounded on three sides by water. Golfing, hiking, biking, swimming, tennis, sightseeing, fishing, and bird watching available. Inside, the inn has California redwood beams from trees estimated to be over 450 years old. TV/game room. Fireplace, deck overlooking lake and pond. Historic Edenton was original colonial capital of North Carolina. The town retains the elegant charm of a bygone era including many of the most beautiful older homes in the country.

Hosts: Peter L. Bogus
Rooms: 5 (PB) $80-100

Full Breakfast
Credit Cards: A, B, C
Notes: 2, 5, 7, 9, 10, 11, 12, 14

## ELLERBE

### Ellerbe Springs Inn

2537 North Highway 220, 28338
(910) 652-5600; (800) 248-6467
www.ellerbesprings.com

Ellerbe Springs Inn is a beautiful, historic country inn on 50 acres of rolling hills. Established in 1857, the manor has been completely renovated and redecorated. Fourteen charming guest rooms feature antique furniture, private bathrooms, and cable TVs. Historic cottage overlooking lake has two suites. First-floor dining room serves breakfast, lunch, and dinner daily. Easy drive from Charlotte, Greensboro, Raleigh, and Myrtle Beach. National Register of Historic Places.

Host: Beth Cadieu
Rooms: 16 (PB) $54-98
Full Breakfast
Credit Cards: A, B, D
Notes: 2, 3, 4, 5, 7, 8, 9, 10, 12, 14

Ellerbe Springs Inn

## EMERALD ISLE

### Emerald Isle Inn & Bed & Breakfast By the Sea

502 Ocean Drive, 28594
(252) 354-3222
e-mail: adetwiller@coastalnet.com

7 No smoking; 8 Children welcome; 9 Social drinking allowed; 10 Tennis nearby; 11 Swimming nearby; 12 Golf nearby; 13 Skiing nearby; 14 May be booked through a travel agent; 15 Handicapped accessible.

Emerald Isle Inn Bed and Breakfast is the only bed and breakfast in Emerald Isle. It offers four unique accommodations, including the newly featured King Suite with ocean view. Enjoy a Continental plus breakfast and freshly ground coffee daily. The inn features porches with rockers, swings, ocean/bay views, and friendly conversation. With direct beach access, experience the warm blue Atlantic, colorful sunsets, and restful sounds of waves breaking on white sands, only steps from guests' suite. In-state checks accepted. AAA- and Mobil-rated.

Hosts: Marilyn and A. K. Detwiller
Rooms: 4 (PB) $75-165
Continental Breakfast
Credit Cards: A, B
Notes: 5, 7, 10, 11, 12, 14

## FRANKLIN

## *Buttonwood Inn*

50 Admiral Drive, 28734
(828) 369-8985; (888) 368-8985

A quaint, small mountain inn awaits those who prefer a cozy country atmosphere. Before hiking, golfing, gem mining, or horseback riding, enjoy a breakfast of puffy scrambled eggs and apple sausage ring or eggs Benedict, Dutch babies, blintz souffle, strawberry omelet, or stuffed French toast.

Rooms: 4 (PB) $60-87
Full Breakfast
Credit Cards: None
Notes: 2, 5, 7, 8, 9, 10, 11, 12

## *The Franklin Terrace*

159 Harrison Avenue, 28734
(828) 524-7907; (800) 633-2431
e-mail: stay@franklinterrace.com
www.franklinterrace.com

The Franklin Terrace, built as a school in 1887, is listed in the National Register of Historic Places. Wide porches and large guest rooms filled with period antiques will carry guests to a time gone by when southern hospitality was

at its best. Antiques, crafts, and gifts are for sale on the main floor. Within walking distance of Franklin's famous gem shops, clothing boutiques, and fine restaurants. Air conditioning. Cable TV. Open April 1 through November 15. Smoking permitted outside only. Children over the age of three are welcome. Social drinking permitted in rooms only.

Hosts: Ed and Helen Henson
Rooms: 9 (PB) $52-69
Full Breakfast
Credit Cards: A, B, C, D
Notes: 2, 10, 11, 12, 14

The Heritage Inn

## *The Heritage Inn*

43 Heritage Hollow Drive, (Just off Route 441 Business), 28734
(828) 524-4150; (888) 524-4150
FAX (828) 524-8167; e-mail: heritage@smnet.net

In Heritage Hollow, a quaint seven-acre country village within the town of Franklin, with restaurants, antique and mountain craft shops within walking distance. Near Cowee Valley where guests can try their hands at gem mines. Area also offers hiking trails, white-water rafting, waterfalls, golfing, country auctions, antiques, and seasonal skiing. Within 45-minute-drive of Great Smoky Mountains National Park, Cherokee Indian Reservation and Harrah's Casino. Gorgeous mountain views.

Innkeepers: Tina and Jim Bottomley
Rooms: 6 (PB) $75
Full Breakfast
Credit Cards: A, B, C
Notes: 2, 5, 7, 9, 10, 11, 12, 13, 14

NOTES: Credit cards accepted: A MasterCard; B Visa; C American Express; D Discover; E Diner's Club; F Other; 2 Personal checks accepted; 3 Lunch available; 4 Dinner available; 5 Open all year; 6 Pets welcome;

## GLENDALE SPRINGS

### Glendale Springs Inn & Restaurant

7414 NC Highway 16, P.O. Box 117, 28629
(336) 982-2103; FAX (336) 982-4036
e-mail: lsmith7689@aol.com
www.glendalespringsinn.com

Since 1892 the Glendale Springs Inn has been a welcome landmark for visitors to Ashe County and the Blue Ridge Parkway. Excellent water, pure mountain air, a superb dining menu, and a good night's rest continue to restore weary travelers. Enjoy the safe, unhurried mountain way of life. Canoe the exquisite New River. Explore back roads, scenic byways, and the region's many park trails. Visit the nearby university town. Return for afternoon tea or an evening cappuccino on the eastern Continental Divide's friendliest front porch. Smoking permitted outside.

Host: Amanda Smith
Rooms: 9 (PB) $95-115
Full Breakfast
Credit Cards: A, B, C, D
Notes: 2, 3, 4, 5, 7, 8, 9, 12, 13, 15

Glendale Springs Inn

## GREENSBORO

### Greenwood

205 North Park Drive, 27401
(336) 274-6350; (800) 535-9363

"A culinary escape," where a New Orleans chef prepares abundant breakfasts to order and

Greenwood

evening desserts in this 1900s chalet in the park. Candlelight packages include room service to five distinctive rooms with private baths. Dinner by special arrangement.

Hosts: Bob and Dolly Guertin
Rooms: 5 (PB) $95-175
Full Breakfast
Credit Cards: A, B, C, D, E
Notes: 2, 5, 7, 9, 10, 11, 12, 14

## HENDERSONVILLE

### Apple Inn

1005 White Pine Drive, 28739-3951
(704) 693-0107; (800) 615-6611

There's no place like home, unless it's the Apple Inn. Only two miles from downtown Hendersonville, the inn is on three acres featuring charmingly comfortable rooms, each with modern private bath that awaits guests' arrival. Delicious home-cooked breakfasts (served al fresco, weather permitting), fresh flowers, and antiques complement the ambiance of this turn-of-the-century home. Enjoy billiards, tennis, swimming, hiking, antiquing, bird watching, or just plain relaxing. Create tomorrow's memories amidst yesterday's charm!

Hosts: Bob and Pam Hedstrom
Rooms: 5 (PB) $85-140
Cottage: 1 (PB)
Full Breakfast
Credit Cards: A, B
Notes: 2, 5, 7, 9, 10, 11, 12, 13, 14

7 No smoking; 8 Children welcome; 9 Social drinking allowed; 10 Tennis nearby; 11 Swimming nearby; 12 Golf nearby; 13 Skiing nearby; 14 May be booked through a travel agent; 15 Handicapped accessible.

## Asheville Accommodations/ Carolina Mornings, Inc.

109 Circadian Way, Chapel Hill, 27516
(800) 770-9055; (888) MORNINGS (667-6467)
FAX (919) 929-5061
e-mail: carolinamornings@mindspring.com
www.carolinamornings.com

**12.** Experience a tasteful blend of European and American antiques and culture in an elegantly warm setting. Gourmet breakfast served in the formal dining room or on a covered porch with Turkish tiles. TV/VCR in all rooms. Rich video library. Walk to downtown Hendersonville. $85-175.

**38.** Offering a comfortable, homelike atmosphere, each charmingly decorated room bears the name of an apple. Relax on the secluded parklike grounds in hammocks and rockers or play badminton, horseshoes, or croquet. Mountain views with delicious home-cooked breakfasts. $79-125.

## The Waverly Inn

783 North Main Street, 28792
(828) 693-9193; (800) 537-8195
FAX (828) 692-1010; e-mail: waverlyinn@ioa.com

Listed in the National Register of Historic Places, the Waverly Inn is the oldest inn in

The Waverly Inn

Hendersonville. The recently renovated inn has something for everyone, including claw-foot tubs and king- and queen-size canopied beds. Convenient to restaurants, shopping, Biltmore Estate, Carl Sandburg home, Blue Ridge Parkway, and Flat Rock Playhouse. Member of NCBBI and IIA. Picnic lunch available.

Hosts: John and Diane Sheiry
Rooms: 15 (PB) $109-195
Full Breakfast
Credit Cards: A, B, C, D, E
Notes: 2, 5, 8, 9, 10, 11, 12, 14

## HICKORY

Hickory

## Hickory Bed & Breakfast

464 7th Street Southwest, 28602
(828) 324-0548; (800) 654-2961
fax (828) 324-0443
e-mail: www.hickoryb&b@conninc.com
www.hickoryonline.com/hickoryb&b

Enjoy this 1908 two-story Georgian-style home on one and one-half acres in a quiet residential area. The rooms are decorated and furnished with the enjoyment and comfort of guests in mind. Air conditioned throughout, and gas-log fireplaces in some rooms. Blocks from fabulous furniture shopping and gourmet restaurants. Full, long-remembered breakfasts are a tradition. Four rooms with private baths.

Hosts: Bob and Pat Lynch
Rooms: 4 (PB) $85-115
Full Breakfast
Credit Cards: A, B, D
Notes: 2, 5, 7, 11

NOTES: Credit cards accepted: A MasterCard; B Visa; C American Express; D Discover; E Diner's Club; F Other; 2 Personal checks accepted; 3 Lunch available; 4 Dinner available; 5 Open all year; 6 Pets welcome;

## HIGHLANDS

### Colonial Pines Inn

541 Hickory Street, 28741
(828) 526-2060

A quiet country guest house with lovely mountain views. Comfortably furnished with antiques and many fine accessories. One-half mile from Highlands' fine dining and shopping area. Full breakfast includes egg dishes, homemade breads, fresh fruit, coffee, and juice. Two separate guest houses with kitchens and fireplaces are great for families. Children over 12 welcome.

Hosts: Chris and Donna Alley
Rooms: 6 (PB) $80-120
Suites: $110-140
Guest House: $110-250
Full Breakfast
Credit Cards: A, B
Notes: 2, 5, 7, 9, 10, 11, 12, 13

Colonial Pines Inn

### The Laurels: Freda's Bed & Breakfast

3309 Horse Cove Road, 28741
(828) 526-2091

The Laurels is in historic Horse Cove, two and one-half miles from Highlands, on seven acres. Serves an English tea in the afternoon. Two fireplaces warm the cool evenings. A large English country breakfast features fruit, bacon, ham, eggs, pancakes. The hosts grind their own whole wheat that makes crunchy toast. Homemade jams and lemon curd. Fish the one-half-acre pond stocked with rainbow trout. No smoking.

The Laurels

Hosts: Warren and Freda Lorenz
Rooms: 5 (PB) $70-80
Full Breakfast
Credit Cards: None
Notes: 2, 7, 8, 9, 15

### Long House Bed & Breakfast

P.O. Box 2078. 28741
(828) 526-4394; (877) 841-9222 (toll-free)

Long House Bed and Breakfast is a rustic mountain retreat at the 4,000-foot level in the Blue Ridge Mountains. There are lots of hiking trails, waterfalls, and scenic areas within easy reach. The town of Highlands boasts of unique shopping and dining experiences. A full breakfast is served family-style and is usually one of the highlights of a visit. If guests are looking for cool summer days spent in the great outdoors, this is the place.

Long House

7 No smoking; 8 Children welcome; 9 Social drinking allowed; 10 Tennis nearby; 11 Swimming nearby; 12 Golf nearby; 13 Skiing nearby; 14 May be booked through a travel agent; 15 Handicapped accessible.

Hosts: Lynn and Valerie Long
Rooms: 4 (PB) $85-135
Full Breakfast
Credit Cards: A, B
Notes: 2, 5, 7, 8, 9, 10, 11, 12

## Ye Olde Stone House Bed & Breakfast

1337 South Fourth Street, 28741
(828) 526-5911

This house built of stone is a mile from town. Rooms are bright, cheerful, and comfortably furnished. Perfect places for relaxing include a sunroom, porch, 30-foot deck, and attached year-round gazebo, all with view. Two fireplaces provide gathering spots. After a restful night's sleep, rise to the smell of freshly brewed coffee and a full country breakfast. Separate, completely furnished chalet and log cabin with fireplaces and meadow views. Breakfast is included in the rates for the bed and breakfast only. Featured on the cover of 1996 edition of *The Annual Directory of American and Canadian Bed & Breakfasts*.

Hosts: Jim and Rene Ramsdell
Rooms: 4 (PB) $85-100
Chalet and cabins: $120-180
Full Breakfast
Credit Cards: A, B
Notes: 2, 5, 7, 8, 9, 10, 11, 12, 13

## HIGH POINT

## The Bouldin House Bed & Breakfast

4332 Archdale Road, Archdale, 27263
(336) 431-4909; (800) 739-1816

Fine lodging and hospitality amidst America's finest home furnishings showrooms—relaxed and casual; yet elegant. Each guest room has been wonderfully decorated and appointed for guests' comfort complete with king-size bed, ceiling fan, fireplace, and spacious, modern bath. Early morning coffee and tea service, Chef's Choice gourmet breakfasts, and evening refreshments including home-baked goodies from the Bouldin House kitchen await guests. Relax on the wraparound veranda, stroll on the grounds or chat with new friends.

Hosts: Larry and Ann Miller
Rooms: 4 (PB) $85-120
Full Breakfast
Credit Cards: A, B, C, D
Notes: 2, 5, 7, 9, 10, 12, 14

## KILL DEVIL HILLS

## Cypress House Bed & Breakfast

500 North Virginia Dare Trail, 27948
(252) 441-6127; (800) 554-2764
FAX (252) 441-2009; e-mail: cypresshse@aol.com
www.cypresshouseinn.com

This large beach house with cypress-wood interior is 500 feet from ocean beach. Quiet and restful. Ideal for relaxing and romance. Close to fine restaurants, golf, hang-gliding, kayaking, scuba diving, wind surfing, deep-sea fishing, shopping, and other attractions. Three-night minimum stay required for holidays.

Hosts: Karen Roos and Leon Faso
Rooms: 6 (PB) $75-120
Full Breakfast
Credit Cards: A, B, C, D
Notes: 2, 5, 7, 9, 10, 11, 12, 14

Cypress House

---

NOTES: Credit cards accepted: A MasterCard; B Visa; C American Express; D Discover; E Diner's Club; F Other; 2 Personal checks accepted; 3 Lunch available; 4 Dinner available; 5 Open all year; 6 Pets welcome;

## LAKE LURE

### Asheville Accommodations/ Carolina Mornings, Inc.

109 Circadian Way, Chapel Hill, 27516
(800) 770-9055; (888) MORNINGS (667-6467)
FAX (919) 929-5061
e-mail: carolinamornings@mindspring.com
www.carolinamornings.com

**11.** With a rare and wonderful combination of elegance and rustic charm, this inn rests on the shores of a mountain lake. Canoes, swimming, fishing, and a daily afternoon cruise with the owners make this a memorable bed and breakfast stay. $89-145.

## LAUREL SPRINGS

### Burgiss Farm Bed & Breakfast

294 Elk Knob Road, 28644
(800) 233-1505; e-mail: tburgiss@aol.com
www.breakfastinn.com

Honeymooners and anniversary couples love Burgiss Farm! This 1897 farmhouse high in the mountains has lots of space and privacy. Mountain biking, dancing at the barn, wading in the clear cool mountain water. Guests can select their breakfast from seven different selections and choose the time. Complimentary wine made by host. By reservations only. Best time to call is around 10 P.M.

Hosts: Nancy and Tom Burgiss
Rooms: 2 (PB) $90-135
Full Breakfast
Credit Cards: A, B
Notes: 2, 5, 7, 8, 9, 10, 12, 13

## LAWSONVILLE

### Southwyck Farm Bed & Breakfast

1070 Southwyck Farm Road, 27022-9768
(336) 593-8006 (phone/FAX)
e-mail: sowyckfarm@mindspring.com
www.southwyck.com

Southwyck Farm is in the foothills of the Blue Ridge Mountains near Hanging Rock State Park and the Dan River. The hosts have created the ambiance of an English country home and cottage complete with sporting clays and bass pond with dock. Enjoy walking on trails that roam 38 acres of rolling countryside or enjoy canoeing down the Dan River. The furnishings are a mix of 18th-century English, American, and Oriental antiques, complemented by waterfowl art. Full air conditioned.

Hosts: Diana Carl and David Haskins
Rooms: 6 (4 PB; 2 SB) $90-130
Full Breakfast
Credit Cards: A, B
Notes: 2, 3, 4, 5, 7, 8, 9, 11, 12, 14

## LITTLE SWITZERLAND

### Alpine Inn

Highway 226 A, P.O. Box 477, 28749
(828) 765-5380

Alpine Inn is a small, quaint establishment with rustic mountain charm. An excellent view, from all rooms, of mountain ranges and valleys. One mile from the Blue Ridge Parkway. Guest rooms are cozy and comfortable with a homelike atmosphere. There is a variety of accommodations from a one bedroom to a full apartment. Breakfasts, which are optional, are hearty and healthful and range from $1 to $5. Full vegetarian breakfast available. Breakfast is served on the main balcony. Commune with nature's sunrises!

Hosts: Sharon E. Smith and William M. Cox
Rooms: 14 (PB) $38-50
Full and Continental Breakfast
Credit Cards: A, B
Notes: 2, 8, 9, 12

## MARSHALL

### Marshall House Bed & Breakfast Inn

100 Hill Street, P.O. Box 865, 28753
(828) 649-9205; FAX (828) 649-2999
e-mail: twaq42a@prodigy.com

7 No smoking; 8 Children welcome; 9 Social drinking allowed; 10 Tennis nearby; 11 Swimming nearby; 12 Golf nearby; 13 Skiing nearby; 14 May be booked through a travel agent; 15 Handicapped accessible.

Truly in the mountains, overlooking the quaint town of Marshall and the French Broad River, this 1903 house is decorated with fancy chandeliers, mirrors, and lots of antiques. Resident cats add extra charm, and the porch is for rocking in this very relaxed atmosphere. Listed in the National Register of Historic Places, the house welcomes all in an atmosphere of bygone days. Continental plus breakfast served. Pets are welcome. Self-provided social drinking permitted. Limited handicapped accessibility.

Hosts: Ruth and Jim Boylan
Rooms: 9 (2 PB; 7 SB) $39-75
Continental Breakfast
Credit Cards: A, B, C, D, E
Notes: 5, 6, 8, 11, 12, 13, 14

## MOCKSVILLE

### Boxwood Lodge

Highway 601 South at 132 Becktown Road, 27028
(336) 284-2031

Boxwood Lodge, a Colonial Revival 25-room country mansion by Delano and Aldrich, is on 51 acres of beautifully wooded land. Convenient to I-85 or I-40 travelers. Enjoy a nearby game of golf, a leisure walk, fishing, a game of billiards, afternoon tea, reading by the fireside in the library, or just browsing around the lodge. Smoking permitted in designated areas only.

Host: Martha Hoffner
Rooms: 8 (5 PB; 3 SB) $95-145
Cabin: $85-95
Continental Breakfast
Credit Cards: A, B, C
Notes: 2, 12, 14

## MURPHY

### Huntington Hall Bed & Breakfast

272 Valley River Avenue, 28806
(828) 837-9567; (800) 824-6189
FAX (828) 837-2527; e-mail: huntington@grove.net

Each of the five spacious guest rooms, one of which is a separate cottage, has a personality of its own with period furnishings. Individual heating and air conditioning units, color cable TV and private baths are part of each room. A full breakfast, afternoon refreshments, and nightly turndown services are part of a guest's day. Huntington Hall is charming, relaxing, and inviting—an escape from hurry and worry—a place to be pampered.

Hosts: Curt and Nancy Harris
Rooms: 5 (PB) $65-125
Full Breakfast
Credit Cards: A, B, C, D
Notes: 2, 5, 7, 8, 9, 10, 12, 14

## NEW BERN

### The Aerie

509 Pollock Street, 28562
(252) 636-5553; (800) 849-5553
FAX (252) 514-2157
e-mail: aeriebb@coastalnet.com

Experience the best in New Bern hospitality at the Aerie inn bed and breakfast. Relax and enjoy the warmth of this 1880s Victorian inn. In the heart of the historic district, just one block from Tryon Palace and Historic Gardens and within an easy walk from many shops, restaurants, and attractions. The Aerie offers

The Aerie

seven spacious guest rooms with private baths, gourmet breakfast with a choice of three entrées and a 1,500-square-foot herbal garden.

Hosts: Doug and Donna Bennetts
Rooms: 7 (PB) $89-99
Full Breakfast
Credit Cards: A, B, C, D
Notes: 2, 5, 7, 10, 12, 14

## Harmony House Inn

215 Pollock Street, 28560
(252) 636-3810 (phone/FAX); (800) 636-3113
e-mail: harmony@cconnect.net
www.harmonyhouseinn.com

The Harmony House Inn is in the historic district of New Bern and is listed in the National Register of Historic Places. This unusually spacious house has eight guest rooms, the spacious two-room Benjamin Ellis Suite, and the newly decorated, romantic Eliza Ellis Suite with heart-shaped Jacuzzi. All rooms are furnished with ceiling fans, central air conditioning, cable TVs, private telephones, and decorative fireplaces. Within walking distance to quaint shops, fine dining restaurants, and many historic sites. The Harmony House, rated three-diamonds by AAA, welcomes business travelers. Complimentary local calls and off-street parking. Many extras.

Hosts: Ed and Sooki Kirkpatrick
Rooms: 10 (PB) $99-155
Full Breakfast
Credit Cards: A, B, C, D, E
Notes: 2, 5, 7, 8, 9, 11, 12, 14

## OCEAN ISLE BEACH

## The Winds Oceanfront Inn & Suites

310 East First Street, 28469
(800) 334-3581; FAX (910) 579-2884
e-mail: info@thewinds.com
www.thewinds.com

This delightful inn, surrounded by palm trees and lush subtropical landscaping, is on the oceanfront on an island beach just 20 minutes from North Myrtle Beach, South Carolina. The Winds features oceanfront rooms and one-, two-, and three-bedroom suites with kitchens and seaside balconies. Also four- and six-bedroom beach houses. Amenities include daily housekeeping, three heated pools (one indoors), whirlpool, beach volleyball, fitness room, rental bicycles, golf on more than 102 courses, and free tennis on the island. Complimentary hot breakfast buffet. Ask about free summer golf.

Hosts: Miller and Helen Pope
Rooms: 73 (PB) $59-182
Continental Breakfast
Credit Cards: A, B, C, D, E, F
Notes: 3, 5, 7, 8, 9, 10, 11, 12, 14, 15

## OCRACOKE ISLAND

## Berkley Manor Bed & Breakfast

P.O. Box 220, 27960-0220
(252) 928-5911; (800) 832-1223
e-mail: berkley@beachlink.com
www.berkleymanor.com

Ocracoke Island has been described as a taste of the Caribbean on the East Coast. Come take a quiet walk on the East Coast's most pristine beach. Sleep in and enjoy the privacy of this secluded island estate, head to the gracious dining room where a full breakfast awaits guests, delight in breathtaking island views from the four-story tower. Guests will find all of this and more at Berkley Manor Bed and Breakfast.

Hosts: Robert and Amy Attaway
Rooms: 12 (PB) $75-165
Full Breakfast
Credit Cards: A, B, C, D
Notes: 2, 5, 7, 9, 11, 14

## Oscar's House

Route 12, Box 206, 27960
(252) 928-1311

Oscar's House was built in 1940 for the family of the last Ocracoke lighthouse keeper. After

---

7 No smoking; 8 Children welcome; 9 Social drinking allowed; 10 Tennis nearby; 11 Swimming nearby; 12 Golf nearby; 13 Skiing nearby; 14 May be booked through a travel agent; 15 Handicapped accessible.

World War II, the family moved into this house. In 1984, Oscar's House became a bed and breakfast and has received guests and friends from all over the world. Many wonderful meals, stories, good times, and some surprises have been shared here. Please join this experience of world-wide community. Ocracoke Island offers 15 miles of wilderness beach and a small village situated around a natural harbor.

Host: Ann Ehringhaus
Rooms: 4 (4 S2B) $55-65
Full Breakfast
Credit Cards: A, B
Notes: 2, 7, 9, 11

# OLD FORT

## *The Inn at Old Fort and Gardens*

106 West Main Street, 28762
(828) 668-9384; (800) 471-0637 PIN 1709

The Inn at Old Fort is a restored two-story Victorian country home built in 1880. The Inn, decorated with antiques, is set on over three and one-half acres. The grounds are shaded by walnut and hemlock trees over 100 years old. The terraced lawn includes a variety of gardens. Along with a front porch for rocking and large, comfortable bedrooms, a parlor and a library are for guests' use.

Hosts: Chuck and Debbie Aldridge
Rooms: 4 (PB) $50-70
Continental Breakfast
Credit Cards: None
Notes: 2, 5, 7, 8, 9, 10, 11, 12, 14

# PILOT MOUNTAIN

## *The Blue Fawn Bed & Breakfast*

3052 Siloam Road, P.O. Box 986, 27041
(336) 374-2064; (800) 948-7716

The Blue Fawn Bed and Breakfast offers country charm in a restored, circa 1892, Greek

The Blue Fawn

Revival farmhouse overlooking the Yadkin River Valley. Featuring two guest rooms and one suite. Each room is furnished with period antiques, reminding guests of that simpler time. Explore the rolling countryside or simply relax and view it from one of the porches. Area attractions include Pilot Mountain, canoeing, hiking, golfing, and quiet rest and relaxation. Restricted smoking.

Hosts: Terri and Geno Cella
Rooms: 3 (PB) $65-85
Full Breakfast
Credit Cards: None
Notes: 2, 3, 4, 5, 8, 9, 11, 12

## *Scenic Overlook Bed & Breakfast*

144 Scenic Overlook Lane, 27043
(336) 368-9591; e-mail: scenic@idt.net
www.scenicoverlook.com

Large luxurious three-room suites, all with spectacular view of lake and Pilot Mountain, on 50 acres. Full amenities including whirlpool for two, fireplaces, full breakfast served in suite or on deck, boating included in price.

Hosts: Gayle and Alan Steinbicker
Rooms: 4 (PB) $95-155
Full Breakfast
Credit Cards: A, B, C, D, E
Notes: 2, 5, 7, 9, 10, 12, 14

NOTES: Credit cards accepted: A MasterCard; B Visa; C American Express; D Discover; E Diner's Club; F Other; 2 Personal checks accepted; 3 Lunch available; 4 Dinner available; 5 Open all year; 6 Pets welcome;

## RALEIGH

The Oakwood Inn

## The Oakwood Inn Bed & Breakfast

411 North Bloodworth Street, 27604
(919) 832-9712; (800) 267-9712
e-mail: oakwoodbb@aol.com
www.members.aol.com/oakwoodbb/

A Victorian retreat nestled in the heart of Raleigh's historic oakwood district. Six elegant guest rooms, each with private bath, warm fireplace, and private telephone lines. Richly furnished with period antiques and surrounded by well-manicured gardens. The Polk Room, the most popular, will ensure a relaxed stay with its oversized bed, warm fireplace, and clawfoot tub. Enjoy afternoon tea on the swing of a private veranda as evening settles in.

Hosts: Bill and Darlene Smith Christian and Diane
    Collinet
Rooms: 6 (PB) $85-135
Full Breakfast
Credit Cards: A, B, C, D, E
Notes: 2, 5, 7, 9, 10, 11, 12, 14

## ROBBINSVILLE

## Blue Boar Inn

200 Santeetlah Road, 28771
(828) 479-8126; FAX (828) 479-2415
e-mail: innkeeper@blueboarinn.com
www.blueboarinn.com

Once a lodge catering to hunters of bear, boar, turkey, and deer, the inn is now a renovated, stylish, upscale country house hotel nestled in the heart of the misty Smoky Mountains and the unspoiled shores of Lake Santeetlah. Eight spacious, elegant guest rooms, each with private porch, sitting area, king- or queen-size beds, large bath, central heat/air conditioning, TV, telephone, refrigerator. Near Cherohala Skyway and Joyce Kilmer Forest. Lake Santeetlah access.

Hosts: Pamela Glenn and Valjawan Deer
Rooms: 8 (PB) $135-165
Full Breakfast
Credit Cards: A, B, C
Notes: 2, 3, 4, 7, 8, 9, 11, 14, 15

## SALISBURY

## Rowan Oak House

208 South Fulton Street, 28144-4845
(704) 633-2086; (800) 786-0437
www.bbonline.com/nc/rowanoak/

"Romantic" and "lavish" describe this Queen Anne Victorian mansion: wraparound porch, rocking chairs, elaborate woodwork, stained glass, and original fixtures. Bedrooms are enormous with central air conditioning, English and American antiques, fruit, and flowers. One room has a double Jacuzzi and gas log fireplace. A full gourmet breakfast will be served with silver, crystal, and china. Murder

Rowan Oak House

---

mystery weekends available. In the heart of the historic district, one mile from I-85, exit 76B. Thirty minutes to High Point furniture shopping. Charlotte Motor Speedway.

Hosts: Barbara and Les Coombs
Rooms: 4 (PB) $110-135
Full Breakfast
Credit Cards: A, B, C, D
Notes: 2, 5, 7, 9, 10, 11, 12, 14

## SALUDA

### The Oaks

339 Greenville Street, 28773
(828) 749-9613; (800) 893-6091
FAX (828) 749-9613

Charm and comfort await guests in this beautifully furnished 1894 Victorian home in the North Carolina mountain town of Saluda. Thirty-five miles from Greenville, Asheville, and Spartanburg, the Oaks is well positioned for hiking to waterfalls or exploring antique shops. All four bedrooms are attractively furnished with period and antique furniture, four-poster beds, cable TVs, and private baths. Guests will enjoy rocking on the wraparound porch, reading in the library, and fabulous full breakfasts.

Hosts: Crowley and Terry Murphy
Rooms: 4 (PB) $95-150
Full Breakfast
Credit Cards: A, B, C, D
Notes: 2, 5, 7, 8, 9, 10, 12

The Oaks

## SOUTHERN PINES

Knollwood House

### Knollwood House

1495 West Connecticut Avenue, 28387
(919) 692-9390

A luxurious English manor house appointed with 18th-century antiques and contemporary comforts. On three acres of longleaf pines, dogwoods, magnolias, holly trees, and hundreds of flowering shrubs. Less than 100 feet to the 15th fairway of a championship golf course. And there are more than 42 courses just minutes away. Tennis and swimming. Suites and guest rooms, all with private baths. Meeting rooms, wedding facilities, and catering are available. Smoking permitted in designated areas only.

Hosts: Mimi and Dick Beatty
Rooms: 6 (PB) $100-150
Full Breakfast
Credit Cards: A, B
Notes: 2, 5, 7, 9, 10, 11, 12, 14

## SOUTHPORT

### Lois Jane's Riverview Inn

106 West Bay Street, 28461
(910) 457-6701; (800) 457-1152
e-mail: butchpat@webtv.net

Ships and sailboats, barges and tugboats—enjoy the gentle view from the veranda at Lois Jane's Riverview Inn while relaxing in the rocking chairs. Inclement weather allows soft relaxation in the parlor or library. In the heart

NOTES: Credit cards accepted: A MasterCard; B Visa; C American Express; D Discover; E Diner's Club; F Other; 2 Personal checks accepted; 3 Lunch available; 4 Dinner available; 5 Open all year; 6 Pets welcome;

of Southport, this historic home was built in the 1890s by Lois Jane's grandfather, faithfully restored by her children in 1995, and furnished with period furniture and accessories, many of them family heirlooms. Wine and hors d'oeuvres in the evening.

Hosts: Butch and Pat Janusik
Rooms: 4 (2 PB; 2 SB) $75-100
Full Breakfast
Credit Cards: A, B
Notes: 2, 5, 7, 9, 11, 12

## SPARTA

### Turby-villa

2072 NC Highway 18 North, 28675
(336) 372-8490

The Turby-villa is on 20 acres of beautiful mountain farmland. Breakfast is selected from a menu and served on a glassed-in porch with a beautiful view of the mountains. The bed and breakfast is 10 miles from the Blue Ridge Parkway, which is maintained by the National Park Service, on Highway 18, 2 miles from Sparta. Dinner available by prior arrangement. Smoking permitted outside only.

Host: Maybelline Turbiville
Rooms: 3 (PB) $53
Full Breakfast
Credit Cards: None
Notes: 2, 3, 5, 6, 7, 8, 9, 10, 11, 12, 13

## SPRUCE PINE

### Ansley/Richmond Inn

51 Pine Avenue, 28777
(828) 765-6993

This lovely half-century-old elegant country inn, specializing in pampering guests, is nestled into the hills overlooking the town of Spruce Pine and the Blue Ridge Parkway just four miles to the south. Ideal for hiking, crafts, skiing, golf, and gem mining, the inn has seven luxurious rooms, all with private baths, and

serves a full breakfast each morning and a complimentary glass of wine in the evening.

Hosts: Bill Ansley and Lenore Boucher
Rooms: 7 (PB) $55-75
Full Breakfast
Credit Cards: A, B, D
Notes: 2, 5, 7, 8, 9, 10, 11, 12, 13, 14

## STATESVILLE

### Madelyn's in the Grove

P.O. Box 249, Union Grove, 28689
(704) 539-4151; (800) 948-4473
FAX (704) 539-4080; e-mail: madelyns@yadtel.net
www.madelyns.com

Fresh flowers and homemade cookies await guests' arrival at the new location in Union Grove. Madelyn's in the Grove now has five comfortable bedrooms, in-room telephones, TVs, a Jacuzzi, and a garden tub. A perfect location for the business traveler and tourist, just two miles from I-77 and 12 minutes from I-40. Return from dinner and sit in the gazebo or on the deck and watch the stars or listen to the birds. It's peacefulness at its best.

Hosts: Madelyn and John Hill
Rooms: 5 (PB) $75-100
Full Breakfast
Credit Cards: A, B, C
Notes: 2, 3, 5, 7, 9, 10, 12, 14

## TABOR CITY

### Four Rooster Inn

403 Pireway Road, Route 904, 28463
(910) 653-3878; (800) 653-5008
FAX (910) 653-3878
e-mail: 4rooster@intrstar.net
www.bbonline.com/nc/rooster

"Such a fine place, we crowed over their outstanding hospitality, beautiful antiques and excellent food"—*Southern Living* magazine. Experience the gracious hospitality of the Old South in the charm of a small-town setting. This family home has been restored to a comfortable elegance with antiques, china and

7 No smoking; 8 Children welcome; 9 Social drinking allowed; 10 Tennis nearby; 11 Swimming nearby; 12 Golf nearby; 13 Skiing nearby; 14 May be booked through a travel agent; 15 Handicapped accessible.

crystal, beautiful fabrics, and fine linens. Afternoon tea awaits guests' arrival. Turndown service is accented with chocolates at bedtime. Awaken to a tray of coffee or tea and the morning news at guests' door. A full southern gourmet breakfast is served in the dining room. Myrtle Beach golf courses begin four miles from the inn.

Hosts: Gloria and Bob Rogers
Rooms: 4 (2 PB; 2 SB) $60-90
Full Breakfast
Credit Cards: A, B, C, D, E
Notes: 2, 5, 7, 9, 10, 12, 14

## TRYON

### The Foxtrot Inn Bed and Breakfast

800 Lynn Road, P.O. Box 1561, 28782
(828) 859-9706; (888) 676-8050

This 1915 architect-designed home is on six wooded acres and offers guests many options and amenities to enhance their stay. Beginning each day with a gourmet breakfast, guests will enjoy walking the trails through the woods, lounging at the pool, and amiable evenings reading, playing cards, or watching TV in the living room and game room. A two-bedroom guest house with fully equipped kitchen, deck, fireplace, and cable TV are also available.

Host: Wim Woody
Rooms: 4 (PB) $75-125
Full Breakfast
Credit Cards: None
Notes: 2, 5, 7, 8, 9, 10, 11, 12, 13, 14

The Foxtrot Inn

### Stone Hedge Inn

300 Howard Gap Road, P.O. Box 366, 28782
(704) 859-9114; (800) 859-1974

A stunning 28-acre estate in the shadow of Tryon Mountain, surrounded by gardens and meadows. Two rooms in the main house; three guest house rooms, one with a fireplace; and a poolside cottage with a fireplace; each has private bath, telephone, cable TV, and air conditioning. A lavish breakfast is served in the dining room where picture windows afford mountain views. Dinner by candlelight in crystal globes is a mix of contemporary specials and traditional favorites. Limited handicapped accessibility.

Hosts: Tom and Shaula Dinsmore
Rooms: 6 (PB) $95-120
Full Breakfast
Credit Cards: A, B
Notes: 2, 4, 5, 7, 8, 9, 10, 11, 12

## UNION GROVE

### Madelyn's in the Grove

P.O. Box 249, 28689
(704) 539-4151; (800) 948-4473
FAX (704) 539-4080; e-mail: madelyns@yadtel.net
www.madelyns.com

Fresh flowers and homemade cookies await guests' arrival at the new location in Union Grove. Madelyn's in the Grove now has five comfortable bedrooms, in-room telephones, TVs, a Jacuzzi, and a garden tub. A perfect location for the business traveler and tourist, just two miles from I-77 and 12 minutes from I-40. Return from dinner and sit in the gazebo or on the deck and watch the stars or listen to the birds. It's peacefulness at its best.

Hosts: Madelyn and John Hill
Rooms: 5 (PB) $75-100
Full Breakfast
Credit Cards: A, B, C
Notes: 2, 3, 5, 7, 9, 10, 12, 14

NOTES: Credit cards accepted: A MasterCard; B Visa; C American Express; D Discover; E Diner's Club; F Other; 2 Personal checks accepted; 3 Lunch available; 4 Dinner available; 5 Open all year; 6 Pets welcome;

## WARSAW

### Squire's Vintage Inn

748 NC Highwy 24 and 50, 28398
(910) 296-1831; FAX (910) 296-1431

"You're inn for something special." The rural setting adds to the privacy and relaxed atmosphere for a feeling of getting away from it all. After a restful night's sleep, guests can gaze out at the beautiful garden or take a walk on brick sidewalks and rustic paths flanked by tall pines and towering oaks. Adjacent is the famous Country Squire Restaurant. Weekend package available. Take exit 364 from I-40. AAA-rated and Mobil Travel Guide. Free HBO.

Host: Iris Lennon
Rooms: 16 (PB) $52-79
Continental Breakfast
Credit Cards: A, B, C, E
Notes: 2, 3, 4, 5, 7, 8, 9, 12, 14, 15

## WASHINGTON

### Pamlico House

400 East Main Street, 27889
(252) 946-7184; (800) 948-8507
FAX (252) 948-8507
www.bbonline.com/nc/pamlico

In the center of a small, historic town, this stately Colonial Revival homes has large rooms that are a perfect foil for the carefully chosen antique furnishings. Guests are drawn

Pamlico House

to the classic Victorian parlor or to the spacious wraparound porch for relaxing conversation. Take a self-guided walking tour of the historic district or a stroll along the picturesque waterfront. Be sure to visit the brand-new Estuarium just two blocks away.

Hosts: George and Jane Fields
Rooms: 4 (PB) $65-85
Full Breakfast
Credit Cards: A, B, C, D
Notes: 2, 5, 7, 9, 10, 11, 12, 14

## WAYNESVILLE

### Asheville Accommodations/ Carolina Mornings, Inc.

109 Circadian Way, Chapel Hill, 27516
(800) 770-9055; (888) MORNINGS (667-6467)
FAX (919) 929-5061
e-mail: carolinamornings@mindspring.com
www.carolinamornings.com

**9.** With four charming guest rooms, this wonderful turn-of-the-century home is graced with antique furnishings, oak paneling, cabinets, and mantels. Enjoy a full home-baked breakfast and rock on the veranda with its panoramic view of the mountains. Walk to Main Street's shops and restaurants. $65-90.

**42.** From the balconies and veranda to elegant interiors reminiscent of the French countryside, everything spells romance. Bedrooms are lavishly decorated. All have fireplaces; some have Jacuzzis and wet bars. Be pampered with a gourmet breakfast bedside. $115-225.

### Grandview Lodge

466 Lickstone Road, 28786
(828) 456-5212; (800) 255-7826
www.bbonline.com/nc/grandview/

A country inn in the western North Carolina mountains; open all year. Southern home cooking, with breakfast featuring homemade

---

7 No smoking; 8 Children welcome; 9 Social drinking allowed; 10 Tennis nearby; 11 Swimming nearby; 12 Golf nearby; 13 Skiing nearby; 14 May be booked through a travel agent; 15 Handicapped accessible.

breads, jams, and jellies. Dinner includes fresh vegetables, freshly baked breads, and desserts. Meals, served family style, are included in the rates. Private bath and cable TV. Reservations required.

Hosts: Stan and Linda Arnold
Rooms: 11 (PB) $105-115
Full Breakfast
Credit Cards: None
Notes: 2, 4, 5, 7, 8, 9, 10, 11, 12, 13, 14

## Mountain Creek

146 Chestnut Walk, 28786
(828) 456-5509; (800) 557-9766
FAX (828) 456-6728; e-mail: guylah@aol.com
www.bbonline.com/nc/mcbb

This 1950s ex-corporate retreat lodge is nestled on six acres surrounded by the lull of two creeks. There is a 1,600-square-foot wrap-around deck overlooking the mountain range, 100 feet above the creek, mill wheel, and trout pond. The lodge has original knotty pine and wormy chestnut walls, with cedar-lined closets. Each of the six rooms is uniquely decorated with its own private bath, two rooms with a whirlpool tub and two rooms with a balcony overlooking the treetops. Innkeepers are avid cyclists both on road and off.

Hosts: Hylah and Guy Smalley
Rooms: 6 (PB) $90-120
Full Breakfast
Credit Cards: A, B, D
Notes: 2, 5, 7, 9, 10, 12, 13, 14

## The Old Stone Inn

109 Dolan Road, 28786
(828) 456-3333; (800) 432-8499

Nestled on six and one-half acres of wooded hillside in the Smoky Mountains, the inn has the feel of a rustic hunting lodge. Cozy, simple rooms have wonderful beds with handmade quilts, porches with rockers and lots of privacy. Romantic candlelight dinners by the fire feature superb regional cuisine. Elegant breakfasts

The Old Stone Inn

at guests' own private table highlight every visit. Close to all mountain activities and within walking distance to the craft and antique shops of Waynesville.

Hosts: Robert and Cindy Zinser
Rooms: 18 (PB) $94-164
Suites: 4 (PB) $150
Full Breakfast
Credit Cards: A, B, D
Notes: 2, 4, 9, 10, 11, 12

## The Swag Country Inn

2300 Swag Road, 28786
(828) 926-0430; (800) 789-7672
FAX (828) 926-2036

Four-star rustic country inn in the Great Smoky Mountains at 5,000 feet above sea level. Private hiking/walking entrance into the Great Smoky Mountains National Park. All three meals included in rates. Open May through October. Amenities include racquet ball, croquet, horseshoes, small pond with small boat, hiking trails, exceptional cuisine, and more.

Host: Deener Matthews
Rooms: 17 (PB) $235-490
Full Breakfast
Credit Cards: A, B, C, D
Notes: 2, 3, 4, 7, 8, 9, 14, 15

NOTES: Credit cards accepted: A MasterCard; B Visa; C American Express; D Discover; E Diner's Club; F Other; 2 Personal checks accepted; 3 Lunch available; 4 Dinner available; 5 Open all year; 6 Pets welcome;

## WAYNESVILLE AREA

### *Windsong: A Mountain Inn*

459 Rockcliffe Lane, Clyde, 28721
(828) 627-6111; www.windsongbb.com

Enjoy a secluded, romantic interlude at this contemporary log inn high in the breathtaking Smoky Mountains. Though the inn is small and intimate, the rooms are large and bright, with high-beamed ceilings, pine log walls, and Mexican tile floors. Rooms have a fireplace, tub for two, separate shower, and private deck or patio. Guest lounge with billiards. Full breakfast included. On 25 acres, with pool, outdoor hot tub, tennis, hiking, and lovable animals. For families with children, there is the Pond Lodge, a separate two-bedroom log guest house with full kitchen. The full breakfast is included in the main inn. Open year-round. Children 12 and older welcome in the main inn. All ages welcome in the Pond Lodge.

Hosts: Russ and Barbara Mancini
Rooms: 7 (PB) $120-175
Full Breakfast
Credit Cards: A, B, C, D
Notes: 2, 5, 7, 9, 10, 11, 12, 13, 14

Windsong

## WILMINGTON

Anderson Guest House

### *Anderson Guest House*

520 Orange Street, 28401
(910) 343-8128

An 1851 Italianate townhouse with separate guest quarters overlooking the private garden. Furnished with antiques, ceiling fans, and working fireplaces. Drinks on arrival. A delightful gourmet breakfast is served. Smoking permitted in designated areas only. Inquire about accommodations for children.

Hosts: Landon and Connie Anderson
Rooms: 2 (PB) $75-90
Full Breakfast
Credit Cards: None
Notes: 2, 5, 6, 9, 10, 12

### *Catherine's Inn*

410 South Front Street, 28401
(910) 251-0863; (800) 476-0723

Experience the gracious atmosphere of this restored 1883 classic Italianate home featuring wrought-iron fence and gate, a Colonial Revival wraparound front porch, and two-story screened rear porch. The 300-foot private lawn, overlooking the Cape Fear River, is beautifully landscaped with a fountain and gazebo for guests to enjoy the beautiful sunsets. Catherine's Inn offers deluxe personal services;

7 No smoking; 8 Children welcome; 9 Social drinking allowed; 10 Tennis nearby; 11 Swimming nearby;
12 Golf nearby; 13 Skiing nearby; 14 May be booked through a travel agent; 15 Handicapped accessible.

Catherine's Inn

Come and enjoy this 1837 home in historic Wilmington. The three guest rooms all offer private baths, bathrobes, hair dryers, cable TV/VCRs, telephones. Complimentary refreshments are always available, and a hearty full breakfast will start the day. Walk to great restaurants, museums, galleries, even carriage and riverboat rides. Atlantic beaches are a short drive. Corporate rates, fax on-site, central air conditioning, three-diamond-rated by AAA.

Hosts: Vickie and Greg Stringer
Rooms: 3 (PB) $75-119
Full Breakfast
Credit Cards: A, B, C
Notes: 2, 5, 7, 10, 11, 12, 14

charming rooms, each with private bath; central air conditioning and ceiling fans; cozy library with cable TV and VCR; horseshoes, croquet, and bicycles at guests' disposal. Complimentary refreshments. Off-street parking. Corporate rates available. Smoking permitted in designated areas only. Children over 10 welcome.

Host: Catherine and Walter Ackiss
Rooms: 5 (PB) $80-115
Suite: $175
Full Breakfast
Credit Cards: A, B, C
Notes: 2, 5, 9, 10, 11, 12, 14

Graystone Inn

## The Curran House

312 South Third Street, 28401
(910) 763-6603; (800) 763-6603
FAX (910) 763-5116

## Graystone Inn

100 South Third Street, 28401
(910) 763-2000; FAX (910) 763-5555
e-mail: www.graystoneinn.com

Palatial mansion, built in 1906, is the most imposing structure downtown and a historic landmark. Vast ground floor includes fireplaces in each room, hand-carved oak Renaissance-style staircase, and library paneled in Honduras mahogany. Frequently used as a set for the movie industry. New owners have completely remodeled/ redecorated in period furnishings and fixtures. Fireplaces, PC data ports, TVs available, two suites, one junior suite, and four large rooms. Easy access to all downtown attractions. Children over 12 welcome.

The Curran House

NOTES: Credit cards accepted: A MasterCard; B Visa; C American Express; D Discover; E Diner's Club; F Other; 2 Personal checks accepted; 3 Lunch available; 4 Dinner available; 5 Open all year; 6 Pets welcome;

Hosts: Paul and Yolanda Bolda
Rooms: 7 (PB) $159-299
Full Breakfast
Credit Cards: A, B, C, D, E, F
Notes: 2, 5, 9, 10, 11, 12, 14

## The Inn on Orange

410 Orange Street, 28401
(910) 815-0035; (800) 381-4666

The Inn on Orange is a lovely 1875 Italianate Victorian home. It offers four bedrooms, all with private baths and two with sitting rooms. A full breakfast is served each morning in the elegant dining room or around the small backyard swimming pool. The Inn is in the heart of the largest historic district in North Carolina. It is just a short walk to the Cape Fear River and Wilmington's great restaurants, shopping, and night spots.

Hosts: The Vargas Family
Rooms: 4 (PB) $75-115
Full Breakfast
Credit Cards: A, B, C, D
Notes: 2, 5, 7, 9, 11, 12

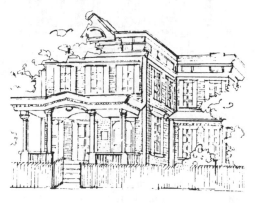

The Inn on Orange

## Live Oaks Bed & Breakfast

318 South Third Street, 28401
(910) 762-6733; (888) 762-6732
www.liveoaks.com

In the historic downtown area, this circa 1883 home has been restored by its present owners

Live Oaks

to its original grandeur and decorated in a Victorian style with antiques and reproductions. Within walking distance are wonderful shops and restaurants, antiquing, museums, and galleries. Take a horse-drawn carriage ride or the walking tour or a house tour and relive a bit of the past. Golf and beaches just 20 minutes away. Children over 12 welcome.

Hosts: Margi and Doug Erickson
Rooms: 3 (PB) $100-135
Full Breakfast
Credit Cards: A, B, C, D
Notes: 2, 5, 6, 7, 9, 11, 12, 14

## Rosehill Inn

114 South Third Street, 28401
(910) 815-0250; (800) 815-0250
FAX (910) 815-0350; www.rosehill.com

Rosehill Inn is an exceedingly comfortable Neoclassical Revival home in the heart of Wilmington's historic district. Just a few minutes' walk from the Cape Fear River with abundant dining and shopping destinations. Restored in 1995, the house offers a wonderful combination of antique charm and beauty with the finest in up-to-date conveniences. Breakfast is served in the formal dining room fresh each morning. Come experience the romance. AAA three-diamond-rated. Mobil three-stars. Cable TV, telephones with fax modem jacks.

7 No smoking; 8 Children welcome; 9 Social drinking allowed; 10 Tennis nearby; 11 Swimming nearby; 12 Golf nearby; 13 Skiing nearby; 14 May be booked through a travel agent; 15 Handicapped accessible.

Rosehill Inn

Hosts: Laurel Jones and Dennis Fietsch
Rooms: 6 (PB) $85-165
Full Breakfast
Credit Cards: A, B, C, D
Notes: 2, 5, 7, 9, 12, 14

## Taylor House Inn Bed & Breakfast

14 North Seventh Street, 28401
(910) 763-7581; (800) 382-9982

In the downtown historic district, just blocks from the Cape Fear River. A haven of warm southern hospitality and thoughtfulness. The five bedrooms are filled with period antiques, fresh flowers, and beautiful linens. A full gourmet breakfast is served in the formal dining room by candlelight. A slice of heaven—be pampered and enjoy the Cape Fear area.

Hosts: Scott and Karen Clark
Rooms: 5 (PB) $85-135
Full Breakfast
Credit Cards: A, B, C
Notes: 2, 5, 7, 8, 9, 10, 11, 12, 14

## The Verandas

202 Nun Street, 28401
(910) 251-2212

Grand and elegant, beautiful and award-winning, restored 1854 antebellum mansion with four verandas and terrace on quiet historic street. Eight luxurious guest rooms, with private marble bathrooms, pamper guests at affordable prices. Gourmet breakfasts. Complimentary beverages. Telephones, modem jacks, color TV, and individual climate control. Enchanted blend of elegance, history, luxury, charm, and hospitality. "An Inn Second to Nun!" Two-night minimum on weekends.

Hosts: Dennis Madsen and Charles Pennington
Rooms: 8 (PB) $120-180
Full Breakfast
Credit Cards: A, B, C, D
Notes: 2, 5, 7, 9, 10, 12

The Verandas

## The Worth House

412 South Third Street, 28401
(910) 762-8562; (800) 340-8559
www.bbonline.com/nc/worth

Romantic Queen Anne Victorian inn in historic district, short walk to riverfront, restaurants, and shopping. Antiques, period furniture, and art in parlor, library, and formal dining room. Seven guest rooms, all with private baths and sitting areas, some with fireplaces and enclosed porches. Full breakfast, free soft drinks, and snacks. Laundry facilities. Large-screen TV, room telephones, fax, copier, and modem link available.

NOTES: Credit cards accepted: A MasterCard; B Visa; C American Express; D Discover; E Diner's Club; F Other; 2 Personal checks accepted; 3 Lunch available; 4 Dinner available; 5 Open all year; 6 Pets welcome;

The Worth House

Rooms: 7 (PB) $80-125
Full Breakfast
Credit Cards: A, B. C
Notes: 2, 5, 7, 9, 10, 11, 12, 14

## WILSON

## *Miss Betty's Bed & Breakfast Inn*

600 West Nash Street, 27893-3045
(919) 243-4447; (800) 258-2058 (reservations)

Selected as one of the "Best Places to Stay in the South," Miss Betty's is comprised of four beau-

Miss Betty's

tifully restored historic properties. In a gracious setting in the downtown historic section, where quiet Victorian elegance and charm abound in an atmosphere of all modern-day conveniences. Guests may browse for antiques at Miss Betty's or in any of the numerous antique shops that have given Wilson the title of "Antique Capital of North Carolina." A quiet town also known for its famous eastern Carolina barbecue, Wilson features four beautiful golf courses, numerous tennis courts, and an Olympic-size pool. Midway between Maine and Florida, along the main north-south route I-95.

Hosts: Betty and Fred Spitz
Rooms: 10 (PB) $60-80
Full Breakfast
Credit Cards: A, B, C, D, E, F
Notes: 2, 5, 7, 9, 10, 11, 12, 14, 15

## WINSTON-SALEM

## *A. T. Zevely Inn*

803 South Main Street, 27101
(336) 748-9299; (800) 928-9299
FAX (336) 721-2211

A. T. Zevely Inn, circa 1844. National register, museum-quality restoration. Only inn in historic Old Salem. Moravian style. Rooms have king- or queen-size beds, private bath, TV, and telephone. Some have fireplaces and/or whirlpool/steam baths. Complimentary breakfast and evening wine and cheese. AAA- and Mobil-rated. Full breakfast served on weekends; Continental breakfast on weekdays. Featured in *Country Living*, *Tasteful*, *Washington Post Travel*, *Southern Living*, and *Home Across America* cable program.

Host: Linda Anderson
Rooms: 12 (PB) $85-205
Full and Continental Breakfast
Credit Cards: A, B, C
Notes: 2, 5, 6, 8, 9, 10, 11, 12, 14, 15

7 No smoking; 8 Children welcome; 9 Social drinking allowed; 10 Tennis nearby; 11 Swimming nearby;
12 Golf nearby; 13 Skiing nearby; 14 May be booked through a travel agent; 15 Handicapped accessible.

## Brookstown Inn Bed & Breakfast

200 Brookstown Avenue, 27101
(336) 725-1120; (800) 845-4262
FAX (336) 773-0147; e-mail: broj6@aol.com

Built in 1837 as a textile mill, the building has been converted to a cozy inn with the original structure carefully preserved. Today, the inn's southern hospitality and authentic Early American decor let guests escape to the charm of yesteryear. The modern conveniences of full-size irons and ironing boards, hair dryers, and coffee makers have been added along with voice mail, TVs, AM/FM radios, and data ports. The inn's state of the art exercise facility will insure that guests don't miss out on their daily routine. The inn offers complimentary Continental breakfast, wine and cheese reception nightly, and homemade cookies with milk each evening. The morning newspaper and evening turndown service is the inn's pleasure.

Host: Gary Colbert, General Manager
Rooms: 71 (PB) $100-155
Continental Breakfast
Credit Cards: A, B, C, E
Notes: 5, 7, 8, 9, 12, 14, 15

## The Henry F. Shaffner House

150 South Marshall Street, 27101
(336) 777-0052; (800) 952-2256
FAX (336) 777-1188

Standing as a monument to turn-of-the-century elegance and English Victorian regency, the Henry F. Shaffner House is the perfect choice for an unforgettable weekend or special event. This breathtaking bed and breakfast was built in 1907 as the home of Winston-Salem businessman, Henry F. Shaffner, co-founder of Wachovia Loan & Trust Co. It has been meticulously restored and refurbished and reflects a quiet, romantic intimacy guaranteed to charm even the most seasoned traveler. Guests will absolutely fall in love with this historic home.

The Henry F. Shaffner House

Host: Shirley B. Ackeret, manager
Rooms: 9 (PB) $99-239
Full Breakfast
Credit Cards: A, B, C
Notes: 2, 4, 5, 7, 8, 9, 10, 12, 14

## Lady Anne's Victorian Bed & Breakfast

612 Summit Street, 27101
(336) 724-1074
www.bbonline.com/nc/ladyannes

Warm southern hospitality surrounds guests in this 1890 historic Victorian. An aura of romance touches every suite and room, all of which are individually decorated with period antiques and treasures, while skillfully including modern luxuries, such as private baths with two-person Jacuzzis, balconies, porches, cable TV with HBO, stereos with music and tapes, telephones, room refrigerators, coffee makers, and microwaves. An evening dessert/tea tray and a delicious full breakfast are served on fine china and lace. Near downtown attractions, performances, restaurants, and shops. Near Old Salem historic village. Smoking is not permitted inside. Children over 12 welcome.

Host: Shelley Kirley
Rooms/Suites: 4 (PB) $60-180
Full Breakfast
Credit Cards: A, B, C, D
Notes: 5, 7, 9, 10, 11, 12

NOTES: Credit cards accepted: A MasterCard; B Visa; C American Express; D Discover; E Diner's Club; F Other; 2 Personal checks accepted; 3 Lunch available; 4 Dinner available; 5 Open all year; 6 Pets welcome;

# South Carolina

## AIKEN

### Historic Holley House Hotel

235 Richland Avenue, 29801
(803) 648-4265; FAX (803)649-6910
e-mail: holleyinfo@holleyhousehotel.com
www.holleyhousehotel.com

The Historic Holley House Hotel has been established in the heart of historic downtown Aiken since 1927. Recent renovations have completely restored this historic hotel to recreate the charm and decor of the roaring 20's. Each room is uniquely decorated in Art Deco and traditional styles. There are also suites available with sleeper sofas. Enjoy a delicious Continental breakfast served in the Carolina courtyard, poolside, or served conveniently to any floor. Close to equestrian stables, numerous restaurants, two theatres, and a museum.

Rooms: 35 (PB) $70-90
Continental Breakfast
Credit Cards: A, B, C, D, E
Notes: 5, 6, 7, 8, 9, 10, 11, 12, 14, 15

### White House Inn

240 Newberry Street Southwest, 29801
(803) 649-2935

The White House Inn is a two-story Dutch Colonial home, furnished with antiques, in a parklike surrounding. Guests start their day with a full breakfast, visit the antique shops or the historical district of Old Aiken, golf, horseback ride, and finish the evening with dinner at one of the fine restaurants near the inn. Government rate honored. Weddings hosted.

White House Inn

Hosts: Mary Ann and Hal Mackey
Rooms: 4 (PB) $69-109
Full Breakfast
Credit Cards: A, B, C, D, E
Notes: 2, 5, 7, 9, 10, 12, 14

## BEAUFORT

### The Rhett House Inn

1009 Craven Street, 29902
(843) 524-9030; (888) 480-9530
FAX (843) 524-1310
e-mail: rhetthse@hargray.com
www.rhetthseinn.com

Nestled in historic Beaufort is an authentic inn that beautifully recreates the feeling of the Old South, when this was the most cultivated and enchanting town of its size in America. All of the guest rooms have been individually decorated for guests' comfort and convenience. All guest rooms have TVs, telephones, private baths, and eight rooms feature fireplaces and Jacuzzis. Enjoy afternoon tea with linzer tortes or homemade chocolate chip cookies in front of the fire or out on the veranda. In the morning, guests will wake up to the smell of freshly

7 No smoking; 8 Children welcome; 9 Social drinking allowed; 10 Tennis nearby; 11 Swimming nearby; 12 Golf nearby; 13 Skiing nearby; 14 May be booked through a travel agent; 15 Handicapped accessible.

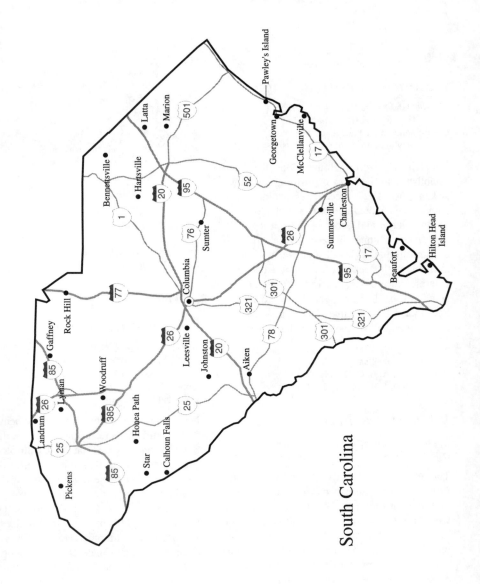

South Carolina

brewed coffee and homemade bread and muffins. Picnic lunches available. Children five and older welcome.

Hosts: Marianne and Steve Harrison
Rooms: 17 (PB) $125-225
Full Breakfast
Credit Cards: A, B, C
Notes: 2, 5, 7, 9, 10, 11, 12, 14, 15

TwoSuns Inn

## TwoSuns Inn Bed & Breakfast

1705 Bay Street, 29902-5406
(843) 522-1122 (phone/FAX); (800) 532-4244
e-mail: twosuns@islc.net; www.twosunsinn.com

Enjoy the charm of Beaufort's most popular bed and breakfast. The panoramic bay view is spectacular, the historic setting idyllic, and the atmosphere casually elegant with antiques, collectibles (including a mini-banana museum just for fun) and modern amenities. Set in a certified historic 1917 grand home, TwoSuns features an afternoon "tea and toddy," comfortable king- or queen-size beds, sumptuous breakfasts and gracious, resident owners. Highly rated nationally and enjoyed by more than 11,000 since 1990.

Hosts: Carrol and Ron Kay
Rooms: 6 (PB) From $105
Full Breakfast
Credit Cards: A, B, C, D, E
Notes: 2, 5, 7, 9, 10, 11, 12, 14, 15

## BENNETTSVILLE

## The Breeden Inn and Carriage House

404 East Main Street, 29512
(843) 479-3665; (888) 335-2996
FAX (843) 479-7998
www.bbonline.com/sc/breeden

In Bennettsville's historic district, this 1886 mansion offers the opportunity to experience true southern hospitality. Well-preserved architectural delights and beautiful antique decor highlight the interior in three period houses. The inn is 20 minutes off I-95. A great halfway point between Florida and New York. Enjoy bird watching on the two-acre backyard habitat, swim or sun by the pool, browse in the inn's collectibles shop, walk Bennettsville's sidewalk-lined streets, relax on the rocker-lined veranda and portico. Cable TV and telephone in all rooms. Come...a good night's sleep and a delicious, elegant breakfast in a wonderful, warm old home await.

Hosts: Wesley and Bonnie Park
Rooms: 10 (PB) $85-125
Full Breakfast
Credit Cards: A, B, C
Notes: 2, 5, 7, 8, 10, 11, 12, 14

The Breeden Inn

NOTES: Credit cards accepted: A MasterCard; B Visa; C American Express; D Discover; E Diner's Club; F Other; 2 Personal checks accepted; 3 Lunch available; 4 Dinner available; 5 Open all year; 6 Pets welcome; 7 No smoking; 8 Children welcome; 9 Social drinking allowed; 10 Tennis nearby; 11 Swimming nearby; 12 Golf nearby; 13 Skiing nearby; 14 May be booked through a travel agent; 15 Handicapped accessible.

## CALHOUN FALLS

### Latimer Inn Bed & Breakfast

1387 Highway 81, P.O. Box 295, 29628
(864) 391-2747

On South Carolina's Heritage Corridor Nature Route, through historic Abbeville County rich in Civil War history, guests can find Latimer Inn Bed and Breakfast. Home was built in 1907, and it has been completely remodeled with private baths, Jacuzzis, fireplaces, veranda, sitting room, and a gift shoppe. Adjacent to Lake Russell, a fisherman's paradise. Gourmet breakfasts are prepared by local chef and artist. Smoking limited to designated areas. Call for information about children's accommodations.

Hosts: Harrison and Anne Sawyer
Rooms: 17 (PB) $49-99
Full Breakfast
Credit Cards: A, B, C, D, E
Notes: 2, 3, 4, 5, 6, 9, 10, 11, 12, 13, 14

## CHARLESTON

### Ann Harper's Bed & Breakfast

56 Smith Street, 29401
(843) 723-3947

This circa 1870 home is in Charleston's historic district. Two rooms with connecting bath and sitting area with TV. The owner is a retired medical technologist and enjoys serving a full breakfast. Two-night minimum stay requested. Extra charge for single night. Smoking in designated areas only. Children over 10 welcome.

Host: Ann D. Harper
Rooms: 2 (PB) $85-115
Full Breakfast
Credit Cards: None
Notes: 2, 5, 9, 10, 11, 12

Ashley Inn

### Ashley Inn Bed & Breakfast

201 Ashley Avenue, 29403
(843) 723-1848; (800) 581-6658

Circa 1832 historic home offers seven bedrooms, beautifully decorated with antique canopied beds. A place to be pampered and sleep in until the aroma of sizzling sausage and home-baked biscuits announces a full breakfast on the columned piazza overlooking the garden and fountain. Tour nearby historic sites on complimentary bicycles and return to more pampering with afternoon tea, sherry, and sumptuous home-baked goods. Private baths, color TV, off-street parking, and very special southern hospitality. AAA three-diamond-rated. Featured on TV's *Country Inn Cooking*. Children over 10 welcome.

Hosts: Bud and Sally Allen; Lynn Bartosh
    (innkeeper)
Rooms: 7 (PB) $79-190
Full Breakfast
Credit Cards: A, B, C, D
Notes: 2, 5, 7, 9, 10, 11, 12, 14

### Barksdale House Inn

27 George Street, 29401
(843) 577-4800; FAX (843) 853-0482

One of Charleston's most luxurious 14-room inns. A 200-year-old home featuring individu-

Barksdale House Inn

robes and towels. Turndown service. Afternoon refreshments. Quiet garden. Cable TV
and HBO. Private steam baths. Whirlpool tubs.
Friendly professional staff. Described by *Elegant Small Hotels*, 1996, as "Garden-centered,
history-laden, romantic and intimate." Highly
recommended.

Host: Katharine Hastie
Rooms: 11 (PB) $99-229
Continental Breakfast
Credit Cards: A, B, C, D
Notes: 2, 5, 7, 9, 10, 11, 12, 14

ally designed rooms, some with whirlpool tubs
and fireplaces. Flowers daily with newspaper,
tea, sherry, turndown service with chocolates.
Fountain in courtyard and free parking.

Rooms: 14 (PB) $90-195
Continental Breakfast
Credit Cards: A, B

27 State Street

## *The Battery Carriage House Inn (1843)*

20 South Battery, 29401
(800) 775-5575

Stay in the carriage house of this landmark
antebellum mansion at White Point Gardens
(on the waterfront), the most elegant residential
district of old and historic Charleston. Eleven
rooms. Ample street parking. Silver tray Continental breakfast in room or garden. Fluffy

## *Bed & Breakfast at 27 State Street*

27 State Street, 29401
(843) 722-4243

Guests can surround themselves with history
and southern hospitality in the French Quarter
of the old walled city of Charlestowne. Stroll to
major points of interest, dining, shopping, and
touring. Guests enter the courtyard with their
own personal key. Enjoy sea breezes on the
veranda. Private entrances and private baths.
Antiques, reproductions, high poster queen-
size beds. Newspaper, fresh flowers, fruit,
cable TV, telephones, and bicycles, Continental
plus breakfast.

The Battery Carriage House Inn

Hosts: Paul and Joye Craven
Rooms: 5 (PB) $110-180
Continental Breakfast
Credit Cards: None
Notes: 2, 5, 7, 8, 9, 10, 11, 12

7 No smoking; 8 Children welcome; 9 Social drinking allowed; 10 Tennis nearby; 11 Swimming nearby;
12 Golf nearby; 13 Skiing nearby; 14 May be booked through a travel agent; 15 Handicapped accessible.

## The Belvedere

40 Rutledge Avenue, 29401
(843) 722-0973
www.belvedereinn.com

A Colonial Revival mansion built in 1900 with an exquisite Adamesque interior taken from the circa 1800 Belvedere plantation house. In the downtown historic district, on Colonial Lake, within walking distance of historical points of interest, restaurants, and shopping. Guests are welcome to use the public areas and piazzas in this romantic, beautifully restored and refurbished mansion.

Hosts: David S. Spell and Rick Zender
Rooms: 3 (PB) $150-175
Continental Breakfast
Credit Cards: None
Notes: 2, 5, 7, 9, 10, 11, 12, 14

The Belvedere

## Brasington House Bed & Breakfast

328 East Bay Street, 29401
(843) 722-1274

Elegant accommodations in a splendidly restored Greek Revival Charleston single house, furnished with antiques, in Charleston's beautiful historic district. Four lovely, well-appointed guest rooms with central heat and air conditioning include private baths, telephones, cable TVs, and tea-making services. King-, queen-size, and twin beds available. Included is a bountiful fam-

Brasington House

ily-style breakfast, wine and cheese served in the living room, liqueurs and chocolates available in the evening. Off-street parking.

Hosts: Dalton K. and Judy Brasington
Rooms: 4 (PB) $115-154
Full Breakfast
Credit Cards: A, B
Notes: 2, 7, 9, 10, 11, 12

## Cannonboro Inn Bed & Breakfast

184 Ashley Avenue, 29412
(843) 723-8572; (800) 235-8039
FAX (843) 723-8007; e-mail: cannon@cchat.com

This circa 1853 historic home offers six beautifully decorated bedrooms with four-poster and canopied beds. The aroma of freshly brewed coffee and home-baked French puff muffins entice guests to a delicious breakfast on the columned piazza overlooking the garden. After breakfast guests can tour nearby historic Charleston on complimentary bicycles, on foot, or by horse-drawn carriage. Return in the afternoon to relax in the parlor and enjoy high tea with fresh home-baked treats such as raspberry almond shortbread and English toffee bars, or guests might enjoy sherry and mint juleps. Off-street parking, private baths, cable TV, central air conditioning, and warm professional staff. Children 10 and older welcome.

NOTES: Credit cards accepted: A MasterCard; B Visa; C American Express; D Discover; E Diner's Club; F Other; 2 Personal checks accepted; 3 Lunch available; 4 Dinner available; 5 Open all year; 6 Pets welcome;

Cannonboro Inn

Hosts: Bud and Sally Allen (owners);
    Lynn Bartosh (innkeeper)
Rooms: 6 (PB) $79-190
Full Breakfast
Credit Cards: A, B, C, D
Notes: 2, 5, 7, 9, 10, 11, 12, 14

## Country Victorian Bed & Breakfast

105 Tradd Street, 29401-2422
(843) 577-0682

Rooms have private entrances and contain antique iron and brass beds, old quilts, oak and wicker antique furniture, and braided rugs over the heart-of-pine floors. Homemade benne seed cookies (a Charleston tradition) will be waiting. The house, built in 1820, is within

Country Victorian

easy walking distance of restaurants, antique shops, churches, art galleries, museums, and all points of historical interest. Many extras are provided. Featured in *Country Quilts* magazine. Children over 10 are welcome.

Host: Diane Deardurff Weed
Rooms: 2 (PB) $85-140
Continental Breakfast
Credit Cards: None
Notes: 2, 5, 7, 9, 10, 11, 12

East Bay

## East Bay Bed & Breakfast

301 East Bay Street, 29401
(843) 722-4186; FAX (803) 720-8528

Elegant 200-year-old Federal single house and birthplace of Civil War heroine Phoebe Pember. Easy walk to Old City Market, King Street shops, College of Charleston, Medical University, restaurants, and day-spa. Exquisitely decorated. Silver tray service. Private carriage house also available. Meeting and reception space. Desks, fax, telephone, cable TV, and off-street parking. Smoking permitted on piazzas only. Inquire about accommodations for children.

Host: Carolyn Rivers; Joe Belbusti (manager)
Room: (PB) $125-185
Continental Breakfast
Credit Cards: A, B, C
Notes: 2, 5, 9, 10, 11, 12, 14

**7** No smoking; **8** Children welcome; **9** Social drinking allowed; **10** Tennis nearby; **11** Swimming nearby; **12** Golf nearby; **13** Skiing nearby; **14** May be booked through a travel agent; **15** Handicapped accessible.

1837 Bed & Breakfast

## 1837 Bed & Breakfast and Tea Room

126 Wentworth Street, 29401
(843) 723-7166
www.fodors.com/bnb

These delightful accommodations are in a wealthy cotton planter's home and brick carriage house, now owned by two artists. In the center of the historic district. Full gourmet breakfast is served in the formal dining room or on the outside piazzas. Visit with others while enjoying such specialties as sausage pie, raspberry french toast, ham frittata with mornay sauce, sausage and grits casserole, and home-baked breads—pecan cinnamon buns, banana nut muffins, and sour cream coffee cake. Afternoon tea is served. Canopied four-poster rice beds, verandas, rockers, and southern hospitality. Smoking permitted in designated areas only.

Hosts: Sherri Weaver and Richard Dunn
Rooms: 8 (PB) $69-135
Full Breakfast
Credit Cards: A, B, C
Notes: 2, 5, 10, 11

## Fulton Lane Inn

202 King Street, 29401
(843) 720-2600; (800) 720-2688

Set off King Street on a quiet pedestrian lane in the heart of the antique and historic district. Many rooms have cathedral ceilings or fireplaces, canopied beds, and large whirlpool baths to give a special romantic feeling of a bygone era. The gracious southern hospitality includes a silver-service breakfast, wine and sherry, turndown with chocolates, and a newspaper. AAA four-diamonds. No smoking.

Host: Beth Babcock
Rooms: 27 (PB) $120-285
Continental Breakfast
Credit Cards: A, B, D, E
Notes: 2, 5, 7, 8, 9, 10, 11, 12, 14, 15

## HarbourView Inn

2 Vendue Range, 29401
(888) 843-8439; FAX (843) 853-4034

Deep in the heart of the historic district, overlooking Waterfront Park and the famous Charleston Harbor, the HarbourView Inn affords guests comforts found nowhere else on the peninsula. Along with the modern amenities of a first-class hotel, HarbourView Inn offers the elegance of a time gone by. Enjoy their signature Portside Breakfast delivered to rooms daily, all day snacks, flavored iced teas, afternoon wine and cheese, milk and freshly baked cookies in the evening, plus turndown services with a sweet dream candy, all compliments of the HarbourView Inn.

Rooms: 52 (PB) $129-299
Continental Breakfast
Credit Cards: A, B, C, D, E
Notes: 5, 8, 9, 10, 11, 12, 14, 15

## Historic Charleston Bed & Breakfast

57 Broad Street, 29401
(843) 722-6606; (800) 743-3583
FAX (843) 722-9589
www.charleston.net/com/bed&breakfast

Representing more than 50 bed and breakfast properties in and around Charleston's historic

---

NOTES: Credit cards accepted: A MasterCard; B Visa; C American Express; D Discover; E Diner's Club; F Other; 2 Personal checks accepted; 3 Lunch available; 4 Dinner available; 5 Open all year; 6 Pets welcome;

district. Accommodations include private homes and carriage houses. Call for details.

**Ashley Avenue.** Two lovely rooms with a full breakfast. The first room is on the second floor with a private hall bath. The second room is a suite on the third floor with a rooftop view, full bath, and separate sitting room. $130-200.

**Broad Street.** Third-floor suite with kitchen, sitting room, queen-size bedroom, and bath. Also available is an accommodation with private entrance, kitchen, king-size bedroom, and bath with shower only. $115-135.

**Chapel Street.** Private entrance, garden level. Queen-size bed, living room, kitchen, private bath, lovely antiques. Lovely garden with fountain. $135-150.

**Church Street.** Two rooms on third floor. Both rooms have private baths and beautiful harbor views from piazza. $110-115.

**East Bay.** Spacious one-bedroom apartment and a two-bedroom carriage house. $125-225.

**Hasell Street.** Carriage house with living room, full kitchen with breakfast area, and private patio. Two bedrooms, one full bath with washer and dryer. Off-street parking. $170-215.

**Limehouse Street.** Carriage house with living room, kitchen, second-floor bedroom with queen-size bed and full bath. Off-street parking. $100-125.

**Water Street.** Third-floor suite with bedroom, full bath, living room, small kitchen, and large porch with a lovely harbor view. $195-215.

**Wentworth Street.** Carriage house with two separate units to be rented individually or as an entire unit. The first unit has a large room with queen-size four-poster bed, full bath, refrigerator, and separate sink in one room, large patio

with seating. Off-street parking. No inside smoking. The second unit has two rooms, one with queen-size bed, fireplace, bath (shower only); additional room has fireplace, sofa, wet bar, and small refrigerator. Bikes and patio seating available. Off-street parking. Non-smoking. $90-120.

## *John Rutledge House Inn*

116 Broad Street, 29401
(843) 723-7999; (800) 476-9741

This national landmark was built in 1763 by John Rutledge, a framer and signer of the U.S. Constitution. Large rooms and suites in the main and carriage houses offer the ambiance of historic Charleston. Rates include wine and sherry upon arrival, turndown service with brandy and chocolate, and breakfast with newspaper delivered to guests' room. Free parking. AAA-rated four diamonds and Mobil-rated four stars. Historic Hotels of America. Nonsmoking rooms available. Limited handicapped accessibility.

Rooms: 19 (PB) $170-355
Continental Breakfast
Credit Cards: A, B, C, D, E
Notes: 2, 5, 8, 9, 10, 11, 12, 14

## *King George IV Inn*

32 George Street, 29401
(843) 723-9339; (888) 723-1667
FAX (843) 723-7749; www.virtualcities.com
www.bbonline.com/sc/kinggeorge/

"Step into the past, feel the history of Charleston around you." Historic inn circa 1790s. Named Peter Freneau House after a prominent Charlestonian, merchant, shipowner, Jeffersonian politician in charge of President Thomas Jefferson's election. The inn is Federal style, four stories tall, three levels of old Charleston porches. All rooms have decorative fireplaces, tall ceilings, plaster moldings, hardwood floors, antiques. Parking, air conditioning, private baths, refrigerators, Continental

7 No smoking; 8 Children welcome; 9 Social drinking allowed; 10 Tennis nearby; 11 Swimming nearby; 12 Golf nearby; 13 Skiing nearby; 14 May be booked through a travel agent; 15 Handicapped accessible.

plus breakfast. In the heart of historic district, five-minute walk to the historic market. Personal checks accepted in advance.

Hosts: Debra, Terry, and Debbie
Rooms: 10 (8 PB; 2 SB) $89-165
Continental Breakfast
Credit Cards: A, B
Notes: 2, 5, 7, 9, 10, 11, 12, 13

## Kings Courtyard Inn

198 King Street, 29401
(843) 723-7000; (800) 845-6119

Kings Courtyard Inn, circa 1853, is in the heart of the antique and historic district. Convenient to attractions, shops, and restaurants. Rate includes Continental breakfast, newspaper, and wine and sherry served in the lobby. Turndown service with chocolate and brandy. AAA four diamonds. Historic Hotels of America. Double, king-, and queen-size beds and suites are available. Nonsmoking rooms available.

Host: Reg Smith
Rooms: 41 (PB) $125-260
Continental Breakfast
Credit Cards: A, B, C, D, E
Notes: 2, 5, 8, 9, 10, 11, 12, 14, 15

Kings Courtyard Inn

## The Kitchen House (Circa 1732)

126 Tradd Street, 29401
(843) 577-6362; FAX (843) 965-5615

The Kitchen House

Nestled in the heart of the historic district, the Kitchen House is a completely restored 18th-century dwelling. Southern hospitality and a decanter of sherry await guests' arrival. The refrigerator and pantry are stocked for breakfast. Absolute privacy, cozy fireplaces, antiques, patio, and colonial herb gardens. This pre-Revolutionary home was featured in *Colonial Homes* magazine and the *New York Times*. Complete concierge services. Honeymoon packages.

Host: Lois Evans
Rooms: 3 (1 PB; 2 SB) $150-250
Full Breakfast
Credit Cards: A, B
Notes: 2, 5, 7, 8, 9, 10, 11, 12, 14

## The Lodge Alley Inn

195 East Bay Street, 29401
(843) 722-1611; (800) 845-1004
FAX (843) 577-7497

Nestled in the historic district within strolling distance of fine dining and attractions. Luxurious inn rooms and suites surround an enchanting courtyard with fountain. Many rooms/suites appointed with pine floors, oriental carpets, fireplaces, and period reproductions

NOTES: Credit cards accepted: A MasterCard; B Visa; C American Express; D Discover; E Diner's Club; F Other; 2 Personal checks accepted; 3 Lunch available; 4 Dinner available; 5 Open all year; 6 Pets welcome;

reflecting Charleston's European heritage. Enjoy amenities including complimentary valet parking, complimentary Continental breakfast, daily newspaper, afternoon sherry, and turndown service with chocolates.

Host: Greg Overmier
Rooms; 95 (PB) $144-360
Continental Breakfast
Credit Cards: A, B, C
Notes: 5, 8, 9, 12, 14, 15

## Palmer Home Bed & Breakfast

5 East Battery, 29401
(843) 853-1574; (888) 723-1574

Fabulous rooms with a view overlooking Charleston Harbor and historic Fort Sumter. Locally known as the "Pink Palace," it is one of the 50 most famous homes in Charleston. The forerunner of the submarine, *The David*, was invented in this house. The Palmer House is in the center of the historic district. Off-street parking and bicycles are provided for guests.

Room: 3 (PB) $100-150
Continental Breakfast
Credit Cards: None
Notes: 2, 5, 7, 9, 11, 12

## The Planters Inn

112 North Market Street, 29401
(843) 722-2345; (800) 845-7082
www.plantersinn.com

The Planters Inn is the heart and soul of historic Charleston, steps away from landmark houses, gardens, and Waterfront Park. The newly renovated inn has 62 spacious rooms and suites featuring oversized private baths and large closets. Guests are treated to refreshments each afternoon and turndown service each night. The acclaimed Peninsula Grill serves dinner seven nights a week. AAA-rated four diamonds. Silver-service breakfast and valet parking available.

Host: Larry Spelts
Rooms: 62 (PB) $105-250
Continental Breakfast

Credit Cards: A, B, C, D, E
Notes: 2, 4, 5, 7, 8, 9, 10, 11, 12, 14, 15

## Rutledge Victorian Inn and Guest House

114 Rutledge Avenue, 29401
(843) 722-7551; (888) 722-7553
FAX (843) 727-0065

Elegant century-old Charleston house in the downtown historic district. All rooms have fireplaces, 12-foot ceilings, hardwood floors, 10-foot doors and windows, and antiques. Lovely round 120-foot porch overlooks the park and Roman columns, the remains of the Confederate Soldiers Reunion Hall. Air conditioning, private baths, TVs, telephones, fax, turndown service, parking, refreshments, and Continental plus breakfast. A 5- to 20-minute walk to all historic sights. Smoking permitted on porches only. Water and lots of beaches nearby. Detached kitchen house, built in 1832, with two bedrooms, private garden is also available. Children 12 and older welcome.

Hosts: Lyn and Norm
Rooms: 10 (7 PB; 3 SB) $60-155
Continental Breakfast
Credit Cards: A, B
Notes: 2, 5, 7, 9, 10, 12, 14

Rutledge Victorian Inn

7 No smoking; 8 Children welcome; 9 Social drinking allowed; 10 Tennis nearby; 11 Swimming nearby; 12 Golf nearby; 13 Skiing nearby; 14 May be booked through a travel agent; 15 Handicapped accessible.

## Thomas Lamboll House

19 King Street, 29401
(843) 723-3212; (888) 874-0793
FAX (843) 723-5222; e-mail: Lamboll@aol.com

This Charleston single house was built in 1735 by Thomas Lamboll, a notable colonial judge, and is just off the Battery in the heart of the historic district. It offers two large, handsome bedrooms with private baths and French doors leading onto the piazza. The bedrooms are centrally air conditioned and have fireplaces, cable TVs, and telephones. Each room is tastefully furnished with reproduction and antique furniture. Will accommodate eight people. A Continental breakfast is served in the dining room on the first floor. Off-street parking available.

Rooms: 2 (PB) $95-145
Continental Breakfast
Credit Cards: A, B
Notes: 2, 5, 7, 8, 9, 10, 11, 12

Two Meeting Street Inn

## Two Meeting Street Inn

2 Meeting Street, 29401
(843) 723-7322

"The Belle of Charleston's bed and breakfasts." This Queen Anne-Victorian mansion, circa 1890-92, has welcomed guests for more than 50 years. In the historic district overlooking the Battery, the inn charms its visitors with exquisite Tiffany windows, canopied beds, oriental rugs, and English antiques. The day starts with freshly baked muffins served in the oak-covered dining room or courtyard, then afternoon tea, and ends with evening sherry on the wraparound piazza. The epitome of southern hospitality and turn-of-the-century luxury. Two-night minimum stay requested for weekends and holidays.

Hosts: The Spell Family
Rooms: 9 (PB) $145-275
Continental Breakfast
Credit Cards: None
Notes: 2, 5, 7, 10, 11, 12

## Vendue Inn

19 Vendue Range, 29401
(843) 577-7970; (800) 845-7900
FAX (843) 577-2913
www.charleston.net/com/vendueinn

Elegant 18th-century-style inn by harbor/Waterfront Park, heart of the historic district. Charming, friendly ambiance. Beautifully decorated rooms and suites, many with harbor views, Jacuzzis, marble baths, and fireplaces. Includes full buffet breakfast, wine/cheese, evening cordials, turndown service. Larger suites offer full breakfast, fresh fruit, and wet bar. Limited smoking rooms. Excellent restaurant, the Library, features American cuisine with southern flair. Rooftop Terrace Bar offers city's best view of harbor/city. AAA four-diamond inn.

Hosts: Coyne and Linda Edmison
Rooms: 45 (PB) $120-235
Full Breakfast
Credit Cards: A, B, C, D, E
Notes: 2, 3, 4, 5, 8, 9, 10, 11, 12, 14, 15

## Victoria House Inn

208 King Street, 29401
(843) 720-2944; (800) 933-5464

Built in 1889, this Romanesque-style building has 18 elegantly renovated guest rooms. Modern amenities are provided in every room, including a stocked refrigerator. Guests receive evening turndown service, and wine and sherry are served in the lobby. Continental breakfast and newspaper delivered to the room each morning.

---

NOTES: Credit cards accepted: A MasterCard; B Visa; C American Express; D Discover; E Diner's Club; F Other; 2 Personal checks accepted; 3 Lunch available; 4 Dinner available; 5 Open all year; 6 Pets welcome;

AAA four diamonds. Nonsmoking rooms available. Limited handicapped accessibility.

Host: Beth Babcock
Rooms: 18 (PB) $140-255
Continental Breakfast
Credit Cards: A, B, D, E
Notes: 2, 5, 8, 9, 10, 11, 12, 14

## Villa de la Fontaine Bed & Breakfast

138 Wentworth Street, 29401
(843) 577-7709

This columned Greek Revival mansion is in the heart of the historic district. It was built in 1838 and boasts a three-quarter- acre garden with fountain and terraces. Restored to impeccable condition, it is furnished with museum-quality furniture and accessories. The hosts are retired American Society of Interior Designers interior designers and have decorated the rooms with 18th-century American antiques. Several of the rooms feature canopied beds. Breakfast is prepared by a master chef who prides himself on serving a different menu every day. Off-street parking. Minimum-stay requirements for weekends and holidays. There are four rooms and two suites.

Hosts: William Fontaine and Aubrey Hancock
Rooms: 6 (PB) $100-150
Full Breakfast
Credit Cards:None
Notes: 2, 5, 7, 9, 10, 11, 12

## Woodlands Resort & Inn

125 Parsons Road, Summerville, 29483
(803) 875-2600; (800) 774-9999
FAX (803) 875-2603

Woodlands Resort and Inn nestled in the woods on 42 acres, just 23 miles west of Charleston, with 19 handsomely appointed rooms. No two are exactly alike, but all feature residential advantages such as fireplaces, sitting areas, heated towel racks, whirlpool baths, and personal amenities. Signature yellow roses and iced split of Perrier-Jouet champagne greet each guest upon arrival. Turndown service includes house-made cookies. Dine in the five-diamond dining room. Heated swimming pool, clay tennis courts, croquet lawn, and bicycles are just a few of the many things available during a stay in South Carolina's only five-diamond, Relais et Chateaux property. Breakfast is served at the five-diamond restaurant, which opens at 7:00 A.M., or guests can order room service.

Host: Marty Wall
Rooms: 19 (PB) $295-350
Credit Cards: A, B, C, D, E
Notes: 2, 3, 4, 5, 7, 9, 10, 11, 12, 14, 15

## COLUMBIA

## Richland Street Bed & Breakfast

1425 Richland Street, 29201
(803) 779-7001; FAX (803) 256-3725

Built in 1992 Victorian design with southern appeal. Historic district in walking distance to restaurants, tours of historic homes, art museum, State House, parks. Spacious eight rooms with private baths. Designed for the corporate or casual traveler. Continental-plus breakfast. Telephones, TV's, and fax. Smoke free. Personal checks accepted in advance. Camel's AAA four-diamond inn.

Host: Naomi S. Perryman
Rooms: 8 (PB) $89-150
Continental Breakfast
Credit Cards: A, B, C
Notes: 2, 5, 7, 9, 15

Richland Street

7 No smoking; 8 Children welcome; 9 Social drinking allowed; 10 Tennis nearby; 11 Swimming nearby; 12 Golf nearby; 13 Skiing nearby; 14 May be booked through a travel agent; 15 Handicapped accessible.

## GAFFNEY

### Jolly Place: A Bed & Breakfast Inn

405 College Drive, 29340
(864) 489-4638

Jolly Place is a comfortable, spacious, craftsman-style home, built in 1920. It is on the National Register of Historic Places, centrally located in Gaffney's historic district, and decorated with antiques, collectibles, and period furnishings. It is a grand house of simple elegance. Relax or discuss business in any of several commons areas. Central air conditioning. Remote-controlled, color/cable TV. Senior citizen, government, and corporate rates. Personal check, traveler's check, and cash accepted.

Hosts: Henry and Mary Mason Jolly
Rooms: 5 (PB) $65-110
Full Breakfast
Notes: 2, 5, 7, 8, 9, 10, 11, 12, 14

## GEORGETOWN

### Ashfield Manor Bed & Breakfast

3030 South Island Road, 29440
(843) 546-0464; (800) 483-5002

The inn offers southern hospitality in the style of a real southern plantation. Ashfield Manor has an elegant but comfortable country setting. All rooms are oversized and redecorated with period furnishings, private entrance, and color cable TV. Enhanced Continental menu for breakfast served in guests' room, the parlor, or on the 57-foot screened porch overlooking a lake with wildlife—even an alligator!

Hosts: Dave and Carol Ashenfelder
Rooms: 4 (2 PB; 2 SB) $55-65
Continental Breakfast
Credit Cards: A, B, D
Notes: 2, 5, 7, 8, 10, 12, 14

King's Inn at Georgetown

### King's Inn at Georgetown

230 Broad Street, 29440
(843) 527-6937 (phone/FAX); (800) 251-8805
www.bbonline.com/sc/kingsinn/

Magnificent moldings, crystal chandeliers, and gleaming original floors grace the foyer and three antique-filled parlors of this 1825 Federal manse. Exquisitely decorated guest rooms provide the ultimate in romantic relaxation, from canopied king-size beds adjoining private piazzas to dreamy four-postered queen-size rooms with an in-room Jacuzzi tub for two. Rooms are furnished with telephones and modem hook-ups. Guests will find swimming facilities on the premises. The garden breakfast room overlooks lap pool and screened porch. Among *Country Inns* 1995 Top 12 Inns.

Hosts: Marilyn and Jerry Burkhardt
Rooms: 7 (PB) $89-139
Full Breakfast
Credit Cards: A, B, C
Notes: 2, 3, 4, 5, 7, 8, 9, 10, 11, 12, 14

### 1790 House

630 Highmarket Street, 29440
(843) 546-4821; (800) 890-7432
e-mail: jwiley5211@aol.com
www.1790house.com

Meticulously restored, this 200-year-old Colonial plantation-style inn is in the heart of historic Georgetown. Spacious, luxurious rooms with sitting areas and central heat and air. Stay

---

NOTES: Credit cards accepted: A MasterCard; B Visa; C American Express; D Discover; E Diner's Club; F Other; 2 Personal checks accepted; 3 Lunch available; 4 Dinner available; 5 Open all year; 6 Pets welcome;

1790 House

in the Rice Planters Room, the beautiful romantic cottage with Jacuzzi, or in one of the other lovely rooms. Gourmet breakfasts. Walk to shops, restaurants, and historic sights. Just a short drive to Brookgreen Gardens, Myrtle Beach, and the Grand Strand—a golfer's paradise. One hour to Charleston. Rated excellent by ABBA, three diamonds by AAA and Mobil.

Hosts: John and Patricia Wiley
Rooms: 6 (PB) $95-135
Full Breakfast
Credit Cards: A, B, C, D, E
Notes: 2, 5, 7, 8, 9, 10, 12, 14

## The Shaw House

613 Cypress Court, 29440
(843) 546-9663

A spacious two-story Colonial home in a serene natural setting overlooking Willowbank Marsh. It is a wonderful setting for bird watching. The rooms are spacious—all private

The Shaw House

baths—have many antiques, are air conditioned, carpeted. Queen-size rice beds, a full southern breakfast. Nighttime chocolate on pillows along with turndown service. Walk to restaurants, shops, and historic sights. A golfer's paradise. Beaches 10 minutes away. Children permitted.

Hosts: Mary and Joe Shaw
Rooms: 3 (PB) $60-70
Full Breakfast
Credit Cards: C
Notes: 2, 5, 8, 9, 10, 11, 12, 14, 15

## "ShipWright's"

609 Cypress Court, 29440
(843) 527-4475

Serving guests with hospitality plus. Quiet, spacious with a tasteful decor of heirlooms and antiques. Experience the breathtaking view of the Avenue of Live Oaks and the Alive Marshes of the Black River while rocking on the large porch or gazing out the parlor window. Taste Grandma Eicher's pancakes, freshly ground coffee, and fresh fruit. Guests say, "I feel like I just visited my best friend."

Host: Leatrice Wright
Rooms: 2 (PB) $60
Full Breakfast
Credit Cards: None
Notes: 2, 5, 7, 8, 9, 10, 11, 12

## HARTSVILLE

## Missouri Inn

314 East Home Avenue, 29550
(843) 383-9553

Missouri Inn offers the graciousness of a southern home and the amenities of a small European luxury hotel. Guests will find the inn on a quiet, tree-lined street of stately homes in the historic district. Tastefully furnished with antiques and oriental rugs, the inn has five guest rooms all with private baths. Catering and corporate retreats are available.

7 No smoking; 8 Children welcome; 9 Social drinking allowed; 10 Tennis nearby; 11 Swimming nearby; 12 Golf nearby; 13 Skiing nearby; 14 May be booked through a travel agent; 15 Handicapped accessible.

Hosts: Kyle and Kenny Segars
Rooms: 5 (PB) $85
Continental Breakfast
Credit Cards: A, B, C
Notes: 2, 5, 9, 10, 12, 14

## HILTON HEAD ISLAND

### *Ambiance*

8 Wren Drive, 29928
(843) 671-4981

Marny welcomes guests to sunny Hilton Head Island. This cypress home, nestled in subtropical surroundings, is in Sea Pines Plantation. Ambiance reflects the hostess's interior decorating business by the same name. All the amenities of Hilton Head are offered in a contemporary, congenial atmosphere. The climate is favorable year-round for all sports. Ambiance is across the street from a beautiful beach and the Atlantic Ocean. Smoking outside only.

Host: Marny Kridel Daubenspeck
Rooms: 2 (PB) $85
Continental Breakfast
Credit Cards: None
Notes: 2, 5, 7, 9, 10, 11, 12, 14

## HONEA PATH

### *Sugarfoot Castle's Bed & Breakfast*

211 South Main Street, 29654
(864) 369-6565

Enormous trees umbrella this circa 1880 brick Victorian home. Fresh flowers grace the 14-inch-thick walled rooms furnished with family heirlooms. Enjoy the living room's interesting collection or the library's comfy chairs, TV, VCR, books, fireplace, desk, and game table. Upon rising, guests will find coffee and freshly squeezed orange juice outside their doors, followed by a breakfast of fresh fruit, cereal, hot breads, and beverages served in the dining room by candlelight. Rock away the world's

Sugarfoot Castle

cares on the screened porch overlooking peaceful gardens. Children over 10 welcome. Smoking permitted outside. All rooms double occupancy. TVs in all rooms.

Hosts: Cecil and Gale Evans
Rooms: 3 (SB) $66-76
Continental Breakfast
Credit Cards: A, B
Notes: 2, 5, 7, 9, 10, 11, 12

## JOHNSTON

### *The Cox House Inn*

478 Lee Street, 29832
(803) 275-2707; FAX (803) 275-4253

Victorian-style architecture. Four suites, each with private bath and full kitchen, separate living area. Ideal for the independent traveler. Central heat and air conditioning, cable TV, private telephone, just one block from the Main

The Cox House Inn

---

NOTES: Credit cards accepted: A MasterCard; B Visa; C American Express; D Discover; E Diner's Club; F Other; 2 Personal checks accepted; 3 Lunch available; 4 Dinner available; 5 Open all year; 6 Pets welcome;

Street of Johnston, population 2,500. Guests will find the inn on Highway 121, that connects I-26 with I-20, along western corridor of South Carolina in historic Edgefield County. Innkeeper is not on site at night.

Rooms: 4 (PB) $55-65
Credit Cards: A, B
Notes: 2, 5, 8, 9, 12

## LANDRUM

### The Red Horse Inn

310 North Campbell Road, 29356
(864) 895-4968

The Red Horse Inn is on 190 acres in the midst of horse country. Charming Victorian cottages are exquisitely furnished and decorated. Each offers a kitchen, separate bedroom, sitting area with a fold-out bed, full bath, TV, air conditioning, and beautiful mountain views from the rocking porch. Three cottages have Jacuzzis and three have lofts. Inquire about accommodations for pets. Pets are welcome within certain limits. Additional charge for extra person up to four per cottage.

Hosts: Mary and Roger Wolters
Cottages: 5 (PB) $145
Continental Breakfast
Credit Cards: A, B, D
Notes: 2, 5, 7, 8, 9, 10, 12, 14

## LATTA

### Abingdon Manor

307 Church Street, 29565
(843) 752-5090; (888) 752-5090
www.bbonline.com/sc/abingdon

Six miles from I-95 and halfway between New York City and Miami, this 8,000-square-foot Greek Revival mansion is the closest AAA four-diamond property in the Carolinas along I-95. Completed in 1905, the inn is listed in the national register. Filled with unique architec-

tural details, and furnished with antiques, the house is comfortably elegant. Feather beds, robes, high-quality linens, turndown service, complimentary wine and sherry among the many amenities included.

Hosts: Michael and Patty Griffey
Rooms: 5 (PB) $105-140
Full Breakfast
Credit Cards: A, B, C, D
Notes: 2, 5, 7, 9, 10, 12, 14

## LEESVILLE

### The Able House Inn

244 East Columbia Avenue, 29070
(803) 532-2763 (phone/FAX)

Able House Inn treats guests the way they love to be treated, because the inn cherishes every guest. Every room has its own private bath. Plush towels, linens, and extra pillows. Generous amounts of fresh-made tea and coffee. Continental plus breakfast included. Restaurants within a five-minute drive. Refrigerator, ice, TV, and VCR, living and dining rooms, sunroom, free use of pool and patio. Limited smoking permitted. Closely supervised children over 12 welcome. Turndown/candy services every night.

Hosts: Jack and Annabelle Wright
Rooms: 5 (PB) $65-75
Continental Breakfast
Credit Cards: A, B
Notes: 2, 5, 9, 10, 11, 12

The Able House Inn

## LYMAN (GREENVILLE/SPARTANBURG)

### Walnut Lane Bed & Breakfast

110 Ridge Road, 29365
(864) 949-7230; FAX (864) 949-1633
e-mail: walnut110@aol.com

Reminiscent of the grand plantations of yesterday, the Walnut Lane Bed and Breakfast stands as a beacon of the past on its lush acreage surrounded by an abundance of fruit trees. Conveniently between Spartanburg and Greenville. Surrounded by great area outlet shopping, art centers, concert facilities, many fine universities, and cultural centers. For business or leisurely travelers the Walnut Lane is where guests want to be. Chair lift available in house. Evening refreshments served with full gourmet breakfast.

Hosts: Marie and Park Urquhart
Rooms: 4 (PB) $80-105
Full Breakfast
Credit Cards: A, B, C, D
Notes: 2, 3, 4, 5, 7, 9, 10, 11, 12, 14

## MARION

### Montgomery's Grove

408 Harlee Street, 29571
(843) 423-5220; (877) 646-7721
www.bbonline.com/sc/montgomery

Montgomery's Grove is an 1893 Victorian manor nestled among five acres of century-old trees. Listed in the national historic register, it's known for unique architecture, dramatic 14-foot interior archways, woodwork, and five beautifully appointed bedrooms. Sip tea on wraparound porches or stroll under Spanish moss-draped trees to Marion's quaint shops and restaurants. Minutes from I-95, the perfect midway stopping point north or south. Close to the fun and excitement of Myrtle Beach.

Hosts: Coreen and Rick Roberts
Rooms: 5 (3 PB; 2 SB) $80-100
Full Breakfast
Credit Cards: None
Notes: 2, 3, 4, 5, 8, 9, 10, 11, 12, 14

## MCCLELLANVILLE

### Laurel Hill Plantation

8913 North Highway 17, P.O. Box 190, 29458
(843) 887-3708; (888) 887-3708
www.bbonline.com/sc/laurelhill/

Laurel Hill faces the Intracoastal Waterway and the Atlantic Ocean. Porches provide a scenic view of marshes and creeks. The house is furnished in charming country and primitive antiques that reflect the Low Country lifestyle. Thirty miles north of Charleston, and only 60 miles south of Myrtle Beach. Smoking is allowed in designated areas only. Children at hosts' discretion

Hosts: Jackie and Lee Morrison
Rooms: 4 (PB) $95-115
Full Breakfast
Credit Cards: A, B, C, D, E, F
Notes: 2, 5, 9, 10, 11, 12, 14

Laurel Hill Plantation

## PAWLEY'S ISLAND

### Cassena Inn

294 Atlantic Ave, 29585 (location)
P.O. Box 6141, Columbia, 29260 (mailing)
(843) 237-3760

This 1950s oceanfront inn is on a small residential island where the rice planters of the 1800s spent their summers. Guests are encouraged to soak up the sun on the beautiful beach and catch up on their reading in a rocking chair on the screened porch. More adventurous guests can visit the historic sites of Georgetown, tour local plantations, experience Brookgreen, America's largest and finest sculpture garden, play championship golf, and enjoy fine dining all within 15 miles. Deep sea fishing, kayak rentals, and tours available.

Rooms: 4 (PB) $75-85
Continental Breakfast
Notes: 2, 8, 9, 10, 11, 12

## PICKENS

### The Schell Haus Bed & Breakfast & Confederate Center

117 Hiawatha Trail, 29671
(864) 878-0078; FAX (864) 878-0066
e-mail: schellhs@bellsouth.net

An enchanting Victorian home tucked away in the foothills of the beautiful Blue Ridge Mountains on the Cherokee Foothills Scenic Highway. Guests are afforded a full view of Table Rock, a natural table-like formation, and wooded acreage, which provide a perfect backdrop for any trip. Four state parks, picturesque lakes, and nearby waterfalls highlight the natural environment of Upcountry South Carolina and invite nature walks, hiking, biking, golfing, and water based activities. Outdoor kennels available for pets.

Hosts: Sharon and Jim Mahanes
Rooms: 6 (PB) $80-160
Full Breakfast
Credit Cards: A, B, D
Notes: 2, 5, 6, 7, 8, 9, 10, 11, 12, 14

## ROCK HILL

### Harmony House Bed & Breakfast

3485 Harmony Road, Catawba, 29704
(803) 329-5886; (888) 737-0016
www.bbonline.com/sc/harmony

Victorian-style farmhouse built in 1991. Nestled on a 36-acre countryside tract just four miles off I-77 on the outskirts of Rock Hill. Beautifully decorated with antiques and fam-

Harmony House

ily treasures. Two common sitting areas, one with TV/VCR, Primestar satellite, movies, games, stocked refrigerator with drinks, snacks, etc. Peace and tranquility are definite assets, with city life just minutes away. Ample attractions nearby. Full breakfast served. Smoking is permitted outside. Children six and older welcome.

Hosts: Winky and Cecil Staton
Rooms: 4 (PB) $70-90
Full Breakfast
Credit Cards: None
Notes: 2, 5, 7, 12, 14

## STARR

### The Gray House

111 Stone's Throw Avenue, 29684
(864) 352-6778; FAX (864) 352-6777

This turn-of-the-century home is the perfect romantic getaway with beautiful gardens, tranquil pond, quiet walking trails and horse-drawn carriage rides (by appointment). Two suites, Jasmine and Rose rooms, offer private baths with whirlpools and private dining alcoves. Breakfast served in guests' suite. Restaurant serves Southern fare. Two-bedroom farmhouse also available with stocked 12-acre pond, situated on secluded 100-acre farm. Two bedrooms with private baths, whirlpool, and bidet.

Host: Kathy T. Stone
Rooms: 4 (PB) $90-150
Full Breakfast
Credit Cards: A, B, C, E
Notes: 2, 3, 4, 5, 7, 8, 9, 10, 11, 12, 14, 15

7 No smoking; 8 Children welcome; 9 Social drinking allowed; 10 Tennis nearby; 11 Swimming nearby; 12 Golf nearby; 13 Skiing nearby; 14 May be booked through a travel agent; 15 Handicapped accessible.

## SUMMERVILLE

### Bed & Breakfast of Summerville

304 South Hampton Street, 29483
(843) 871-5275

Sleep in the slave quarters of an 1862 house in a quiet historic district. Near restaurants, antique and specialty shops. Queen-size bed, telephone, TV, kitchenette, bath with shower, bikes, and pool. Short drive to Charleston, Middleton, and Magnolia Gardens. Winter breakfast is self-prepared from the stocked refrigerator. For the rest of the year, breakfast in the greenhouse is an option. Advance reservation, please.

Hosts: Dusty and Emmagene Rhodes
Room: 1 (PB) $60-70
Continental Breakfast
Credit Cards: None
Notes: 2, 5, 7, 9, 10, 11, 12

## SUMTER

### Bed and Breakfast of Sumter

6 Park Avenue, 29150
(803) 773-2903; (888) 786-8372

This restored 1896 Prairie-style home sits in the heart of Sumter's historic district across from Memorial Park. Large front porch with swings and rocking chairs. Gracious guest rooms with antiques, fireplaces. Formal Victorian parlor and TV sitting room. Cable. Fax. Gourmet

Bed & Breakfast of Sumter

breakfast (fruit, entrée, home-baked breads). Antique shops, Swan Lake, and golf courses are all nearby. AAA-rated three diamonds.

Hosts: Charles, Joyce, and Kathryn Thielman
Rooms: 4 (PB) $75
Full Breakfast
Credit Cards: A, B, D
Notes: 2, 5, 7, 10, 12, 14

## WOODRUFF

The Nicholls-Crook Plantation

### The Nicholls-Crook Plantation House Bed & Breakfast

120 Plantation Drive, 29388
(864) 476-8820 (phone/FAX)
www.bbonline.com/sc/nicholls

Be surrounded with the atmosphere of times gone by in this Georgian-style plantation house built in 1793 and listed in the National Register of Historic Places. Delight in historic ambiance enhanced by period antique furnishings and beautiful gardens. A bountiful breakfast adds to guests' pleasures. Guest rooms are cozy and inviting. Near Spartanburg, Greenville, Cowpens, and Kings Mountain battlefields, historic Walnut Grove Plantation, BMW Zentrum, antique shopping, and more. Take exit 28 from I-26. Smoking permitted outside only. Children over six welcome.

Hosts: Suzanne and Jim Brown
Rooms: 3 (2 PB; 1 SB) $85-95
Full Breakfast
Credit Cards: C
Notes: 2, 5, 7, 9, 12, 14

NOTES: Credit cards accepted: A MasterCard; B Visa; C American Express; D Discover; E Diner's Club; F Other; 2 Personal checks accepted; 3 Lunch available; 4 Dinner available; 5 Open all year; 6 Pets welcome;

# Tennessee

## Woodlawn

110 Keith Lane, 37303
(615) 745-8211; (615) 745-6029

Woodlawn is an elegant bed and breakfast in historic downtown Athens. The antebellum Greek Revival mansion is filled with family antiques. Built in 1858 by Alexander Keith, it was a Union hospital during the Civil War. Listed in the National Register of Historic Places. Thirteen-foot ceilings, large bedrooms with private baths. Halfway between Chattanooga and Knoxville off I-75. The *Tennessean* calls Woodlawn a classic bed and breakfast. On five acres, Woodlawn is filled with warm, friendly southern hospitality in the heart of Athens.

Hosts: Barry and Susan Willis
Rooms: 4 (PB) $60-140
Full Breakfast
Credit Cards: A, B, D
Notes: 2, 5, 7, 9, 10, 11, 12, 13, 14

## BRISTOL

## New Hope Bed & Breakfast

822 Georgia Avenue, 37620
(423) 989-3343; (888) 989-3343

All the charm of a late Victorian home, yet comfort and convenience were high on the agenda when decorating decisions were being made. "Come home to New Hope" is the hosts' motto. There are four guest rooms with large private baths. A full breakfast is always served. Arrange for a guided walking tour of the historic neighborhood or call ahead and inquire about the murder mystery weekends.

Hosts: Tom and Tonda Fluke
Rooms: 4 (PB) $85-135
Full Breakfast
Credit Cards: A, B, C
Notes: 2, 5, 7, 12, 14

## CHATTANOOGA

## Adams Hilborne Mansion Inn

801 Vine Street, 37403
(423) 265-5000; FAX (423) 265-5555

Cornerstone to the Fort Wood historic district, this majestic Romanesque Victorian mansion is built in castlelike proportions of native mountain stone. The Adams Hilborne pampers guests with fine antiques, original artwork, and exquisite fabrics in all the oversized guest suites. The Designer Showhouse for the city of Chattanooga and winner of the prestigious National Trust Great American Home Awards. The reception rooms are resplendent with heavily carved moldings, coffered ceilings, 16-foot-tall

Adams Hilborne Mansion Inn

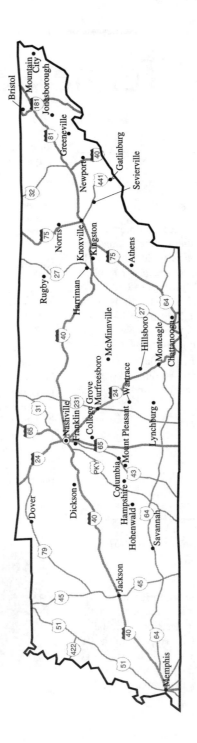

Tennessee

arched pocket doors with silver-plated hinges.
Fine candlelight dining in the restaurant.
Restaurant is handicapped accessible. Minutes
from the Tennessee Aquarium, Civil War sites,
and Tennessee River.

Hosts: Wendy and Dave Adams
Rooms: 10 (PB) $100-295
Continental Breakfast
Credit Cards: A, B, C, E
Notes: 2, 4, 5, 7, 8, 9, 10, 11, 12, 14

Bluff View Inn

## Alford House Bed & Breakfast

5515 Alford Hill Drive, 37419
(423) 821-7625

A traditional, family-owned, 18-room home at
lower Lookout Mountain. Minutes from great
dining, museums, Civil War sites, live theatres,
Tennessee Aquarium, hiking, boating, Coolidge
Park, and more, including the only school for
carousel animal-carving in the United States.
Antiques and Victorian era atmosphere fill the
home. Guest rooms reflect Chattanooga's past
and present. Enjoy early coffee, breakfast, and
afternoon tea on the upper balcony or in the
dining room. On cool evenings warm up by the
fire with a good book, or visit with other guests.
Off-street parking for guests. Offseason and
weeknight discounts. Limited accommodations
for children.

Host: Rhoda Alford
Rooms: 3 (PB) $75-95
Suite: 1 (PB) $160
Full and Continental Breakfast
Credit Cards: None
Notes: 2, 5, 7, 9, 10, 11, 12, 14

## Bluff View Inn

411 East Second Street, 37403
(423) 265-5033; FAX (423) 757-0124

Overlooking the Tennessee River, in the Bluff
View Art District, the Bluff View Inn offers
refined accommodations in three turn-of-the-
century restored homes. Guests enjoy Old

World elegance, a spectacular view, and an
exciting blend of gourmet restaurants, gardens,
galleries, meeting rooms, banquet halls, private
parlors, terrace cafés, working artists' studios,
the Bocce Court Terrace, and the new Bluff
View Scenic Overlook. Conveniently connected to downtown Chattanooga's major
attractions and the popular North Shore via the
Tennessee Riverwalk and Walnut Street Pedestrian Bridge. Private parking.

Host: Julie Poston, innkeeper
Rooms: 16 (PB) $115-250
Full Breakfast
Credit Cards: A, B, C, D
Notes: 2, 3, 4, 5, 7, 8, 9, 12

## The Captain's Quarters Bed & Breakfast Inn

13 Barnhardt Circle
Fort Oglethorpe, GA 30742-3601
(706) 858-0624; (800) 710-6816
FAX (706) 861-4053
e-mail: innkeeper@captains-qtrs-inn.com
www.captains-qtrs-inn.com

Circa 1902, this beautifully renovated Classic
Renaissance Revival home was built by the
US Army for two captains and their families.
Rooms are individually decorated and some
have working fireplaces. The spacious common areas are filled with family antiques. A
hot tub spa is available with robes and slippers provided. In the suburbs of Chattanooga
on the northern border of the Chickamauga

NOTES: Credit cards accepted: A MasterCard; B Visa; C American Express; D Discover; E Diner's Club;
F Other; 2 Personal checks accepted; 3 Lunch available; 4 Dinner available; 5 Open all year; 6 Pets welcome;
7 No smoking; 8 Children welcome; 9 Social drinking allowed; 10 Tennis nearby; 11 Swimming nearby;
12 Golf nearby; 13 Skiing nearby; 14 May be booked through a travel agent; 15 Handicapped accessible.

and Chattanooga National Military Park, just 20 minutes from the Tennessee Aquarium and Lookout Mountain. Smoking permitted outside only. Children over 10 welcome. Cat in residence. No pets. Three-course breakfast served.

Hosts: Betty and Daniel McKenzie
Rooms: 7 (PB) $89-129
Full Breakfast
Credit Cards: A, B, C, D
Notes: 2, 5, 7, 9, 10, 12, 14

## COLLEGE GROVE

### Peacock Hill Country Inn

6994 Giles Hill Road, 37046
(615) 368-7727; (800) 327-6663
www.bbonline.com/tn/peacock/

Ten luxury accommodations on a 700-acre cattle farm, convenient to Franklin and Nashville. A historic 1850s farmhouse, two-story log cabin, a two-level granary suite and new/old McCall House. Private baths with whirlpools, European showers, king-size beds, fireplaces. Fireside suppers by reservation. Featured in *Country Inns, National Geographic Travel, Southern Living, Romantic Homes*, and *Travel Holiday*. Carmel's AAA four-diamond inn. No smoking.

Hosts: Anita and Walter Ogilvie
Rooms: 10 (PB) $125-225
Full Breakfast
Credit Cards: A, B, C, D
Notes: 2, 3, 4, 5, 7, 8, 9, 10, 11, 12, 14, 15

## COLUMBIA

### Natchez Trace Bed & Breakfast Reservation Service

P.O. Box 193, Hampshire, 38461
(931) 285-2777; (800) 377-2770
e-mail: natcheztrace@worldnet.att.net
www.bbonline.com/natcheztrace

**Sweetwater Inn.** Milepost 409. Thirteen miles from Columbia and just five miles from I-65,

this 1901 farmhouse has been newly restored to elegant perfection. Double wraparound porch provides view of the Middle Tennessee countryside. The Columbia area is the antebellum home capital of Tennessee. A gourmet breakfast is served on fine linens and china. $100-125.

## DICKSON

### East Hills Bed & Breakfast Inn

100 East Hills Terrace, 37055
(615) 441-9428; FAX (615) 446-2181
www.bbonline.com/tn/easthills/

This fully restored traditional home with southern charm was built in the late 1940s by the current owner's father. The house is near Luther Lake, Greystone Golf Course, and is only six miles from Montgomery Bell State Park; convenient to shopping, hospital, restaurants, and downtown area. Large living room, library/den with fireplace, and TV for guests to enjoy. Furnished throughout with period antiques. The long front porch has rocking chairs and a swing. Enjoy the big front yard with lots of trees.

Hosts: John and Anita Luther
Rooms: 5 (PB) $65-95
Cottage: 1
Full and Continental Breakfast
Credit Cards: A, B, C, D
Notes: 2, 5, 7, 10, 11, 12, 14, 15

East Hills

## DOVER

### Riverfront Plantation Inn

190 Crow Lane, P.O. Box 349, 37058
(931) 232-9492

Experience the southern hospitality of this splendidly restored Civil War-era home. The inn features five elegant guest rooms with private baths, screened porches, and a gourmet plantation breakfast. The historic waterfront estate is adjacent to Fort Donelson National Battlefield and minutes from Land Between the Lakes.

Hosts: Lynn and Fulton Combs
Rooms: 5 (PB) $95-115
Full Breakfast
Credit Cards: A, B, C, D
Notes: 2, 3, 4, 5, 7, 9, 10, 11, 12, 14

## FRANKLIN

### Blueberry Hill Bed & Breakfast

4591 Peytonsville Road, 37064
(615) 791-9947
www.bbonline.com/tn/blueberry

Blueberry Hill is eight miles from historic Franklin—rich in Civil War history. It is perched near the top of a high hill with breathtaking views of the rolling hills and valleys of Middle Tennessee from the great room, deck, porch, and gardens. The original house was built in the Federal style with fireplaces in every room. There are two guest rooms with four-poster beds and gas log fireplaces. Full breakfast with blueberry specialties.

Hosts: Art and Joan Reesman
Rooms: 2 (PB) $75-85
Full Breakfast
Credit Cards: A, B, D
Notes: 2, 5, 7, 9, 12

### Natchez Trace Bed & Breakfast Reservation Service

P.O. Box 193, Hampshire, 38461
(931) 285-2777; (800) 377-2770
e-mail: natcheztrace@worldnet.att.net
www.bbonline.com/natcheztrace

**Blueberry Hill Bed and Breakfast.** Twelve miles from the Natchez Trace and convenient to Franklin, I-65, and Nashville, this home has a breathtaking view of the valley. A replica of a Federal-period home, there are old heart-pine flooring and a fireplace in every room. The modern addition boasts a great room with books, a piano, a pub table, and large-screen TV, with a collection of movies. Queen-size beds; full breakfast with blueberry specialties. Children over 10 welcome. Open only on weekends. $70-80.

**Namaste Bed and Breakfast.** Milepost 436. Set in the lovely Leipers Creek valley near the village of Leipers Fork, this country home is only two and one-half miles from the Natchez Trace. There are facilities for horses; the trail along the trace is just minutes away. Large guest rooms with private baths. Enjoy a full breakfast and look out over the peaceful setting. Swimming pool and exercise room available. $85.

**Sweeney Hollow.** Just three miles from the Trace. Guests will find their own suite, with sitting room and private porch in this brick ranch home. Complete privacy since there are accomodations for one group only! The drive leads guests through beautiful horse country in the rolling hills outside of Leipers Fork, 20 minutes from Franklin. Satellite TV, videos. An Irish farmhouse breakfast is their specialty on Sunday mornings. $125.

### The Old Marshall House Bed & Breakfast

1030 John Williams Road. 37067
(615) 591-4121; (800) 863-5808
FAX (615) 591-4174
e-mail: marshallhouse@acelink.net
www.oldmarshallhouse.com

Beautiful 1869 Victorian farmhouse in serene coutry setting. Convenient location to all attractions and restaurants. Charming and comfortable guest accommodations including an 1850s log cabin. Queen- and king-size beds,

---

7 No smoking; 8 Children welcome; 9 Social drinking allowed; 10 Tennis nearby; 11 Swimming nearby; 12 Golf nearby; 13 Skiing nearby; 14 May be booked through a travel agent; 15 Handicapped accessible.

fireplaces, antique furnishings, private bathrooms—two with oversized claw-foot tubs. Porches and parlors, beautiful gardns, ponds, and stream. Enjoy southern hospitality at its best! Multiple-night and mid-week discounts.

Hosts: Glenn and Ursula Houghton
Rooms: 3 (PB) $90-150
Full Breakfast
Credit Cards: A, B, C, D
Notes: 2, 5, 7, 9, 10, 11, 12, 14

Eight Gables

## GATLINBURG

### Buckhorn Inn

2140 Tudor Mountain Road, 37738
(423) 436-4668; FAX (423) 436-5009
e-mail: buckhorninn@msn.com

A favorite destination for discriminating travelers to Gatlinburg and the Great Smoky Mountains for more than 60 years, Buckhorn Inn is situated in the heart of the renowned Crafts Community and less than a mile from the Great Smoky Mountains National Park. A 20-acre private pine and hemlock forest cocoon guests in comfortable privacy, while the ever-changing views of the mountains never fail to inspire them. Private nature trail and labyrinth. Superb four-course dinner served nightly except on Sunday.

Hosts: Lee and John Mellor
Rooms: 12 (PB) $115-150
Full Breakfast
Credit Cards: A, B, D
Notes: 2, 3, 4, 5, 7, 9, 10, 11, 12, 13, 14, 15

### Eight Gables and Magnolia Tea Room

219 North Mountain Trail, 37738
(423) 430-3344; (800) 279-5716

Guests of this bed and breakfast are welcomed by a peaceful mountain setting. It features a unique design and decor. Comfort is assured in the spacious guest rooms, each decorated with an individual theme and style. Each first-floor guest room has a private

entrance, and all of the second-floor guest rooms are graced with cathedral ceilings and arched windows. Gathering rooms for relaxing and visiting. Full sit-down breakfast. Dramatic surroundings inside and out. Everything a guest might need marks this tribute to southern hospitality. AAA four-diamond-rated. Dinner available on Saturday only. Lunch served Tuesday through Friday.

Hosts: Don and Kim Cason
Rooms: 12 (PB) $109-179
Full Breakfast
Credit Cards: A, B, C, D
Notes: 2, 3, 5, 7, 8, 9, 10, 11, 12, 13, 14

## GREENEVILLE

### Hilltop House Bed & Breakfast Inn

6 Sanford Circle, 37743
(423) 639-8202

Come and experience the serenity of a 1920s manor house overlooking the Nolichucky River Valley with the Appalachian Mountains in the background. All three guest rooms have private baths and spectacular mountain views, and two have their own verandas. Enjoy afternoon tea at 4:00 P.M. each day and sumptuous breakfasts. Nearby golf, mountain hiking and biking, trout fishing, canoeing, white-water rafting, horseback riding, or antiquing. The house is beautifully furnished with oriental rugs, English antiques, and reproduction pieces. Children over three welcome.

NOTES: Credit cards accepted: A MasterCard; B Visa; C American Express; D Discover; E Diner's Club; F Other; 2 Personal checks accepted; 3 Lunch available; 4 Dinner available; 5 Open all year; 6 Pets welcome;

Host: Denise M. Ashworth
Rooms: 3 (PB) $75-80
Full Breakfast
Credit Cards: A, B, C
Notes: 2, 3, 4, 5, 7, 8, 9, 12, 14

## Nolichuckey Bluffs

400 Kinser Park Lane, 37743
(423) 787-7947; (800) 842-4690
FAX (423) 787-9247; e-mail: cabins@usit.net

Luxury bed and breakfast and fully equipped large, two-bedroom cabins. Full breakfasts with home-baked goodies. Laundry and exercise area. Spectacular mountain views in a beautiful country setting. Children's playground, trails, and picnic pavilion. Asheville, North Carolina, Gatlinburg, antiques, historical spots, and Appalachian Trail nearby. Enjoy evenings around the fireplace as someone puts another roll in the player piano, or enjoy freshly baked cookies while watching the sun set behind the mountains. Pets welcome on a limited basis.

Hosts: Patricia and Brooke Sadler
Rooms: 7 (PB) $70-95
Full Breakfast
Credit Cards: A, B, D
Notes: 2, 5, 6, 7, 8, 10, 11, 12, 14

## HAMPSHIRE

## Natchez Trace Bed & Breakfast Reservation Service

P.O. Box 193, Hampshire, 38461
(931) 285-2777; (800) 377-2770
e-mail: natcheztrace@worldnet.att.net
www.bbonline.com/natcheztrace

**Ridgetop Bed and Breakfast.** Milepost 392. Contemporary cedar home furnished with antiques, set on 170 acres of wooded hills near the village of Hampshire, between Columbia and Hohenwald. Picture windows look out over the woods; have coffee on the spacious deck. Clear streams, a waterfall, birds, and

wildflowers. Near Meriwether Lewis Park, Metal Ford, and Jackson Falls on the trace. The hosts are experts on local wildflowers. Full breakfast served. There is one guest room in the home, a cottage for up to four people, and an 1830 log cabin with fireplace. $75-95.

## HILLSBORO

## Lord's Landing Bed & Breakfast

375 Lord's Landing Lane, 37342
(931) 467-3830; FAX (931) 467-3032
e-mail: lordslanding@blomand.net
www.lordslanding.com

Central Tennessee's 50-acre paradise awaits guests from near and far. Drive in for a relaxing retreat, or fly in to the 2,400 x 80-foot turf airstrip for a quiet getaway. Near the base of the Cumberland Plateau, the main house boasts breathtaking views from every window. A leisurely stroll takes guests to the seven-bedroom, seven-bath country cottage, beautifully decorated with antiques and fine furnishings. Fireplaces and Jacuzzi tubs in most rooms. Swimming pool.

Hosts: Denny and Pam Neilson
Rooms: 7 (PB) $95-150
Full Breakfast
Credit Cards: A, B, C, D
Notes: 2, 3, 4, 5, 8, 11, 12, 14

Lord's Landing

---

## HOHENWALD

### Natchez Trace Bed & Breakfast Reservation Service

P.O. Box 193, Hampshire, 38461
(931) 285-2777; (800) 377-2770
e-mail: natcheztrace@worldnet.att.net
www.bbonline.com/natcheztrace

**Armstrong's Bakery Bed and Breakfast.** Just seven miles from the Natchez Trace in Hohenwald, this home has been freshly restored and opened as a bed and breakfast. Once the town jail, it is now beautifully decorated with antiques and has a comfortable balcony that can be used as a sitting area for two of the guest rooms. "High Forest" in German, Hohenwald is known for its small-town charm and outdoor activities, including canoeing, cycling, and hunting. Convenient to Meriwether Lewis Park on the trace. Full breakfast. $65.

**Avaleen Springs Bed and Breakfast.** Sixteen miles west of the trace on Highway 412, this is a truly magical 30-acre retreat, a rustic cedar home nestled against a bluff, with a mile-long series of springs and streams that runs under the house. Guests can actually observe creek life through a glass coffee table in the sitting room. Canoeing and fishing in the area, and convenient to the Tennessee River, the Buffalo River, Shiloh Battlefield, and Mousetail Landing State Park. $75-105.

## JACKSON

### Highland Place Bed & Breakfast

519 North Highland Avenue, 38301
(901) 427-1472

This noted historic home of Jackson, known locally as the Hamilton-Butler Mansion, contains a treasure of unique and interesting woodwork and antiques. The architectural jewel of the house is a cherry-paneled library. The one guest room and three suites offer an unusual

Highland Place

degree of flexibility in accommodations. One suite has a custom-built walnut queen-size canopied bed with easy chairs grouped in front of an operating fireplace and is available with an adjoining bedroom, making it suitable for a family of four. The four full baths include one with a restored antique claw-foot tub and one with an oversized tub large enough for two. Dinner available by reservation.

Hosts: Glenn and Janice Wall
Rooms: 4 (PB) $75-135
Full Breakfast
Credit Cards: A, B, C
Notes: 2, 3, 4, 5, 7, 10, 11, 12, 14

## JONESBOROUGH

### Jonesborough Bed & Breakfast

100 Woodrow Avenue, P.O. Box 722, 37659
(423) 753-9223

This beautifully restored home was built in 1848 and is in Jonesborough's historic district. All restaurants and shops are within easy walking distance. To make a visit memorable, guests will find robes, high beds, antique furnishings, fireplaces, large porch with rocking chairs, secluded terrace, air conditioning, and a big breakfast. Private baths. Seasonal rates.

Host: Tobie Bledsoe
Rooms: 3 (PB) $79-99

NOTES: Credit cards accepted: A MasterCard; B Visa; C American Express; D Discover; E Diner's Club; F Other; 2 Personal checks accepted; 3 Lunch available; 4 Dinner available; 5 Open all year; 6 Pets welcome;

Jonesborough

Full Breakfast
Credit Cards: None
Notes: 2, 5, 7, 8, 9, 11, 12

## KINGSTON

## Whitestone Country Inn

1200 Paint Rock Road, 37763
(423) 376-0113; FAX (423) 376-4454

A luxurious, secluded 360-acre country estate on the shores of Watts Bar Lake provides a perfect escape for a getaway. Each of the 15 bedrooms has a fireplace, whirlpool tub, TV/VCR. Fishing and hiking are also available on the property. Surrounded by a wildlife and waterfowl refuge, Whitestone Inn brings guests close to all East Tennessee attractions, but far enough away to find sanctuary, relaxation, and the tranquility of God's creation.

Hosts: Paul and Jean Cowell
Rooms: 16 (PB) $105-200
Full Breakfast
Credit Cards: A, B, C, D
Notes: 2, 3, 4, 5, 7, 8, 10, 11, 12, 14, 15

## KNOXVILLE

## Maplehurst Inn

800 West Hill Avenue, 37920
(423) 523-7773 (phone/FAX); (800) 451-1562
www.maplehurstinn.com

Built in 1917 as a single-family home on the Tennessee River, adjacent to the University of Tennessee. In 1981, the Maplehurst Inn was converted to a European-style bed and breakfast inn. It remains an exquisite inn for special guests in Knoxville's historic and peaceful Maplehurst Park. The Penthouse Honeymoon Suite and the Anniversary Suite have Jacuzzis and king-size beds. Other rooms feature sunken or marble tubs, a fireplace, and a king-size or two double beds. A bodacious buffet breakfast is served each day.

Hosts: Sonny and Becky Harben
Rooms: 11 (PB) $85-149
Full Breakfast
Credit Cards: A, B, C, E
Notes: 2, 5, 7, 9, 10, 12, 14

## Masters Manor Inn

1909 Cedar Lane, 37918
(423) 219-9888; (877) 866-2667
FAX (423) 219-9811
e-mail: rbhallet@nxs.net

This 100-year-old Victorian Inn is in the foothills of the Smoky Mountains. Luxury accommodations, private baths, telephones, cable TV, and data ports. Convenient location to area attractions: national parks, Dollywood, 30 golf courses, Knoxville Zoo, World's Fair Park. Decorated in period antiques, 12-foot ceilings, six fireplaces, two winding staircases, wraparound porch, and a 50-foot magnolia tree. Evening desserts included.

Hosts Dana and Rhonda Hallet
Rooms: 6 (PB) $100-150
Full Breakfast
Credit Cards: A, B, C
Notes: 2, 5, 6, 8, 9, 10, 11, 12, 13, 14, 15

## Mitchell's

1031 West Park Drive, 37909
(423) 690-1488

This bed and breakfast offers a comfortable room in a private home in a pleasant tree-shaded neighborhood near fine shops and restaurants. Parking at a private entrance, double bed, TV, refrigerator, and microwave; roll-away bed and crib available. It is 45 minutes to

---

7 No smoking; 8 Children welcome; 9 Social drinking allowed; 10 Tennis nearby; 11 Swimming nearby; 12 Golf nearby; 13 Skiing nearby; 14 May be booked through a travel agent; 15 Handicapped accessible.

ky Mountains, 25 minutes to Oak
, 1.5 miles to I-75/I-40, and 8 miles to
ntown Knoxville. Ground level is handicapped accessible.

Host: Mary M. Mitchell
Room: 1 (PB) $40
Continental Breakfast
Credit Cards: None
Notes: 2, 5, 6, 8, 9, 10, 11, 12, 15

## LYNCHBURG

### Lynchburg Bed & Breakfast

Mechanic Street, P.O. Box 34, 37352
(931) 759-7158; e-mail: lynchburgbb@cafes.net
www.bbonline.com/tn/lynchburg/

Lynchburg Bed and Breakfast is within walking distance of Jack Daniel's Distillery and
shopping area. The quaint atmosphere of this
two-story, circa 1877 home provides relaxation
and enjoyment in a small town. Each room is
beautifully decorated. Big front porch for a
quiet afternoon view of the beautiful hills of
Tennessee. Continental breakfast served by
personal hostess.

Hosts: Virginia and Mike Tipps
Rooms: 2 (PB) $65-75
Continental Breakfast
Credit Cards: A, B
Notes: 2, 5, 7, 8, 10, 11, 12

"Lynchburg Bed and Breakfast," built 1877

Lynchburg

Mulberry House

### Mulberry House Bed & Breakfast

8 Old Lynchburg Highway, Mulberry, 37359
(615) 433-8461

This 110-year-old home in Mulberry, where
Davy Crockett spent a winter, is nestled in the
hills of Middle Tennessee, only seven miles
from Lynchburg, the home of Jack Daniel's
Tennessee whiskey. Only 45 minutes from
Huntsville, Alabama. There are numerous
craft and antique shops to visit. Buggy rides
available.

Host: Candy Richard
Rooms: 2 (PB) $55
Continental Breakfast
Credit Cards: A, B
Notes: 2, 5, 7, 8, 9, 14

## MCMINNVILLE

### Historic Falcon Manor

2645 Faulkner Springs Road, 37110
(931) 668-4444; FAX (931) 815-4444
e-mail: falconmanor@falconmanor.com
www.falconmanor.com

Relive the 1890s in one of the South's finest
Victorian mansions. Indulge in the luxury of
museum quality antiques. Enjoy owners' tales
of the 10,000-square-foot mansion's history
and their adventures restoring it. Rock on gin-
gerbread verandas shaded by giant trees in this
country setting just minutes from town.
Halfway between Nashville and Chattanooga
with easy access to I-24 and I-40, this is the
ideal base for a Tennessee vacation. The 1997
National Trust Restoration Award winner.

NOTES: Credit cards accepted: A MasterCard; B Visa; C American Express; D Discover; E Diner's Club;
F Other; 2 Personal checks accepted; 3 Lunch available; 4 Dinner available; 5 Open all year; 6 Pets welcome;

Historic Falcon Manor

verandas supply ample space for rock
away the day. Fine dining by candlelig
available every evening. In a 117-year-old
Chautauqua village; abundant hiking, views,
vistas, and natural activities in the area. Also
proximity to Jack Daniel's, University of the
South, Sewanee, and Arnold Engineering
Center with the largest wind tunnel in the
world. National register property. Independent innkeepers. Limited accommodations for
handicapped.

Hosts: George and Charlien McGlothin
Rooms: 7 (PB) $95-105
Full Breakfast
Credit Cards: A, B, C
Notes: 2, 4, 5, 7, 9, 10, 11, 12, 14, 15

Hosts: Wendy and Dave Adams
Rooms: 12 (PB) $95-205
Full Breakfast
Credit Cards: A, B, C
Notes: 2, 4, 5, 7, 8, 9, 10, 11, 12, 14, 15

## MEMPHIS

### Lowenstein-Long House

217 North Waldran, 38105
(901) 527-7174

This beautifully restored Victorian mansion
near downtown is listed in the National Register of Historic Places. Convenient to major
attractions, such as the Mississippi River,
Graceland, Beale Street, the Memphis Zoo,
Brooks Museum, and the Victorian Village.
Free off-street parking.

Hosts: Col. Charles and Dr. Margaret Long
Rooms: 4 (PB) $50-80
Full Breakfast
Credit Cards: None
Notes: 2, 5, 7, 9

Adams Edgeworth Inn

## MOUNTAIN CITY

### Butler House Bed & Breakfast

309 North Church Street, 37683
(423) 727-4119 (phone/FAX); (888) 219-7737
e-mail: bhbb@preferred.com

Nestled in the beautiful Blue Ridge mountains
of eastern Tennessee, this spacious circa 1870
national registry home is sure to please. Two
blocks from downtown Mountain City on 15
acres of lawns gardens, and treed hillsides, and
just minutes from tourist attractions of North
Carolina and Virginia as well as Tennessee.
The upstairs porch is made for rocking and
relaxing, and the comfortably appointed rooms
are all accessible from it.

## MONTEAGLE

### Adams Edgeworth Inn

Monteagle Assembly, 37356
(931) 924-4000; FAX (931) 924-3236

A quaint country inn filled with antiques,
original paintings, and handmade quilts; nestled in an exclusive historic village on top of
Monteagle Mountain. Two hundred feet of

7 No smoking; 8 Children welcome; 9 Social drinking allowed; 10 Tennis nearby; 11 Swimming nearby;
12 Golf nearby; 13 Skiing nearby; 14 May be booked through a travel agent; 15 Handicapped accessible.

and Joan Trathen
(PB) $60-70
akfast
Cards: A, B
otes: 2, 5, 7, 9, 10, 11, 12, 13

## Prospect Hill Bed & Breakfast

801 West Main Street, Highway 67, 37683
(423) 727-0139; e-mail: prospect@mounet.com

Unusual tranquility, superb mountain views, and proximity to nature hikes, fishing, boating, festivals, caverns, galleries, and shopping. Between the mountains where Tennessee, North Carolina, and Virginia join. Circa 1889 solid brick mansion built by a local prospector who served in the Union army. Huge rooms, modern romantic baths, comfortable beds, and fireplaces. Innkeepers have stripped and restored the oak moldings in the formal rooms and are turning two and one-half acres into a parklike setting. Decorating in the second owner's 1910 period with antique dining set and Stickley reproductions. Comfortable hospitality from experienced innkeepers who found a lovely house in the best small town in northeast Tennessee.

Hosts: Robert and Judy Hotchkiss
Rooms: 5 (PB) $89-199
Full Breakfast
Credit Cards: A, B
Notes: 2, 5, 7, 8, 9, 10, 11, 12, 13, 14, 15

## MOUNT PLEASANT

## Natchez Trace Bed & Breakfast Reservation Service

P.O. Box 193, Hampshire, 38461
(931) 285-2777; (800) 377-2770
e-mail: natcheztrace@worldnet.att.net
www.bbonline.com/natcheztrace

**Academy Place Bed and Breakfast.** The site of an 1835 "female academy" and rebuilt in 1906 by the mayor of the town of Mount Pleasant. At his death, the spacious bedrooms were used for boarders; it continues in that tradition as a newly opened bed and breakfast, 15 miles from the Natchez Trace. Each room has a

queen-size bed, comfortable seating, and a writing desk. Hot spa available, as well as basketball, horseshoes, and cable TV. Nearby are historic homes and churches and the Mount Pleasant/Maury Phosphate Museum. Full breakfast. $85-105.

## MURFREESBORO

## Clardy's Guest House

435 East Main Street, 37130
(615) 893-6030; e-mail: rdeaton@bellsouth.net
www.bbonline.com/tn/clardys/

In the historic district, this 20-room Victorian Romanesque home is filled with antiques and features ornate woodwork and fireplaces. An 8-x-8-foot stained-glass window overlooks the magnificent staircase. The area has much to offer history buffs and antique shoppers. Thirty miles from Nashville, just two miles off I-24. Continental plus breakfast served.

Hosts: Robert and Barbara Deaton
Rooms: 3 (2 PB; 1 SB) $45-58
Continental Breakfast
Credit Cards: None
Notes: 2, 5, 7, 8, 9, 10, 11, 12, 14

Clardy's Guest House

## Simply Southern Bed & Breakfast

211 North Tennessee Boulevard, 37130
(888) 723-1199; (615) 896-4988
FAX (615) 867-2899; e-mail: InnSouth@aol.com
www.bbonline.com/tn/simplysouthern
www.citysearch.com/nas/simplysouthern

---

NOTES: Credit cards accepted: A MasterCard; B Visa; C American Express; D Discover; E Diner's Club; F Other; 2 Personal checks accepted; 3 Lunch available; 4 Dinner available; 5 Open all year; 6 Pets welcome;

Simply Southern

In the heart of Tennessee. Four-story home, built 1907. Four spacious rooms plus a suite. Professionally decorated, casual elegance, private baths, and sitting areas. Large Rec Room with pool table, player piano, and karaoke, decorated with old advertising and Coke memorabilia. Amenities reflect innkeepers' desire to provide an experience, not just a place to stay. Across street from Middle Tennessee State University's beautiful campus. Horse farms, quaint villages, Civil War sites nearby. Near Nashville.

Hosts: Carl and Georgia Buckner
Rooms: 5 (PB) $85-99
Suite: 1 $125-145
Full Breakfast
Credit Cards: A, B, C, D
Notes: 2, 5, 7, 9, 10, 11, 12, 14

## NASHVILLE

### Birdsong Lodge

1306 Highway 49 East, 37015
(615) 792-1767

Listed in the National Register of Historic Places, this circa 1912 home sits on a bluff overlooking Sycamore Creek. A short drive from The Narrows of the Harpeth, many Civil War battle sites and monuments, and one of the largest prehistoric Native American communities in North America. Guests also enjoy

antique hunting, birdwatching, fishing, canoeing, golf, horseback riding, biking, and hiking. Front screened porch with swings. Living room with massive fireplace. All three suites have private baths, four-poster beds, chandeliers, telephones, and cable TV. Antiques, artwork, and music create a romantic ambiance. Gourmet candlelight dinners and breakfasts. Pets welcome within limits. Rustic elegance.

Hosts: Bob and Bett Pilling
Suites: 3 (PB) $125-175
Full Breakfast
Credit Cards: A, B, C
Notes: 3, 4, 6, 9, 10, 12, 13,

### Crocker Springs Bed & Breakfast

2382 Crocker Springs Road, Goodlettsville, 37072
(615) 876-8502

Come, relax, and enjoy this country haven just 14 miles from downtown Nashville. Crocker Springs is a restored Tennessee farmhouse built circa 1880, furnished with many antiques. Listen to the rippling sounds of the creek from the porch or sunroom. Hike the wooded ridge and partake of God's beautiful nature. Escape from the busy world. Full breakfast along with sweet rolls or breads. Jack and Bev extend a warm welcome of southern hospitality to each of their guests. Pets and children welcome with prior arrangements.

Hosts: Jack and Bev Spangler
Rooms: 3 (PB) $85-100
Full Breakfast
Credit Cards: A, B, C, D
Notes: 2, 5, 6, 7, 8, 10, 11, 12, 14, 15

### Natchez Trace Bed & Breakfast Reservation Service

P.O. Box 193, Hampshire, 38461
(931) 285-2777; (800) 377-2770
e-mail: natcheztrace@worldnet.att.net
www.bbonline.com/natcheztrace

**Applebrook Bed and Breakfast.** Almost three miles from the terminus of the Natchez Trace

7 No smoking; 8 Children welcome; 9 Social drinking allowed; 10 Tennis nearby; 11 Swimming nearby; 12 Golf nearby; 13 Skiing nearby; 14 May be booked through a travel agent; 15 Handicapped accessible.

and 14 miles from downtown Nashville, this turn-of-the-century farmhouse is nestled on five panoramic acres. There are a swimming pool, five-stall horse barn, and a brook and natural spring. Savor their specialty—apple pancakes with real maple syrup. Convenient to Nashville attractions, as well as Franklin's Civil War sites and antique shops. Large guest rooms with queen-size beds. $95.

**Chigger Ridge.** Less than 10 miles from the trace, near Pegram, this home is perched on a ridgetop with 67 acres of trails and vistas in all directions. The main house, with two guest bedrooms, is a western cedar log home, with vaulted ceilings, skylights, ceiling fans, and porches everywhere. A separate guest house has three more guest rooms, two baths, a complete kitchen, and wraparound deck. Convenient to I-40 and only 30 minutes from Nashville. Guest house available at $279. Bed and breakfast rooms available at $89-99.

**Sweet Annie's Bed and Breakfast.** Milepost 438 at Fairview. Ten miles from the trace, this contemporary country home features a swimming pool and a hot tub. Guests can rent horses and bicycles from hosts, and they are convenient to both the bridle trail along the trace and to Fairview Nature Park's riding trails. Guests can even get a personal fitness workout for an extra charge. $65-80.

# NEWPORT

## Christopher Place, An Intimate Resort

1500 Pinnacles Way, 37821
(423) 623-6555; (800) 595-9441
e-mail: thebestinn@aol.com
www.christopherplace.com

Surrounded by expansive mountain views, this premier southern estate includes over 200 acres to explore, a pool, tennis court, and sauna. Relax by the marble fireplace in the library,

Christopher Place

retreat to the game room, or enjoy a hearty mountain meal in the dining room. Romantic rooms are available with a hot tub or fireplace. Off I-40 at exit 435, just 32 scenic miles from Gatlinburg and Pigeon Forge. Handicapped accessible. AAA-rated four diamonds.

Host: Tim Hall
Rooms: 8 (PB) $150-300
Full Breakfast
Credit Cards: A, B, C, D
Notes: 2, 3, 4, 5, 7, 9, 10, 11, 12, 13, 14, 15

# NORRIS

## Skunk Ridge Christmas Tree Farm

1203 Mountain Road, Clinton, 37716
(423) 494-0214
e-mail:laryhamner@aol.com

Horses, pastures, and woods surround this secluded yet convenient location. I-75, Museum of Appalachia, Lenoir Museum, historic Norris all within three miles. Twenty minutes to Knoxville and Oak Ridge. The Smoky Mountains, Big South Fork, Dollywood, and six TVA lakes within 50 miles. Rustic, two-story country home. Large bedrooms furnished with Appalachian antiques. Swimming in season. Nature trails and a Christmas tree plantation. Children over 12 welcome.

Hosts: Larry and Martha Hammer
Rooms: 2 (1 PB; 2 SB) $65
Full Breakfast
Credit Cards: None
Notes: 2, 5, 7, 9, 10, 11, 12, 13

---

NOTES: Credit cards accepted: A MasterCard; B Visa; C American Express; D Discover; E Diner's Club; F Other; 2 Personal checks accepted; 3 Lunch available; 4 Dinner available; 5 Open all year; 6 Pets welcome;

## RUGBY

### Grey Gables
### Bed 'n' Breakfast Inn

Highway 52, P.O. Box 52, 37733
(423) 628-5252

Nestled on the outskirts of the 1880s English village of Rugby, Grey Gables offers the best of the Victorian English and Tennessee country heritage, creatively blending Victorian and country antiques. Fare includes lodging, evening meal, and country breakfast. Visit the beautiful Cumberland Plateau, historic Rugby, and Grey Gables. In the tradition of the forebears, guests will receive a hearty welcome, a restful bed, and a full table. Reservations required. Lunch available by reservation. Smoking permitted in designated areas only. Limited handicapped accessibility. Limited smoking.

Hosts: Bill and Linda Brooks Jones
Rooms: 8 (4 PB; 4 SB) $115
Full Breakfast
Credit Cards: A, B, C
Notes: 2, 3, 4, 5, 7, 8, 9, 11, 12, 14, 15

### Newbury House at
### Historic Rugby

P.O. Box 8, Highway 52, 37733
(423) 628-2441; (423) 628-2430

Newbury House was Rugby's first boarding house, established in 1880. Victorian era. Beautifully restored features include board-and-batten siding, mansard roof, dormer windows, a lovely front porch, and shared parlor and sunroom. Newbury House lodged both visitors and settlers to British author Thomas Hughes's utopian colony. The national register village offers historic building tours, museum stores, specialty restaurant, and hiking trails. Victorian cottages are available for families with children.

Host: Historic Rugby
Rooms: 5 (3 PB; 2 SB) $68-82
Suite: 1
Full Breakfast
Credit Cards: A, B
Notes: 2, 3, 4, 5, 7, 9, 11

## SAVANNAH

### Natchez Trace Bed & Breakfast
### Reservation Service

P.O. Box 193, Hampshire, 38461
(931) 285-2777; (800) 377-2770
e-mail: natcheztrace@worldnet.att.net
www.bbonline.com/natcheztrace

**White Elephant Bed and Breakfast.** In Savannah, 30 miles from the trace, and only 10 miles from Shiloh National Military Park, this turreted Victorian home has wraparound porches and one and one-half acres of grounds. There are period antique furnishings—even claw-foot tubs—and Civil War memorabilia. The host's passion is Civil War history, and guests can sign up for a personalized tour of Shiloh Battlefield. There is an "overflow room" available for additional guests in a party for $25. $75-105.

### White Elephant
### Bed & Breakfast Inn

304 Church Street, 38372
(901) 925-6410; www.bbonline.com/tn/elephant

Stately 1901 Queen Anne-style Victorian home on one and one-half shady acres in the Savannah historic district. Within walking distance of Tennessee River, downtown shopping, restaurants, and churches. Nearby golf courses and Civil War attractions; 10 miles to Shiloh National Military Park; innkeeper offers

White Elephant

---

7 No smoking; 8 Children welcome; 9 Social drinking allowed; 10 Tennis nearby; 11 Swimming nearby; 12 Golf nearby; 13 Skiing nearby; 14 May be booked through a travel agent; 15 Handicapped accessible.

guided battlefield tours; 12 miles to Pickwick Dam and Lake. Three individually decorated rooms feature antique furnishings, queen-size beds, private baths. Full breakfast. Two parlors, antiques, central heat and air, wraparound porches, croquet, and horseshoes.

Hosts: Sharon and Ken Hansgen
Rooms: 3 (PB) $75-105
Full Breakfast
Credit Cards: None
Rooms: 2, 5, 7, 9, 10, 11, 12, 14

## SEVIERVILLE

### Calico Inn

757 Ranch Way, 37862
(423) 428-3833; (800) 235-1054
www.bbonline.com/tn/calico/

Voted 1998 Inn of the Year, the Calico Inn is an authentic log inn with touches of elegance. It is decorated with antiques, collectibles, and country charm. It has a spectacular mountain view and is on a hilltop with 25 acres surrounding it. Each guest room has its own private bath. Guests will be served a full delicious breakfast daily. Only minutes away from the Great Smoky Mountains National Park, Dollywood, Gatlinburg, hiking, fishing, golfing, and all the attractions, yet completely secluded. Children six and older welcome.

Hosts: Lill and Jim Katzbeck
Rooms: 3 (PB) $89-99
Full Breakfast
Credit Cards: A, B
Notes: 2, 5, 7, 8, 10, 11, 12, 13, 14

Calico Inn

Little Greenbrier Lodge

### Little Greenbrier Lodge

3685 Lyon Springs Road, 37862
(423) 429-2500; (800) 277-8100
e-mail: litlegreenbrier@worldnet.att.net
www.bbonline.com/tn/lgl

Little Greenbrier Lodge is at the entrance to the Great Smoky Mountains National Park. One of the oldest rustic lodges, circa 1939, nestled in the trees overlooking Wears Valley. The inn offers guests today's modern comforts, yet recaptures yesterday's charm with antique Victorian decor. The view of the valley provides a perfect backdrop for the country breakfast, and the lodge provides peace, quiet, and privacy.

Host: Charles and Susan Lebon
Rooms: 10 (8 PB; 2 SB) $65-110
Full Breakfast
Credit Cards: A, B, D
Notes: 2, 3, 4, 5, 7, 9, 11, 12, 13, 14

### Persephone's Farm Retreat

2279 Hodges Ferry Road, 37876
(423) 428-3904; FAX (423) 453-7089
e-mail: unicholson@smokymtnmall.com

A peaceful rural estate nestled by the beautiful French Broad River within a close distance to the Great Smoky Mountains, Dollywood, Factory Outlet Malls, Golf Courses, Music Theatres and other Sevier and Knox County attractions. Elegant rooms with private baths, large porches, spacious grounds, picturesque barn, miniature horses, farm animals, shiitake mushrooms, fruit trees, country road for walks, bonfire area and yard games.

NOTES: Credit cards accepted: A MasterCard; B Visa; C American Express; D Discover; E Diner's Club; F Other; 2 Personal checks accepted; 3 Lunch available; 4 Dinner available; 5 Open all year; 6 Pets welcome;

Hosts: Bob Gonia and Victoria Nicholson
Rooms: 2 (PB) $95
Full Breakfast
Credit Cards: A, B, C
Notes: 2, 7, 8, 9, 10, 11, 12, 13

## Von-Bryan Mountaintop Inn

2402 Hatcher Mountain Road, 37862
(865) 453-9832; (800) 633-1459
FAX (865) 428-8634
e-mail: von-bryan-inn@juno.com
www.vonbryan.com

A magnificent log inn with beautiful Smoky Mountain views from every window, porch, and deck. A climbing, curving road leads to the inn at the top of a 2100-foot mountain and the views are breathtaking. The guest will find it hard to break away long enough to visit Pigeon Forge, Gatlinburg, Dollywood, and Townsend. Amenities include swimming pool, hot tub, whirlpool tubs, steam shower, pool and game tables, exercise room, and library. Seven guest rooms and a three-bedroom cabin all have private baths. A full Smoky Mountains breakfast is served and dessert and beverages for evening enjoyment.

Hosts: The Vaughn Family: D. J., JoAnn, David,
    Patrick, Anna
Rooms: 7 (PB) $100-145
Cabin: $220
Full Breakfast
Credit Cards: A, B, C, D
Notes: 2, 5, 7, 8, 9, 11, 12, 13, 14

## WARTRACE

## Ledford Mill Bed & Breakfast

Route 2, Box 152 B, 37183
(931) 455-2546
www.bbonline.com/tn/ledfordmill/

A welcome change from the daily grind! Enjoy a peaceful night's rest in a historic 1884 gristmill by a waterfall. Turn-of-the-century charm with antique mill workings. Three unique accommodations, all with views of falls, creek, and gardens. Claw-foot tubs, comfy queen-size beds. A beautiful rural setting in southern Middle Tennessee. Near many historic and natural areas. Three miles from Tullahoma. Continental plus breakfast served.

Hosts: Dennis and Kathleen Depert
Rooms: 3 (PB) $85-110
Continental Breakfast
Credit Cards: A, B
Notes: 2, 5, 7, 9, 10, 11, 12, 14

Texas

# Texas

## BJ's Prairie House Bed & Breakfast

508 Mulberry Street, 79601
(915) 675-5855; (800) 673-5855

Nestled in the heart of Abilene is a 1902 home furnished with antiques and modern luxuries combined to create a warm, homelike atmosphere. Downstairs, there are high ceilings and hardwood floors. The living room invites cozy conversation or curling up with a book in comfortable recliners or watching TV or movies. Upstairs are four unique bedrooms (Love, Joy, Peace, and Patience), each beautifully decorated. Breakfast includes homemade breads, fresh fruits, and other scrumptious delights and is served in the dining room that is decorated with a collection of blue-and-white china collected from around the world.

Hosts: BJ and Bob Fender
Rooms: 4 (2 PB; 2 SB) $65-75
Continental Breakfast
Credit Cards: A, B, C, D
Notes: 2, 5, 7, 9, 12

## AMARILLO

## Parkview House Bed & Breakfast

1311 South Jefferson, 79101
(806) 373-9464; FAX (806) 373-3166
e-mail: parkviewbb@aol.com
www.members.aol.com/parkviewbb

This 1908 Prairie Victorian in the heart of the Texas panhandle has been lovingly restored

Parkview House

by the present owners to capture its original charm. It is furnished with antiques and comfortably updated. Guests may relax, read, or engage in friendly conversation on the wicker-filled front porch; browse through the garden; or soak leisurely in the romantic hot tub under stars. Convenient to biking, jogging, tennis, hiking, and the award-winning musical drama *Texas* in Palo Duro State Park. Old Route 66, antique shops, restaurants, various museums, and West Texas A&M University are nearby. Continental plus breakfast. Smoking outside only. Inquire about accommodations for children.

Hosts: Nabil and Carol Dia
Rooms: 5 (3 PB; 2 SB) $65-85
Cottage: $135
Continental Breakfast
Credit Cards: A, B, C
Notes: 2, 5, 7, 9, 10, 12, 14

NOTES: Credit cards accepted: A MasterCard; B Visa; C American Express; D Discover; E Diner's Club; F Other; 2 Personal checks accepted; 3 Lunch available; 4 Dinner available; 5 Open all year; 6 Pets welcome; 7 No smoking; 8 Children welcome; 9 Social drinking allowed; 10 Tennis nearby; 11 Swimming nearby; 12 Golf nearby; 13 Skiing nearby; 14 May be booked through a travel agent; 15 Handicapped accessible.

## AUSTIN

### Austin-Lake Travis Bed & Breakfast

4446 Eck Lane, 78734
(512) 266-3386; (888) 764-LTBB (5822)
(reservations only)
e-mail: LTBINNB@aol.com
www.laketravisbb.com

This unique waterfront retreat is a 20-minute drive from downtown Austin. Cliffside location, crystal water, hills, and expansive view provide the setting for a luxurious getaway. The natural beauty of the surroundings is reflected in the hill country home with each of the four guest suites having a deck with view of the lake. "Intimate resort" describes the amenities available: private boat dock, pool, hot tub, fitness center, massage and spa services, and sailing/boat charters. Inside is a stone fireplace, game room, pool table, and library/theater. Nearby are a boat and Jet Ski rentals, horseback riding, bicycling, hiking, steam train, and wineries to tour. Breakfast is served in bed.

Hosts: Judy and Vic Dwyer
Rooms: 4 (PB) $145-195
Full Breakfast
Credit Cards: A, B, C
Notes: 5, 7, 9, 10, 11, 12, 14

### Austin's Wildflower Inn

1200 West 22 1/2 Street, 78705
(512) 477-9639; FAX (512) 474-4188
e-mail: kjackson@io.com

Austin's Wildflower Inn, built in the early 1930s, is a lovely Colonial-style two-story home tucked away in a very quiet neighborhood of tree-lined streets in the center of Austin. Convenient to the University of Texas, the state capitol, and the downtown shopping and entertainment district. Every room has been carefully restored to create an atmos-

Austin's Wildflower Inn

phere of warmth and comfort. "I invite you to come and relax here and enjoy our beautiful grounds and have one of our special breakfasts in our lovely back garden. I wish you happiness and prosperity, and may your road lead to mine."

Host: Kay Jackson
Rooms: 4 (2 PB; 2 SB) $79-94
Full Breakfast
Credit Cards: A, B, C
Notes: 2, 5, 7, 9, 10, 11, 12

### Bed & Breakfast Texas Style

4224 West Red Bird Lane, Dallas, 75237
(972) 298-8586; (800) 899-4538
FAX (972) 298-7118; e-mail: bdtxstyle1@aol.com
www.bnbtexasstyle.com

**Bed and Breakfast on Castle Hill.** This very private, one-bedroom efficiency is tucked between the trees and gardens behind the large residence and is very centrally located. There is a king-size bed, nice sitting area, and beautiful built-in kitchen. Perfect setting for business travelers or visitors to Austin who want peace and solitude, as well as convenience. Breakfast goodies are provided. $95.

**Carter Lane Bed and Breakfast.** This large sprawling residence in a quiet area of bustling Austin has two guest areas, a well-stocked fish pond, pool, picnic area, and a weight and exercise room. The home is newly decorated with upscale furnishings; each guest room has a pri-

---

NOTES: Credit cards accepted: A MasterCard; B Visa; C American Express; D Discover; E Diner's Club; F Other; 2 Personal checks accepted; 3 Lunch available; 4 Dinner available; 5 Open all year; 6 Pets welcome;

vate bath. Guests are encouraged to relax in the hammock by the lake, or work out while watching a video in the exercise room. Weekday breakfasts are Continental. On weekends guests will be served a full breakfast with all the trimmings. The lucky guest who lands a bass from the lake may enjoy having it for breakfast. The host will also prepare vegetarian and healthy recipes. $75-85.

The Brook House

## The Brook House Bed & Breakfast

609 West 33rd Street, 78705
(512) 459-0534

The Brook House was built in 1922 and restored to its present country charm. It is seven blocks from the University of Texas with easy access to local restaurants and live music. Enjoy one of six guest rooms, each of which has a private bath, TV, and telephone. A full breakfast is served daily in the dining room which has a fireplace or, weather permitting, outside on the veranda. No smoking in rooms. Partial handicapped accessibility.

Host: Barbara Love
Rooms: 6 (PB) $72-99
Full Breakfast
Credit Cards: A, B, C, D, E, F
Notes: 2, 5, 6, 8, 9, 10, 11, 12

## Carrington's Bluff

1900 David Street, 78705
(800) 871-8908; e-mail: governorstan@earthlink

Carrington's Bluff is Austin's "Country Inn in the City." Inside this 1877 English country house, guests will find rooms filled with English and American antiques, accented with English country fabrics and decor. The smell of fresh-brewed gourmet coffee beckons from the kitchen. Full breakfast of fresh fruit, homemade granola, choice of yogurts, bakery items, and the hot house specialty entrée, all served on fine china. A 500-year-old native oak is visible from spacious porch. A few minutes away is the University of Texas, the state capitol, parks, museums, fine shopping, excellent restaurants, and Austin's famous Sixth Street. Featured in *Innstyle* magazine, March 1998.

Host: Lisa Kloss
Rooms: 8 (PB) $59-119
Full Breakfast
Credit Cards: A, B, C, D, E, F
Notes: 2, 5, 6, 7, 8, 9, 10, 11, 12, 14

Carrington's Bluff

## Gregg House & Gardens

4201 Gregg Lane, 78744
(512) 448-0402; FAX (512) 462-0512
e-mail: jhayes@qsigroup.com

Two in-town country retreats on three acres of wood property await guests 10 minutes from downtown Austin. Two fish ponds, a beautiful waterfall, decks, a huge patio, hardwood floors, stone fireplace, swimming pool, and hot tub. LBJ presidential library and shopping 15 minutes away. Full kitchen, TV rooms, living/dining, and laundry available for guests' use. Bus stop at corner of property; airport 10 minutes. Hosts will help guests with their special interests and provide directions and maps. Large organic gardens.

Hosts: Nelda and Jim Haynes
Rooms: 4 (PB) $50-60; 2 (SB) $40-45
Credit Cards: None
Notes: 2, 4, 5, 7, 9, 10, 11, 12

The McCallum House

## The McCallum House

613 West 32nd Street, 78705
(512) 451-6744; FAX (512) 451-4752
e-mail: McCallum@austinTx.net

Six blocks from UT, two miles from the capitol and downtown, and located in a historic residential area. There are three guest rooms and a suite in the main house, and a large suite in an adjoining building on the grounds. All accommodations have private baths, kitchen facilities, color TVs, private telephones with answering machines, private verandas, hair dryers, irons and ironing boards, sitting and working areas. Suites have VCRs and one has a whirlpool tub.

Hosts: Roger and Nancy Danley
Rooms: 5 (PB) $94-149
Full Breakfast
Credit Cards A, B, D
Notes: 2, 5, 7, 9, 10, 11, 12, 13

## BEN WHEELER

## Bed & Breakfast Texas Style

4224 West Red Bird Lane, Dallas, 75237
(972) 298-8586; (800) 899-4538
FAX (972) 298-7118; e-mail: bdtxstyle1@aol.com
www.bnbtexasstyle.com

**The Arc Ridge Guest Ranch.** This 600- acre ranch in East Texas near Canton and Tyler has its own lake. Three guest houses have two bedrooms, living room, complete kitchen, and shower. Fishing and paddleboats are available. No hunters allowed in this environmentally protected area. Breakfast will be left in the refrigerator for guests to prepare themselves. Family rates will be considered. Two-night minimum stay. $95.

## BOERNE

## Guadalupe River Ranch

605 F.M. 474, 78006
(830) 537-4837; (800) 460-2005
FAX (830) 537-5249; e-mail: grranch@gvtc.com
www.guadaluperiverranch.com

The main lodge was built in 1929 (formerly owned by actress Olivia de Havilland) and restored to its original elegance. With 360 acres, the ranch provides one of the most spectacular views in the Texas Hill Country. The Guadalupe River Ranch is known for its memorable cuisine, fine wines, Vintner Events, and it also offers a variety of activities: river tubing, canoeing, horseback riding, body treatments and pampering spa services, and hiking trails. If one is seeking rest and relaxation, find a hammock, or the overlook swing. Enjoy the peace and serenity.

Host: Elisa McClure
Rooms: 43 (PB) $219-309
Full Breakfast
Credit Cards: A, B, C, D
Notes: 2, 3, 4, 7, 8, 9, 12, 14, 15

NOTES: Credit cards accepted: A MasterCard; B Visa; C American Express; D Discover; E Diner's Club; F Other; 2 Personal checks accepted; 3 Lunch available; 4 Dinner available; 5 Open all year; 6 Pets welcome;

## BRADY

Brady House

## *Brady House*

704 South Bridge, 76825
(915) 597-5265; (888) 272-3901
e-mail: bradyhs@centex.net

Brady is at the geographic center of Texas: the northern gateway to the Hill Country, the southern door to the Texas plains, and the portal to West Texas. Six blocks south of the square, Brady House, amid its acre of landscaped grounds has three spacious guest rooms, each with private bath. The Craftsman-style home built in 1908 is furnished to reflect not only the period but also family collections.

Hosts: Bobbie and Kelly Hancock
Rooms: 3 (PB) $85-95
Full Breakfast
Credit Cards: A, B, C, D
Notes: 3, 4, 5, 7, 10, 11, 12

## BRECKENRIDGE

## *Bed & Breakfast Texas Style*

4224 West Red Bird Lane, Dallas, 75237
(972) 298-8586; (800) 899-4538
FAX (972) 298-7118; e-mail: bdtxstyle1@aol.com
www.bnbtexasstyle.com

**The Keeping Room Bed and Breakfast.** This large two-story brick inn is a place for comfort and refuge from the busy world. It was built in 1929 and has been faithfully restored to "better than original" condition. There are two large suites, Bluebonnet and Walker, that each have a sitting room, a bedroom with queen-size beds and matching day bed, and a private bath. The other two rooms, Goodwin and Rustic, also have queen-size beds and share a hall bath. All rooms have TVs. Guests will be pampered with a hearty breakfast of biscuits, sausage, eggs, muffins, juice, and coffee. $65-75.

## BROADDUS

## *Sam Rayburn Lake Bed & Breakfast "The Cole House"*

Route 1 Box 258, 75929
(409) 872-3666

Within the piney woods of deep East Texas is this cozy guest house, bed and breakfast, that has been in operation since 1984. All electric home, with full kitchen, including microwave, everything furnished, central heating and cooling, and carpeted throughout. Five-room cottage with a great view of Sam Rayburn Lake. Charcoal grill and other facilities available. Rental boats available at near-by marina, also launching for private boats.

Hosts: Gene and Jean Cole
Rate for House: $55
Continental Breakfast
Notes: 2, 5, 7, 8, 9, 11, 13, 14, 15

Sam Rayburn Lake

## BRYAN

### Bed & Breakfast Texas Style

4224 West Red Bird Lane, Dallas, 75237
(972) 298-8586; (800) 899-4538
FAX (972) 298-7118; e-mail: bdtxstyle1@aol.com
www.bnbtexasstyle.com

**Wilderness Bed and Breakfast.** This charming home is at the end of a cul-de-sac just three miles from Texas A&M University. There are three bedrooms, two with queen-size beds, one with twin beds, and a private sitting room with a sleeper-sofa. The master suite downstairs has a private bath; the two rooms upstairs share a hall bath. Breakfast may be Continental with homemade breads or muffins, lots of fruit and cereals, or it may be a traditional Canadian/Texan-style breakfast. This is a nonsmoking facility. Children over 15 years welcome. $75-85.

**Cardinal's Retreat.** This lovely home is on acreage that attracts birds and critters for fun viewing out the back patio. A visit with Reba and Bob will be the highlight of your trip, as they share one hall bath. Many antiques are found throughout the home, also a lovely angel collection that fills a large glass cabinet in the cozy den. breakfast will be homemade bread or muffins, fruit, cereal, and beverages, coffee, tea, and juice. There is a siamese cat in the residence. The George Bush Library is very near this Bed and Breakfast. $75.

## CANTON

### Heavenly Acres Guest Ranch

660 Van Zandt Circle, Box 2816, 75147
(800) 283-0341; (903) 887-3016

Heavenly Acres fits many guests' personal visions of what Heaven must be like. An 83-acre East Texas ranch between Dallas and Tyler. Just 12 miles southwest of Canton, known for its First Monday Trade Days. There are five cabins which are designed to be guests'

very own "home-away-from-home" and have the capacity of 41 beds. All kitchens are fully equipped and stocked with breakfast items for guests to prepare at their own convenience.

Hosts: Diana and Bruce Avellanet
Rates: $35-95
Full or Continental Breakfast
Credit Cards: A, B, C, D
Notes: 2, 3, 4, 5, 7, 8, 9, 11, 12, 15

### Bed & Breakfast Texas Style

4224 West Red Bird Lane, Dallas, 75237
(972) 298-8586; (800) 899-4538
FAX (972) 298-7118; e-mail: bdtxstyle1@aol.com
www.bnbtexasstyle.com

**Lacy Creek Bed and Breakfast.** This large style home sits on a farm just outside Canton and has four bedrooms available for guests that wish a quiet retreat in the country. There is a pool for relaxing in the summer, and a large game room with a wood-burning stove for fall and winter evenings. The bedroom upstairs has its own private entrance and sitting area. The other rooms are great for families or groups of ladies. Children are welcome here. Hearty breakfast of sausage and egg casserole, hash browns, homemade muffins, and fruit, or stuffed French toast with strawberry syrup. Smoking only on deck or porches. $75-95.

### Texas Star Bed & Breakfast

Route 1, Box 187, Edgewood, 75117
(903) 896-4277; FAX (903) 896-7061
e-mail: ohohm@aol.com

Enjoy a peaceful day in the country nestled among large oaks, cedar trees, and green pasturelands in the gently rolling hills of East Texas. Each of the six rooms reflects a different theme of Texas history—Spanish, Native American, Old West, German, Texas country. Private baths, private entrances, and private patios are available. Full course country breakfasts. Five minutes from the world-famous First Monday Trade Days in Canton. Dinner

---

NOTES: Credit cards accepted: A MasterCard; B Visa; C American Express; D Discover; E Diner's Club; F Other; 2 Personal checks accepted; 3 Lunch available; 4 Dinner available; 5 Open all year; 6 Pets welcome;

for groups is available by advance request. Capacity up to 20. Private cabin now available.

Hosts: David and Marie Stoltzfus
Rooms: 6 (4 PB; 2 SB) $65-85
Full Breakfast
Credit Cards: A, B, C, D
Notes: 2, 4, 5, 7, 12

## CASTROVILLE

### Bed & Breakfast Texas Style

4224 West Red Bird Lane, Dallas, 75237
(972) 298-8586; (800) 899-4538
FAX (972) 298-7118; e-mail: bdtxstyle1@aol.com
www.bnbtexasstyle.com

**Le Parc Bed and Breakfast.** This wonderful historic town with the Medina River running through it can now boast of a recently opened bed and breakfast cottage and a Tea Room next door. The cottage has three bedrooms with private baths, a lovely sitting room, and front porch with a swing and patio. Two have private entrances. Each room has a TV with VCR. Full breakfast served in Tea Room. A fourth bedroom upstairs in the Tea Room has a private bath. Enjoy the park, town square across the street, and the French restaurant just two blocks away. Jaye and Gene are veterans of the bed and breakfast industry and are eager for guests to enjoy their special hospitality. Castroville is just 22 miles from the Riverwalk in downtown San Antonio and convenient to Sea World and Fiesta Texas. No children. No pets. Smoking on the porch. $80-95.

## CLEBURNE

### Bed & Breakfast Texas Style

4224 West Red Bird Lane, Dallas, 75237
(972) 298-8586; (800) 899-4538
FAX (972) 298-7118; e-mail: bdtxstyle1@aol.com
www.bnbtexasstyle.com

**Cleburne Guest House.** This lovely historical Queen Anne Victorian house was built near the turn of the century and is near downtown Cle-

burne. There are four guest rooms, two with private baths and two sharing a hall bath. All rooms have color TVs and fresh flowers. Coffee bar and refrigerator upstairs for guests' needs. A Continental breakfast will be served in the main dining room or out on the New Orleans-style patio. Area attractions include antiquing, candlewalk, Springfest, and Hot Air Balloon Festival. Walk to antique malls, tearoom, and shopping. $95-115.

## CLIFTON

### Bed & Breakfast Texas Style

4224 West Red Bird Lane, Dallas, 75237
(972) 298-8586; (800) 899-4538
FAX (972) 298-7118; e-mail: bdtxstyle1@aol.com
www.bnbtexasstyle.com

**The Sweetheart Cottage.** A historic home, once damaged in a tornado, now restored for a perfect weekend getaway. A loft room has a queen-size bed, and a pull-out sofa is available downstairs. Country breakfast fare is left in the complete kitchen for the guests to prepare. No smoking. Two-night minimum stay required. $85-125.

## COLLEGE STATION

### Bed & Breakfast Texas Style

4224 West Red Bird Lane, Dallas, 75237
(972) 298-8586; (800) 899-4538
FAX (972) 298-7118; e-mail: bdtxstyle1@aol.com
www.bnbtexasstyle.com

**Country Gardens.** A sense of peace and tranquility will descend on guests as they enter this little country hideaway on four acres. Stroll through the wooded glen, fruit orchard, grapevines, and berry patches and enjoy the birds and wildflowers. The hosts will prepare a delicious breakfast of wheat pancakes or homemade bread; coffee, tea, or milk; and fruit in season. $65-75.

7 No smoking; 8 Children welcome; 9 Social drinking allowed; 10 Tennis nearby; 11 Swimming nearby; 12 Golf nearby; 13 Skiing nearby; 14 May be booked through a travel agent; 15 Handicapped accessible.

**Crystal Lake Cottage.** Nestled in the woods on a large private lake is this two-bedroom guesthouse just behind the owner's home. It has a private entrance, off-street parking, walking trails around the lake, and lovely gardens. There is a nice sitting room, small kitchen, and a full bath in the cottage. Patty and Byron want to interact with their guests and will invite them into the main residence for a full breakfast of homemade rolls, omelets, and sausage. Fruit and coffee, tea or milk will also be served. She is a teacher, and Byron is with TAMU. About one-half mile to the University. No smoking. Double $125.

## COMFORT

### *The Comfort Common*

717 High Street, P.O. Box 539, 78013
(830) 995-3030
e-mail: comfortcommon@hctc.net
www.bbhost.com/comfortcommon

Historic limestone hotel, circa 1880, listed in the National Register of Historic Places. Rooms and suites are furnished with antiques. The downstairs of the hotel features numerous shops filled with American antiques. A stay at the Comfort Common will put guests in the heart of the Texas Hill Country with Fredericksburg, Kerrville, Boerne, Bandera, and San Antonio all a brief 15-30 minutes away. Fiesta Texas theme park is only 20 minutes away. Featured in *Southern Living* and *Travel &*

The Comfort Common

*Leisure* magazines. Also selected by *Fodor's Travel Publications* as one of the Best Bed and Breakfasts.

Hosts: Jim Lord and Bobby Dent
Rooms: 9 (PB) $65-110
Full Breakfast
Credit Cards: A, B, C, D
Notes: 2, 5, 7, 9, 12

## CORPUS CHRISTI

Bay Breeze

### *Bay Breeze Bed & Breakfast*

201 Louisiana Parkway, 78404
(361) 882-4123; (887) 882-4123
e-mail: baybreeze@baybreezebb.com
www.baybreezebb.com

Within view of the sparkling bay waters, this fine older home features bedroom suites with private baths that radiate the charm and ambiance of days gone by. Less than a five-minute drive from the business district and city marinas, where sea vessels of every description are berthed. One can enjoy fine dining, recreation, or purchase shrimp direct from the net. Travel only a short distance to the Bayfront Convention Center, art and science museums, the Columbus ships, the preservation homes of Heritage Park, and the Harbor Playhouse Community Theater. Beach nearby.

Hosts: Frank and Perry Tompkins
Rooms: 4 (PB)
Full Breakfast
Credit Cards: A, B
Notes: 2, 5, 7, 9, 10, 11, 12

NOTES: Credit cards accepted: A MasterCard; B Visa; C American Express; D Discover; E Diner's Club; F Other; 2 Personal checks accepted; 3 Lunch available; 4 Dinner available; 5 Open all year; 6 Pets welcome;

## The Ginger Rose Bed & Breakfast

7030 Dunsford Drive, 78413
(361) 992-0115; (877) 894-8109
e-mail: ginrose@ flash.net
www.GingerRose.com

The Ginger Rose is easily accessible to all bayfront activities and the beach, but allows the guest to escape the tourist traffic for a quiet night's sleep. There is a private pool and a tennis court. Rooms have private baths, cable TV, stained glass, and antiques. A typical breakfast might be blackberry pancakes with Grand Marnier syrup. Arrangements with several of the best restaurants, tourist attractions, and merchants in town allow special discounts for guests.

Hosts: Peg and Pete Braswell
Rooms: 2 (PB) $60-75
Full Breakfast
Notes: 2, 5, 7, 9, 10, 11, 14

## Sand Dollar Hospitality

3605 Mendenhall Drive, 78415
(361) 853-1222; (800) 528-7782
FAX (361) 814-1285
e-mail: bednbreakfast@aol.com
www.ccinternet.net/sand-dollar

**Bay Breeze.** Within view of the sparkling bay waters, this fine older home offers four accommodations, all with private baths. Guests are invited to enjoy the large sunroom, the 1930s billiard table, watch TV, or just relax. A five-minute drive to the business district and city marinas, where guests can enjoy fine dining and recreation or purchase shrimp direct from the net. It is only a short stroll to the city's finest bayfront park and fishing pier. Resident cat. Full breakfast. Smoking permitted outside only. $65-90.

**Colley House (formerly the Seagull).** New England antiques collected by the hosts, a retired navy couple, add to the charm and ambiance of this lovely home. Only one block

from Corpus Christi Bay, this 50-year-old home is in a quiet up-scale neighborhood just a five-minute walk from the city's largest bayside park. Guests are invited to relax in the enclosed patio/den with TV, wet bar, and cozy surroundings. Two bedrooms with private baths are available. Older children are welcome. Full breakfast. Smoking permitted outside only. $75.

**Ginger Rose.** Within a quiet gated community, reminiscent of the medieval cities of Provence, this scenic home offers a guest room with private bath, a heated pool, and access to nearby tennis courts. This charming French Provincial-style home is midway between downtown and the gulf beaches—driving time being 25 minutes in either direction. A full gourmet breakfast served. Smoking permitted outside only. $70-75.

**Smith Place.** A colorfully landscaped back yard with pool and hot tub is the setting for two charming guest houses—the Garden Room and the Lodge. The sleeping accommodations for the Garden Room include a queen-size bed in the bedroom and a queen-size sofa bed in the adjoining sitting room. The Lodge has just a queen-size bed and easy chair. Other amenities include private entrances, off-street parking, refrigerator, microwave, coffee center, and cable TV. Breakfast provisions are brought in daily. Small pets permitted. $90.

## DALLAS

## Bed & Breakfast Texas Style

4224 West Red Bird Lane, Dallas, 75237
(972) 298-3586; (800) 899-4538
FAX (972) 298-7118; e-mail: bdtxstyle1@aol.com
www.bnbtexasstyle.com

**Artist's Haven.** This private home offers two upstairs guest rooms with lovely amenities and shared bath. One room has twin beds, and the other room has a king-size bed. Breakfast is Continental plus, with fruit, pastries, and

7 No smoking; 8 Children welcome; 9 Social drinking allowed; 10 Tennis nearby; 11 Swimming nearby; 12 Golf nearby; 13 Skiing nearby; 14 May be booked through a travel agent; 15 Handicapped accessible.

beverages. Cat in residence. No smoking. Children are welcome. $85.

**The Cloisters.** This lovely home is one block from White Rock Lake in a secluded area of Dallas. There are two guest rooms, each with a private bath. Both rooms have double beds, one with an antique Mexican headboard that is a conversation piece. Breakfast will be lots of protein, eggs, and/or blueberry pancakes. A bicycle is available for riding around the lake. No smoking. $85.

**Fan Room.** The antique fan displayed in this lovely twin bedroom is the focal point and was the start of a large collection of fans. The home is near Prestonwood, Marshall Fields, and the Galleria Mall. Southfork Ranch is a 15-minute drive north. A full country breakfast includes jalapeño muffins for first-time Texas visitors. Second bedroom near the kitchen with a double bed and private bath. $70.

**The Southern House.** A new three-story modified prairie-style home fits right in with the large historic homes in the State-Thomas area, in the Arts District of Dallas. The two bed and breakfast rooms share one bath; the Heritage Room is exquisitely decorated with a full-size bed, the luxurious bath features a black antique-footed tub and shower. The Artist's Room has a queen bed and is the owner's actual studio and office. The computer and fax machine are available for guests' use. The McKinney Trolley and Hard Rock Café are two blocks away. The Myerson Symphony Hall and Art Museum are walking distance away. $125-150.

**Tudor Mansion.** Built in 1933 in an exclusive neighborhood in the shadow of downtown, this Tudor-style mansion offers queen-size bed and private bath. A full gourmet breakfast of cheddar on toast, Texas-style creamed eggs with jalapeño, or fresh vegetable omelet is served. The bus line is three blocks away. Spanish and French are spoken. Three miles from downtown. Close to a public golf course. $80.

## DEL RIO

## The 1890 House

609 Griner Street, 78840
(830) 775-8061; (800) 282-1360
FAX (830) 775-4667; www.1890house.com

Nestled in the heart of Del Rio guests will find this magnificent turn-of-the-century Victorian home. It boasts five charming guest rooms, private soaking tubs, and Jacuzzi. Intimate and elegant. Fireplaces, verandas, and candlelight breakfasts. Make this visit an international event by traveling three miles south of the border to Acuna, Mexico.

Hosts: Alberto and Laura Galvan
Rooms: 5 (PB)
Full Breakfast
Credit Cards: A, B, C, D
Notes: 5, 7, 8, 9, 10, 11, 12

## EL PASO

## Cowboys & Indians Board & Bunk

P.O. Box 13752, 79913
(505) 589-2653; www.softaid.net/cowboys

Lie back and enjoy the wonderful panoramic view of Franklin Mountains and desert sunsets of southern New Mexico. Bunk down in one of the four theme rooms that are comfortable and decorated to make guests feel like they are a part of the Old West. Relax in the large gathering room. The grub is the best in southwestern- and chuckwagon-style cooking. Special packages for year-round golf, horseback riding, sightseeing, seminars, and workshops. Lunch and dinner available but catered only. Smoking permitted outside only. Children over 12 welcome. One room is handicapped accessible.

Hosts: Irene and Don Newlon
Rooms: 4 (PB) $67-89 per night
Full and Continental Breakfast

NOTES: Credit cards accepted: A MasterCard; B Visa; C American Express; D Discover; E Diner's Club; F Other; 2 Personal checks accepted; 3 Lunch available; 4 Dinner available; 5 Open all year; 6 Pets welcome;

Credit Cards: A, B, C, E
Notes: 2, 4, 5, 7, 8, 9, 10, 11, 12, 15

## FORT DAVIS

### The Veranda Country Inn

210 Court Avenue, P.O. Box 1238, 79734
(888) 383-2847; e-mail: info@veranda.com
www.theveranda.com

The Veranda is a spacious historic inn built in 1883. This unique adobe building, with 2-foot-thick walls and 12-foot ceilings, has fourteen large rooms and suites furnished with antiques and collectibles. Its walled gardens and quiet courtyards provide travelers with a change of pace and lifestyle in mile-high Fort Davis. A large, separate Carriage House is next to the gardens in the shade of a large pecan tree. The Veranda is within minutes of sites renowned for astronomy, historical forts and buildings, and scenic hiking, biking, and bird watching.

Hosts: Paul and Kathie Woods
Rooms: 14 (PB) $80-120
Carriage House: $100-145
Full Breakfast
Credit Cards: A, B, D
Notes: 2, 5, 7, 9,

The Veranda Country Inn

## FORT WORTH

### Bed & Breakfast at the Ranch

8275 Wagley Robertson Road, 76131
(817) 232-5522; (888) 593-0352
e-mail: bbranch@flash.net
www.fortworthians.com/bbranch

Bed & Breakfast at the Ranch

A true taste of Texas on 15 acres. Bed and Breakfast at the Ranch offers four spacious rooms with their own private baths. Two rooms have special tubs—a Jacuzzi and antique claw-foot tub. Three rooms have their own private patio. The spacious living room offers a stone fireplace, TV with video library, board games, upright grand piano, and library of books. Enclosed patio room is complete with hot tub, patio furniture, wet bar, guest refrigerator, and free pinball. Gourmet breakfast served by resident innkeeper—full on weekends and Continental on weekdays. Grounds offer tennis, putting green, gazebo, swing, and smokehouse. Unique!

Hosts: Scott and Cheryl Stewart
Rooms: 4 (PB) $85-159
Full or Continental Breakfast
Credit Cards: A, B, C
Notes: 2, 4, 5, 7, 8, 9, 10, 12, 14, 15

### Bed & Breakfast Texas Style

4224 West Red Bird Lane, Dallas, 75237
(972) 298-3586; (800) 899-4538
FAX (972) 298-7118; e-mail: bdtxstyle1@aol.com
www.bnbtexasstyle.com

**Bloomsbury House.** Escape to this beautifully restored 1908 two-story Queen Anne home in one of Texas's largest historic neighborhoods, just south of downtown. Guests will be pampered in one of the four guest bedrooms; each room has its own private bath. Enjoy desserts upon arrival and full home-cooked breakfast in the morning. Attractions in Fort Worth include the Sundance Square, Kimbell Art Museum, and Billy Bob's (famous "kicker dance" club). $99-110.

7 No smoking; 8 Children welcome; 9 Social drinking allowed; 10 Tennis nearby; 11 Swimming nearby; 12 Golf nearby; 13 Skiing nearby; 14 May be booked through a travel agent; 15 Handicapped accessible.

## The Texas White House

1417 Eighth Avenue, 76104
(817) 923-3597; (800) 279-6791
FAX (817) 923-0410

This historically designated, award-winning country-style home has been restored to its original 1910 grandeur of simple, yet elegant decor. Within five minutes of downtown, medical center, Fort Worth zoo, the cultural district, botanic gardens, water gardens, and Texas Christian University. Three guest rooms with sitting areas and private baths with claw-foot tubs. Breakfast served in either the dining room or sent to guests' room. Amenities include telephone, TV, early morning coffee service, afternoon snacks and beverages, secretarial services, laundry service for extended stays, and off-street parking.

Hosts: Jamie and Grover McMains
Rooms: 3 (PB) $100-125
Full Breakfast
Credit Cards: A, B, C, D
Notes: 2, 5, 7, 9, 10, 11, 12, 14

### FREDERICKSBURG

## Das College Haus

106 West College, 78624
(830) 997-9047; (800) 654-2802
www.dascollegehaus.com

Visit historic Fredericksburg and stay at Das College Haus, just three blocks from downtown. Spacious rooms with private baths; all have access to the porches, balcony with porch swing, and wicker rockers, where guests can relax and visit. Das College Haus is beautifully

Das College Haus

appointed with comfortable period furniture and original art for a wonderful "at home" atmosphere. Enjoy a full breakfast served in the old-fashioned dining room. Central heat and air, cable TV, VCR, and a collection of movies. Coffee makers and refrigerators in rooms.

Host: Myrna Dennis
Rooms: 4 (PB) $95-110
Full Breakfast
Credit Cards: A, B
Notes: 2, 5, 7, 9, 10, 11, 12, 15

## Magnolia House

101 East Hackberry, 78624
(800) 880-4374; FAX (830) 997-0766
e-mail: magnolia@hctc.net
www.magnolia-house.com

Built circa 1923 and restored in 1991, this inn exudes southern hospitality in a grand and gracious manner. Outside magnolias, a bubbling fishpond with waterfall set a soothing mood. Inside, a beautiful living room, formal dining room, and sunroom provide areas for guests to mingle. Two beautiful suites, with fireplaces, and three romantic rooms have been decorated thoughtfully with antiques. Beautiful, bountiful breakfast and complimentary beverages make this a memorable experience.

Hosts: Joyce and Patrick Kennard
Rooms: 5 (PB) $95-140
Full Breakfast
Credit Cards: A, B, C, D
Notes: 2, 5, 7, 9, 10, 11, 12

## Moonbeam Cottage

514 West Austin Street, 78624
(830) 997-5612

Completely private cottage located in the historic district one block off Main Street offering city convenience and country charm in the shadow of a 1904 home surrounded by beautiful country gardens. Central heat and air, full kitchen, microwave. One bedroom with luxuries, both with shower for two. Queen sofa bed can accommodate two extra people. Front porch swing and rocker. Telephone, cable TV, and Continental breakfast included. Contact Gastehaus Schmidt.

Hosts: Judy Vincent
Rooms: 1 (PB) $85 per night
Continental Breakfast
Notes: 5, 7, 12, 14

## Schmidt Barn Bed & Breakfast

Gästehaus Schmidt Reservation Service
231 West Main, 78624
(210) 997-5612; FAX (210) 997-8282
e-mail: gasthaus@ktc.com
www.fbglodging.com

The remnants of an 1860s limestone barn were lovingly saved to turn it into a guest house. Stone walls, brick floors, timber beams maintain century-old charm. Bathroom invites guests to a long soak in a sunken tub. Quilts, antique linens, samplers, and a collection of toys enliven the wooden-beamed loft bedrooms. Hosts live next door. Featured in *Country Living* and *Travel and Leisure*. German Continental plus breakfast is left for guests to enjoy at their leisure.

Hosts: Charles and Loretta Schmidt
Rooms: 1 (PB) $90
Continental Breakfast
Credit Cards: A, B
Notes: 2, 5, 6, 8, 9, 10, 11, 12, 14

## GAINESVILLE

## Alexander Bed & Breakfast Acres, Inc.

3692 C.R. 201, 76240-7819
(903) 564-7440; (800) 887-8794
e-mail: abba@texoma.net
www.bbhost.com/alexanderbbacres

Three-story Queen Anne Victorian home on 65 peaceful acres of woods and meadows. Large wraparound porch for lounging; walking trails; near two large lakes, antiques, country farms, and zoo. Each bedroom decorated with different theme: western, antique, canopied, or

Amish. Full breakfast included. Separate conference room and extra lodging on third floor. Two-story guest cottage offers three bedrooms sharing one and one-half baths, kitchen, laundry, living area, and large screened porch. Children welcome in cottage only. Dinner available by arrangement.

Hosts: Jim and Pamela Alexander
Rooms: 8 (5 PB; 3 SB) $60-125
Full Breakfast
Credit Cards: A, B, C, D
Notes: 2, 4, 5, 7, 9, 11, 12, 14

## GALVESTON

## Inn at 1816 Postoffice

1816 Postoffice Street, 77550
(409) 763-9444; e-mail: INN1816@aol.com
www.bbonline.com/tx/1816

Built in 1886, this beautiful Victorian home is located in Galveston's East End Historic District and has been lovingly restored and furnished with antiques and fine furniture. Five separate and unique rooms, all with private baths. Guests can walk to Strand Shopping District, Galveston Arts District, Grand Opera House, many casual and fine restaurants, historic trolley station, and Galveston Bay Harbor. Accommodations include game room with pool table and board games and use of bicycles for touring purposes. Gourmet breakfast served in dining room with fresh coffee and tea. Appetizers and refreshments in afternoon. Gourmet picnic baskets available for extra fee.

Rooms: 5 (PB) $125-195
Full Breakfast
Credit Cards: A, B, C, D
Notes: 2, 5, 7, 9, 11, 12

## The Queen Anne Bed & Breakfast

1915 Sealy Avenue, 77550-2312
(409) 763-7088; (800) 472-0930

This home is a four-story Queen Anne-style Victorian in the historic home district, built in

1905. Stained-glass windows, beautiful floors, large rooms, pocket doors, and 12-foot ceilings with transom windows; beautifully redecorated in 1991. Walk to the historic shopping district, restaurants, 1894 opera house, and museums. A short drive to the beach. A visit to Queen Anne is to be anticipated, relished, and long-remembered.

Hosts: Ron and Jackie Metzger
Rooms: 5 (3 PB; 2 SB) $90-150
Full Breakfast
Credit Cards: A, B, C
Notes: 2, 5, 7, 9, 10, 11, 12, 13, 14

## GALVESTON ISLAND

### Bayview Inn with Hot Tub and Boatpier

P.O. Box 1326, 77553
(409) 741-0705

Waterfront casual luxury and elegance in a romantic setting complete with huge swaying palms, exotic waterfowl, and hot tub. Water views from all rooms with private baths; furnished with fabulous rare antiques from world travels. Boat dock. Golf course and beach two minutes away. Ms. Pat is an island character well worth meeting. Her specialty is adult getaways. Nearby are flight and car museums, historical homes, IMAX, rainforest-pyramid, trolley, fishing, beach, boating; 45 minutes to Houston. Discount for weekly or monthly rates.

Host: Ms. Pat Hazlewood
Rooms: 3 (PB) $65-145
Continental Breakfast
Credit Cards: F
Notes: 2, 5, 7, 9, 10, 11, 12, 13

## GARLAND

### Bed & Breakfast Texas Style

4224 West Red Bird Lane, Dallas, 75237
(972) 298-8586; (800) 899-4538
FAX (972) 298-7118; e-mail: bdtxstyle1@aol.com
www.bnbtexasstyle.com

**Catnip Creek.** Right on Spring Creek, the hot tub on the deck overlooks a wooded creek. The guest room has a queen-size bed, private bath, and private entrance. Breakfast has granola and cinnamon-raisin biscuits or other homemade muffins and breads. Weekend guests are treated to a healthy quiche or pancakes. Herbal teas and specially blended coffees are offered. Bicycles are provided. Just 30 minutes from downtown Dallas and very near Hypermart, the newest tourist attraction of the metroplex. Also near Southfork Ranch. $60-75.

## GEORGETOWN

### Claibourne House

912 Forest, 78626
(512) 930-3934; (512) 913-2272 (voice mail)
FAX: (512) 869-0202

Claibourne House is three blocks west of the historic courthouse square in the heart of old Georgetown. Built in 1896, this spacious Victorian residence was restored during 1987-88 and adapted as a bed and breakfast inn. Guests are graciously accommodated in four bedrooms, each with private bath. An intimate upstairs sitting room and downstairs grand hall and parlor and wraparound porch are available for guests. The guest rooms are handsomely furnished with treasured family furniture, antiques, and distinctive fine art.

Host: Clare Easley
Rooms: 4 (PB) $85-125
Continental Breakfast
Credit Cards: A, B
Notes: 2, 5, 7, 9

### Heron Hill Farm Bed & Breakfast

1350 County Road 143, 78626
(512) 863-0461; (800) 439-3828

New, old-fashioned Texas farmhouse built in 1996 especially for bed and breakfast. House sits high on a hill overlooking 13 acres of wildlife habitat and a large vegetable garden.

NOTES: Credit cards accepted: A MasterCard; B Visa; C American Express; D Discover; E Diner's Club; F Other; 2 Personal checks accepted; 3 Lunch available; 4 Dinner available; 5 Open all year; 6 Pets welcome;

Heron Hill Farm

Pick own veggies in season. The four guest rooms, each with private bath, are on the second floor. Rooms feature country decor which mixes new and antique furniture. Three rooms have queen-size beds, one room has two twin antique white iron beds. Full breakfast served daily. Enjoy antiquing, hiking, biking, and swimming and boating at local lake; golf also available nearby. Inner Space Caverns and Lady Bird Johnson Wildflower Center make good day trips.

Hosts: Ed and Linda Devine
Rooms: 4 (PB) $80
Full Breakfast
Credit Cards: A, B
Notes: 2, 5, 7, 8, 9, 11, 12

## GLADEWATER

# Honeycomb Suites

111 North Main Street, 75647
(800) 594-2253; FAX (903) 845-2448
e-mail: sho4go@internetwork.net
www.honeycombsuites.com

Specializing in romantic getaways, offering seven suites, each in a different motif. Five suites are above scratch-recipe bakery in the antique district of Gladewater. Two suites (including the honeymoon suite) are in an adjacent building. Four suites have whirlpool tubs for two. Saturday

evenings, candlelight dinners with horse-drawn carriage rides are available by reservation. Romance packages and gift certificates are available. Gladewater is 120 miles east of Dallas or 60 miles west of Shreveport.

Hosts: Bill and Susan Morgan
Rooms: 7 (PB) $85-150
Full Breakfast
Credit Cards: A, B, C, D
Notes: 2, 3, 4, 5, 7, 9, 10, 11, 12

## GLEN ROSE

# Bed & Breakfast Texas Style

4224 West Red Bird Lane, Dallas, 75237
(972) 298-8586; (800) 899-4538
FAX (972) 298-7118; e-mail: bdtxstyle1@aol.com
www.bnbtexasstyle.com

**Hummingbird Lodge.** The motto of the owners for this extraordinary bed and breakfast is "Come find the trees and streams, the deer and the birds, the peace. Come find yourself." Just about two miles south of Glen Rose off the beaten path, surrounded by cedar trees and small hills, a weary city dweller will find complete serenity. There are large porches and decks with rocking chairs; the "hummers" are most entertaining; or just curl up with a book down by the hot tub in the swinging hammock. There are well-marked walking trails, a waterfall, and a pond for the energetic fisherman. There are six guest rooms, all with private baths. A full gourmet breakfast is provided. $85-115.

# Bussey's Something Special

202 Hereford Street, P.O. Box 1425, 76043
(817) 897-4843; (877) 426-2233

Relax in a private country cottage in downtown Glen Rose historic district. Family-friendly with crib upstairs. Enjoy hand-crafted lounges, artwork, books, games, and toys. Seashell and oak bathroom with shower (no tub). Experience the Early American decor in a private cozy cottage with tropical bath, whirlpool jet

7 No smoking; 8 Children welcome; 9 Social drinking allowed; 10 Tennis nearby; 11 Swimming nearby; 12 Golf nearby; 13 Skiing nearby; 14 May be booked through a travel agent; 15 Handicapped accessible.

Bussey's Something Special

tub/shower, and small kitchen. Both cottages have a king-size bed. Continental plus breakfast, private front porches, and attractive decor. Sweetheart packages available upon request. No hosts on premises

Hosts: Susan and Morris Bussey
Cottage: 2 (PB) $80-100
Continental Breakfast
Credit Cards: A, B, C, D
Notes: 2, 5, 7, 8, 10, 11, 12, 14

## Ye Ole Maple Inn

1509 Van Zandt, P.O. Box 1141, 76043
(254) 897-3456; texasguides.com/mapleinn.html

Built circa 1950, the inn is decorated with several antique pieces throughout. Two rooms, each with its own private bath. Den with a grand fireplace and small library for reading pleasure. Breakfast includes fresh fruit or fruit compote, breakfast sausage or Black Forest Ham, orange juice and coffee or tea with an entree such as Oatmeal waffles, Maple Baked Eggs or Egg-Sausage-Apple Casserole. Dessert is served every evening. Area activities include the Fossil Rim Wildlife Refuge, Creation Museum, Dinosaur State Park, Texas Amphitheatre, and the Somervell Country Golf Course. No pets, children, or smoking.

Host: Roberta Maple
Rooms: 2 (PB) $80-85
Credit Cards: A, B, C
Notes: 2, 5, 7, 12, 15

## GRANBURY

## Dabney House Bed & Breakfast

106 South Jones, 76048
(817) 579-1260; (800) 566-1260

Craftsman-style home built in 1907 boasts its original hardwood floors, ceiling beams, stained and beveled glass, and fixtures. Long-term business rates available per request as well as a whole-house rental discount. Hosts offer a candlelight romantic dinner or group lunches per reservation only. Custom special occasion baskets available by advance order only. Special discounts for certified peace officers and firefighters.

Hosts: John and Gwen Hurley
Rooms: 4 (PB) $60-105
Full Breakfast
Credit Cards: A, B, C
Notes: 2, 5, 7, 9, 10, 11, 12, 14

## Pearl Street Inn Bed & Breakfast

319 West Pearl Street, 76048
(817) 579-7465; (888) PEARL ST

Relax and reminisce in the stately, stylish comfort of a 1912 Prairie-style home. Three blocks from Granbury's historic square, this tastefully restored historical home features antique furnishings, two porches, cast-iron tubs, pocket doors, outdoor hot tub, and scrumptious breakfasts. Enjoy live theater, state parks, drive-in

Pearl Street Inn

movies, antique shopping, or festivals in a charming country setting, 30 miles south of the Dallas/Fort Worth metroplex. Enjoy overnight accommodations in a delightful home "where days move gently in all seasons."

Host: Danette D. Hebda
Rooms: 5 (PB) $59-109
Full Breakfast
Credit Cards: None
Notes: 2, 5, 7, 9, 10, 11, 12, 14

## HOUSTON

### The Lovett Inn

501 Lovett Boulevard, 77006
(713) 522-5224; (800) 779-5224
FAX (713) 528-6708; e-mail LovettInn@aol.com
www.lovettinn.com

Once the home of Houston mayor and federal court judge Joseph C. Hutcheson, the Lovett Inn has all of the amenities of a first-class hotel. Within walking distance to some of the city's finest restaurants, clubs, and shopping. The George R. Brown Convention Center, downtown, Greenway Plaza, Texas Medical Center, Hobby Airport, and the Galleria are also nearby. Each room has been comfortably decorated to evoke the inn's historic past, while adding such modern amenities as in-room telephones, remote color TV, and private bathrooms. To accommodate the most discriminating traveler, suite accommodations, meeting rooms, fax service, and in-room whirlpool are available.

Host: Tom Fricke
Rooms: 9 (8 PB; 1 SB) $85-150
Continental Breakfast
Credit Cards: A, B, C, D
Notes: 5, 6, 7, 8, 9, 10, 11, 12, 14

### Patrician Bed & Breakfast Inn

1200 Southmore Boulevard, 77004-5826
(713) 523-1114; (800) 553-5797;
FAX (713) 523-0790; e-mail: southmor@swbell.net
www.texasbnb.com

Visitors can relax in this immense, three- story mansion built in 1919. The inn is centrally

Patrician

located and less than 2 miles south of downtown Houston. Take a short walk to Hermann Park, Museum of Fine Arts, and Rice University. The breakfast is served gourmet-style and may include creamy French toast slathered with cream cheese and orange marmalade, orange mandarin coffee cake, fresh fruit, and orange juice.

Host: Patricia Thomas
Rooms: 5 (PB) $90-135
Full Breakfast
Credit Cards: A, B, C, D, E
Notes: 5, 7, 9, 12, 14

### Robin's Nest

4104 Greeley, 77006
(713) 528-5821; (800) 622-8343
FAX (713) 521-2154; www.houstonbnb.com

Historic, circa 1898, two-story wooden Queen Anne. Feather beds atop fine mattresses, convenience of central location, and a full breakfast make the stay worthwhile. The rooms are spacious, furnished in eclectic Victorian with custom-made drapes, bed covers, etc. Robin's Nest is decoratively painted in concert with her sister "painted ladies." In the Museum and Arts district, surrounded by museums, art galleries, downtown, excellent restaurants, and the theater district. Inquire about accommodations for pets and children.

---

**7** No smoking; **8** Children welcome; **9** Social drinking allowed; **10** Tennis nearby; **11** Swimming nearby; **12** Golf nearby; **13** Skiing nearby; **14** May be booked through a travel agent; **15** Handicapped accessible.

Host: Robin Smith
Rooms: 4 (PB) $75-120
Full Breakfast
Credit Cards: A, B, C, D
Notes: 2, 5, 7, 9, 10, 11, 12, 13

Sara's

## Sara's Bed & Breakfast Inn

941 Heights Boulevard, 77008
(713) 868-1130; (800) 593-1130

This Queen Anne Victorian is in the historic Heights district of Houston, only four miles from downtown, a neighborhood of historic homes, many of which are in the National Register of Historic Places. Each bedroom is uniquely furnished, having either single, double, queen-, or king-size beds. The balcony suite consists of two bedrooms, two baths, kitchen, living area, and balcony. Children welcome only in balcony suite.

Hosts: Donna and Tillman Arledge
Rooms: 14 (12 PB; 2 SB) $70-150
Continental Breakfast
Credit Cards: A, B, C, D, E, F
Notes: 2, 5, 7, 8, 9, 10, 11, 12, 14

## INGRAM

## Lazy Hills Guest Ranch

P.O. Box G, 78025
(800) 880-0632; (830) 367-5600;
FAX (830) 367-5667; e-mail: lhills@ktc.com

Surrounded by the panoramic beauty of the Texas Hill Country, Lazy Hills has a wide variety of fun activities, comfortable accommodations, and delicious, family meals. Guest rooms are furnished with comfortable twin or queen beds and will sleep from four to six people comfortably. Electric heat, air conditioning, bathrooms with showers, and pleasant porches. Some have fireplaces. Breakfast, lunch, and dinner served daily. Accommodations include swimming pool, game room, tennis courts, a community telephone and community TV, and coin-operated laundry facilities. Activities include horseback riding, hiking, bird watching, golf, and fishing. No pets. Children are welcome.

Hosts: Bob and Carol Steinruck and family
Rooms: 25 (PB) $75-95
Full Breakfast
Credit Cards: A, B
Notes: 7, 8, 10, 11, 12, 14

## JEFFERSON

## 1st Bed & Breakfast in Texas—Pride House

409 Broadway, 75657
(800) 894-3526; (903) 665- 2675;
FAX (903) 665-3901; e-mail: jefftx@mind.net
www.jeffersontexas.com

Breathtaking Victorian mansion in historic steamboat port, Texas' favorite small town—where a weekend is never enough. Luxurious accommodations, luscious interiors, and legendary breakfasts. Within driving distance of Shreveport and Texarkana. Eleven rooms, each with private bath. Mobil rated, HAT approved, member TH&MA. Hot and cold drinks and snacks included and available around the clock. German and English spoken. No pets. Smoking outside only.

Hosts: Carol Abernathy and Christel Frederick
  (innkeepers); Sandy Spalding (owner)
Rooms: 11 (PB) $75-150
Full Breakfast
Credit Cards: A, B, C, D
Notes: 2, 5, 7, 8, 9, 10, 12, 14

NOTES: Credit cards accepted: A MasterCard; B Visa; C American Express; D Discover; E Diner's Club; F Other; 2 Personal checks accepted; 3 Lunch available; 4 Dinner available; 5 Open all year; 6 Pets welcome;

McKay House

## McKay House
## Bed & Breakfast Inn

306 East Delta Street, 75657
(903) 665-7322
(800) 468-2627 (reservations 9 A.M.-5 P.M.)

Jefferson is a riverport town from the frontier days of the Republic of Texas. It has historical mule-drawn tours, 30 antique shops, boat rides on the Big Cypress Bayou, and a mysterious lake made famous by Walt Disney. The McKay House, an 1851 Greek Revival cottage, offers period furnishings, cool lemonade, porch swings, and fireplaces. Seven rooms that vary from the keeping room to the garden suite (with his and her antique footed tubs). A full gentleman's breakfast is served in the garden conservatory. Victorian nightclothes are laid out for guests. VIP guests have included Lady Bird Johnson, Alex Haley, and Fabio. Mobil Travel Guide.

Owner: Peggy Taylor
Innkeepers: Lisa and Roger Cantrell
Rooms: 4 (PB) $139 weekend; $89 weekday
Suites: 3 (PB) $169
Full Breakfast
Credit Cards: A, B, C
Notes: 2, 5, 7, 8, 11, 12

## Old Mulberry Inn

209 Jefferson Street, 75657
(903) 665-1945; (800) 263-5319;
FAX (903) 665-9123;
e-mail: mulberry@jeffersontx.com
www.jefferson.com/oldmulberryinn

A gracious new inn in the style of Jefferson's fine antebellum homes offers guests the best of the old and the new. Adding to the charm are antique heartpine floors, tastefully eclectic furnishings, and designer touches throughout. Soak in a footed tub, relax by the fireplace in the library, or swing on the spacious porch. Five unique rooms. Private baths. Cable TV. Gourmet breakfast. 24-hour refreshments. Walk to tour homes, shopping, museums.

Hosts: Donald and Gloria Degn
Rooms 5 (PB) $100-125
Full Breakfast
Credit Cards: A, B, C, D
Notes: 5, 7, 9, 11, 12, 14

Urquhart House of Eleven Gables

## Urquhart House of
## Eleven Gables

301 East Walker Street, 75657
(903) 665-8442; (888) 922-8442

The Urquhart House of Eleven Gables is an experience of luxuries and historical elegance. Turn-of-the-century quality of life comes alive with period decor and antiques. Further creating the yesteryear ambiance are equestrian carriages and wagons clip-clopping the street that fronts the wraparound porch of this expansive 1890 Queen Anne house. Antique wicker swing and furniture occupy the abundantly pleasant wraparound porch inviting guests to come and "sit a spell." Gourmet breakfast served with antique linens, crystal, and china.

7 No smoking; 8 Children welcome; 9 Social drinking allowed; 10 Tennis nearby; 11 Swimming nearby; 12 Golf nearby; 13 Skiing nearby; 14 May be booked through a travel agent; 15 Handicapped accessible.

Host: Joyce Jackson
Rooms: 2 (PB) $125
Full Breakfast
Credit Cards: A, B, C, D, E
Notes: 2, 5, 7, 8, 9, 12, 14

## KINGSLAND

### The Antlers Hotel

Route 2, Box 430, 78639
(800) 383-0007; FAX (915) 388-6488
www.theantlers.com

Historic, lakeside hotel built by the railroad in
1901. All antique-filled rooms and suites are
luxurious with private entrances off wide
porches. Game room with TV/VCR, pool
table, and treadmill. Fifteen acres of grounds
include nature trails, orchard, and over a thou-
sand feet of waterfront for swimming, fishing,
and boating. Boat slips available. Listed on
National Register of Historic Places. Great
weather, wildflowers, bird watching, and golfing in the Texas Hill Country.

Hosts: Lori and Anthony Mayfield
Rooms: 6 (PB) $120-140
Continental Breakfast
Credit Cards: A, B, C, D
Notes: 2, 3, 4, 5, 7, 9, 11, 12, 15

## KINGSVILLE

### B Bar B Ranch Inn

325 East County Road 2215, 78363
(361) 296-3331; FAX (361) 296-3337
e-mail: bbarb@rivnet.com
www.b-bar-b.com

Quietly nestled beneath the rippling leaves of a
south Texas mesquite grove, this 80-acre working ranch is host to a wide variety of native
plants and wildlife. Originally part of the historic King Ranch, the B Bar B is a bird watching hot spot. The hosts also offer fishing and
hunting trips. Their gourmet restaurant is sure
to tempt guests' taste buds.

Hosts: Luther and Patti Young
Rooms: 16 (PB) $85-125

Full Breakfast
Credit Cards: A, B, D
Notes: 2, 4, 5, 11, 12, 14

## LEANDER

### Trails End Bed & Breakfast

12223 Trail End Road, #7, 78641
(512) 267-2901

Trails End Bed and Breakfast located near
Austin and Lake Travis in Texas Hill Country.
Our quiet country setting is elegant and entertaining. We offer fine food, quaint hospitality,
decks, nature hikes, pool, monogrammed robes,
telephones in rooms, and gardens. Take home
happy memories and a gift from the Bed and
Breakfast Store. Fishing, water sport, and golfing
close by. Much exploring in nearby quaint town.

Hosts: JoAnn and Tom Patty
Rooms: 3 (PB) $75-185
Full Breakfast
Notes: 2, 3, 4, 5, 7, 8, 9, 10, 11, 12, 13, 14

Trails End

## MASON

### Hasse House Ranch

P.O. Box 779, 76856
(888) 41-HASSE (414-2773)

The Hasse House, circa 1883, is where country
quality lives in historical architecture laced

Hasse House Ranch

with modern conveniences. Complete with period furniture, microwave, dishwasher, washer-dryer, central air, two bedrooms, two baths, living room, and complete kitchen. Guests may explore the 320-acre ranch with two-mile nature trail and abundant wildlife. Owner lives in town so party will be only one in the house. "Let us invite you to the complete peace of rural living."

Host: Laverne Lee
Rooms: 2 (PB) $95
Continental Breakfast
Credit Cards: A, B
Notes: 2, 5, 8, 9, 12

## The Lott Home
## Bed & Breakfast Cottages

311 East Kilpatrick Street, 75773
(888) 232-LOTT (5688); e-mail:
lotthomecottages@tyler.net

The Lott Home Cottages, circa 1918, offers old-fashioned southern hospitality at its best. The charming, romantic cottages include queen-size beds, private baths, cable TV, antique furnishings, and a kitchen, with microwave, refrigerator, and coffee maker, fully stocked with refreshments and snacks. Each cottage has its own private porch with wooden rockers for guests to relax and view a beautiful East Texas sunset. Treat oneself to an unforgettable night, relive a moment in time and take home wonderful memories at the Lott Home Bed and Breakfast Cottages.

Hosts: Mark and Sharon Chamblee
Rooms: 2 (PB) $95
Full Breakfast
Credit Cards: A, B, D
Notes: 2, 5, 7, 9, 10, 12, 14, 15

## Gruene Homestead Inn

832 Gruene Road, 78130
(830) 606-0216; FAX (830) 625-6390
e-mail: homestead@compuvision.com

The inn's 20 guest suites are housed in several historic homes and cottages, dating from the late 1860s, that have been carefully restored and decorated in unique styles ranging from elegant Victorian to "Texas Country." Relaxation and romance are the keys to the graceful beauty of this hill country inn. On eight acres and less then two minutes from historic Gruene and the Guadalupe River. One room is handicapped accessible.

Hosts: Ed and Billie Miles
Rooms: 18 (PB) $95-135
Credit Cards: A, B, D
Notes: 2, 5, 7, 9, 11, 12, 15

## Karbach Haus Bed & Breakfast

487 West San Antonio Street, 78130
(830) 625-2131; (800) 972-5941;
FAX (830) 629-1126; www.bbhost.com/karbach

Meticulously restored turn-of-the-century mansion on an acre estate in downtown New Braunfels. Walk to fine restaurants, museums, antique stores, local attractions. Experience *Gemutlichkeit* of a German *Gasthaus* with amenities of a small resort. Spacious guest rooms have private tile baths (some with Jacuzzis), queen- or king-size beds, cable TV, VCR, robes, ceiling fans, down quilts, and many antiques. Central heat/air conditioning, swimming pool and spa, video library, butler's pantry with guest refrigerator, ice machine. World-class German-style breakfasts. Long-term rentals available. Owner/hosts on premises.

7 No smoking; 8 Children welcome; 9 Social drinking allowed; 10 Tennis nearby; 11 Swimming nearby; 12 Golf nearby; 13 Skiing nearby; 14 May be booked through a travel agent; 15 Handicapped accessible.

Hosts: Captain Ben Jack Kinney, USN (retired) and
   Kathleen Karbach Kinney, Ph.D.
Rooms: 6 (PB) $105-175
Full Breakfast
Credit Cards: A, B, D
Notes: 2, 5, 7, 9, 10, 11, 12, 14

## Prince Solms Inn

295 East San Antonio Street, 78130
(800) 625-9169; FAX (830) 625-9169

100-year-old landmark
in historic New Braun-
fels. Gateway to the
breathtaking Texas Hill
Country. Rated ninth
best historic inn by
*Texas Highways* Maga-
zine. Two blocks from
museum, water sports,
and shopping. Ideal for family gatherings,
small weddings, and corporate retreats.
Romance Package which includes dinner in
renowned Wolfgang's Keller Restaurant, rated
one of the ten most romantic restaurants by
*Ultra* Magazine. Country breakfast served.
Restaurant on premises. Smoking permitted in
courtyard only.

Hosts: Larry Patton, Carmen Morales, and Beverly
   Talbot
Rooms: 10 (PB) $95-159
Four-Room Cottage: $229
Continental Breakfast
Credit Cards: A, B, C, D
Notes: 2, 4, 5, 7, 8, 9, 10, 11, 12, 14

## PADRE ISLES

## Sand Dollar Hospitality

35 Mendenhall Drive, Corpus Christi, 78415
(512) 853-1222; (800) 528-7782
FAX (512) 814-1285
www.ccinternet.net/sand-dollar

**Coguina Bay.** Two great suites, each with a
king-size bed, private bath, ceiling fan with
view of pool and hot tub offered on this canal
home in Padre Isles. The host, an accomplished

mariner also offers sailing charters on his 33
foot sail boat. Jet ski rentals are also available.
A full buffet-style breakfast is served in the
dining room overlooking the water. $120.

**Fortuna Bay.** This enchanting hideaway on
Texas's North Padre Island is cradled between
the Laguna Madre and the Gulf of Mexico. A
unique bed and breakfast inn, Fortune Bay
presently consists of three one-bedroom fully
furnished condominiums in a 10-unit complex.
Each unit has a living room with cable TV, a
bedroom with a queen-size bed, a fully
equipped kitchen with microwave, and a
washer and dryer. There is also an outside grill
near the pool. The three-story, red-tile-roof
structure is at the intersection of five canals.
Provisions for a Continental plus breakfast are
supplied. A complimentary boat ride through
the canal system is offered. Weekly and
monthly rates are available. $96.

**Island Retreat.** Overlooking a major canal on
North Padre Island, this attractive two-bedroom, two-bath home is available in total for
families or couples traveling together. The
home can accommodate six people in air-conditioned comfort. One bedroom has sleeping
room for four. The refrigerator is stocked with
fruit and other breakfast provisions for guests
to self serve. There are two decks, one with a
hammock, the other built out over the water.
Children are welcome. Also small, well-
behaved pets are permitted with a $50 damage
deposit. The gulf beaches are just minutes
away, across the island. Ten dollars for each
additional person school-age or older. $150.

**Sunrise on the Water.** This bright and beautiful white stucco home is on one of the major
canals on North Padre Island and is just 5 minutes from the gulf beaches. The larger of the
two guest suites faces the water and has a balcony large enough for seating. A second bedroom has twin beds and its own private bath.
Both rooms have their own TVs and telephones. $90-110.

NOTES: Credit cards accepted: A MasterCard; B Visa; C American Express; D Discover; E Diner's Club;
F Other; 2 Personal checks accepted; 3 Lunch available; 4 Dinner available; 5 Open all year; 6 Pets welcome;

## ROCKPORT

### Sand Dollar Hospitality

35 Mendenhall Drive, Corpus Christi, 78415
(361) 853-1222; (800) 528-7782
FAX (361) 814-1285
www.ccinternet.net/sand-dollar

**Anthony's by the Sea.** The innkeepers at Anthony's offer four guest bedrooms in the guest wing of the residence plus two guest cottages. All units throughout the inn include a refrigerator, cable TV and VCR. A spacious plant-filled patio with lounge chair and tables connects the main house and the two guest cottages. There guests will also find a barbecue grill for guests' use. Off to the side is a swimming pool and hot tub. A full breakfast is served. The renowned Aransas Wildlife Refuge is less than an hour's drive away. Group, weekly, and monthly rates available. $66-95.

**The Blue Heron.** This Federal-style brick home was built in 1890 and after withstanding the hurricane of 1919 was reconstructed with the addition of porches and verandas in the 1930s. Great accommodations include four suites, two with half-baths and two with full. Outside, the rose and herb garden invites visitors to sit and relax under the massive live-oak tree. A full buffet style breakfast is served in the formal dining room. $95-105.

**Chandler House.** The upper-level veranda of this 123-year-old house offers a view of the gulf and the town's shopping area with its many specialty shops and galleries. Each of the two large upstairs bedrooms has two queen-size beds and its own private bath. The downstairs bedroom has a king-size bed, a private attached bath, fireplace, and TV. The common area includes a great room with fireplace and parlor games and a spacious breakfast room. Lunch is also available and open to the public at the unique Chandler House Tea Room. Children over 12 welcome at $25 per each child. $100-150.

**Cygnet.** A cozy, secluded country cottage on 16 acres with a double bed, top of the line queen-size sleeper sofa, kitchenette, TV/VCR, and country Jacuzzi outside. This delightful country retreat is about five miles south of Rockport and was designed to provide guests with privacy and comfort. Guests will be provided with farm-fresh eggs, homemade bread, cereals, milk, and fresh fruit. Five dollars for each additional person. $70.

**The Habitat.** A unique haven of seven plus acres, in the heart of the Lamar Peninsula and near the Aransas Wildlife Refuge, this bed and breakfast consists of four log cabins. Each cabin has a fully stocked kitchen, screened front porch, and outdoor grill. Bird watchers will have a chance to identify and photograph a myriad of bird life in and around the two-acre lake that fronts each cabin. Self-serve Continental breakfast. No pets. $70.

**Hoope's House.** Elegant but casual, this lovely home combines modern luxury with Old World charm. With its gleaming hardwood floors, twelve-foot ceilings with crown molding, this home is one of the oldest and most illustrious homes in the area. Commanding a panoramic view of Rockport Harbor, the inn is also within walking distance of museums, shops, and galleries. There are four guest rooms in the main house, each with a private bath. In addition there are four garden rooms across from the pool and hot tub. These too, have private bath, telephone, and TV.

## ROCKWELL

### Bed & Breakfast Texas Style

4224 West Red Bird Lane, Dallas, 75237
(972) 298-8586; (800) 899-4538
FAX (972) 298-7118; e-mail: bdtxstyle1@aol.com
www.bnbtexasstyle.com

**Barton on Boydstun.** Individual cottage suites are on this large property right near downtown

7 No smoking; 8 Children welcome; 9 Social drinking allowed; 10 Tennis nearby; 11 Swimming nearby; 12 Golf nearby; 13 Skiing nearby; 14 May be booked through a travel agent; 15 Handicapped accessible.

Rockwall. Other buildings are an art gallery, working studio, and the Bois d'Arc Chapel. The cottages are new and built specifically for guests. Each one has its own screened porch and small kitchen. Perfect place for a small wedding or honeymoon retreat. Breakfast is a prepared treat that is left in the cottage for guests to zap in the microwave. $110-140.

## ROUND TOP

### The Settlement at Round Top

2218 Hartfield Road, P.O. Box 176, 78954
(406) 249-5015; (888) ROUNDTOP
FAX (409) 249-5587
e-mail: stay@thesettlement.com
www.thesettlement.com

The Settlement at Round Top is a luxurious pioneer-era adult retreat on 35 picturesque acres. This charming little complex includes 10 private guest rooms and suites in wonderfully restored log cabins and Berman cottages and houses including porches with rockers, fireplaces, private whirlpools, original art, fine linens, towering oaks, antique roses, miniature horses, and wildflowers in season. Featured in *Country Living, Country Home,* and *The Dallas Morning News.* Full breakfast on weekends and Continental weekdays.

Hosts: Karen and Larry Beevers
Rooms: 10 (PB) $95-200
Full Breakfast
Credit Cards: A, B, C, D
Notes: 2, 3, 4, 5, 7, 9, 10, 11, 12, 14

The Settlement at Round Top

## SAN ANTONIO

### Beckmann Inn & Carriage House

222 East Guenther Street, 78204
(210) 229-1449; (800) 945-1449
FAX (210) 229-1061; www.beckmanninn.com

This elegant Victorian inn is in the heart of San Antonio in the King William Street Historic District. The wraparound porch welcomes guests to this beautiful home. All rooms are colorfully decorated, featuring ornately carved Victorian queen-size beds, antiques, private baths, TVs, telephones, refrigerators, desks, and robes. Ride the trolley or take the Riverwalk to the Alamo, restaurants, shops, Mexican market, and much more. Guests receive gracious and warm hospitality during their stay. Gourmet breakfast with a breakfast dessert. AAA three-diamond-rated, Mobil three-star-rated, and IIA-rated excellent.

Hosts: Betty Jo and Don Schwartz
Rooms: 5 (PB) $99-140
Full Breakfast
Credit Cards: A, B, C, D, E
Notes: 2, 5, 7, 8, 9, 11, 12, 14

Beckmann Inn

### The Belle of Monte Vista

505 Belknap Place, 78212
(210) 732-4006; FAX (210) 732-4006

J. Riley Gordon designed this Queen Anne-style Victorian as a model home. Built in 1890 with limestone, the house has been beautifully restored and is located in the elegant Monte Vista historic district just two miles from the Alamo and Riverwalk. Inside, guests will find eight fireplaces, stained-glass windows, a hand-carved oak staircase, and Victorian furnishings. The host, Jim Davis, serves a full southern breakfast and will help guests plan their day.

Hosts: Jim Davis and Jeanette Duval
Rooms: 5 (2 PB; 3 SB) $50-85
Full Breakfast
Credit Cards: A, B, C
Notes: 2, 5, 7, 8, 9, 10, 12

## Bonner Garden Bed & Breakfast

145 East Agartia, 78212
(800) 396-4222; FAX (210) 733-6129
e-mail: noels@onr.com
www.travelbase.com

An award-winning replica of an Italian Renaissance villa built in 1910 for internationally known artist Mary Bonner. The original villa was built in Italy in the early 1600s. Fireplaces, tile, fixtures, etc., were imported from Italy. A large swimming pool and a rooftop patio provide enjoyable respites for guests. Guest rooms have private baths, some with Jacuzzi, TVs, VCRs, and telephones. A film library and Texarkana library are available for guests' enjoyment. A full gourmet breakfast is served.

Hosts: Jan and Noel Stenoien
Rooms: 5 (PB) $85-115
Full Breakfast
Credit Cards: A, B, C, D, E
Notes: 2, 5, 7, 9, 10, 11, 12, 14

Bonner Garden

Brackenridge House

## Brackenridge House: A Bed & Breakfast Inn

230 Madison, 78204
(210) 271-3442; (800) 221-1412
FAX (210) 226-3139; e-mail: benniesueb@aol.com
www.brackenridgehouse.com

Native Texan owners and innkeepers will guide guests through their visit to this beautiful Greek Revival home in historic King William. Gourmet breakfast served in formal dining room or veranda, hot tub, private baths, and country Victorian decor add to guests' comfort and pleasure. Pets and children are welcome in the carriage house. AAA-, Mobil-, and HAT-rated.

Owners and Innkeepers: Bennie and Sue Blansett
Rooms: 5 (PB) $89-200
Guest house: 2 (PB) $125-250
Full Breakfast
Credit Cards: A, B, D, E
Notes: 2, 5, 6, 7, 8, 9, 10, 11, 12, 14

## The Columns on Alamo

1037 South Alamo, 78210
(800) 233-3364
www.bbonline.com/tx/columns

Resident innkeepers welcome guests to their gracious 1892 Greek Revival home and guest house in the historic King William area. Blocks from Riverwalk, restaurants, shopping,

7 No smoking; 8 Children welcome; 9 Social drinking allowed; 10 Tennis nearby; 11 Swimming nearby; 12 Golf nearby; 13 Skiing nearby; 14 May be booked through a travel agent; 15 Handicapped accessible.

The Columns on Alamo

convention center, and Alamo; short drive to Sea
World and Fiesta Texas. Marvelous antiques and
period reproductions, queen- and king-size
beds, Jacuzzis, fireplace, telephones, TVs, large
common areas, verandas, gardens, off-street
parking. Full gourmet breakfast is served in the
main house. Smoke free except for verandas,
outdoors. Two-night minimum Saturday.

Hosts: Ellenor and Art Link
Rooms: 11 (PB) $89-155
Full Breakfast
Credit Cards: A, B, C, D, E, F
Notes: 5, 7, 9, 10, 12, 14

## Noble Inns

107 Madison Street, 78204
(210) 225-4045; (800) 221-4045
FAX (210) 227-0877; e-mail: nobleinns@aol.com
www.nobleinns.com

Noble Inns

Noble Inns operates two luxury Victorian properties in downtown San Antonio's King
William historic district. Meticulously
restored, the 1890-era bed and breakfasts are
decorated with period antiques and offer full
modern amenities. All accommodations feature private, marble bath with two-person
Jacuzzi or claw-foot tub; antique mantel gas
fireplace; sumptuous fabrics, wallpapers; color
cable TV with HBO; telephone with data port
and voice mail. Full and Continental breakfasts. Beautiful patios, outdoor pool and heated
spa or indoor swim spa. Transportation in classic 1960 Rolls Royce available.

Hosts: Don and Liesl Noble
Rooms: 9 (PB) $130-185
Full and Continental Breakfast
Credit Cards: A, B, C, D, E, F
Notes: 2, 5, 7, 9, 10, 11, 12, 14

## The Ogé House on the Riverwalk

209 Washington Street, 78204
(800) 242-2770; FAX (210) 226-5812
e-mail: ogeinn@swbell.net; www.ogeinn.com

Elegant historic antebellum mansion shaded by
massive pecans and oaks, on one and one-half
landscaped acres along the banks of the famous
San Antonio Riverwalk in the King William
Street historic district. The inn, beautifully decorated with antiques, has large verandas and a
grand foyer. All rooms have air conditioning,
telephones, and TVs, many with fireplaces.
Dining, entertainment, convention centers,
trolley, and the Alamo are steps away. Featured
in the *New York Times*, *Glamour*, *Victoria*,
*Southern Living*, Travel channel. IIA-rated
excellent, Mobil three-star-rated. Complimentary *Wall Street Journal*, *New York Times*, and
*San Antonio Express News*. Smoking
restricted. Gourmet breakfast.

Hosts: Patrick and Sharrie Magatagan
Rooms: 10 (PB) $145-205
Full Breakfast
Credit Cards: A, B, C, D, E
Notes: 2, 5, 9, 10, 12, 14

NOTES: Credit cards accepted: A MasterCard; B Visa; C American Express; D Discover; E Diner's Club;
F Other; 2 Personal checks accepted; 3 Lunch available; 4 Dinner available; 5 Open all year; 6 Pets welcome;

## Riverwalk Inn

329 Old Gailbeau Road, 78204
(210) 212-8300; (800) 254-4440
FAX (210) 229-9422

The Riverwalk Inn is five two-story log homes, circa 1840, that have been restored on the San Antonio Riverwalk and are tastefully decorated in period antiques. Amenities include fireplaces, refrigerators, private baths, telephones, balconies, 80-foot porch, and conference area. Continental plus breakfasts and desserts served. Swimming nearby. Smoking permitted outside only. No children.

Hosts: Johnny Halpenny; Jan and Tracy Hammer
Rooms: 11 (PB) $110-175
Continental Breakfast
Credit Cards: A, B, C, D
Notes: 2, 5, 10, 11, 12, 14

## The Victorian Lady Inn

421 Howard Street, 78212
(210) 224-2524; (800) 879-7116
www.viclady.com

This 1898 historic mansion offers spacious guest rooms furnished with period antiques. High-back beds, claw-foot tubs, fireplaces, and verandas complete guests' pampered retreat. Savor a fabulous full breakfast each morning. Relax in the outdoor hot tub or in-ground pool

The Victorian Lady Inn

surrounded by tropical palms and banana trees. The Alamo, Riverwalk, convention center, and trolley are just blocks away. Package plans, corporate rates, and meeting space available.

Hosts: Joe and Kathleen Bowski
Rooms: 8 (PB) $79-135
Full Breakfast
Credit Cards: A, B, C, D
Notes: 2, 5, 7, 9, 10, 11, 12, 14

## A Yellow Rose

229 Madison, 78204
(210) 229-9903; (800) 950-9903
www.bbonline.com/tx/yellowrose/

A Yellow Rose bed and breakfast is an 1878 Victorian home in the King William Street Historic District. It has five wonderful guest rooms appointed with antiques, and each has private bath, cable TV, and queen-size bed. Off-street, covered parking is also provided. Breakfast is served daily in the elegant 18th-century dining room, and afterwards or in the afternoon or evening guests will enjoy relaxing on the veranda. Two blocks from the Riverwalk, one block from the 50¢ trolley, five blocks from the Alamo and convention center, and within three blocks three of the finest restaurants in San Antonio.

Hosts: Deb Field-Walker and Kit Walker
Rooms: 5 (PB) $95-140
Full Breakfast
Credit Cards: A, B, C, D
Notes: 5, 7, 9, 12, 14

## SANDIA

## Sand Dollar Hospitality

35 Mendenhall Drive, Corpus Christi, 78415
(361) 853-1222; (800) 528-7782
FAX (361) 814-1285
www.ccinternet.net/sand-dollar

**Knolle Farm and Ranch Bed and Breakfast.**
A true Texas ranch experience with sufficient

7 No smoking; 8 Children welcome; 9 Social drinking allowed; 10 Tennis nearby; 11 Swimming nearby; 12 Golf nearby; 13 Skiing nearby; 14 May be booked through a travel agent; 15 Handicapped accessible.

"citified" amenities to make for a comfortable and enjoyable stay. There are four guest rooms. There are eight stalls as well as outside paddock and arena. Additional attractions and/or activities include canoeing, fishing, skeet shooting, and bird watching. Ten dollars for each additional person. $125.

## SEABROOK

### Bed & Breakfast Texas Style

4224 West Red Bird Lane, Dallas, 75237
(972) 298-8586; (800) 899-4538
FAX (972) 298-7118; e-mail: bdtxstyle1@aol.com
www.bnbtexasstyle.com

**Crew's Quarters.** Right on Galveston Bay at the channel where shrimp boats and ocean liners go in and out, this Cape Cod-style cottage is available for families or romantic getaways. It will sleep seven to nine people with two bedrooms downstairs, each with a private bath. A loft room upstairs with two double beds and a twin bed has a half-bath. A large deck with chairs is perfect for sunning and watching birds and boats. Continental breakfast. $75-95.

## SMITHVILLE

### Katy House Bed & Breakfast

201 Ramona Street, P.O. Box 803, 78957
(512) 237-4262; (800) 843-5289;
FAX (512) 237-2239; e-mail thekatyh@onr.com
www.katyhouse.com

Consider this an invitation to visit the Katy House, named for the M-K-T Railroad. In the beautiful old road town of Smithville, Texas, this charming turn-of-the-century residence is handsomely decorated in American antiques and railroad memorabilia. All guest rooms offer a queen-size bed and private bath.

Smithville is also the hometown of the movie, *Hope Floats.*

Hosts: Bruce and Sallie Blalock
Rooms: 5 (PB) $68-115
Full Breakfast
Credit Cards: A, B, C
Notes: 2, 5, 7, 12, 14

### Bed & Breakfast Texas Style

4224 West Red Bird Lane, Dallas, 75237
(972) 298-8586; (800) 899-4538
FAX (972) 298-7118; e-mail: bdtxstyle1@aol.com
www.bnbtexasstyle.com

**The Doll House.** A private guest area on the second level of this residence in the Lost Pines area near Bastrop is available for visitors. The large sitting-bedroom is furnished with lovely antiques and collectibles and has its own private bath. There is a small kitchen area with refrigerator and microwave. If guests prefer to eat in, Continental fixings will be left in the room. A hearty breakfast downstairs in the dining area will be served by the gracious hosts. Two decks are available for bird watching or sunning. A lovely patio is a few steps down the trail. The state park is a few miles away. Two public golf courses are within a 10-minute drive. $110-125.

## SOUTH PADRE ISLAND

### Brown Pelican Inn

207 West Aries, P.O. Box 2667, 78597
(956) 761-2722

The Brown Pelican Inn is a place to relax, make oneself at home, and enjoy personalized service. The porches are a great spot to sit and watch the sun set over the bay. The inn is comfortably furnished with European and American antiques; all guest rooms have private baths, and most rooms have spectacular bay views. Breakfast in the parlor includes freshly baked bread or muffins, fresh fruit, cereal, juice, and gourmet coffee or tea. Children over 12 welcome.

Hosts: Vicky and Ken Conway
Rooms: 8 (PB) $73-108
Continental Breakfast
Credit Cards: A, B
Notes: 2, 5, 7, 9, 10, 11, 12, 14, 15

## TEXARKANA

# Mansion on Main Bed & Breakfast Inn

802 Main Street, 75501
(903) 792-1835; www.bbonline.com/tx/mansion/

Historic Victorian mansion accented with 14 Ionic columns around the veranda. Six romantic rooms and suites, each with private bath. Cross the threshold to timeless values, comfortable lodging for business and leisure travelers, and hospitality that confirms the city of Texarkana's motto of "Twice as Nice." Guests enjoy luxury beds in rooms and suites authentically furnished with period antiques and pleased amenities. A classic "Gentleman's Breakfast" served in the dining room, prepared by a trained chef. Visitors will drive right past

Mansion on Main

any motel to get to luxury lodging, fine food, and southern hospitality.

Hosts: Inez and Lee Hayden
Rooms: 6 (PB) $60-109
Full Breakfast
Credit Cards: A, B, C
Notes: 2, 5, 7, 8, 12, 14, 15

## TYLER

# Bed & Breakfast Texas Style

4224 West Red Bird Lane, Dallas, 75237
(972) 298-8586; (800) 899-4538
FAX (972) 298-7118; e-mail: bdtxstyle1@aol.com
www.bnbtexasstyle.com

**Vintage Farm Home.** This newly renovated, circa 1836-1864, home, once an original dogtrot plantation home, sits in the piney woods of East Texas. Catch the morning sun or evening breeze on the large veranda where rocking chairs and a swing invite relaxation. Take a stroll through the trails during dogwood or fall foliage season. The guest room has a king-size bed and private bath. Breakfast is served downstairs in the cozy nook. $85-125.

# Rosevine Inn Bed & Breakfast

415 South Vine, 75702
(903) 592-2221; e-mail: rosevine@iamerica.net
www.bbonline.com/tx/rosevine

Rosevine Inn is in the historic Brick Street district. Come rest and relax at Rosevine Inn. Amenities include a lovely courtyard with fountain and fireplace. There are also an outdoor hot tub and game room complete with billiards for guests' enjoyment. There are now two suites available. A full gourmet breakfast is served, and picnic lunches are available. The hosts look forward to meeting guests and welcoming them to the Rose Capital of the World.

7 No smoking; 8 Children welcome; 9 Social drinking allowed; 10 Tennis nearby; 11 Swimming nearby; 12 Golf nearby; 13 Skiing nearby; 14 May be booked through a travel agent; 15 Handicapped accessible.

A picnic lunch is available. Children more than two-years-old welcome.

Hosts: Bert and Rebecca Powell
Rooms: 7 (PB) $85-150
Full Breakfast
Credit Cards: A, B, C, D, E
Notes: 2, 3, 5, 7, 8, 9, 10, 11, 12, 14

## VICTORIA

### *Friendly Oaks Bed & Breakfast*

210 East Juan Linn Street, 77901
(512) 575-0000; e-mail: innkprbill@aol.com
www.bbhost.com/friendlyoaks

In the shelter of ancient live oaks, history comes alive at the Friendly Oaks Bed and Breakfast in a preservation area of 200 restored Victorian homes. Each of four guest rooms has a private bath, its own individual decor reflecting the preservation efforts of Victoria. A conference room provides a quiet setting for retreats, meetings, seminars, parties, showers, and small weddings. Here "Bed means Comfortable, Breakfast means Scrumptious."

Hosts: Bill and Cee Bee McLeod
Rooms: 4 (PB) $55-80
Full Breakfast
Credit Cards: A, B, C, D
Notes: 2, 5, 7, 9, 10, 11, 12, 14, 15

## WACO

### *The Judge Baylor House*

908 Speight Avenue, 76706
(888) JBAYLOR; FAX (817) 756-0711
e-mail: jbaylor@iamerica.net
www.eyeweb.com/jbaylor

Two blocks from Baylor University and its Armstrong Browning Library, five minutes from Waco Convention Center. A two-story red brick home with five spacious and beautifully appointed guest rooms. All have private baths and either king-, queen-size, or twin beds. Sitting in the swing hanging from a large ash tree in the front lawn, playing the grand piano, or enjoying a new book, guests are sure to relax and feel at home.

Hosts: Bruce and Dorothy Dyer
Rooms: 5 (PB) $69-89
Full Breakfast
Credit Cards: A, B, C
Notes: 2, 6, 7, 8, 9, 10, 12, 14, 15

## WAXAHACHIE

### *BonnyNook Inn*

414 West Main Street, 75163
(972) 938-7207

Queen Anne Victorian Painted Lady. Elaborate gardens with a bit of whimsy. Elegant décor but not frilly. Refined furnishings yet comfy. Graceful candlelight table with wholesome food. Friendly hosts with the CVB thrown in. In all, more than a place to rest, relax, and reflect. Old World elegance with 20th-century comforts.

Hosts: Bonnie and Vaughn Franks
Rooms: 5 (PB) $85-115
Full Breakfast
Credit Cards: A, B, C, D, E
Notes: 2, 4, 5, 7, 8, 9, 10, 12, 14

## WIMBERLEY

### *Rancho Cama Bed & Breakfast*

2595 Flite Acres Road, 78676-5706
(512) 847-2596; (800) 594-4501
FAX (512) 847-7135
e-mail: ranchocama@aol.com

NOTES: Credit cards accepted: A MasterCard; B Visa; C American Express; D Discover; E Diner's Club; F Other; 2 Personal checks accepted; 3 Lunch available; 4 Dinner available; 5 Open all year; 6 Pets welcome;

Romantic getaway in charming Guest House. Queen bed, sitting area, electric organ, private bath. Cozy Bunk House comfortably sleeps six, featuring extra-long twin beds, double bed, and bunk beds with shared bath. Both houses have color/cable TV, courtesy telephone, refrigerator, coffee maker, air conditioning, and ceiling fans. Homemade breakfast. Pool, hot tub, swings, rockers. On a miniature horse and donkey ranch, with Nigerian Dwarf Goats, and lots of deer. Live oak setting with unobscured view of the Hill Country.

Rancho Cama

Hosts: Curtis and Nell Cadenhead
Rooms: 3 (1 PB; 2 SB) $70-90
Full Breakfast
Notes: 2, 5, 7, 9, 11, 12

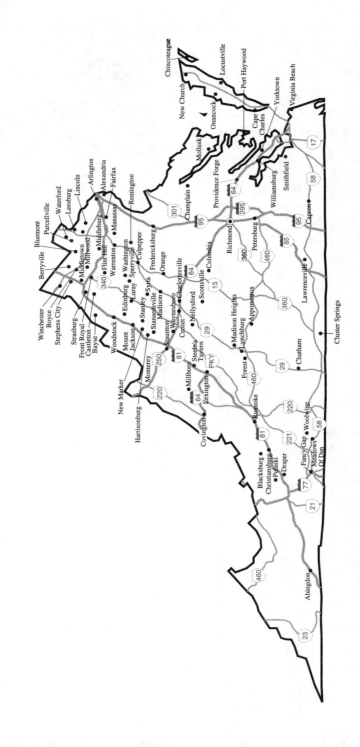

Virginia

# Virginia

Inn on Town Creek

## ABINGDON

## Inn on Town Creek

P.O. Box 1745, 445 East Valley Street, 24212-1745
(540) 628-4560; FAX (540) 628-9611
www.naxs.com/abingdon/innontowncreek/
  index.htm

A historic creek is the theme of this bed and breakfast on four acres of beautifully land-scaped property. Multilevel brick patios and rock gardens provide tranquil privacy; air-conditioned, antique-filled rooms and the cordial-ity of the innkeepers offer a peaceful getaway to the discerning guest. Near fine dining, enter-tainment. Ample parking. Smoking outside. Children 10 and older welcome.

Hosts: Dr. Roger and Linda Neal
Rooms: 5 (4 PB; 1 SB) $100-250
Full Breakfast
Credit Cards: A, B
Notes: 2, 5, 7, 9, 10, 11, 12, 14

## River Garden Bed & Breakfast

19080 North Fork River Road, 24210-4560
(540) 675-0335; (800) 952-4296

River Garden is nestled in the foothills of the Clinch Mountains, on the bank of the north fork of the Holston River outside historic Abingdon. Furnished with traditional, antique, and period furniture, each room has its own riverside deck overlooking the gentle rapids. Private exterior entrance, queen- or king-size bed, full bath, and central heat and air. Guests are also granted kitchen privileges. Common areas include living room, den, dining room, and recreation room.

Hosts: Carol and Bill Crump
Rooms: 4 (PB) $60-70
Full Breakfast
Credit Cards: None
Notes: 2, 5, 7, 9, 11, 12, 14

## Summerfield Inn

101 West Valley Street, 24210
(540) 628-5905; (800) 668-5905;
FAX (540) 628-7515
www.Summerfieldinn.com

Elegant 1920s era home, centrally in Abing-don's historic district, within walking distance of Barter Theatre, Virginia Creeper Trail, restaurants, and fine shops. Enjoy American and European antiques in a quiet and casual atmosphere. Relax in comfortable parlors, library, and large wraparound porch with swing and rockers. Bedrooms are decorated with floral touches, artwork, oriental carpets,

Summerfield Inn

brass- or four-poster beds, antiques, and whirlpool baths. Full breakfast.

Hosts: Janice and Jim Cowan
Rooms: 7 (PB) $90-130
Full Breakfast
Credit Cards: A, B, C, D
Notes: 2, 5, 7, 9, 10, 12, 14, 15

## ALEXANDRIA

### Alexandria and Arlington Bed & Breakfast Network

P.O. Box 25319, 22202-9319
(703) 549-3415; (888) 549-3419
FAX (703) 549-3411; e-mail: aabbn@juno.com

Offering more than 50 private homes, bed and breakfasts, and inns, this network offers something for everyone coming to Washington, D.C., Virginia, and Maryland. Stay in a 1750s Old Town Alexandria townhouse or a glamorous high-rise apartment. Hosts range from retired politicians and admirals to New Age entrepreneurs. All hosts are dedicated to guests' comfort, safety, and enjoyment of a visit in or near Washington, D.C.

Contact: Leslie Garrison
Rooms: 100+ (PB and SB) $60-325
Full and/or Continental Breakfast
Credit Cards: A, B, C
Notes: 2, 5, 6, 8, 9, 10, 11, 12, 14

### Amanda's Bed & Breakfast Reservation Service

3538 Lakeway Drive, Ellicott City, MD 21042-1226
(443) 535-0008; (800) 899-7533
FAX (443) 535-0009; e-mail: AmandasRS@aol.com
www.Amandas-BBRS.com

**150.** In historic Alexandria, a town with an interesting past and current features such as the renovated Torpedo Factory with artist shops and restaurants. The historic buildings and other shops are within easy access. Guests can walk to the Metro with access to Washington, D.C. If driving, there are several areas in the region to tour: Mount Vernon, Arlington Cemetery, and the horse country around Leesburg. Two rooms for bed and breakfast. Two-night minimum. $85-95.

### The Morrison House

116 South Alfred Street, 22314
(703) 838-8000; (800)367-0800
FAX (703) 548-2489
e-mail: mhresrv@morrisonhouse.com
www.morrisonhouse.com

This small boutique Mobil four-star, AAA four-diamond inn, built in the style of an 18th-century manor house, offers 45 elegantly appointed guest rooms, 24-hour butler, concierge and room service, and complimentary Continental breakfast served in the parlor each morning. Home of award-winning Elysium Restaurant. It is hard to imagine that one is only minutes from downtown Washington, D.C., strolling along cobblestone streets to one-of-a-kind shops, local "pubs," and historical landmarks just outside the grand entrance.

Rooms: 45 (PB) $150-295
Continental Breakfast
Credit Cards: A, B, C, E
Notes: 2, 3, 4, 5, 7, 8, 9, 10, 11, 12, 14, 15

NOTES: Credit cards accepted: A MasterCard; B Visa; C American Express; D Discover; E Diner's Club; F Other; 2 Personal checks accepted; 3 Lunch available; 4 Dinner available; 5 Open all year; 6 Pets welcome;

## APPOMATTOX

### The Babcock House Bed & Breakfast Inn

Route 6, Box 1421, 106 Oakleigh Avenue, 24522
(804) 352-7532; (800) 689-6208
FAX (804) 352-5754
e-mail: richguild@earthlink.net
www.babcockhouse.com

A restored turn-of-the-century inn in down-town Appomattox, less than three miles from the famous surrender site which ended the Civil War. The inn has five rooms and one suite. All rooms have private baths, ceiling fans, cable TV, and air conditioning.

Hosts: Debbie Powell, Luella Coleman
Rooms: 6 (PB) $85-110
Full Breakfast
Credit Cards: A, B, C, D
Notes: 2, 3, 4, 5, 7, 8, 9, 10, 12, 14, 15

## ARLINGTON

### The Bed & Breakfast League, Ltd./ Sweet Dreams and Toast, Inc.

P.O. Box 9490, Washington, D.C. 20016-9490
(202) 363-7767; FAX (202) 363-8396
e-mail: bedandbreakfast-washingtondc@erols.com

**298.** A short ride to the Pentagon and Crystal City, this bed and breakfast is in a quiet, secluded area, but has easy access to Washington. Two pretty, antique-filled guest rooms have a double bed or two twin beds, each with a private bath. The hosts offer the use of a computer and fax in their office and, better still, their lovely garden with a pond. She is a costume historian, he a retired military officer; both are widely traveled, very interesting people. Parking is on-street and easy.

Rates: $70-80
Credit Cards: A, B, C, E
Notes: 2, 5, 7, 9

## BASYE

### Sky Chalet Mountain Lodges

P.O. Box 300, 22810
(540) 855-2147; (877) 867-8439
FAX (540) 856-2436
e-mail: skychalet@skychalet.com
www.skychalet.com

Romantic, rustic, mountaintop hideaway in the Shenandoah Valley. The property features spectacular, panoramic mountain and valley views. The Ridge Lodge has individual bed-rooms with private baths. The Treetop Lodge has bedrooms, private baths, living rooms, working fireplaces, decks, and some kitchens. All are welcome: individuals, couples, honey-mooners, families, children, groups, retreats, pets. Continental breakfast delivered to guests. Unique Old World Lodge with unbelievable views for receptions and special events. Hiking, restaurants, resort, attractions, activities, airport nearby. "The Mountain Lovers' Paradise" since 1937.

Hosts: Mona and Ken Seay
Rooms: 10 (PB) $34-79
Continental Breakfast
Credit Cards: A, B, D, E
Notes: 2, 5, 6, 8, 9, 10,11, 12, 13, 14

Sky Chalet Mountain Lodges

## BERRYVILLE

### Berryville Bed & Breakfast

100 Taylor Street, 22611
(540) 955-2200; (800) 826-7520
e-mail: bvillebb@shentel.net

Enjoy the in-town comfort and elegance of the Berryville Bed and Breakfast while exploring

Berryville

the small town of Berryville and Clarke County, in the heart of the Shenandoah Valley. Known for its apple orchards and horse farms, it is a perfect area for unwinding after a hectic week or for celebrating a special occasion. The house, built in 1915, is in the English country style and offers an acre of grounds for guests' enjoyment. The master suite features a fireplace. An abundant breakfast is served to each guest, and Berryville and the surrounding area offer restaurants for other meals to suit every taste and price range. "Come join us and name your pleasure."

Hosts: Don and Jan Riviere
Rooms: 4 (2 PB; 2 SB) $85-145
Full Breakfast
Credit Cards: A, B, C, D
Notes: 2, 5, 7, 9, 12

## *Blue Ridge Bed & Breakfast*

2458 Castleman Road, 22611
(540) 955-1246; (800) 296-1246
FAX (540) 955-4240; e-mail: blurdgbb@shentel.net
www.blueridgebb.com

A Colonial Williamsburg reproduction furnished with lovely antiques; near the Shenandoah River on 11 acres complete with Christmas trees. Perfect getaway; ideal for weekend bikers and hikers. Only 90 minutes from Washington, D.C. $65-100.

## BLACKSBURG

## *L'Arche Bed and Breakfast*

301 Wall Street, 24060
(703) 951-1808

An oasis of tranquility just one block from the Virginia Tech campus, L'Arche Bed and Breakfast is an elegant turn-of-the-century Federal Revival home among terraced gardens in downtown Blacksburg. Spacious rooms have traditional antiques, family heirlooms, handmade quilts, and private baths. Delicious full breakfasts feature homemade breads, cakes, jams, and jellies.

Host: Vera G. Good
Rooms: 5 (PB) $85
Full Breakfast
Credit Cards: A, B
Notes: 2, 5, 10, 12, 13, 15

L'Arche

## BLUEMONT

## *Blue Ridge Bed & Breakfast*

2458 Castleman Road, Berryville, 22611
(540) 955-1246; (800) 296-1246
FAX (540) 955-4240; e-mail: blurdgbb@shentel.net
www.blueridgebb.com

Perfect for hiking the Appalachian Trail or biking. This retreat on the Shenandoah River 50 miles west of Washington D.C., is a restful stopover for a bed and meals. From $30.

NOTES: Credit cards accepted: A MasterCard; B Visa; C American Express; D Discover; E Diner's Club; F Other; 2 Personal checks accepted; 3 Lunch available; 4 Dinner available; 5 Open all year; 6 Pets welcome;

## BOYCE

### Amanda's Bed and Breakfast Reservation Service

3538 Lakeway Drive, Ellicott City, MD 21042-1226
(443) 535-0008; (800) 899-7533
FAX (443) 535-0009; e-mail: AmandasRS@aol.com
www.Amandas-BBRS.com

**333.** Near Winchester and Front Royal at the northern end of Skyline Drive and the Shenandoah Valley. A rural getaway on the river, built in 1780 and 1820. Fireplaces and private baths, lots of books, full breakfast, and scenery. $80-125.

### Blue Ridge Bed & Breakfast

2458 Castleman Road, Berryville, 22611
(540) 955-1246; (800) 296-1246
FAX (540) 955-4240; e-mail: blurdgbb@shentel.net
www.blueridgebb.com

**A.** In the heart of fox hunt country. Lovely modern stone and clapboard house has a true western ranch house feel. Complete fox hunting arrangements available seven days a week for experienced riders, including complete care for horse and tack. Groom quarters available. Indoor ring. In the middle of 60 acres with beautiful views of mountains, a swimming pool, stable house, and kennel. $75-115.

**B.** Historic estate built in 1748 is graced by a lovely English hostess. In the National Register of Historic Places and featured in major books and the *Washington Post*. Over 1,000 spring bulbs, wicker-filled porch, acreage to hike, in-ground pool, and two lakes on property. George Washington really did sleep here, as well as Col. John S. Mosby. $100.

**C.** Beautiful view of the Blue Ridge to enjoy. Guests might even get a ride in a horse and buggy in this farm country. Less than two hours from the nation's capital. $55.

## CAPE CHARLES

### Amanda's Bed & Breakfast Reservation Service

3538 Lakeway Drive, Ellicott City, MD 21042-1226
(443) 535-0008; (800) 899-7533
FAX (443) 535-0009; e-mail: AmandasRS@aol.com
www.Amandas-BBRS.com

**122.** Lovely, quiet, rural setting along the Chesapeake Bay featuring unspoiled land, abundant wildlife, game birds, miles of private beach, and nature's most fabulous sunsets. This two-story brick home has a great view of the bay and is decorated with antiques, reproductions, and collectibles. Four rooms with private baths. Full breakfast. $85.

**138.** Restored 1910 Colonial Revival. Just steps from a public beach on the bay. Relax on one of the porches, sample the cool breezes off the bay, or bike through the historic town. Guests set their own pace to explore. Four guest rooms share two baths. Full breakfast. $75-85.

**183.** Cape Charles is the only public beach in area. This majestic home with a wraparound porch is just a few blocks from the beach. Walk and watch the beautiful sunsets over the bay. The Eastern Shore has a unique natural splendor for guests' enjoyment. In the house, the Corinthian columns form the grand staircase leading to some of the bedrooms. A gourmet breakfast is served in the spacious sun-filled dining room. $80-110.

### Sea Gate Bed & Breakfast

9 Tazewell Avenue, 23310
(757) 331-2206 (phone/FAX)
e-mail: seagate@pilot.infl.net
www.bbhost.com/seagate

In the sleepy town of Cape Charles, closest to the beach on Chesapeake Bay on Virginia's undiscovered Eastern Shore. The day begins with a country breakfast followed by leisure,

---

7 No smoking; 8 Children welcome; 9 Social drinking allowed; 10 Tennis nearby; 11 Swimming nearby; 12 Golf nearby; 13 Skiing nearby; 14 May be booked through a travel agent; 15 Handicapped accessible.

Sea Gate

hiking, bird watching, bathing, or exploring the historic area. Tea prepares guests for the glorious sunsets over the bay. Sea Gate is the perfect place to rest, relax, and recharge—away from the crush of modern America. Winter special available. Two guest rooms have toilet and sink in room and share a bath across the hall. Smoking restricted. Children seven and older welcome.

Host: Chris Bannon
Rooms: 4 (2 PB; 2 SB) $80-90
Full Breakfast
Credit Cards: None
Notes: 2, 5, 10, 11, 12, 14

## Wilson-Lee House Bed & Breakfast

403 Tazewell Avenue, 23310
(757) 331-1WLH (331-1954)
e-mail: WLHBnb@aol.com
www.wilsonleehouse.com

Wilson-Lee House

At the geographic center of historic Cape Charles, Wilson-Lee House is an example of the finest architecture of its time. Built in 1906, this Colonial Revival home is the work of Norfolk architect James W. Lee. A modified four-square house with four rooms per floor, it has been restored to its original elegance and has been configured to accommodate the needs of a late-20th-century bed and breakfast. Six and one-half baths were added for guests' comfort, and the butler's pantry was redesigned with the guests' in mind. The grand foyer with its Ionic colonnade is bright and especially welcoming. The Eastern Shore pace is deliciously slow, and sunsets on the Chesapeake Bay are breathtaking. Come rock on the porch, ride a bicycle built for two, and let the hosts arrange a romantic sunset sail, followed by a relaxing cookout on the deck.

Hosts: David Phillips and Leon Parham
Rooms: 6 (PB) $85-120
Full or Continental Breakfast
Credit Cards: A, B, C
Notes: 2, 5, 7, 9, 10, 11, 12, 14

## CAPRON

## Sandy Hill Farm Bed & Breakfast

11307 Rivers Mill Road, 23829
(804) 658-4381

Enjoy gracious southern hospitality and experience the pleasures of an unspoiled rural setting at this ranch-style farmhouse. Eleven miles from I-95 at exit 20, this working peanut and cotton farm also offers animals to visit and places to stroll in addition to a lighted tennis court on the grounds. Day trips to Williamsburg, Richmond, and Norfolk are within two hours. Fresh fruits and homemade breads are served at breakfast. Open March 25 through December 10. Reservations necessary.

Host: Anne Kitchen
Rooms: 2 (PB) $50
Full Breakfast
Credit Cards: None
Notes: 3, 4, 6, 8, 9, 10

NOTES: Credit cards accepted: A MasterCard; B Visa; C American Express; D Discover; E Diner's Club; F Other; 2 Personal checks accepted; 3 Lunch available; 4 Dinner available; 5 Open all year; 6 Pets welcome;

## CASTLETON

### Blue Ridge Bed & Breakfast

2458 Castleman Road, Berryville, 22611
(540) 955-1246; (800) 296-1246
FAX (540) 955-4240; e-mail: blurdgbb@shentel.net
www.blueridgebb.com

**A.** Fabulous pre-Civil War house built in 1850, in a lovely country setting in the middle of five and one-half acres with small pond. Close to Thornton River, Inn at Little Washington, and Skyline Drive. Lovely mountain views. Two bedrooms and a suite with Jacuzzi are available. $95-125.

## CHAMPLAIN

### Linden House Bed & Breakfast & Plantation

11770 Tidewater Trail, P.O. Box 23, 22438
(804) 443-1170; (800) 622-1202

Stay in one of the top-rated inns in Virginia. Rated A-plus by the ABBA and three diamonds by AAA. The 250-year-old mansion with carriage house is decorated in 18th- century reproductions and antiques. The beautifully landscaped yard and garden with gazebo and arbor provide room to relax and enjoy the quiet and serene setting. Only 45 minutes south of Fredericksburg and 75 minutes north of Williamsburg. The recently completed Linden House Ball Room with large porches and fountain on the patio overlooking the pond.

Hosts: Ken and Sandra Pounsberry
Rooms: 6 (PB) $85-135
Full Breakfast
Credit Cards: A, B, C, D, F
Notes: 2, 4, 5, 7, 8, 9, 11, 12, 14, 15

## CHARLOTTESVILLE

### Clifton–The Country Inn

1296 Clifton Inn Drive, 22947
(804) 971-1800; (888)971-1800

FAX (804) 971-7098; e-mail: reserve@cstone.net
www.cliftoninn.com

A restored 18th-century manor house hotel, built by Thomas Jefferson's son-in-law with 14 antique-appointed rooms and suites, all with wood-burning fireplaces. Outdoor pool, heated spa, and clay tennis court, available on 40 wooded and manicured acres, five miles east of downtown Charlottesville. Clifton offers elegant prix-fixe, impeccable service and an award-winning wine list. Midweek rates and bicentennial packages available year round.

Host: Keith Halford
Rooms: 14 (PB) $165-415
Full and Continental Breakfast
Credit Cards: A, B, C, E, F
Notes: 2, 4, 5, 7, 9, 10, 11, 12, 13, 14, 15

### Guesthouses Bed & Breakfast

P.O. Box 5737, 22905
(804) 979-7264 (12:00-5:00 P.M. weekdays)
FAX (804) 293-7791
e-mail: guesthouses_bnb_reservations@
   compuserve.com
www.va-guesthouses.com

**Afton House.** A mountain retreat with panoramic views east to valleys and hills, this spacious home is on the old road up the mountain pass. There are four bedrooms, mostly furnished with antiques. One has a private adjoining bath, and three share two hall baths. Full breakfast is served. Antique shop on the premises and others in the village. $75-80.

**Alderman House.** This large, formal Georgian home is authentic in style and elegant in decor. It was built by the widow of the first president of the University of Virginia in the early 1900s and is about one mile from the university. Breakfast is served with true southern hospitality. Two guest rooms, each with adjoining private bath. Air conditioning. No smoking in the house. $100.

**Auburn Hill.** An antebellum cottage on a scenic farm that was part of the original

7 No smoking; 8 Children welcome; 9 Social drinking allowed; 10 Tennis nearby; 11 Swimming nearby; 12 Golf nearby; 13 Skiing nearby; 14 May be booked through a travel agent; 15 Handicapped accessible.

Jefferson plantation. The main house was built by Jefferson for one of his overseers. It is convenient to Monticello and Ash Lawn, just six miles east of the city. The cottage has a sitting room with fireplace, sleeper sofa, bedroom with four-poster bed, and connecting bath and shower. Guests may use the pool in summer. Scenic trails, walks, and views. Air conditioning. No smoking. Supplies provided for guests to prepare breakfast. Weekly rates available. $125-150.

**Buck's Elbow Mountain Cottage.** Mountaintop retreat with 360-degree views. Buck's Elbow Mountain is the highest point in Albemarle County and looks down on the Skyline Drive and Appalachian Trail, which run adjacent to the farm. Wake up and see the Valley of Virginia without getting out of bed. The cottage is contemporary with lots of glass, a cathedral ceiling in the living room, full kitchen, two bedrooms, and one and one-half baths, one with a Jacuzzi with views. Two-night minimum stay. Air conditioned. $200.

**Cross Creek.** A spectacular wood, stone, and glass "cottage" on a hilltop nine miles west of Charlottesville, Cross Creek is a perennial favorite. The living room, dining room, half-bath, and kitchen are built around a massive central stone fireplace. A deck provides a wonderful wooded view. Two bedrooms are on the lower level with a full bath across the hall. Air conditioning. Supplies provided for guests to prepare breakfast. $150-200.

**Foxbrook.** This lovely home just blocks north of the bypass is convenient to either downtown or the university area. Guest quarters consist of a sitting room overlooking a lovely garden, a bedroom, and a large bath with separate shower and sunken tub. Full breakfast. Air conditioned. No smoking. $100.

**Indian Springs.** This new cottage with a rustic feel is in a lovely wooded setting on a private lake. The lake is stocked and has a small dock for fishing, basking in the sun, or swimming at guests' own risk. There is a large main room, a sitting area with a sofa bed, dining area, kitchen, and bath. This cottage has complete privacy. TV and air conditioning. Supplies are provided for guests to prepare breakfast. $125-200.

**Ingwood.** In a lovely villa on six wooded acres in one of Charlottesville's most prestigious neighborhoods, Ingwood is an elegant, separate-level suite with its own drive and private entrance. The bedroom is appointed with antiques and has adjoining bath. The sitting room includes a fireplace, pullman kitchen, and sofa for an extra person. A second bedroom with twin beds and private bath is also available. Sliding glass doors open to a secluded terrace with a view of the woods. Air conditioning. Breakfast supplies are left in the suite for guests to prepare. $150-200.

**Ivy Rose Cottage.** An original cypress cottage, handmade by the host, is surrounded by gardens and offers mountain views. The ground floor has a double drawing room, separated by a screen, with a sitting area and a hand-wrought-iron bed. There is a rainforest sunroom with adjoining kitchen and bath with shower. Upstairs is creatively furnished with stained glass and lace curtains. It has heart-pine floors, an antique bed, and a half-bath. The host is a potter and the cottage showcases her work and that of her father, photographer Stan Jorstad. Full breakfast. Gas log stove. Air conditioned. Smoking outside only. $150-200.

**Meadow Run.** Enjoy relaxed rural living in this new Contemporary/Classical home six miles west of Charlottesville. Guest rooms share a bath. Guests are welcome to browse in the boat lover's library, play the grand piano, or lounge in the living room. Many windows offer bucolic vistas of the southwest range. Fireplaces in the kitchen and living room add to the homey, friendly feel. Air conditioning. $80-100.

**Millstream.** A lovely, large house about 20 minutes north of Charlottesville up a long driveway lined with old box bushes. The house, with a brick English basement, was built before the Civil War and enlarged in 1866. There are two guest rooms, each with private bath. Guests may enjoy the fireplace in the library or the mountain views from the living room. Full breakfast. No smoking. Air conditioning. $100.

**Nicola Log Cabin.** This is a romantic 200-year-old log cabin on a 150-acre farm in historic Ivy eight miles west of Charlottesville, with spectacular views of the Blue Ridge Mountains. The one-room cabin has a bedroom, sleeper-sofa, a new bath with shower, microwave oven, refrigerator, and wood-burning stove. Children's playset and tennis court available. Supplies provided for guests to prepare breakfast. $100-150.

**Northfields.** This gracious home is on the northern edge of Charlottesville. The guest room has a TV, private bath, and air conditioning. There is another bedroom available with a double four-poster bed and private hall bath. A full gourmet breakfast is served. No smoking. $68-72.

**Northwood.** This 1920s city house is convenient to the historic downtown area of Charlottesville, only a few blocks from Thomas Jefferson's courthouse and the attractive pedestrian mall with many shops and restaurants. The guest quarters have a private adjoining bath. Many of the furnishings are antique, and next to the bedroom there is a small, comfortable sitting room with TV. Window air conditioning. $68-72.

**Pocahontas.** A large white clapboard house built in the 1920s as a summer retreat in the countryside near Ivy, west of Charlottesville. The large porch and beautiful gardens provide a wonderful place to stop and enjoy life passing by. A large guest room, furnished in Victorian pieces, greets guests with a bright and sunny warmth and offers a private adjoining bath with shower. Other rooms are available for larger groups or families on special weekends. No air conditioning but the house stays cool through the use of attic fans and large, high-ceilinged rooms. $80-100.

**Polaris Farm.** In the middle of rolling farmland dotted with horses and cattle, this architect-designed brick home offers guests an atmosphere of casual elegance. The accommodations consist of a ground-floor room with an adjoining bath, and two upstairs rooms that share a bath. There are gardens and terraces where one can view the Blue Ridge Mountains; a spring-fed pond for swimming, boating, and fishing; miles of trails for walking or horseback riding (mounts available at nearby stables). Air conditioning. $50-100.

**Recoletta.** An older Mediterranean-style house built with flair and imagination. The red tile roof, walled gardens with fountain, and artistic design create the impression of a secluded Italian villa within walking distance of the University of Virginia, shopping, and restaurants. Many of the beautiful antique furnishings are from Central America and Europe. The charming guest room has a beautiful brass bed and a private hall bath with shower. Air conditioning. $80-100.

**The Rectory.** This charming home in a small village five miles west of Charlottesville was a church rectory. It is furnished with lovely antiques and has an English garden in the back. The guest room overlooking the formal rose garden has its own entrance and adjoining full bath. Air conditioning. No smoking allowed. $80-100.

7 No smoking; 8 Children welcome; 9 Social drinking allowed; 10 Tennis nearby; 11 Swimming nearby; 12 Golf nearby; 13 Skiing nearby; 14 May be booked through a travel agent; 15 Handicapped accessible.

**Rolling Acres Farm.** A lovely brick Colonial home in a wooded setting on a small farm, this guest house has two bedrooms with a hall bath upstairs. The house is furnished with many Victorian pieces. No smoking. Air conditioning. $68-72.

**The Rutledge Place.** These hosts are only the third family to own this elegant Virginia farmhouse built around 1840 with magnificent mountain views. The original brick structure has been left intact, adding only a bathroom wing. The guest accommodations are light and airy in the English basement and offer a large bedroom, a sitting room, and a full bath. The home is furnished with antiques from the hosts' family homes in the Valley of Virginia. The suite opens to a brick terrace and gardens facing the mountains. Full breakfast. Air conditioned. No smoking allowed. $125.

**Upstairs Slave Quarters.** A fascinating place to stay if guests want interesting decor with the privacy of their own entrance. There is a harmonious mixture of antiques and art objects. The guest suite consists of a sitting room with a fireplace and two bedrooms with bath (tub only). A sleeper-sofa in the sitting room for extra guests. Adjacent to the University of Virginia and fraternity row, it is especially convenient for university guests. Air conditioning. $120-150.

## High Meadows— Virginia's Vineyard Inn

Highmeadows Lane, Scottsville, 24590
(804) 286-2218; (800) 232-1832
e-mail: peterhmi@aol.com
www.highmeadows.com

Enchanting 19th-century European-style auberge with tastefully appointed spacious guest rooms, private baths, and period antiques. Two-room suites available. Several common rooms, fireplaces, and tranquility. Pastoral setting on 50 acres. Privacy, relaxing walks, and

High Meadows

gourmet picnics. Virginia wine tasting and romantic candlelit dining nightly. Virginia Architectural Landmark. National Register of Historic Places. Two-night minimum stay on weekends and holidays. Closed December 24-25. One room is handicapped accessible.

Hosts: Peter Sushka and Mary Jae Abbitt
Rooms: 14 (PB) $90.52-192.42
Full Breakfast
Credit Cards: A, B, C, D, F
Notes: 2, 4, 6, 7, 8, 9, 10, 11, 12, 13, 14

## The Inn at the Crossroads

5010 Plank Road, P.O. Box 6519, 22906
(804) 979-6452

Listed in the National Register of Historic Places, the inn has been welcoming travelers since 1820. Today it continues this tradition, offering hospitality and comfort reminiscent of a bygone era. On four acres in the foothills of the Blue Ridge Mountains and convenient to

The Inn at the Crossroads

NOTES: Credit cards accepted: A MasterCard; B Visa; C American Express; D Discover; E Diner's Club; F Other; 2 Personal checks accepted; 3 Lunch available; 4 Dinner available; 5 Open all year; 6 Pets welcome;

Charlottesville, Monticello, and the Skyline Drive. Enjoy magnificent panoramic mountain views and a delicious country breakfast served in the keeping room.

Hosts: John and Maureen Deis
Rooms: 5 (PB) $85-115
Cottage: $125
Full Breakfast
Credit Cards: A, B
Notes: 2, 5, 7, 9, 10, 11, 12, 13, 14

The Inn at Monticello

## The Inn at Monticello

Route 20 South, 1188 Scottsville Road, 22902
(804) 979-3593; FAX (804) 296-1344
e-mail: innatmonticello@mindspring.com
www.innatmonticello.com

Just two miles from Jefferson's Monticello, Michie Tavern, and Ash Lawn-Highland, the Inn at Monticello is the perfect place to rest and relax after visiting the historic sites in the area. The 1850 country manor house has five bedrooms, all with private baths, each decorated with antiques and fine reproductions. Each room has a special feature, such as a fireplace, porch, or romantic canopied beds. The comfortable elegance of the inn is enhanced by the gourmet breakfast served each morning, and the Virginia wine tasting offered each afternoon. Limited handicapped accessibility.

Hosts: Norm and Becky Lindway
Rooms: 5 (PB) $125-145
Full Breakfast
Credit Cards: A, B, C
Notes: 2, 5, 7, 9, 10, 12, 13, 14

## The Mark Addy

56 Rodes Farm Drive, Nellysford, 22958
(804) 361-1101; (800) 278-2154
FAX (804) 361-2425
www.synweb.com/rockfish/mark.html

Dr. Everett's "most commanding estate in Nelson County" has been beautifully restored and lovingly appointed. The charming rooms and luxurious suites enjoy magnificent views of the beautiful Blue Ridge. The Mark Addy is between Charlottesville and Wintergreen Resort, to encourage either relaxation or adventure. Be surrounded by 12.5 acres of serenity and the romance of a bygone era. The elegant and imaginative "cuisine de grandmère" will delight all tastes.

Host: John Storck Maddox
Rooms: 9 (PB) $90-135
Full Breakfast
Credit Cards: A, B
Notes: 2, 3, 4, 5, 7, 9, 10, 11, 12, 13, 14, 15

The Mark Addy

## Palmer Country Manor

Route 2, Box 1390, Palmyra, 22963
(804) 589-1300; (800) 253-4306
FAX (804) 589-1716

A gracious 1830 estate on 180 secluded acres, Palmer Country Manor is only minutes from historic Charlottesville; Monticello, Thomas Jefferson's beloved home; Ash Lawn, home of James Monroe; Michie Tavern, one of Virginia's oldest homesteads; and some of Virginia's finest wineries. Come and enjoy one of

7 No smoking; 8 Children welcome; 9 Social drinking allowed; 10 Tennis nearby; 11 Swimming nearby; 12 Golf nearby; 13 Skiing nearby; 14 May be booked through a travel agent; 15 Handicapped accessible.

10 private cottages. Each features a living area with fireplace, color TV, private bath, and a deck. On the grounds, enjoy the swimming pool, five miles of trails, and the fishing pond; use one of the bikes; or take a hot-air balloon ride. Golf is available nearby.

Hosts: Gregory and Kathleen Palmer
Rooms: 12 (10 PB: 2 SB) $77.50-185
Full Breakfast
Credit Cards: A, B, C, D, E
Notes: 2, 3, 4, 5, 8, 9, 11, 12, 14

## CHATHAM

### Eldon—The Inn at Chatham

1037 Chalk Level Road, State Road 685, 24531
(804) 432-0935

Classically restored 1835 historic plantation manor home. One-half mile from Chatham, "Virginia's prettiest town." Four guest rooms, private baths, and full gourmet country breakfast. Formal garden, wooded country setting with original dependencies (smokehouse, ice house, and servants' cottage). In-ground swimming pool, pergola. Intimate gourmet restaurant with a Culinary Institute of America graduate as chef and CHIC graduate as pastry chef. Former home of Virginia's governor and U.S. secretary of the navy, Claude A. Swanson. Member BBAV. Smoking permitted in designated areas only.

Hosts: Joy and Bob Lemm
Rooms: 4 (3 PB; 1 SB) $65-130
Full Breakfast
Credit Cards: A, B
Notes: 2, 4, 5, 7, 9, 10, 11, 12, 14

Eldon

## CHINCOTEAGUE

### Amanda's Bed & Breakfast Reservation Service

3538 Lakeway Drive, Ellicott City, MD 21042-1226
(443) 535-0008; (800) 899-7533
FAX (443) 535-0009; e-mail: AmandasRS@aol.com
www.Amandas-BBRS.com

**362.** Island visitors can enjoy this seaside restored Victorian while sitting on the porch with a cool breeze. The ponies on the island are a must-see along with the many birds and animals at the national wildlife refuge. Rooms are air conditioned should the weather not cooperate. Each room is decorated with antiques, most with private baths. A full breakfast is served as well as afternoon tea. Seasonal rates. $95-135.

**369.** In town but just a short drive or bike ride to the beach and wildlife area. Walk to shops and restaurants. Charming and romantic ambiance. A brick courtyard, fountains, and a rose garden enhance this large shore home. Rooms are furnished with antiques and art from the 18th and 19th centuries. Once two houses now joined to create one rambling bed and breakfast. $90-150.

### Cedar Gables Seaside Inn

6095 Hopkins Lane, P.O. Box 1006, 23336
(757) 336-1096; (888) 491-2944
FAX (757) 336-1291
e-mail: cdrgbl@shore.intercom.net
www.intercom.net/user/cdrgbl

Cedar Gables Seaside Inn is a romantic waterfront bed and breakfast overlooking picturesque Assateague Island. The inn has upscale amenities such as a heated swimming pool, hot tub, dock, secluded shade garden, etc. The rooms all have Jacuzzis, fireplaces, telephones, central heat and air conditioning, TVs, VCRs, exterior and interior entrances, and decks overlooking the water. A must for the discriminating traveler.

NOTES: Credit cards accepted: A MasterCard; B Visa; C American Express; D Discover; E Diner's Club; F Other; 2 Personal checks accepted; 3 Lunch available; 4 Dinner available; 5 Open all year; 6 Pets welcome;

Cedar Gables Seaside Inn

Hosts: Fred and Claudia Greenway
Rooms: 4 (PB) $130-175
Full Breakfast
Credit Cards: A, B, C, D
Notes: 2, 7, 9, 10, 11, 12, 14

## The Channel Bass Inn

6228 Church Street, 23336
(757) 336-6148; (800) 249-0818
FAX (757) 336-0600
www.channelbass-inn.com

This imposing house  was built in 1892 and became the Channel Bass Inn during the 1920s. Today this elegant Chincoteague landmark has six guest rooms, beautifully furnished, spacious, and quiet. Some rooms have view of Chincoteague Bay; all have comfortable sitting areas for reading and relaxing. Afternoon tea, with "world-famous" scones, and a full breakfast included. Close to wildlife refuge and unspoiled beaches of Assateague Island. Bicycles and beach equipment available for guests' use. Mobil two-star rating. Tea room open to public. Nonsmoking. Children eight and older welcome.

Hosts: David and Barbara Wiedenheft
Rooms: 6 (PB) $89-175
Full Breakfast
Credit Cards: A, B, C, D
Notes: 2, 7, 9, 10, 11, 12, 14

## The Garden and the Sea Inn

Virginia Eastern Shore, Route 710
P. O. Box 275, New Church, 23415
(757) 824-0672

Casual elegance and warm hospitality in a charming Victorian inn near Chincoteague and beautiful Assateague wildlife refuges and the beach. Large, luxurious rooms, romantically designed with custom beds, designer fabrics, stained glass, oriental rugs, bay windows, private baths, and skylights. Suites with whirlpools, walk-in showers, and TVs. Hearty Continental breakfast. Romantic, candlelit gourmet dinners created by chef and innkeeper Tom Baker. Patio, gardens, porches. Boating, tennis, and golf nearby. Handicapped suite available. Mobil three-star-rated. Smoking permitted in designated areas only. Children over 12 welcome.

Hosts: Tom and Sara Baker
Rooms: 6 (PB) $75-175
Continental Breakfast
Credit Cards: A, B, C, D
Notes: 2, 4, 6, 9, 10, 11, 12, 14, 15

The Garden and the Sea Inn

## Inn at Poplar Corner

4248 Main Street, 23336
(757) 336-6115; (800) 336-6787
FAX (757) 336-5776

The Inn at Poplar Corner is a romantically decorated Victorian home, with marbletop tables

Inn at Poplar Corner

and dressers, high-back walnut beds, and lace curtains. All guest rooms feature whirlpool tubs and are air conditioned for guests' comfort. After enjoying the free use of bicycles to tour Chincoteague National Wildlife Refuge and beach, guests can enjoy afternoon tea on the wraparound veranda featuring wicker rockers, tables, and chairs. Full breakfast.

Room: 4 (PB) $99-149
Full Breakfast
Credit Cards: A, B
Notes: 2, 7, 9, 10, 11, 12, 14

## Miss Molly's Inn

4141 Main Street, 23336
(757) 336-6686; (800) 221-5620
FAX (757) 336-0600
e-mail: msmolly@shore.intercom.net
www.missmollys-inn.com

Built in 1886, Miss Molly's Inn is a charming Victorian on the bay, two miles from Chincoteague National Wildlife Refuge and five miles from Assateague National Seashore. All rooms are air conditioned and furnished with

Miss Molly's Inn

period antiques. Room rate includes a traditional English afternoon tea (with Barbara's superlative scones) and a full breakfast. Marguerite Henry stayed in this grand old home while writing *Misty of Chincoteague*. Complimentary bicycles and beach equipment. Mobil two-star rating. Nonsmoking. Children eight and older welcome.

Hosts: David and Barbara Wiedenheft
Rooms: 7 (5 PB: 2 SB) $69-155
Full Breakfast
Credit Cards: A, B, C, D
Notes: 2, 7, 9, 10, 11, 12, 14

The Watson House

## The Watson House

4240 North Main Street, 23336
(757) 336-1564; (800) 336-6787
FAX (757) 336-5776

The Watson House has been tastefully restored with Victorian charm. Nestled in the heart of Chincoteague, the home is within walking distance of shops and restaurants. Each room has been comfortably decorated, including air conditioning, private baths, and antiques. A full, hearty breakfast and afternoon tea are served in the dining room or on the veranda. Enjoy free use of bicycles to tour the island. Chincoteague National Wildlife Refuge and its beach are two minutes away, offering nature trails, surf, and Chincoteague's famous wild ponies. AAA-rated three diamonds. Smoking permitted in designated areas only. Inquire about accommodations for children.

NOTES: Credit cards accepted: A MasterCard; B Visa; C American Express; D Discover; E Diner's Club; F Other; 2 Personal checks accepted; 3 Lunch available; 4 Dinner available; 5 Open all year; 6 Pets welcome;

Hosts: David and Jo Anne Snead;
   Tom and Jacque Derrickson
Rooms: 6 (PB) $69-115
Full Breakfast
Credit Cards: A, B
Notes: 2, 7, 9, 10, 11, 12, 14

## CHRISTIANSBURG

Evergreen

## Evergreen—
## The Bell-Capozzi House

201 East Main Street, 24073
(504) 382-7372; (888) 382-7372
FAX (540) 382-0034; www.bnt.com/evergreen

Charming Victorian Inn in Christiansburg's historic East Main Street Area. Close drives to I-81, the Blue Ridge Parkway, Virginia Tech, and Radford University. Five guest rooms and one private cottage. Private baths, air conditioning, Godiva chocolates. library, VIB bears, concert grand piano, traditional southern breakfast: homemade biscuits, country ham, cheese grits, eggs, pancakes, Gevalia coffee and tea. In-ground pool, gazebo, swings, and rocking chairs.

Hosts: Rocco Capozzi and Barbara Bell-Capozzi
Rooms: 5 (PB) $95-135.
Full Breakfast
Credit Cards: A, B, C, D, F
Notes: 2, 5, 7, 9, 11, 12, 14

## The Oaks Victorian Inn

311 East Main Street, 24073
(540) 381-1500; (800) 336-6257
FAX (540) 381-3036; www.bbhost.com/theoaksinn

Award-winning Queen Anne inn, listed in the National Register of Historic Places. Warm hospitality, comfortable, relaxed elegance, and memorable breakfasts are the hallmark of the Oaks. Antique-filled rooms with fireplaces, Jacuzzis, and canopied king- or queen-size beds. Surrounded by lawns, perennial gardens, and 300-year-old oak trees, the inn faces Main Street, once part of the Wilderness Trail blazed by Daniel Boone and Davy Crockett. Near Roanoke and the Blue Ridge Parkway. Mountain winery tours nearby, hiking, bike trails, golf, tennis, fishing, antiquing, and historic sites in the area. AAA four-diamond award for four consecutive years. Member of Independent Innkeepers Associations.

Hosts: Margaret and Tom Ray
Rooms: 7 (PB) $125-160
Full Breakfast
Credit Cards: A, B, C, D
Notes: 2, 5, 7, 9, 10, 12, 14

## CLUSTER SPRINGS

## Oak Grove Plantation

1245 Cluster Springs Road, P.O. Box 45, 24535
(804) 575-7137

Operated from May to September by descendants of the family who built the house in 1820. Full country breakfast in the Victorian dining room. Hiking, biking, bird watching, and wildflower walks on 400 acres of grounds. Near Buggs Island for swimming, boating, and fishing; Danville to tour the last capital of the Confederacy; and Appomattox. One hour

Oak Grove Plantation

7 No smoking; 8 Children welcome; 9 Social drinking allowed; 10 Tennis nearby; 11 Swimming nearby; 12 Golf nearby; 13 Skiing nearby; 14 May be booked through a travel agent; 15 Handicapped accessible.

north of Raleigh-Durham. One handicapped-accessible room.

Host: Pickett Craddock
Rooms: 4 (1 PB; 3 SB) $55-120
Full Breakfast
Credit Cards: None
Notes: 2, 4, 8, 9, 10, 11, 12, 14

## COLUMBIA

### Upper Byrd Farm Bed & Breakfast

6452 River Road West, 23038
(804) 842-2240

A turn-of-the-century farmhouse nestled in the Virginia countryside on 26 acres overlooking the James River. Enjoy fishing or tubing. Canoe rentals available. Visit Ash Lawn and Monticello plantations. See the state's capitol, or simply relax by the fire surrounded by antiques and original art from around the world. Breakfast is special. Children 12 and older welcome. Open on weekends only in winter. Winter Green skiing area is one hour away.

Hosts: Ivona Kaz-Jespen and Maya Laurinaitis
Rooms: 4 (SB) $70
Full Breakfast
Credit Cards: None
Notes: 2, 7, 9, 11, 12, 13

## COVINGTON

### Blue Ridge Bed & Breakfast

2458 Castleman Road, Berryville, 22611
(540) 955-1246; (800) 296-1246
FAX (540) 955-4240; e-mail: blurdgbb@shentel.net
www.blueridgebb.com

**A.** This Gothic mansion, built in 1874 in the Allegheny Mountains, is nestled within 44 acres of fabulous manicured lawns and formal gardens. It has 14 fireplaces. Close to George Washington National Forest and excellent restaurants. Jacuzzi. Full afternoon tea. $75-140.

Milton Hall

### Milton Hall Bed & Breakfast Inn

207 Thorny Lane, 24426
(540) 965-0196; e-mail: milton_h@CFW.com

Milton Hall Bed and Breakfast Inn is a Virginia Historic Landmark, listed in the National Register of Historic Places. This country manor house, built by English nobility in 1874, is on 44 acres adjoining the George Washington National Forest and one mile from I-64, exit 10. Spacious rooms are decorated in the style of the period. All guest rooms have fireplaces and private baths. A full breakfast and afternoon tea are included with a stay.

Hosts: Eric and Suzanne Stratmann;
    George and Pearl Keddie
Rooms: 6 (PB) $85-110
Full Breakfast
Credit Cards: A, B
Notes: 2, 3, 5, 6, 8, 9, 10, 11, 12, 13, 14

## CROZET

### Guesthouses Bed & Breakfast

P.O. Box 5737, 22905
(804) 979-7264 (12:00-5:00 P.M. weekdays)
FAX (804) 293-7791
e-mail: guesthouses_bnb_reservations@
    compuserve.com
www.va-guesthouses.com

**Le Refuge.** About 13 miles west of Charlottesville on Buck's Elbow Mountain, this contemporary home was designed by the architect host. The house has a wonderful relaxed, casual atmosphere and magnificent views. It is near the Appalachian Trail and there are plenty of trails for hiking. The upstairs guest suite has a sitting alcove, private bath, and its own balcony. The downstairs guest room, has views in two directions, comfortable seating, and a private hall bath. Resident canines will greet guests and escort them into a house full of art work, eclectic furnishings. and charm. $100-150.

## CULPEPER

### Fountain Hall Bed & Breakfast

609 South East Street, 22701-3222
(540) 825-8200; (800) 29-VISIT
e-mail: fhbnb@aol.com; www.fountainhall.com

A warm welcome awaits guests. This grand bed and breakfast is highlighted with beautiful antiques, spacious rooms, and formal gardens. Relax on own private porch, stroll the grounds, or curl up with a good book. Enjoy a filling breakfast featuring freshly baked croissants, fresh fruits, yogurt and berries, brewed coffee, and more. Attractions: wineries, hiking, biking, canoeing, museum, battlefields, antique/craft shops, Skyline Drive, Montpelier. Golf courses nearby. Mobil three-star- and AAA three-diamond-rated. BBAV approved. Continental plus breakfast.

Hosts: Steve and Kathi Walker
Rooms: 6 (PB) $95-150

Fountain Hall

Continental Breakfast
Credit Cards: A, B, C, D, E, F
Notes: 2, 5, 7, 12, 13, 14, 15

## DRAPER

### Claytor Lake Homestead Inn

Route 651, Brown Road, Route 1, Box 184 E5, 24324
(540) 980-6777; (800) 676-LAKE

The inn originated as a two-room log cabin over a century ago. The old Doc Brown house was renovated in 1990. The inn has six guest rooms, four overlooking the lake. The inn offers boating, fishing, and summer swimming on its own beach. Rooms are decorated with antiques, reproductions, and period furnishings from the old Hotel Roanoke. A full country breakfast is served in the dining room overlooking the lake. The inn is only a mile from the New River hiking, biking, and horse trail. The Draper golf course is five miles away. There are 550 feet of waterfront with private sand beach, fishing, and boating. Antique shops are nearby in Pulaski.

Rooms: 6 (3 PB: 3 SB) $95
Full Breakfast
Credit Cards: A, B, C, D
Notes: 2, 4, 5, 7, 8, 9, 11, 12, 13, 14, 15

## EDINBURG

### Edinburg Inn Bed & Breakfast, Ltd.

218 South Main Street, 22824
(540) 984-8286

This circa 1850 Victorian home is in the heart of the Shenandoah Valley on the edge of town next to Stoney Creek and the historic Edinburg Mill. The inn is reminiscent of Grandma's country home, with a full country breakfast which includes homemade breads and muffins, local country eggs, bacon and sausage. Game room with board games, new and vintage magazines and books, TV, VCR, and video library. Enjoy outdoor games on spacious grounds and

Edinburg Inn

wraparound porch with swing, rockers, and wicker. Walk to nearby restaurant and antique and craft shops. Short drive to caverns, battlefields, fishing, hiking, canoeing, horseback riding, and vineyards. Reservations appreciated.

Hosts: Judy and Clyde Beachy
Rooms: 3 (PB) $75
Full Breakfast
Credit Cards: None
Notes: 2, 5, 7, 8, 9, 10, 11, 12, 13

## FAIRFAX

### The Bailiwick Inn

4023 Chain Bridge Road, 22030
(703) 691-2266; (800) 366-7666
www.bailiwickinn.com

In the heart of the historic city of Fairfax, 15 miles west of the nation's capital. George

The Bailiwick Inn

Mason University is just down the street, and Mount Vernon and Civil War battlefields are nearby. In the National Register of Historic Places. Fourteen rooms with queen-size feather beds and private baths, fireplaces, Jacuzzis, and bridal suite. Afternoon tea. Candlelight dinner served by reservation. Small meetings and weddings.

Hosts: Annette and Bob Bradley
Rooms: 14 (PB) $135-309
Full Breakfast
Credit Cards: A, B, C
Notes: 2, 4, 5, 7, 8, 12, 14

## FANCY GAP

### The Doe Run at Groundhog Mountain

Mile Post 189 Blue Ridge Parkway, 24328
(540) 398-2212; (800) 325-6189
FAX (540) 398-2833; FAX (540) 398-3050
e-mail: doerun@tcia.net; www.doerunlodge.com

Romantic getaways, family vacations, business retreats, breathtaking views, quiet pastoral setting. Two-bedroom mountainside chalets with equipped kitchens. Full service restaurant and bar (in season.) Live weekend entertainment (in season.) Three miles from historic Mabry Mill. Heated pool, hiking trails, stocked fish pond, three lit tennis courts, and meeting facilities. Jacuzzis and hot tubs. TV/VCR and fireplace. Reduced rates and services January through March.

Rooms: 100 (PB) $109-260
Continental and Full Breakfast
Credit Cards: A, B, C
Notes: 2, 3, 4, 5, 6, 7, 8, 9, 10, 11, 12, 14

## FLINT HILL

### Blue Ridge Bed & Breakfast

2458 Castleman Road, Berryville, 22611
(540) 955-1246; (800) 296-1246
FAX (540) 955-4240; e-mail: blurdgbb@shentel.net
www.blueridgebb.com

NOTES: Credit cards accepted: A MasterCard; B Visa; C American Express; D Discover; E Diner's Club; F Other; 2 Personal checks accepted; 3 Lunch available; 4 Dinner available; 5 Open all year; 6 Pets welcome;

**A.** Lovely stone home built in 1812 with working fireplaces in bedrooms; a working cattle farm adjacent to Shenandoah National Park. With Virginia's Blue Ridge Mountains in the background, this inn offers guests a beautiful setting. Scenic pasture lands are surrounded by stone fences. Close to Inn at Little Washington and Old Rag Mountain. Hot tub. $100-140.

## FOREST

### Blue Ridge Bed & Breakfast

2458 Castleman Road, Berryville, 22611
(540) 955-1246; (800) 296-1246
FAX (540) 955-4240; e-mail: blurdgbb@shentel.net
www.blueridgebb.com

**A.** This summer kitchen has been converted to a lovely private cottage. The main mansion was built in 1830. It is in the middle of 600 acres. It has a private Jacuzzi and fireplace. Hostess gives private tours. Close to Thomas Jefferson's birthplace, Peaks of Otter, Blue Ridge Parkway, and Smith Mountain Lake. $135-170.

## FREDERICKSBURG

### Amanda's Bed & Breakfast Reservation Service

3538 Lakeway Drive, Ellicott City, MD 21042-1226
(443) 535-0008; (800) 899-7533
FAX (443) 535-0009; e-mail: AmandasRS@aol.com
www.Amandas-BBRS.com

**310.** Combine a visit to the Civil War sites between Antietam-Gettysburg and Fredericksburg. A Classical Revival-style home with high ceilings, wide heart-pine floors, acorn and oak leaf moldings, and a two-story front portico. On 10 acres of grounds filled with a fine balance of mature trees and a pond. Two rooms, each with a private bath. Full breakfast served. $105.

### Fredericksburg Colonial Inn

1707 Princess Anne Street, 22401
(540) 371-5666

A restored country inn in the historic district, 32 antique-appointed rooms with private baths, telephones, TVs, refrigerators, and Civil War motif. More than 200 antique dealers, 20 major tourist attractions, and battlefields. Less than one hour from Washington, D.C., Richmond, and Charlottesville. A great getaway. Suites and family rooms available. Wonderful restaurants within walking distance. A nonsmoking facility. Olde Town within walking distance.

Hosts: Brenda Price, Sherrie Beach, and Christine
 Goldsmith
Rooms: 32 (PB) $59-89
Continental Breakfast
Credit Cards: A, B, C
Notes: 5, 7, 15

### La Vista Plantation

4420 Guinea Station Road, 22408
(540) 898-8444; (800) 529-2823
e-mail: lavistabb@aol.com
www.bbonline.com/va/lavista/

This lovely 1838 Classical Revival home is just outside historic Fredericksburg. On 10 quiet acres, the grounds present a fine balance of mature trees, flow-ers, shrubs, and farm fields. The pond is stocked with bass. Choose from a spacious two-bedroom apartment that sleeps six with a kitchen and a fireplace, or a formal room with a king-size mahogany rice-carved four-poster bed, fireplace, and Empire furniture. Homemade jams and farm-fresh eggs for breakfast.

Hosts: Michele and Edward Schiesser
Rooms: 1 (PB) $105
Apartment: 1
Full Breakfast
Credit Cards: A, B
Notes: 2, 5, 7, 8, 9, 10, 12, 14

7 No smoking; 8 Children welcome; 9 Social drinking allowed; 10 Tennis nearby; 11 Swimming nearby; 12 Golf nearby; 13 Skiing nearby; 14 May be booked through a travel agent; 15 Handicapped accessible.

## FRONT ROYAL

### Chester House

43 Chester Street, 22630
(540) 635-3937; (800) 621-0441
FAX (540) 636-8695; www.chesterhouse.com

A stately Georgian mansion with extensive formal gardens on two acres in Front Royal's historic district. Quiet, relaxed atmosphere in elegant surroundings, often described as an oasis in the heart of town. Easy walking distance to antique and gift shops and historic attractions; a short drive to Skyline Caverns, Skyline Drive, Shenandoah River, golf, tennis, hiking, skiing, horseback riding, fine wineries, and excellent restaurants.

Hosts: Bill and Ann Wilson
Rooms: 7 (5 PB; 2 SB) $65-190
Continental Breakfast
Credit Cards: A, B, C
Notes: 2, 5, 9, 10, 11, 12, 14

### Killahevlin

1401 North Royal Avenue, 22630
(540) 636-7335; (800) 847-6132
FAX (540) 636-8694; e-mail: kllhvln@shentel.net
www.vairish.com

Historic Edwardian mansion with spectacular views. Spacious bedrooms, professionally designed and restored with working fireplaces,

Killahevlin

private baths, and whirlpool tubs. Private Irish pub for guests. Complimentary beer and wine. Close to Skyline Drive, Shenandoah National Park, hiking, golf, tennis, canoeing, horseback riding, antiquing, fine dining, wineries, and live theater. Property was built in 1905 for William E. Carson, father of Skyline Drive. National Register of Historic Places and Virginia landmarks register.

Hosts: Susan O'Kelly-Lang
Rooms: 6 (PB) $125-225
Full Breakfast
Credit Cards: A, B, C, D, E, F
Notes: 2, 5, 7, 9, 10, 11, 12, 14

## HARRISONBURG

### Blue Ridge Bed & Breakfast

2458 Castleman Road, Berryville, 22611
(540) 955-1246; (800) 296-1246
FAX (540) 955-4240; e-mail: blurdgbb@shentel.net
www.blueridgebb.com

**A.** Ten miles west of Harrisonburg off Route 33. Beautiful seven and-a-half-acre estate close to George Washington National Forest. Huge boxwoods with lots of tunnels, terrace, patios, and gazebo; built in 1925 out of matched river rock. There are 128 varieties of wildflowers as well as hiking trails and stocked trout streams. Full breakfast. $65 and up.

### Kingsway Bed & Breakfast

3955 Singers Glen Road, 22802
(540) 867-9696

In this private home enjoy the warm hospitality, carpentry, and homemaking skills of your hosts who make guests' comfort their priority. This ranch-style home is in a rural area of the beautiful Shenandoah Valley, just four and one-half miles from downtown. On the mountains to the east, drive the scenic Skyline Drive, visit the caverns, historic Monticello, New Market battlefield, Natural Bridge, antique shops, flea markets, and Valley Mall. Inquire about accommodations for pets. In-ground pool.

NOTES: Credit cards accepted: A MasterCard; B Visa; C American Express; D Discover; E Diner's Club; F Other; 2 Personal checks accepted; 3 Lunch available; 4 Dinner available; 5 Open all year; 6 Pets welcome;

Hosts: Chester and Verna Leaman
Rooms: 2 (PB) $60-65
Full Breakfast
Credit Cards: B
Notes: 2, 5, 6, 7, 8, 11, 12, 13, 14

## LAWRENCEVILLE

### Blue Ridge Bed & Breakfast

2458 Castleman Road, Berryville, 22611
(540) 955-1246; (800) 296-1246
FAX (540) 955-4240; e-mail: blurdgbb@shentel.net
www.blueridgebb.com

**A.** Built in 1785, this mansion is filled with all-period antiques. Ideal location between I-85 and I-95. On 27 acres, close to Fort Christina, Civil War battlefield, many Civil War re-enactments, horse racing, and charter fishing on Lake Gaston. Also has two cabins on property complete with fireplaces and small kitchens. Full country breakfasts; will also do dinners and weddings. $95-125.

## LEESBURG

### The Norris House Inn & Stonehouse Tea Room

108 Loudoun Street, SW, 20175-2909
(703) 777-1806; (800) 644-1806
FAX (703) 771-8051; e-mail: inn@norrishouse.com
www.norrishouse.com

The Norris House Inn

Elegant accommodations in the heart of historic Leesburg. The six charming guest rooms are all furnished with antiques, and three of the rooms have working fireplaces. Full country breakfasts served and evening libations served. Convenient in-town location with several restaurants nearby. Only one hour's drive to Washington, D.C. In the heart of the Virginia hunt country, rich in colonial and Civil War history. Lots of antiquing and wineries. The perfect place for special romantic getaways, small meetings, and weddings. The inn is open daily by reservation. Children over 12 are welcome.

Hosts: Pam and Don McMurray
Rooms: 6 (SB) $95-140
Full Breakfast
Credit Cards: A, B, C, D, E, F
Notes: 2, 5, 7, 9, 10, 11, 12, 14

## LEXINGTON

### Applewood Inn

Buffalo Bend Road, P.O. Box 1348, 24450
(540) 463-1962; (800) 463-1902
e-mail: applewd@cfw.com
www.applewoodbb.com

Spectacular passive solar country retreat on 35 hilltop acres between the Shenandoah Valley's historic Lexington and Natural Bridge with views of the Blue Ridge Mountains. Romantics and nature lovers alike enjoy the huge porches, quilt-covered queen-size beds, private baths, hot tub, hiking trails, picnic llama treks, poolside barbecues, and hearty whole-grain country breakfasts. Nearby are museums, Washington and Lee University, Virginia Military Institute, the Virginia Horse Center, summer theater, and wonderful scenic back roads.

Hosts: Linda and Chris Best
Rooms: 4 (PB) $80-129
Full Breakfast
Credit Cards: A, B, C
Notes: 2, 5, 6, 7, 8, 11, 12, 15

---

7 No smoking; 8 Children welcome; 9 Social drinking allowed; 10 Tennis nearby; 11 Swimming nearby; 12 Golf nearby; 13 Skiing nearby; 14 May be booked through a travel agent; 15 Handicapped accessible.

## A Bed & Breakfast at Llewellyn Lodge

603 South Main Street, 24450
(540) 463-3235; (800) 882-1145
e-mail: LLL@rockbridge.net; www.LLodge.com

The great in-town location of this charming Colonial, combined with the warm and friendly atmosphere, makes it the perfect home base for exploring this historic town. Ellen and John are "personalized guidebooks" in helping guests get the most out of their visit. Refreshments are served upon arrival and guests receive lots of advice on hiking, cycling, fly-fishing, golf, and other outdoor activities. A full breakfast is served including Belgian waffles, Ellen's special omelets, meats, and homemade muffins. The decor combines traditional with antique furnishings. Walking distance to Lee Chapel, Stonewall Jackson House, Washington and Lee University, and Virginia Military Institute.

Hosts: Ellen and John Roberts
Rooms: 6 (PB) $65-98
Full Breakfast
Credit Cards: A, B, C, D
Notes: 2, 5, 7, 9, 10, 11, 12, 14

## Historic Country Inns

11 North Main Street, 24450
(877) 463-2044; FAX (540) 463-7262

Three historic homes restored and furnished with antiques, paintings, and amenities. In center of historic district are Alexander-Withrow, circa 1789, and McCampbell Inn, circa 1809. Museums, shops, Virginia Military Institute, and Washington and Lee University within walking distance. Maple Hall, circa 1850, six miles north of Lexington at the intersection of I-81 and Route 11, offers tennis, swimming, fishing, trails, and working fireplaces. Nightly dining for inn guests and public. Smoking permitted in designated areas only. Limited handicapped accessible.

Hosts: Don Fredenburg (innkeeper);
   Meredith Family (owners)
Rooms: 44 (PB)
Continental Breakfast
Credit Cards: A, B
Notes: 2, 4, 5, 8, 9, 10, 11, 14

The Hummingbird Inn

## The Hummingbird Inn

30 Wood Lane, P.O.Box 147, Goshen, 24439
(540) 997-9065; (800) 397-3214
e-mail: hmgbird@cfw.com
www.hummingbirdinn.com

On a tranquil acre of landscaped grounds, the Hummingbird Inn, a unique carpenter Gothic villa, offers accommodations in an early Victorian setting. Comfortable rooms are furnished with antiques and combine an old-fashioned ambiance with modern convenience. Some have whirlpool tubs and fireplaces. Architectural features include wraparound verandas on the first and second floors, original pine floors of varying widths, a charming rustic den dating from the early 1800s, and a solarium. A wide trout stream defines one of the property lines, and the old red barn was once the town livery. Full breakfasts include unique area recipes.

Hosts: Diana and Jerry Robinson
Rooms: 5 (PB) $85-135
Full Breakfast
Credit Cards: A, B, C, D
Notes: 2, 4, 5, 6, 7, 9, 13, 14

---

NOTES: Credit cards accepted: A MasterCard; B Visa; C American Express; D Discover; E Diner's Club; F Other; 2 Personal checks accepted; 3 Lunch available; 4 Dinner available; 5 Open all year; 6 Pets welcome;

Steeles Tavern Manor

## Steeles Tavern Manor Country Inn

P.O. Box 39, Highway 11, 24476
(540) 377-6444; (800) 743-8666
FAX (540) 377-5937; www.steelestavern.com

WDBJ7-TV "A place that specializes in putting the romance back into a relationship." Find romance at the Manor. Guests are spoiled with flowers, afternoon teas, candlelight dinners, as well as sumptuous breakfasts in bed or in the dining room. Languish in a guest room with double Jacuzzis, fireplaces, TV/VCRs. Hike the 55 acres with fishing pond, falls, and panorama of the Blue Ridge Parkway, winery, and much more.

Host: Eileen Hoernlein
Rooms: 5 (PB) $120-185
Full Breakfast
Credit Cards: A, B, D
Notes: 2, 4, 5, 7, 9, 12, 13, 14

## Stoneridge Bed & Breakfast

Stoneridge Lane, P.O. Box 38, 24450
(540) 463-4090; (800) 491-2930
FAX (540) 463-6078
www.webfeat-inc.com/stoneridge

Get reacquainted at this romantic 1829 antebellum home on 36 secluded acres. Five guest rooms with private baths, ceiling fans, and queen-size beds, some featuring private balconies, double Jacuzzis, and fireplaces. Relax on the large front porch and enjoy the sunset over Short Hills Mountains. Virginia wines are available and a gourmet country breakfast is served in the candlelit dining room or on the back patio. Central air conditioning. Just five minutes south of historic Lexington.

Hosts: Norm and Barbara Rollenhagen
Rooms: 5 (PB) $95-160
Full Breakfast
Credit Cards: A, B, C, D
Notes: 2, 5, 7, 8, 9, 14

## LINCOLN

## Springdale Country Inn

Lincoln, 20160 (mailing)
18348 Lincoln Road, Purcellville, 20132 (location)
(540) 338-1832; (800) 388-1832
FAX (540) 338-1839

Restored historic landmark 45 miles west of Washington, D.C., on six acres of secluded terrain with babbling brooks, foot bridges, and terraced gardens. Meal service for groups, e.g. weddings; breakfast included in room price. Fully air conditioned. New heating system and seven fireplaces.

Hosts: Nancy and Roger Fones
Rooms: 9 (6 PB; 3 SB) $95-200
Full Breakfast
Credit Cards: A, B, D
Notes: 2, 5, 7, 8, 9, 10, 11, 12, 14, 15

## LOCUSTVILLE

## Amanda's Bed & Breakfast Reservation Service

3538 Lakeway Drive, Ellicott City, MD 21042-1226
(443) 535-0008; (800) 899-7533
FAX (443) 535-0009; e-mail: AmandasRS@aol.com
www.Amandas-BBRS.com

**143.** This 18th-century Colonial is near Wachapreague and just one mile from the ocean. Quiet and comfortable. Water sports nearby. One room with private bath. Continental breakfast. $95.

7 No smoking; 8 Children welcome; 9 Social drinking allowed: 10 Tennis nearby; 11 Swimming nearby; 12 Golf nearby; 13 Skiing nearby; 14 May be booked through a travel agent; 15 Handicapped accessible.

## LURAY

### Blue Ridge Bed & Breakfast

2458 Castleman Road, Berryville, 22611
(540) 955-1246; (800) 296-1246
FAX (540) 955-4240; e-mail: blurdgbb@shentel.net
www.blueridgebb.com

**A.** Fabulous mansion built in 1739. Eighteen acres with ponds, in-ground pool, great mountain views, antique furnishings. Two separate cottages also available. $90-150.

**B.** Large Victorian house with each room providing a private bath and fireplace. Jacuzzi. Bikes and canoes provided. Complete with resident ghost. Full country breakfast and afternoon buffet provided for guests. Mystery weekends available. $98-145.

**C.** Built in 1931, this grand old inn rests on 14 acres of lawn and formal gardens, delighting its guests with a colonial dining room offering traditional menu. A gallery features the art of P. Buckley Moss, who is often a guest at the inn. The Gilded Cage, specializing in antiques and fine art restoration, is on the lower level. Single, double, and family units available. Also suites with private parlors. This inn boasts a banquet room that will accommodate up to 200 people. A solarium and terrace overlook the formal gardens. Eleanor Roosevelt was an honored guest at this inn. Jacuzzi available. $54-124.

### Locust Grove Inn

1456 North Egypt Bend Road, 22835
(540) 743-1804; FAX (540) 843-0751
e-mail: locustg@shentel.net
www.bbonline.com/va/locustgrove/

A time away, a place away—here mountains end, a valley starts, a river runs by. Unforgettable scenery and centuries of history make this restored colonial log house on a large farm a piece of paradise for history and nature lovers.

Five spacious bedrooms, all with private bathrooms, central air conditioning, and beautiful views. Three miles west of Luray on the Shenandoah River. One mile of Shenandoah riverfront.

Hosts: Rod and Isabel Graves
Rooms: 5 (PB) $110-125
Full Breakfast
Credit Cards: A, B, D
Notes: 2, 5, 7, 8, 9, 10, 11, 12, 13, 14

The Woodruff House

### The Woodruff House Bed & Breakfast

330 Mechanic Street, 22835
(540) 743-1494

This 1882 fairy-tale Victorian is beautifully appointed with period antiques, hallmarked silver, and fine china. Each room includes working fireplace and private bathroom. Some rooms have Jacuzzis for two. Escape from reality, come into this fairytale where the ambiance never ends! Awaken to freshly brewed coffees delivered to guests' doors; a gourmet candlelit breakfast follows. Sumptuous candlelit high tea buffet dinner included. Relax in the fireside candlelit garden spa. AAA three-diamond-rated. Mobil three-star. Chef owned and operated *Intimate Weddings and Honeymoons* Inquire about accommodations for children.

Hosts: Lucas and Deborah Woodruff
Rooms: 6 (PB) $98-195
Full Breakfast
Credit Cards: A, B, D
Notes: 2, 4, 5, 7, 9, 10, 11, 12, 13, 14

---

NOTES: Credit cards accepted: A MasterCard; B Visa; C American Express; D Discover; E Diner's Club; F Other; 2 Personal checks accepted; 3 Lunch available; 4 Dinner available; 5 Open all year; 6 Pets welcome;

# LYNCHBURG

## Blue Ridge Bed & Breakfast

2458 Castleman Road, Berryville, 22611
(540) 955-1246; (800) 296-1246
FAX (540) 955-4240; e-mail: blurdgbb@shentel.net
www.blueridgebb.com

**A.** Built in 1874, this fabulous Victorian home is in the National Register of Historic Places and has received the Merit Award from the Lynchburg Historic Association for outstanding exterior renovation. Near Blue Ridge Parkway and Appomatox. $65-109.

**B.** This fabulous house is on a very quiet acre of land. Beautifully landscaped. Both host and hostess are interior decorators. House filled with antiques and reproductions. It is close to many colleges and universities, the entrance to the Blue Ridge Parkway, Wintergreen skiing, and Walton's Mountain. $65-85.

## Federal Crest Inn Bed & Breakfast

1101 Federal Street, 24504
(804) 845-6155; (800) 818-6155
FAX (804) 845-1445
www.inmind.com/federalcrest

Relax and unwind in this elegant 1909 Georgian Revival brick home in a historical district.

Federal Crest Inn

Enjoy unique woodwork, bedroom fireplaces, central air, down comforters, whirlpool tub, canopied queen-size beds, 1950s café, gift shop, antiques, country breakfasts, friendly hosts, and much more. Perhaps there might even be a special invitation to visit the third-floor theater where the original owner built a stage for his children to give plays. Convenient to Jefferson's Poplar Forest and Appomatox.

Hosts: Ann and Phil Ripley
Rooms: 5 (4 PB; 1 SB) $85-125
Full Breakfast
Credit Cards: A, B, C, D
Notes: 2, 5, 7, 9, 12, 13, 14

Lynchburg Mansion Inn

## Lynchburg Mansion Inn Bed & Breakfast

405 Madison Street, 24504
(804) 528-5400; (800) 352-1199
FAX (804) 847-2545; e-mail: Mansioninn@aol.com
www.Lynchburgmansioninn.com

Enjoy luxurious accommodations in a 9,000-square-foot Spanish Georgian mansion on a street still paved in turn-of-the-century brick in a national register historic district. Highly rated inn, known for attention to detail. Remarkable interior cherry woodwork. King- and queen-size beds, lavish linens, private bathrooms, fireplaces, TV, telephones, turn-down with chocolates. Full silver service breakfast. Hot tub. Suites. Well-supervised children welcome. Near

7 No smoking; 8 Children welcome; 9 Social drinking allowed; 10 Tennis nearby; 11 Swimming nearby; 12 Golf nearby; 13 Skiing nearby; 14 May be booked through a travel agent; 15 Handicapped accessible.

Appomattox, Jefferson's Poplar Forest, summer baseball, Blue Ridge, antiquing, colleges.

Hosts: Bob and Mauranna Sherman
Rooms: 5 (PB) $109-144
Full Breakfast
Credit Cards: A, B, C, E
Notes: 2, 5, 7, 8, 9, 10, 11, 12, 14

## MADISON

### Guesthouses Bed & Breakfast

P.O. Box 5737, Charlottesville, 22905
(804) 979-7264 (12:00-5:00 P.M. weekdays)
FAX (804) 293-7791
e-mail: guesthouses_bnb_reservations@
    compuserve.com
www.va-guesthouses.com

**Laurel Run.** A recently built cottage in the woods of Madison County, 30 miles north of Charlottesville. This private cabin offers a great room, kitchen, dining area, and two bedrooms on the first floor. The loft has a double bed and cot. The broad, screened porch offers views of a stream, fields, and woods. Hiking, fishing, and riding are available in nearby Shenandoah National Park. Breakfast supplies are included for the first morning of guests' stay. $100-200.

## MADISON HEIGHTS

### Blue Ridge Bed & Breakfast

2458 Castleman Road, Berryville, 22611
(540) 955-1246; (800) 296-1246
FAX (540) 955-4240; e-mail: blurdgbb@shentel.net
www.blueridgebb.com

**A.** This 80-year-old grand southern Colonial mansion is in the middle of 14 acres with fabulous views of Blue Ridge Parkway. Fishing on the James River. Near Appomatox. $69-85.

## MANASSAS

### Blue Ridge Bed & Breakfast

2458 Castleman Road, Berryville, 22611
(540) 955-1246; (800) 296-1246
FAX (540) 955-4240; e-mail: blurdgbb@shentel.net
www.blueridgebb.com

**A.** In Manassas battlefields, this beautiful restored farmhouse was built upon General McDowell's campsite. Just five miles from I-66 and 35 minutes from Washington, D.C. Antiques, fireplaces, stone walls, barn livestock, and old gas lamps throughout make this a special treat. $88-100.

## MEADOWS OF DAN

### Meadowood Bed & Breakfast

6235 Buffalo Mountain Road, SW, 24120
(540) 593-2600; FAX (540) 593-2700

Meadowood is just a short 1,000 feet off the Blue Ridge Parkway (near milepost 174) on 20 beautiful acres of fields and woods with views of the surrounding mountains. Peaceful and quiet, yet only two and one-half miles from the Chateau Morrisette Winery and two miles from famous Mabry Mill. Old split rail fences, spring-fed streams, park benches, and walking trails abound. A 60-foot front porch looks out over the fields and mountains. Large gathering room with library and warm woodstove is provided. Reservations are suggested. "Just what a

Meadowood

bed and breakfast should be"—*Blue Ridge Country.* "Delightful bed and breakfast just off the Blue Ridge Parkway"—*LA Times.* Children over 12 welcome.

Hosts: Frank and Leona Warren
Rooms: 4-5 (4 PB; 1-2 SB) $75-95
Full Breakfast
Credit Cards: None
Notes: 2, 5, 7, 9, 10, 12

## Spangler's Bed & Breakfast

1340 Mayberry Church Road, 24120-9523
(703) 952-2454

On Country Road 602 within view of the Blue Ridge Parkway at milepost 180, four miles from Mabry Mill, this 1904 farmhouse has a kitchen with fireplace, piano, and four porches. There is also an 1826 private log cabin perfect for one couple. An additional 1987 log cabin has two bedrooms, complete kitchen, and wraparound porch. Fishing in the lake, swimming, three boats, bikes, and volleyball. No smoking inside. No pets.

Hosts: Martha and Harold Spangler
Rooms: 7 (2 PB; 5 SB) $50-60
Full Breakfast
Credit Cards: None
Notes: 2, 7, 8, 9, 10, 11, 12

## MIDDLEBURG

## Blue Ridge Bed & Breakfast

2458 Castleman Road, Berryville, 22611
(540) 955-1246; (800) 296-1246
FAX (540) 955-4240; e-mail: blurdgbb@shentel.net
www.blueridgebb.com

**A.** Two-hundred-year-old cozy commercial inn in the heart of Middleburg with working fireplaces in all bedrooms. Complete facilities for dinner. Accessible to quaint shops and eateries. $95-275.

## The Longbarn

37129 Adams Green Lane, P.O. Box 208, 20118-0208
(540) 687-4137; FAX (504) 687-4044
e-mail: thlongbarn@aol.com
http://member.aol.com/thlongbarn/

Century-old renovated barn in historic Middleburg, VA, surrounded by beautiful woods; European-style garden; swimming, horseback and bicycle riding nearby; golf course available. Air conditioning, fireplaces, and large library for guests' pleasure and comfort. Elegant ambiance in Italian country style; spacious bedrooms with private bath. Delicious breakfast with warm breads and other specialties from Europe. For guests' safety, no indoor smoking.

Host: Chiara Langeley
Rooms: 3 (PB) $105-125
Full Breakfast
Credit Cards: A, B, F
Notes: 2, 5, 7, 9, 10, 11, 12, 14

## MIDDLETOWN

## Blue Ridge Bed & Breakfast

2458 Castleman Road, Berryville, 22611
(540) 955-1246; (800) 296-1246
FAX (540) 955-4240; e-mail: blurdgbb@shentel.net
www.blueridgebb.com

**A.** Historic Victorian home on Main Street close to famous restaurant and theatre. All period furniture. Minutes from many antique shops, Passion play, and small lake with beach. $65.

## Wayside Inn

7783 Main Street, 22645
(877) 869-1797; (540) 869-1797
FAX (540) 869-6038
e-mail: waysiden@shentel.net

The Wayside Inn is an elegantly restored 18th-century inn nestled in the Shenandoah Valley, exit 302 off of I-81. The inn features period furnishings, rare antiques, and an extensive collection of Americana. There are 22 unique

7 No smoking; 8 Children welcome; 9 Social drinking allowed; 10 Tennis nearby; 11 Swimming nearby; 12 Golf nearby; 13 Skiing nearby; 14 May be booked through a travel agent; 15 Handicapped accessible.

Wayside Inn

guest rooms and suites with private baths, and eight charming dining rooms that feature authentic regional American cuisine. Hiking, swimming, fishing, boating, golfing, skiing, and the Wayside Theatre are all nearby. Small pets welcome.

Rooms: 22 (PB) $110-160
Full Breakfast
Credit Cards: A, B, C, D, E
Notes: 3, 4, 5, 6, 7, 8, 9, 10, 11, 12, 13, 14

## MILLWOOD

### Blue Ridge Bed & Breakfast

2458 Castleman Road, Berryville, 22611
(540) 955-1246; (800) 296-1246
FAX (540) 955-4240; e-mail: blurdgbb@shentel.net
www.blueridgebb.com

A. Guests in the 1780s section of this stone mansion can enjoy huge fireplaces in every room. There is easy access through a separate entrance to the Shenandoah River. Easy drive to and from Washington, D.C., which is just an hour away. $70-108.

## MOLLUSK

### Guesthouses on the Water at Greenvale

Route 354, Box 70, 22517
(804) 462-5995

Two separate and private guest houses on 13 acres on the Rappahannock River and Greenvale Creek. Pool, dock, private beach, and bicycles. Each house is furnished with antiques and reproductions and has two bedrooms, two baths, living room, kitchen, and deck. Air conditioned. Enjoy sweeping water views, breathtaking sunsets, and relaxing and peaceful tranquility. Weekly rates available.

Hosts: Pam and Walt Smith
Guest Houses: 2 (PB) $85-125
Continental Breakfast
Credit Cards: A, B
Notes: 2, 5, 9, 11, 12

## MONTEREY

### Highland Inn

Main Street, P.O. Box 40, 24465
(703) 468-2143; (888) INN-INVA (466-4682)

Classic Victorian inn listed in the National Register of Historic Places. Tranquil location in the picturesque village of Monterey, nestled in the foothills of the Allegheny Mountains. There are 17 individually decorated rooms furnished with antiques and collectibles, each with private bath. Full-service dining room and tavern offer dinner Monday through Saturday and Sunday brunch. Antiquing, hiking, fishing, golf, and mineral baths are nearby.

Host: Michael Strand and Cynthia Peel
Rooms: 17 (PB) $55-85
Continental Breakfast
Credit Cards: A, B, C, D
Notes: 2, 4, 5, 8, 9, 11, 12, 13, 14

Highland Inn

NOTES: Credit cards accepted: A MasterCard; B Visa; C American Express; D Discover; E Diner's Club; F Other; 2 Personal checks accepted; 3 Lunch available; 4 Dinner available; 5 Open all year; 6 Pets welcome;

## MOUNT JACKSON

### Amanda's Bed & Breakfast Reservation Service

3538 Lakeway Drive, Ellicott City, MD 21042-1226
(443) 535-0008; (800) 899-7533
FAX (443) 535-0009; e-mail: AmandasRS@aol.com
www.Amandas-BBRS.com

**181.** An 1830 Colonial homestead on seven acres overlooking the George Washington Mountains. Some bedrooms have wood-burning fireplaces, and the antique furniture is for sale. Pool on premises. Area activities include craft fairs, hiking, fishing, tennis, and horseback riding. Five rooms with private baths. Two guest cottages. Full breakfast. $65-85.

### Blue Ridge Bed & Breakfast

2458 Castleman Road, Berryville, 22611
(540) 955-1246; (800) 296-1246
FAX (540) 955-4240; e-mail: blurdgbb@shentel.net
www.blueridgebb.com

**A.** This 1830 stately Colonial is near George Washington Parkway, 10 miles from Bryce. Six bedrooms with working fireplaces. There is also a cozy two and one-half room cottage separate from the main house. Pool. Full breakfast. $65-90.

## NELLYSFORD

### Distinguished Accommodations in the Potomac Region— (Amanda's Bed & Breakfast Reservation Service)

3538 Lakeway Drive, Ellicott City, MD 21042-1226
(443) 535-0008; (800) 899-7533
FAX (443) 535-0009; e-mail: AmandasRS@aol.com
www.Amandas-BBRS.com

**397.** Richness and romance of a bygone era, beautifully restored and lovingly appointed. Sitting atop a verdant knoll, this historic home is surrounded by the magnificence of the Blue Ridge Mountains. Charming rooms or luxurious suites offer elegant comfort, romantic privacy, and incredible views. Enjoy serenity and inspiring surroundings from any of the five porches, the hammock, or a peaceful spot on the 13 acres. Some rooms feature a double whirlpool bath or double sauna. Historic sites within a short drive or stay around the property for quiet contemplation. A delicious and satisfying gourmet breakfast is included. A prix fixe lunch or dinner is available by reservations. From $135.

### Guesthouses Bed & Breakfast

P.O. Box 5737, Charlottesville 22905
(804) 979-7264 (12:00-5:00 P.M. weekdays)
FAX (804) 293-7791
e-mail: guesthouses_bnb_reservations@
   compuserve.com
www.va-guesthouses.com

**The Mark Addy.** Near Nellysford in the Rockfish Valley near the foot of Wintergreen, this inn has magnificent mountain views. Relax on one of the porches or in the library or parlor, or stroll around the beautiful grounds. This inn offers eight guest rooms or suites furnished with lovely antiques and collectibles, each with a private bath. Two rooms have Jacuzzis. A bountiful breakfast is served. Smoking outdoors on the porches only. Not suitable for children under 12. Air conditioned. $95-135.

**Meander Inn.** A 75-year-old Victorian farmhouse on 50 acres of pasture and woods skirted by hiking trails and traversed by the Rockfish River. The inn offers five twin or queen-size bedrooms, some with private baths. A delicious full country breakfast is served each morning. Guests may enjoy the hot tub, wood-burning stove, player piano, deck, or front porch. Wintergreen Resort and Stoney Creek golf and tennis facilities are available to guests. Smoking is permitted outdoors only. Air conditioning. $80-100.

---

7 No smoking; 8 Children welcome; 9 Social drinking allowed; 10 Tennis nearby; 11 Swimming nearby; 12 Golf nearby; 13 Skiing nearby; 14 May be booked through a travel agent; 15 Handicapped accessible.

## The Meander Inn

3100 Berry Hill Road, 22959
(804) 361-1121; FAX (806) 361-1380
e-mail: meanderinn@aol.com
www.symweb.com/rockfish/meander.html

Nestled in the foothills of Virginia's Blue Ridge Mountains, in the peaceful surroundings of the Rockfish Valley, the Meander Inn and its 40 acres, welcomes guests to relax in the distinctively French ambiance. Guests can refresh and regroup in the comfort of country farm-style living. Activities in the surrounding area include skiing, hiking, golf, tennis, horseback riding, fishing, swimming, antique shopping. Historic sites such as Charlottesville's Monticello and the University of Virginia are all within 30 minutes' travel.

Hosts: Conte Alain and Francesca San Giorgio
Rooms: 5 (PB) $105-125
Full Breakfast
Credit Cards: A, B, C, D, E, F
Notes: 2, 4, 5, 7, 10, 11, 12, 13

## Trillium House

P.O. Box 280, 22958
(804) 325-9126; (800) 325-9126
FAX (804) 325-1099

Trillium House was built in 1983 as a small 12-room country hotel. Relax in the great room, garden room, TV room, or the outstanding library. Available to guests at preferred rates: two golf courses, swimming pool, 30 tennis courts, 25 miles of mapped hiking trails. The entry gate to the Wintergreen Mountain Village is one mile from the Blue Ridge Parkway; motorcycle restrictions. Dinner available Friday and Saturday. Inquire about accommodations for pets.

Rooms: 12 (PB) $100-160
Full Breakfast
Credit Cards: A, B
Notes: 2, 5, 7, 8, 9, 10, 11, 12, 13, 14, 15

## NEW CHURCH

## Blue Ridge Bed & Breakfast

2458 Castleman Road, Berryville, 22611
(540) 955-1246; (800) 296-1246
FAX (540) 955-4240; e-mail: blurdgbb@shentel.net
www.blueridgebb.com

**A.** Beautiful Colonial house built in 1790 on 20 acres with fabulous view of Massanetta Mountains, and a fishing creek. Franklin D. Roosevelt slept here in 1936. Ski resort is only 15 miles away. $55-65.

**B.** Beautiful carriage house built in 1873 offers two rooms in the main house. There is a cottage on the premises that offers two rooms decorated with lovely country decor and many oak and wicker antiques. In the heart of a busy Civil War town within easy walking distance of many quaint country shops and restaurants. $60-65.

**C.** Gracious manor house in a beautiful garden setting with fabulous mountain views. Built in 1926 in the middle of one and a half acres of land. Gourmet breakfast served: chef attended cooking school in Europe. Afternoon tea included. Activities include antiquing, museums, caverns, Civil War sites, vineyards, and fine restaurants. $55-90.

## NEW MARKET

## Cross Roads Inn Bed & Breakfast

9222 John Sevier Road, 22844
(540) 740-4157; FAX (540) 740-4255
e-mail: freisitz@shentel.net

This Victorian clapboard home is full of southern hospitality and European charm. The innkeepers serve imported Austrian coffee alongside the homemade breakfasts, and apple strudel is served as an afternoon refreshment. The home is decorated with English floral wallpapers, laced with family antiques, and

NOTES: Credit cards accepted: A MasterCard; B Visa; C American Express; D Discover; E Diner's Club; F Other; 2 Personal checks accepted; 3 Lunch available; 4 Dinner available; 5 Open all year; 6 Pets welcome;

Cross Roads Inn

boasts a wonderful view of New Market Gap and Massanutten Mountain. The historic downtown area is within walking distance.

Hosts: Mary-Lloyd and Roland Freisitzer
Rooms: 6 (PB) $55-100
Full Breakfast
Credit Cards: A, B
Notes: 2, 5, 7, 8, 9, 10, 11, 12, 13

## ONANCOCK

### The Spinning Wheel Bed & Breakfast

31 North Street, 23417
(757) 787-7311
e-mail: BandB@downtownonancock.com
www.downtownonancock.com

An 1890s folk Victorian home with antiques and spinning wheels throughout. Waterfront town listed in the National Register of Historic Places. Calm Eastern Shore getaway from D.C., Virginia, Maryland, Delaware, and New Jersey. Full breakfast. All rooms with private baths, queen-size beds, and air conditioning. Walk to restaurants, shops, and deep-water harbor. Golf and tennis available at private club. Near beach, bay, and ocean. Bicycles, antiques, museums, kayaking, festivals, fishing, wildlife refuge, and Tangier Island cruise. Open May through October. AAA-approved.

Hosts: Karen and David Tweedie
Rooms: 5 (PB) $75-95
Full Breakfast
Credit Cards: A, B, D
Notes: 2, 3, 4, 7, 9, 10, 11, 12, 14

## ORANGE

### Hidden Inn

249 Caroline Street, 22960
(540) 672-3625; (800) 841-1253
FAX (540) 672-5029
e-mail: hiddeninn@ns.gemlink.com
www.innbook.com/hidden.html

A romantic Victorian featuring 10 guest rooms, each with private bath. Jacuzzis, working fireplaces, and private verandas are available. Wicker and rocking chairs on the wraparound verandas; handmade quilts and canopied beds enhance the Victorian flavor. Full country breakfast, afternoon tea, and candlelight picnics. Minutes from Monticello, Montpelier, and Virginia wineries.

Hosts: Ray and Barbara Lonick
Rooms: 10 (PB) $99-169
Full Breakfast
Credit Cards: A, B, C
Notes: 2, 5, 7, 8, 9, 10, 11, 12, 14

## PETERSBURG

### The High Street Inn–
### A Bed & Breakfast

405 High Street, 23803
(804) 733-0505; FAX (804) 861-9433
e-mail: highst@mail.ctg.net; www.ctg.net/owlcat/

An elegant turn-of-the-century Queen Anne mansion (circa 1899) a few blocks' walk to the Old Towne historic district, restaurants, antiques, and Civil War museums. Spacious guest rooms, most with private baths, air conditioning units, and beautiful wood floors. Full breakfast. Discounted rates on weekdays. Easy day trips to Richmond, James River plantations, and Civil War sites. The "purr-fect" base for guests' southern Virginia discovery. Inquire about accommodations for pets. Children over eight welcome.

Hosts: Jim Hillier and Jon Hackett
Rooms: 6 (4 PB: 2 SB) $75-105
Full Breakfast
Credit Cards: A, B, D
Notes: 2, 5, 6, 7, 8, 9, 12, 14

## PORT HAYWOOD

### Tabb's Creek Inn

Route 14, Mathews County, P.O. Box 219, 23138
(804) 725-5136

Private water-view porches make this an especially attractive getaway for those seeking a dose of seclusion. On the banks of Tabb's Creek in Chesapeake Bay, this post-Colonial farm features a detached guest cottage separated by pool and rose garden. Innkeeper is a well-known producing artist. The rooms are decorated with stippling, stenciling, antiques, and beds that soothe. Canoe and paddle boat provided so guests can scoot by sea. Lunch and dinner available upon request. Smoking permitted in designated areas only.

Tabb's Creek Inn

Hosts: Catherine and Cabell Venable
Rooms: 4 (PB) $75-125
Full Breakfast
Credit Cards: None
Notes: 2, 5, 6, 8, 11, 12, 14

## PROVIDENCE FORGE

### Jasmine Plantation
### Bed & Breakfast Inn

4500 North Courthouse Road, 23140
(804) 966-9836; (800) NEW-KENT
FAX (804) 966-5679

Restored 1750s farmhouse on 47 acres with rooms decorated in various period antiques. Secluded, yet only three minutes from I-64 and convenient to Williamsburg, James River Plantations, and Richmond. Fine dining, golf, sporting clays, fishing, and horse racing

Jasmine Plantation

NOTES: Credit cards accepted: A MasterCard; B Visa; C American Express; D Discover; E Diner's Club; F Other; 2 Personal checks accepted; 3 Lunch available; 4 Dinner available; 5 Open all year; 6 Pets welcome;

nearby. Nature areas and walking trails. Full country breakfast. No smoking inside.

Hosts: Joyce and Howard Vogt
Rooms: 6 (4 PB; 2 SB) $80-120
Full Breakfast
Credit Cards: A, B, C
Notes: 2, 5, 7, 12, 14

## PULASKI

### Count Pulaski
### Bed & Breakfast & Gardens

821 North Jefferson Avenue, 24301
(540) 980-1163; (800) 980-1163

Historic home in quiet neighborhood, Southwest Virginia mountain town. Easy to find, near I-81. In the National Register of Historic Places. Furnished with family antiques, owner's paintings, and items collected from living and traveling around the world. All rooms with new queen- or king- size beds, private baths, tubs and showers, ceiling fans, air conditioning, several fireplaces, continuous beverage center. Gardens in season, arched bridge, patio and outdoor furniture, seed or samples of flowers available. Full gourmet breakfast served at guests' convenience by candlelight, with classical music.

Host: Dr. Florence Byrd Stevenson
Rooms: 3 (PB) $95
Full Breakfast
Credit Cards: A, B
Notes: 5, 7, 9, 10, 11, 12

Count Pulaski

## PURCELLVILLE

### Amanda's Bed & Breakfast Reservation Service

3538 Lakeway Drive, Ellicott City, MD 21042-1226
(443) 535-0008; (800) 899-7533
FAX (443) 535-0009; e-mail: AmandasRS@aol.com
www.Amandas-BBRS.com

**114.** A spacious new log home in a meadow setting at the foothills of the Blue Ridge Mountains. Enjoy the sun rise with early morning coffee relaxing in a rocking chair on the front veranda. Convenient to Harpers Ferry and Shepherdstown. Two rooms, each with private bath. One with whirlpool. Continental breakfast. $85-90.

**239.** Be refreshed by a country setting while staying in an 18th-century home. Guest rooms are welcoming and spacious. The four private-bath bedrooms are pleasingly decorated with comfortable beds and easy chairs. One room has a Jacuzzi and one has a fireplace. A full breakfast is served. $100-125.

### Blue Ridge Bed & Breakfast

2458 Castleman Road, Berryville, 22611
(540) 955-1246; (800) 296-1246
FAX (540) 955-4240; e-mail: blurdgbb@shentel.net
www.blueridgebb.com

**A.** Quaint log house just 10 minutes from Harpers Ferry. Hiking, white-water rafting, great restaurants, and a fun flea market. Mixture of antiques and reproductions. TV, room for all guests. Full country breakfast. Beautiful stone fireplace. Hostess is from Australia. $80-90.

## REMINGTON (WARRENTON)

### Highland Farm & Inn, L.L.C.

10981 Lees Mill Road, 22734
(540) 439-0088
http://highlandfarminn.hypermart.net

In Lakota, south of Warrenton, this secluded, 36-acre farm is known for raising thoroughbred

Highland Farm

horses and cattle. Often fox and deer share their pastures. The accommodations, with private baths and queen-size beds, are tastefully furnished with family antiques. Guests may enjoy the spacious solarium or comfortable living room for conversation, cozy fires, and spectacular sunsets. Swim in the in-ground pool, walk along the Rappahannock River, or relax by the waterfall and ponds. Antiquing, Civil War battlefields, horse events, wineries, and fine dining are a short drive away. Enjoy afternoon refreshments and a delightful breakfast. One room is handicapped accessible. Dinners by reservation only. Smoking permitted outside.

Hosts: Ralph and Linda Robinson
Rooms: 3 (2 PB; 1 S1/2B) $60-110
Full Breakfast
Credit Cards: None
Notes: 2, 4, 5, 7, 9, 11, 12, 15

## RICHMOND

## *The Emmanuel Hutzler House*

2036 Monument Avenue, 23220
(804) 355-4885; (804) 353-6900
e-mail: be.our.guest@bensonhouse.com
www.bensonhouse.com

This large Italian Renaissance-style inn has been totally renovated and offers leaded-glass windows, coffered ceilings, and natural mahogany raised paneling throughout the downstairs, and a large living room with marble fireplace for guests' enjoyment. Four guest rooms on the second floor, each have sitting

area and private bath. One suite has a four-poster bed, love seat, and wing chair. The largest suite has a marble fireplace, four-poster mahogany bed, antique sofa, dresser, and a private bath with shower and Jacuzzi. Resident cat. Nonsmoking environment. Children over 12 welcome.

Hosts: Lyn M. Benson and John E. Richardson
Rooms: 4 (PB) $95-155
Continental and Full Breakfasts
Credit Cards: A, B, C, D, E
Notes: 2, 5, 7, 9, 10, 11, 12, 14

## *The William Catlin House*

2304 East Broad Street, 23223
(804) 780-3746

Antiques and working fireplaces await at the William Catlin House, built in 1845, Richmond's first and oldest in the historic district. The luxury of goose down pillows and evening sherry promises a restful night. Each morning a delicious full breakfast and endless pots of steaming hot coffee or tea await guests in the elegant dining room. Numerous nearby historic sites. As seen in *Colonial Homes*, *Southern Living*, and *Mid-Atlantic* magazines.

Hosts: Robert and Josephine Martin

The William Catlin House

Rooms: 5 (3 PB; 2 SB) $75-125
Full Breakfast
Credit Cards: A, B, D
Notes: 2, 5, 7, 8, 9, 10, 14

## ROANOKE

## CrossTrails Bed & Breakfast

5880 Blaksburg Road, Catawba, 24070
(540) 384-8078; (800) 841-8078
e-mail: xtrails@roanoke.infi.net

A mountain valley getaway in scenic Catawba Valley where the Appalachian Trail and TransAmerica Bicycle Trail cross between Roanoke and Blacksburg. World- class hiking and biking just outside the door. The 15 acres adjoining on three sides are national park property. Porches and decks designed to take advantage of commanding views. Rooms have queen-size beds and private baths. Remote carriage house, hot tub, library, cross-country skiing, fly-fishing, shuttles, full breakfast, Homeplace Restaurant nearby.

Hosts: Bill and Katherine Cochran
Rooms: 3 (PB) $70-75
Full Breakfast
Credit Cards: None
Notes: 2, 7, 9, 12

## Stone Manor Bed & Breakfast

1135 Stone Manor Place, Smith Mountain Lake, 24095
(540) 297-1414

On beautiful Smith Mountain Lake–690 feet of waterfront, lighted boardwalk, dockage for boats, fishing, in-ground swimming pool, all-season sunroom boasting a panoramic view of the lake. Golf close by. Resort-like atmosphere. Guest rooms highlight themes of the lake activities. Magnificent lake views and sunsets. Near Roanoke and Blue Ridge Parkway. Children over 12 welcome.

Rooms: 3 (PB) $85-105
Credit Cards: A, B, D
Notes: 2, 5, 7, 9, 11, 12, 14

## SCOTTSVILLE

## Guesthouses Bed & Breakfast

P.O. Box 5737, Charlottesville, 22905
(804) 979-7264 (12:00-5:00 P.M. weekdays)
FAX (804) 293-7791
e-mail: guesthouses_bnb_reservations@
  compuserve.com
www.va-guesthouses.com

**Belle Grove.** In a beautiful setting on a small farm with gardens and rolling pastures, this upstairs guest suite is in a separate building adjacent to the 1750 home that was the original Scottsville courthouse. These accommodations are light and airy with a large bed-sitting room. There is a queen bed, a kitchenette, and dining area furnished with antiques. There are lovely grounds to wander, and a swimming pool available in season. Continental breakfast supplies are left for you. Air conditioning. No smoking indoors. $125-150.

## SMITHFIELD

## Isle of Wight Inn

1607 South Church Street, 23430
(757) 357-3176; (757) 357-0777

This luxurious Colonial bed and breakfast inn is found in a delightful historic river-port town. Several suites with fireplaces and Jacuzzis. Antique shop featuring tallcase clocks and period furniture. More than 60 old homes in town dating from 1750. Just 30 minutes and a ferry ride from Williamsburg and Jamestown; less than an hour from James River plantations, Norfolk, Hampton, and Virginia Beach. No smoking allowed in common areas and some rooms.

Hosts: The Harts and the Earls
Rooms: 10 (PB) $59-119
Full Breakfast
Credit Cards: A, B, C, D
Notes: 2, 5, 8, 9, 10, 11, 12, 14

---

7 No smoking; 8 Children welcome; 9 Social drinking allowed; 10 Tennis nearby; 11 Swimming nearby; 12 Golf nearby; 13 Skiing nearby; 14 May be booked through a travel agent; 15 Handicapped accessible.

## SPERRYVILLE

### Sharp Rock Farm
### Bed & Breakfast

5 Sharp Rock Road, 22740
(540) 987-8020; www.bnb-n-va.com/sharp.htm

Sharp Rock Farm is on 23 acres in an unspoiled valley at the foot of the Blue Ridge Mountains with the Hughes River meandering through the property. It embodies the peace and pleasures of country life at its best with trout fishing, swimming, and six-acre vineyard. Hike nearby Old Rag Mountain. There are spectacular views at every turn. Hosts offer a two-bedroom cottage and a carriage house with privacy plus gourmet breakfasts. Smoking permitted outside only. Nestled in beautiful Rappahanock County.

Hosts: Marilyn and David Armor
Rooms: 3 (2 PB; 1 SB) $125-200
Full Breakfast
Credit Cards: A, B
Notes: 2, 5, 7, 8, 9, 11, 12, 14, 15

Sharp Rock Farm

## STANARDSVILLE

### Edgewood Farm
### Bed & Breakfast

1186 Middle River Road, 22973
(800) 985-3782; FAX (804) 985-6275
e-mail: edgewoodfarm@firstva.com
www.firstnetva.com/edgewoodfarm

Edgewood Farm

Beautifully restored circa 1790 farmhouse on 130 acres in the Blue Ridge foothills. Off the beaten path yet near Skyline Drive, wineries, fine restaurants. antique and craft shops as well as Montpelier, Monticello, Ash Lawn, and University of Virginia. Accommodations include spacious, period-decorated bedrooms with private and shared baths and wood-burning fireplaces in each room. A sumptuous breakfast is served each morning on fine china; coffee, tea, or juice is brought to guests' door each morning before breakfast with the newspaper. Sparkling apple cider, cheese and crackers, and fruit served upon arrival. Lovely views, excellent bird watching, quiet and relaxing atmosphere. Skiing is one hour away.

Hosts: Eleanor and Norman Schwartz
Rooms: 3 (2 PB; 2 SB) $90-110
Full Breakfast
Credit Cards: A, B, C
Notes: 2, 5, 7, 8, 9, 11, 12, 14

## STANLEY

### Jordan Hollow Farm Inn

326 Hawksbill Park Road, 22851
(540) 778-2285; (888) 418-7000
FAX (540) 778-1759
e-mail: jhf@jordanhollow.com

Circa 1700s inn nestled at the base of the Blue Ridge Mountains. Beautiful views, 150 acres to roam, horses to ride. Relax on the spacious porches, walk the trails, and enjoy the llamas

NOTES: Credit cards accepted: A MasterCard; B Visa; C American Express; D Discover; E Diner's Club; F Other; 2 Personal checks accepted; 3 Lunch available; 4 Dinner available; 5 Open all year; 6 Pets welcome;

Jordan Hollow Farm Inn

and other farm animals. Fabulous meals in the restaurant—a restored Shenandoah Valley farmhouse. New Luray Caverns, Shenandoah River, snow skiing. "We welcome you with true southern hospitality!"

Hosts: Betsy Anderson and Gail Kyle
Rooms: 14 (PB) $125-200
Full Breakfast
Credit Cards: A, B, D, E
Notes: 2, 3, 4, 5, 7, 8, 9, 10, 11, 12, 13, 14

## STAUNTON

### Blue Ridge Bed & Breakfast

2458 Castleman Road, Berryville, 22611
(540) 955-1246; (800) 296-1246
FAX (540) 955-4240; e-mail: blurdgbb@shentel.net
www.blueridgebb.com

A. Farm has 190 acres, close to Woodrow Wilson's birthplace. Monticello, Skyline Drive, Blue Ridge Parkway, Shenandoah and Allegheny Mountains all surround this gracious farmhouse. Museum of American Frontier Culture, James Madison University, and Mary Baldwin College, with many antique shops nearby. Weekend packages available. $50-55.

### Frederick House

28 North New Street, 24401
(540) 885-4220; (800) 334-5575
FAX (540) 885-5180
e-mail: ejharman@frederickhouse.com
www.frederickhouse.com

A small hotel in the European tradition. Large, comfortable rooms or suites. Amenities include private baths, air conditioning, TV, telephones, robes, private entrances, and antique furnishings. Some balconies or fireplaces. Gourmet breakfast. Award-winning restoration and gardens. Across from Mary Baldwin College. Near shops, restaurants, and the Woodrow Wilson Birthplace. In central Shenandoah Valley near Skyline Drive and Blue Ridge Parkway.

Hosts: Joe and Evy Harman
Rooms: 20 (PB) $75-170
Full Breakfast
Credit Cards: A, B, C, D, E
Notes: 2, 3, 4, 5, 7, 8, 9, 10, 11, 12, 13, 14

Frederick House

### The Sampson Eagon Inn

238 East Beverley Street, 24401
(540) 886-8200 (phone/FAX); (800) 597-9722

In the Virginia historic landmark district of Gospel Hill, this gracious, circa 1840, town residence has been thoughtfully restored and transformed into a unique inn offering affordable luxury and personal service in an intimate, inviting atmosphere. Each elegant, spacious, air-conditioned room features private bath, sitting area, canopied bed, TV/VCR, telephone, and antique furnishings. Adjacent to the Woodrow Wilson birthplace and Mary Baldwin College, the inn is within two blocks of downtown dining and attractions.

7 No smoking; 8 Children welcome; 9 Social drinking allowed; 10 Tennis nearby; 11 Swimming nearby; 12 Golf nearby; 13 Skiing nearby; 14 May be booked through a travel agent; 15 Handicapped accessible.

The Sampson Eagon Inn

Hosts: Laura and Frank Mattingly
Rooms: 5 (PB) $95-120
Full Breakfast
Credit Cards: A, B, C
Notes: 2, 5, 7, 9, 10, 11, 12, 13

## Thornrose House at Gypsy Hill

531 Thornrose Avenue, 24401
(540) 885-7026

A wraparound veranda and Greek colonnades distinguish this turn-of-the-century Georgian residence. Family antiques, a grand piano, and fireplaces create an elegant, restful atmosphere. Breakfast specialties served in a formal dining room energize guests for sightseeing in the beautiful Shenandoah Valley. Beside a 300-acre park with golf, tennis, swimming, and trails. Other attractions include the Woodrow Wilson birthplace, the Museum of American Frontier Culture, and the nearby Skyline Drive and Blue Ridge Parkway. Children six and older welcome.

Hosts: Suzanne and Otis Huston
Rooms: 5 (PB) $60-90
Full Breakfast
Credit Cards: A, B, C
Notes: 2, 5, 7, 9, 10, 11, 12, 13, 14

### STEELES TAVERN

## Osceola Mill Country Inn

Route 56, 24476
(540) 377-6455

This 1800s grist mill was built by Cyrus McCormick, the inventor of the reaper. The mill itself hosts four guest rooms, the Victorian Manor house has seven, and the Old Mill Store has been converted into a honeymoon cottage with Jacuzzi and fireplace. Also in the Mill, there is a restaurant for dining amongst chestnut timbers and candlelight. The inn is halfway between the towns of Staunton and Lexington and is at the foot of the Blue Ridge Mountains, close to the Appalachian Trail.

Hosts: Mercer Balliro and Brian Domino
Rooms: 12 (PB) $89-169
Full Breakfast
Credit Cards: A, B
Notes: 2, 4, 5, 7, 9, 11, 12, 15

Osceola Mill Country Inn

## Sugar Tree Inn

Highway 56, 24476
(540) 377-2197 (phone/FAX); (800) 377-2197
www.sugartreeinn.com

Sugar Tree, Virginia's mountain inn, is nestled into a mountainside less than a mile from the Blue Ridge Parkway. Guests find romantic seclusion here in rustically elegant surroundings. Each spacious room or suite offers a private wood-burning fireplace and beautiful, comfortable furnishings. There are 40-mile views from the front porch rockers. Hike Sugar Tree trails, explore historic Virginia, shop, or simply relax. Open April 1 through December 1. Great hiking, antiquing, scenery, and historic attractions nearby. One smoking room available; smoking is not permitted in public rooms.

NOTES: Credit cards accepted: A MasterCard; B Visa; C American Express; D Discover; E Diner's Club; F Other; 2 Personal checks accepted; 3 Lunch available; 4 Dinner available; 5 Open all year; 6 Pets welcome;

Rooms: 11 (PB) $100-145
Full Breakfast
Credit Cards: A, B, C, D
Notes: 2, 4, 9, 14, 15

## STEPHENS CITY

### The Inn at Vaucluse Spring

231 Vaucluse Spring Lane, 22655
(540) 869-0200; (800) 869-0525
FAX (540) 869-9546
e-mail: mail@vauclusespring.com
www.vauclusespring.com

Set amidst 100 acres in the orchard country of the Northern Shenandoah Valley, this enclave of four guest houses offers rooms with manor house elegance or log and stone warmth. Ideally located between Winchester's historic sites and Front Royal's Skyline Drive and Shenandoah River. Enjoy fireplaces, Jacuzzis, warm hospitality and gourmet food in an award-winning historic restoration. Beautiful decor and gardens. Large limestone spring. Swimming pool. Dinner available Saturday night.

Hosts: Neil and Barry Myers; Karen and Mike Caplanis
Rooms: 12 (PB) $140-250
Full Breakfast
Credit Cards: A, B
Notes: 2, 5, 7, 9, 12, 14

## STRASBURG

### Hotel Strasburg

213 Holliday Street, 22657
(540) 465-9191; (800) 348-8327
FAX (540) 465-4788; e-mail: thehotel@shentel.net

Like stepping back in time to the 1890s, Hotel Strasburg combines Victorian history and charm to make a special place for lodging and dining. Tastefully decorated with many antique period pieces and an impressive collection of art. Guests are invited to wander through the inn's dining rooms and quaintly renovated sleeping rooms (Jacuzzi suites). Nestled at the foot of Massanutten Mountain near the

entrance to the breathtaking Skyline Drive. Inquire about accommodations for pets.

Hosts: Gary and Carol Rutherford
Rooms: 29 (PB) $74-165
Continental Breakfast
Credit Cards: A, B, C, D, E
Notes: 3, 4, 5, 8, 9, 10, 11, 12, 14

## SYRIA

### Graves' Mountain Lodge

Route 670, 22743
(540) 923-4231; FAX (540) 923-4312
www.gravesmountain.com

This peaceful lodge is on a large cattle and fruit farm in the shadow of the Blue Ridge Mountains next to the Shenandoah National Park. Guests enjoy three meals a day on the American plan while getting rest and relaxation during their visit. Rooms, cabins, and cottages to choose from. Trout stream and farm ponds are available for fishing. Hiking trails and horseback riding are also available for guests' enjoyment. Open mid-March through November. Seasonal rates available. Inquire about accommodations for pets. Both smoking and nonsmoking rooms available.

Hosts: Rachel and Jim Graves
Rooms: 44 (38 PB; 6 SB) $60-100
Cottages: 11 (PB) $55-100
Full Breakfast
Credit Cards: A, B, D
Notes: 2, 3, 4, 6, 7, 8, 9, 10, 11, 12, 14, 15

## VIRGINIA BEACH

### Angie's Guest Cottage

302 24th Street, 23451
(757) 423-4690
www.bbinternet.com/angies

Angie's Guest Cottage is in the heart of the resort area, just one block from the ocean. Early-20th-century beach house that former guests describe as "cute, cozy, quiet, and extra clean with fresh flowers everywhere!" All

7 No smoking; 8 Children welcome; 9 Social drinking allowed; 10 Tennis nearby; 11 Swimming nearby; 12 Golf nearby; 13 Skiing nearby; 14 May be booked through a travel agent; 15 Handicapped accessible.

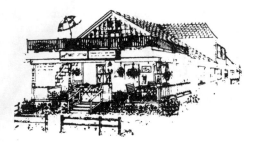

Angie's Guest Cottage

rooms are air conditioned; some have small refrigerators and private entrances. Continental plus breakfast. Sun deck, barbecue pit, and picnic tables. International atmosphere. Closed mid-October through mid-March. Two-night minimum stay. Inquire about accommodations for pets. Also, one- and two-bedroom duplex weekly, and AYH Hostel.

Host: Barbara Yates
Rooms: 6 (1 PB; 5 SB) $60-84
Continental Breakfast
Credit Cards: None
Notes: 7, 8, 9, 10, 11, 12

## Barclay Cottage

400 16th Street, 23451
(757) 422-1956; www.barclaycottage.comm
www.inngetaways.com/va/barclay.html

Enjoy casual sophistication in a warm, historic, innlike atmosphere. Two blocks from the beach and in the heart of the Virginia Beach recreational area, the Barclay Cottage has been decorated in turn-of-the-century style with antique

Barclay Cottage

furniture. The hosts welcome guests to the Barclay Cottage where their theme is "We go where our dreams take us." Open April through October. AAA-approved three diamonds.

Hosts: Peter and Claire
Rooms: 5 (3 PB; 2 SB) $78-108
Full Breakfast
Credit Cards: A, B, C
Notes: 7, 9, 10, 11, 12, 14

## The Picket Fence

209 43rd Street, 23451
(804) 428-8861

The furnishings in this comfortable Colonial home glow with the patina of loving care. The beach is just one block away, and beach chairs and umbrellas are provided for comfort. Near the new Virginia Marine Science Museum. One room and a suite are available year-round. A guest cottage is open May through October.

Host: Kathleen J. Hall
Room: 1 (PB) $60-90
Suite: 1 (PB)
Cottage: 1 (PB)
Full Breakfast
Credit Cards: None
Notes: 2, 3, 5, 7, 9, 10, 11, 12

## WARRENTON

## The Black Horse Inn

8393 Meetze Road, 20187
(540) 349-4020; www.blackhorseinn.com

The Black Horse Inn is an elegant Virginia hunt country estate, only 45 minutes from Washington, D.C. Circa 1850, the original portion of this home served as a hospital during the Civil War. Fireplaces, whirlpool baths, four-poster canopied beds complement the serene setting to provide a relaxing respite for guests. The inn provides an elegant setting for family reunions, weddings, and corporate events. Equine guests are welcome. Activities include fox-hunting, horseback riding, wine-tasting, hiking, shopping at antique and spe-

NOTES: Credit cards accepted: A MasterCard; B Visa; C American Express; D Discover; E Diner's Club; F Other; 2 Personal checks accepted; 3 Lunch available; 4 Dinner available; 5 Open all year; 6 Pets welcome;

The Black Horse Inn

cialty shops in Old Town Warrenton, bicycling, and boating.

Host: Lynn A. Pirozzoli
Rooms: 9 (PB) $125-295
Credit Cards: A, B C
Notes: 2, 5, 7, 9, 10, 11, 12, 14

## WASHINGTON

### Blue Ridge Bed & Breakfast

2458 Castleman Road, Berryville, 22611
(540) 955-1246; (800) 296-1246
FAX (540) 955-4240; e-mail: blurdgbb@shentel.net
www.blueridgebb.com

**A.** Lovely 1850's house on quiet street with great views of mountains. Easy walk to Inn at Little Washington and local theatre. House has lovely antiques including Rose Kennedy chaise lounge and working fireplace in bedroom. $80-125.

### Caledonia Farm—1812

47 Dearing Road, Flint Hill, 22627
(540) 675-3693; (800) BNB-1812

Beautifully restored 1812 stone home and romantic guest house on a farm adjacent to Shenandoah National Park. Listed in the National Register of Historic Places, offers splendor for all seasons in Virginia's Blue Ridge Mountains. Skyline Drive, wineries, caves, historic sites, and superb dining. Fireplaces, air conditioning, hay rides, hot tub, and

bicycles. Only 68 miles to Washington, D.C. Children over 12 welcome.

Host: Phil Irwin
Rooms: 2 (SB) $80
Suites: 2 (PB) $140
Full Breakfast
Credit Cards: A, B, C, D
Notes: 2, 5, 7, 9, 10, 11, 12, 13, 14

Caledonia Farm—1812

### The Foster-Harris House

189 Main Street, Box 333, 22747
(800) 656-0153; www.fosterharris.com

A turn-of-the-century home in a historic village nestled in the foothills of the Blue Ridge Mountains, with country antiques, fresh flowers, and outstanding mountain views. Near Shenandoah National Park. Five-star restaurant in town. All rooms feature private baths and central air conditioning.

Host: John and Libby Byam
Rooms: 4 (PB) $95-170
Full Breakfast
Credit Cards: A, B, D
Notes: 2, 5, 7, 9, 12, 14

## WATERFORD

### Milltown Farms Inn

14163 Milltown Road, P.O. Box 34, 20197-0034
(540) 882-4470; (888) 747-3942
e-mail: paul-barbara@erols.com
http://MilltownFarms.com

Paul and Barbara enjoy sharing their world with guests in this 1765 log and stone home set

7 No smoking; 8 Children welcome; 9 Social drinking allowed; 10 Tennis nearby; 11 Swimming nearby; 12 Golf nearby; 13 Skiing nearby; 14 May be booked through a travel agent; 15 Handicapped accessible.

on 300 acres. Period antiques, feather beds, fireplaces, unlimited pastoral views of horses, cattle, sunsets over the Blue Ridge, and a gourmet breakfast. Health is utmost on the innkeepers' minds. Come and join them. One room is handicapped accessible.

Hosts: Paul and Barbara Mayville
Rooms: 3 (PB) $100-135
Full Breakfast
Credit Cards: A, B, C, D
Notes: 2, 5, 7, 9, 10, 11, 12, 14, 15

## WAYNESBORO

### The Iris Inn

191 Chinquapin Drive, 22980
(540) 943-1991; FAX (540) 942-2093

The Iris Inn, architecturally designed and built in 1991, is on 21 wooded acres on a western slope of the Blue Ridge. It overlooks the historic Shenandoah Valley. Rooms are spacious and comfortable with king- or queen-size beds, all private baths, some whirlpools and fireplaces, porches, rockers, hot tub, full breakfast. Only five minutes to Blue Ridge Parkway and Shenandoah National Park. Near wineries, Monticello, P. Buckley Moss Museum.

Hosts: Wayne and Iris Karl
Rooms: 9 (PB) $80-140
Full Breakfast
Credit Cards: A, B
Notes: 2, 5, 7, 9, 11, 12, 13, 15

## WILLIAMSBURG

### Aldrich House Bed & Breakfast

505 Capitol Ct., 23185
(757) 229-5422; (877) 745-0887
e-mail: spatton@widomaker.com
www.aldrichhouse.com

A short stroll from the Aldrich House will transport guests to the 18th-century and the heart of Colonial Williamsburg. This Colonial saltbox home offers spacious accommodations

and formal living and dining areas in an unpretentious atmosphere. Innkeepers Tom and Sue Patton will help guests make their visit to the colonial past an enjoyable experience.

Rooms: 2 (PB) $100-115
Full Breakfast
Credit Cards: None
Notes: 2, 5, 7, 8, 10, 11, 12

### Amanda's Bed & Breakfast Reservation Service

3538 Lakeway Drive, Ellicott City, MD 21042-1226
(443) 535-0008; (800) 899-7533
FAX (443) 535-0009; e-mail: AmandasRS@aol.com
www.Amandas-BBRS.com

**253.** This Flemish-bond brick home was one of the first homes built on Richmond Road after the restoration of Colonial Williamsburg began in the late 1920s. The house features 18th-century decor, and the owner's apple collection is evident throughout. Four rooms with private baths. Continental plus breakfast. $95-150.

**262.** Three blocks from historic area and across from the College of William and Mary's Alumni House and Zable Stadium. Recent renovations have restored the house to its original charm when built in 1926. Antique furnishings throughout. Five guest rooms, each with private bath. $95-115.

**361.** Williamsburg is well known for its restored historic district and the depth of its history. To take advantage of this, stay a few days in one of Williamsburg's oldest and largest guest houses with 10 guest rooms. Guests are treated to southern hospitality and a full breakfast. Two of the rooms share a bath but this makes a nice family suite. Walk to the historic area and the College of William and Mary. Decorated with 18th-century reproductions and traditional antiques, with canopied or four-poster beds and quilts. $95-160.

NOTES: Credit cards accepted: A MasterCard; B Visa; C American Express; D Discover; E Diner's Club; F Other; 2 Personal checks accepted; 3 Lunch available; 4 Dinner available; 5 Open all year; 6 Pets welcome;

## Anne Marie's Bed & Breakfast

610 Capitol Landing Road, 23185
(757) 564-0225

Gracious hosts at Anne Marie's have a genuine interest in making a visit to Colonial Williamsburg unforgettable. A three-block stroll and guests are in the quiet restored area where history and shops abound. Evenings at Anne Marie's bring relaxation and comfort. Rooms and suite are tastefully furnished with family heirlooms and antiques. Feather beds are covered with fine linens and await guests' slumber. Guests rave about the exceptional full breakfast and the finest of hospitality.

Hosts: Marie and Ann Supplee
Rooms: 2 (PB) $85-110
Full Breakfast
Credit Cards: A, B
Notes: 2, 5, 7, 8, 9, 10, 11, 12, 14

## Candlewick Bed & Breakfast

800 Jamestown Road, 23185
(757) 253-8693; (800) 418-4949

In the heart of Williamsburg, Candlewick invites guests to enjoy the comforts and gracious charm of an earlier era. With 18th-century antiques and reproductions, each of the three guest bedrooms boasts a curtained canopied bed with a plush mattress decked in an antique quilt and absolutely everything necessary for guests' comfort. Following a marvelous night's rest, guests will enjoy a wonderful breakfast in the keeping room. Just a whisper away from the historic area and across the street from College of William and Mary. Children over 12 welcome.

Hosts: Bernie and Mary Peters
Rooms: 3 (PB) $115-125
Full Breakfast
Credit Cards: A, B, C
Notes: 2, 7, 9, 10, 11, 12, 14

## The Cedars

616 Jamestown Road, 23185
(757) 229-3591; (800) 296-3591
www.cedarsofwilliamsburg.com

An eight-minute walk to historic Williamsburg and across from the College of William and Mary, this elegant three-story brick Georgian inn offers tradition, gracious hospitality, and comfort. Scrumptious, bountiful breakfasts are served by candlelight on the tavern porch. The porch also serves as a meeting place for cards, chess, or other diversions. Each guest chamber reflects the romance and charm of the colonial era. Cottage with fireplace can accommodate five people. Off-street parking. Williamsburg's oldest, largest bed and breakfast.

Hosts: Carol, Jim, and Brona Malecha
Rooms: 8 (PB) $95-180
Cottage: 1 (PB) $150-275
Full Breakfast
Credit Cards: A, B
Notes: 2, 5, 7, 8, 9, 10, 12, 14

## Colonial Gardens Bed & Breakfast

1109 Jamestown Road, 23185
(757) 220-8087; (800) 886-9715
e-mail: colgdns@widomaker.com
www.ontheline.com/cgbb

Colonial Gardens offers the perfect escape in a quiet, woodland setting. The charming interior is beautifully furnished with heirloom antiques and original art. Enjoy breakfast in the sunroom overlooking the beautifully landscaped yard. In the evening relax with other guests in the large living room around the game table and comfortable sitting areas. Ideal for Colonial Williamsburg and all area attractions. Outstanding suites and guest rooms with luxury amenities. TV/VCR, telephones. AAA three-diamond-rated.

Hosts: Scottie and Wilmot Phillips
Rooms 4 (PB) $115-145
Full Breakfast
Credit Cards: A, B, C, D
Notes: 2, 5, 7, 9, 10, 11, 12, 14

---

7 No smoking; 8 Children welcome; 9 Social drinking allowed; 10 Tennis nearby; 11 Swimming nearby; 12 Golf nearby; 13 Skiing nearby; 14 May be booked through a travel agent; 15 Handicapped accessible.

## Distinguished Accommodations in the Potomac Region— (Amanda's Bed & Breakfast Reservation Service)

1428 Park Avenue, Baltimore, 21217-4203
(410) 728-DAPR (3277); (800) 360 DAPR (3277)
FAX (410) 728-8957; e-mail: amandasrs@aol.com
www.amandas-bbrs.com

**561.** A three-story brick Georgian home setting the tone of an 18th-century home. Less than a 10-minute walk to historic Williamsburg and across the street from the College of William and Mary. A full breakfast is served. There are eight rooms plus a cottage that are individually and graciously appointed with century reproductions and traditional antiques. Each bedroom has either a canopy or four-poster bed. All rooms have private baths. There is off-street parking. The perfect location for visiting nearby attractions: Jamestown, Yorktown, James River plantations, and Busch Gardens.

## For-Cant-Hill Guest Home

4 Canterbury Lane, 23185-3140
(757) 229-6623; FAX (757) 229-1863

This home is in a lovely wooded area, only five to six blocks from the colonial historic area, overlooking a lake, part of the campus of the College of William and Mary, in the heart of town. The rooms are beautifully decorated in antiques and collectibles for guests' complete comfort. The home is central heated and air conditioned with TVs in each room, and a hearty breakfast is served. The hosts make dinner reservations for guests and provide helpful information on the many attractions offered in the area. Telephone and fax are available in the home. Children over eight welcome.

Hosts: Martha and Hugh Easler
Rooms: 2 (PB) $85
Full Breakfast
Credit Cards: None
Notes: 2, 5, 7, 8, 9, 10, 11, 12, 14

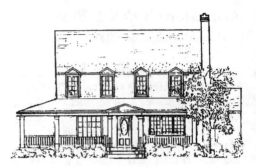

Fox & Grape

## Fox & Grape Bed & Breakfast

701 Monumental Avenue, 23185
(757) 229-6914; (800) 292-3699
www.foxandgrapebb.com

Genteel accommodations five blocks north of Virginia's restored colonial capital. This lovely two-story Colonial with spacious wraparound porch is a perfect place to enjoy one's morning coffee, plan the day's activities, or relax with a favorite book. Furnishings include antiques, counted cross-stitch, duck decoys, and folk art Noah's arks made by the host.

Hosts: Pat and Bob Orendorff
Rooms: 4 (PB) $100-115
Full Breakfast
Credit Cards: A, B, D
Notes: 5, 7, 9

## Hite's Bed & Breakfast

704 Monumental Avenue, 23185
(757) 229-4814

Charming Cape Cod—seven minutes' walk to Colonial Williamsburg. Large rooms cleverly furnished with antiques and collectibles. Each room has a TV, telephone, coffee maker, robes, and beautiful private bathroom with claw-foot tub. In the parlor for guest enjoyment are an antique pump organ and hand-crank Victrola. Guests can relax in the garden and enjoy the swings, birds, flowers, and goldfish pond.

Host: Faye Hite
Rooms: 2 (PB) $90

NOTES: Credit cards accepted: A MasterCard; B Visa; C American Express; E Diner's Club; F Other; 2 Personal checks accepted; 3 Lunch available; 4 Dinner available; 5 Open all year; 6 Pets welcome;

Suite: $100
Full Breakfast
Credit Cards: None
Notes: 2, 5, 7, 8, 10, 12, 14

The Homestay

## The Homestay Bed & Breakfast

517 Richmond Road, 23185
(757) 229-7468 (information)
(800) 836-7468 (reservations)
e-mail: homestaybb@aol.com
http://williamsburg-virginia.com/homestay

Cozy and convenient. Enjoy the comfort of a lovely Colonial Revival home, furnished with turn-of-the-century family antiques and country charm. It is only four blocks to Colonial Williamsburg and just minutes away from Jamestown, Yorktown, and other local attractions. Adjacent to the College of William and Mary. A full breakfast featuring homemade breads and a delicious hot dish is served in the formal dining room. Children 10 and older welcome.

Hosts: Barbara and Jim Thomassen
Rooms: 3 (PB) $80-110
Full Breakfast
Credit Cards: A, B
Notes: 2, 5, 7, 9, 12, 14

## Hughes Guest Home

106 Newport Avenue, 23185-4212
(757) 229-3493
e-mail: LivesIV

Directly opposite the Williamsburg Lodge on Newport Avenue, the Hughes Guest Home has been in operation since 1947. A lovely two-

minute stroll to Colonial Williamsburg's restored district, golfing facilities, and numerous dining facilities including the colonial taverns. The College of William and Mary, Merchant's Square, and several Colonial Williamsburg museums are also within easy walking distance. The house is decorated lavishly with family antiques. Eating facilities are across the street at Williamsburg Lodge and Williamsburg Inn. Lodging only.

Rooms: 3 (1 PB; 2 SB) $60
Credit Cards: None
Notes: 2, 7, 8, 9, 12

## Indian Springs Bed & Breakfast

330 Indian Springs Road, 23185
(800) 262-9165; e-mail: indianspgs@tni.net

Indian Springs is in downtown Williamsburg, nestled in a private, wooded glade. Beautiful gardens adorn the view from each guest room. King suites open onto a shady greenery-filled veranda. The Colonial-style cottage features a king-size feather bed loft, fireplace, and wetbar. A small library has holdings for business and leisure activities. A sunny deck is a birdwatcher's haven. In-room amenities include cable. VCR, refrigerator, private bath, and private entrance.

Hosts: Kelly and Paul Supplee
Rooms: 4 (PB) $75-130
Full Breakfast
Credit Cards: A, B
Notes: 2, 5, 7, 8, 9, 10, 11, 12, 14

## The Inn at 802

802 Jamestown Road, 23185
(757) 564-0845; (800) 672-4086
FAX (757) 564-7018; e-mail: 105313.42@csi.com
www.bbhost.com/innat802

A four-room bed and breakfast close to Colonial Williamsburg and adjacent to the College of William and Mary. Period decor with down comforters and dust ruffles. Four-poster beds. Large, comfortable, and private rooms, all with private bath/showers. Delicious full

7 No smoking; 8 Children welcome; 9 Social drinking allowed; 10 Tennis nearby; 11 Swimming nearby; 12 Golf nearby; 13 Skiing nearby; 14 May be booked through a travel agent; 15 Handicapped accessible.

breakfast served daily. Two fireplaces, library, sun porch.

Hosts: Don and Jan McGarva
Rooms: 4 (PB) $125-145
Full Breakfast
Credit Cards: A, B, C, D
Notes: 2, 5, 6, 7, 8, 9, 10, 11, 12

Newport House

## Newport House

710 South Henry Street, 23185-4113
(757) 229-1775

Newport House was designed in 1756 by Peter Harrison. It is furnished totally in the period, including four-poster canopy beds. Each room has a private bathroom. The full breakfast includes authentic colonial-period recipes. Only five minutes from the historic area (as close as one can walk.) The host is a former museum director and author of many books on colonial history. Enjoy colonial dancing in the ballroom every Tuesday evening.

Hosts: John and Cathy Millar
Rooms: 2 (PB) $130-160
Full Breakfast
Credit Cards: None
Notes: 2, 5, 7, 8, 9, 10, 11, 12, 14

## Piney Grove at Southall's Plantation (1790)

P.O. Box 1359, 23187-1359
(804) 829-2480; FAX (804) 829-6888

Piney Grove is just 20 miles west of Williamsburg in the James River plantation country, among working farms, country stores, and historic churches. The elegant accommodations at this National Register of Historic Places property are in two restored antebellum homes (1790 and 1857). Also on the property is Ashland (1835), Dower Quarter (1835), and Duck Church (1917). Guests are welcome to enjoy the parlor-library, gardens, pool, nature trail, farm animals, or a game of croquet or badminton. Upon arrival, guests are served mint juleps and Virginia wine. Restaurants nearby.

Hosts: Brian, Cindy, Joan, and Joseph Gordineer
Rooms: 6 (PB) $130-170
Full Breakfast
Credit Cards: C, D
Notes: 2, 5, 7, 8, 9, 10, 11, 12, 14

## Primrose Cottage

706 Richmond Road, 23185
(757) 229-6421; (800) 522-1901
www.primrose-cottage.com

A short walk from Colonial Williamsburg, Primrose Cottage is abloom with pansies, primroses, and thousands of tulips. A French double harpsichord, hand-painted antiques, German dollhouse, and the comforts of home including private baths (two bathrooms have Jacuzzis) and king- or queen-size beds await guests. The aroma of Inge's home-cooked breakfast usually rouses even the sleepiest traveler.

Host: Inge Curtis
Rooms: 4 (PB) $95-125
Full Breakfast
Credit Cards: A, B
Notes: 2, 5, 7, 10, 11, 12, 14

## War Hill Inn

4560 Long Hill Road, 23188
(757) 565-0248; (800) 743-0248

Large country estate less than two miles from Williamsburg. Manor House built in 1969 with recycled building materials and patterned after an 18th-century home. Two cottages on grounds, also 18th-century design. Canopy beds, private baths, whirlpool tubs, and fireplaces. Honeymooners as well as families will find their special place at War Hill. AAA three-diamond-rated.

Hosts: Shirley, Bill, Cherie, and Will Lee
Rooms: 7 (PB) $75-100
Suites: 2 (PB) $100-165
Cottage: 2 (PB) $120-180
Full Breakfast
Credit Cards: A, B
Notes: 2, 5, 7, 8, 9, 10, 12, 14

Williamsburg Manor

## Williamsburg Manor Bed & Breakfast

600 Richmond Road, 23185
(757) 220-8011; (800) 422-8011

This 1927 Georgian home was built during the reconstruction of historic Colonial Williamsburg. Recently restored to its original elegance and furnished with exquisite pieces, including antiques and collectibles. Five well-appointed guest rooms with private baths, TVs, and central air conditioning. Guests are treated to a lavish fireside breakfast. Home is available for weddings, private parties, dinners, and meetings. Ideal location within walking distance of the historic area. On-site parking. Off-season rates available.

Host: Laura Reeves
Rooms: 5 (PB) $95-150
Full Breakfast
Credit Cards: A, B
Notes: 2, 5, 7, 8, 9, 10, 11, 12, 14

## Williamsburg Sampler Bed & Breakfast Inn

922 Jamestown Road, 23185
(757) 253-0398; (800) 722-1169
FAX (757) 253-2669
e-mail: WbgSampler@aol.com
www.WilliamsburgSampler.com

An elegant 18th-century plantation-style six-bedroom Colonial proclaimed by Virginia's governor "Inn of the Year." The Washington Post wrote, "decorated with an eclectic assortment of antiques collected by the innkeepers." Lovely rooms and suites with four-poster beds, plus fireplace, wet bar, refrigerator, TV/VCR, and private bath. "Skip lunch"® breakfast. Internationally known as a favorite for honeymoons, anniversaries, or romantic getaways. On-site parking. Walk to historic area. AAA three-diamond and Mobil three-star. Appeared on CBS This Morning.

Hosts: Helen and Ike Sisane
Rooms: 2 (PB) $100
Suites: 2 (PB) $150
Full Breakfast
Credit Cards: A, B
Notes: 2, 5, 7, 9, 10, 11, 12, 14

Williamsburg Sampler

---

7 No smoking; 8 Children welcome; 9 Social drinking allowed; 10 Tennis nearby; 11 Swimming nearby; 12 Golf nearby; 13 Skiing nearby; 14 May be booked through a travel agent; 15 Handicapped accessible.

## WINCHESTER

### Brownstone Cottage Bed & Breakfast

161 McCarty Lane, 22602
(540) 662-1962
e-mail: brnstone@winchesterva.com
www.nvim.com/brownstonebnb

Guests can enjoy the quiet and peaceful country setting of the Brownstone Cottage, a private home nestled in the Shenandoah Valley outside historic Winchester, Virginia. Hospitality and individual attention highlight a stay with hosts, Chuck and Shiela Brown. Wake to the aroma of freshly brewed coffee and the beginning of a full country breakfast featuring Chuck's homemade pancakes or bread. Smoking outside only. Children over 12 welcome.

Hosts: Charles and Shiela Brown
Rooms: 2 (PB) $95
Full Breakfast
Credit Cards: A, B
Notes: 2, 5, 7, 10, 11, 12

## WOODSTOCK

### Azalea House

551 South Main Street, 22664
(540) 459-3500
www.shenwebworks.com/azaleahouse

The Azalea House dates back 100 years when it was built in the Victorian tradition and used as a church manse. The guest rooms are pleasing and comfortable, with antique furnishings and mountain views. Situated in the rolling hills of the Shenandoah Valley near fine restaurants, vineyards, shops, caverns, Civil War sites, hiking, and fishing. A great place to relax! Children over six are welcome.

Azalea House

Hosts: Margaret and Price McDonald
Rooms: 4 (PB) $55-75
Full Breakfast
Credit Cards: C
Notes: 2, 7, 8, 9, 10, 11, 12, 13

### Blue Ridge Bed & Breakfast

2458 Castleman Road, Berryville, 22611
(540) 955-1246; (800) 296-1246
FAX (540) 955-4240; e-mail: blurdgbb@shentel.net
www.blueridgebb.com

C. Gorgeous mansion built in 1892 filled with antiques and hand-stenciled rooms. Hundreds of azaleas. In-ground swimming pool. $45-75.

## WOOLWINE

### The Mountain Rose Inn

1787 Charity Highway, 24185
(540) 930-1057; e-mail: mtrosein@swva.net
www.swva.net/mtroseinn

"Historical country elegance in the Blue Ridge Mountains." Once a part of the Mountain Rose Distillery, this Victorian inn, circa 1901, has five spacious rooms with private baths, working

The Mountain Rose Inn

antique-mantled fireplaces, and six porches. Elegant oil-lamp-lit threecourse breakfast. Swimming pool, trout-stocked creek, and 100 acres of hiking and privacy. Convenient to the Blue Ridge Parkway and Chateau Morrisette Winery. AAA three-diamond-rated. Member of BBAV and PAII. Open year-round.

Hosts: Melodie Pogue and Reeves Simms
Rooms: 5 (PB) $79-99
Full Breakfast
Credit Cards: A, B, D
Notes: 2, 5, 7, 8, 9, 10, 11, 12, 14

## YORKTOWN

### *Marl Inn Bed & Breakfast*

220 Church Street, P.O. Box 572, 23690
(757) 898-3859; (800) 799-6207
FAX (757) 898-3587
e-mail: EugeneM918@aol.com

Only 20 minutes from Williamsburg. Four rooms with private baths. Two are full suites with a bedroom, living room, kitchen. All rooms are on the second floor and have outside private entrances. Bicycles available for guests to tour battlefields and campgrounds of the Revolutionary armies. The beautiful 13-mile Colonial Parkway linking Yorktown with Williamsburg is a particularly attractive route for bicyclists and touring families. Four restaurants, upscale gift and antique shops are within walking distance, swimming and boating in the York River just two blocks from the house.

Rooms: 4 (PB) $95-120
Continental Breakfast
Credit Cards: A, B, C
Notes: 2, 7, 8, 9, 11, 12, 14

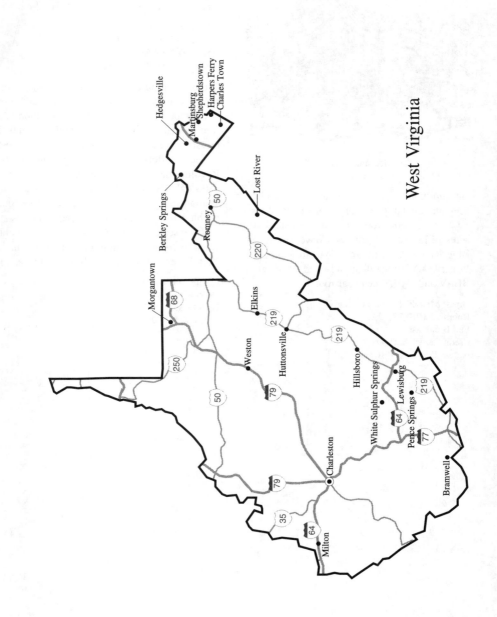

West Virginia

# West Virginia

## BERKELEY SPRINGS

### Blue Ridge Bed & Breakfast

2458 Castleman Road, 22611
(540) 955-1246; (800) 296-1246
FAX (540) 955-4240; e-mail: blurdgbb@shentel.net
www.blueridgebb.com

**A.** Two houses; eight rooms completely redone. Near mineral waters, castle, Roman bath and massage, fish ponds, health resort, golf, and horseback riding. $50-65.

## BRAMWELL

### Three Oaks & a Quilt

P.O. Box 84, 24715
(304) 248-8316

The oaks, to keep guests cool; the quilts, to keep guests warm. Grandfather bought the home in 1904 and it has remained in the family ever since. It was restored in 1985 and 1986, using and reusing everything possible. Most people come to Bramwell to see the coal operators' mansions, which give the feeling of a town having stood still since the early 1900s. One is quickly renewed in the restful, relaxing atmosphere. A fan appliquéd quilt hangs on the front porch wall, one of three dozen at the inn. Children over 12 welcome.

Host: B. J. Kahle
Rooms: 2 (PB) $58.30
Full Breakfast
Credit Cards: None
Notes: 2, 5, 7, 9, 10, 11, 12, 13

## CHARLESTON

### Brass Pineapple Bed & Breakfast

1611 Virginia Street East, 25311
(304) 344-0748; (800) CALL WVA
e-mail: pineapp104@aol.com
www.wvweb.com/brasspineaplebandb

This cozy but elegant 1910 brick home is in Charleston's historic district. The house has been carefully restored to its original grandeur, with antiques throughout, lots of stained glass, and original oak woodwork. Guest rooms are furnished in elegant style with private baths, terry robes, hair dryers, telephones with voice mail, cable TVs, and VCRs. Central air and heat. A small copier and fax are on the first floor. Mints on pillows and turndown, upon request, add that special touch. Tea is available from 5:00 to 7:00 P.M. Generous full or Continental candlelit breakfast is accented with crystal and silver and may be had alfresco in the petite rose garden in season. Smoking

Brass Pineapple

permitted outside only. Open year-round except for holidays. Children eight and older welcome. Limited social drinking permitted. Skiing an hour away.

Host: Sue Pepper
Rooms: 6 (PB) $59-109
Continental and Full Breakfasts
Credit Cards: A, B, C, E, F
Notes: 2, 7, 10, 11, 12, 14

## *Historic Charleston Bed & Breakfast*

110 Elizabeth Street, 25311
(304) 345-8156; (800) CALL WVA
FAX (304) 342-1572
e-mail: bed2brkst@aol.com

The first bed and breakfast in Charleston. This French country home, built in 1907, has three guest rooms with private bath. One of the guest rooms is a bridal suite with whirlpool tub in bath; another is a large room with queen-size bed and an adjoining smaller room with day bed and TV. The third room has an antique iron bed (double-size). Guests may relax in the den by the fire to watch TV or a movie. When weather permits, enjoy the front porch swing. A full breakfast is served. Walk to the state capitol and cultural center.

Hosts: Bob and Jean Lambert (resident owners)
Rooms: 3 (PB) $75-90
Full Breakfast
Credit Cards: A, B, C
Notes: 2, 5, 7, 10, 11, 12, 13, 14

## CHARLES TOWN

## *Gilbert House of Middleway Historic District: A Bed & Breakfast*

P.O. Box 1104, 25414
(304) 725-0637

Near Harpers Ferry and Antietam National Battlefield. Magnificent stone house, circa

Gilbert House

1760, listed in the National Register of Historic Places and the Historic American Building Survey (1938). Spacious, romantic rooms with wood-burning fireplaces and air conditioning. Bridal Suite has curtains around the bed and a claw-foot tub. Many European treasures, some from royal families. In the Middleway historic district. The village is one of the first European settlements in the Shenandoah Valley and is on the original settlers' trail. Colonial-era mill sites, theater at the Old Opera House, horse and auto races, rafting, outlet shopping.

Host: Bernie Heiler
Rooms: 3 (PB) $80-140
Full Breakfast
Credit Cards: A, B, C
Notes: 2, 5, 7, 9, 12, 14

## ELKINS

## *The Post House*

306 Robert E. Lee Avenue, 26241
(304) 636-1792

In the heart of Elkins, this bed and breakfast has five guest rooms, one of which has an adjoining children's room. Sit on the front porch or lounge in the parklike back yard with a children's playhouse. Close to Davis and Elkins College and other cultural and scenic attractions. Easy access to main roads. Certified massage is available. Handmade quilts for sale.

NOTES: Credit cards accepted: A MasterCard; B Visa; C American Express; D Discover; E Diner's Club; F Other; 2 Personal checks accepted; 3 Lunch available; 4 Dinner available; 5 Open all year; 6 Pets welcome;

Host: Jo Ann Post Barlow (owner)
Rooms: 5 (2 PB; 3 SB) $60-65
Continental Breakfast
Credit Cards: None
Notes: 2, 7, 8, 9, 10, 11, 12, 13

The Retreat

## The Retreat

214 Harpertown Road, 26241
(304) 636-2960; (888) 636-2960
e-mail: retreat@neumedia.net

The Retreat is a stately turn-of-the-century home just off the campus of Davis and Elkins College, .6 miles from downtown Elkins, gateway to the 840,000-acre Monongahela National Forest. Elkins was recently selected as one of the top 50 American small towns. Wide porches wrap around the house and five acres of old-growth trees, evergreens, rhododendron, flower and vegetable gardens make the Retreat a secluded spot to get away. Heritage music and art, as well as virtually every type of outdoor recreation, are specialties of the innkeeper.

Host: Leslie Henderson
Rooms: 5 (4 SB) $50-80
Full Breakfast
Credit Cards: A, B
Notes: 2, 5, 7, 8, 9, 10, 11, 12, 13

## Tunnel Mountain Bed & Breakfast

Route 1, Box 59-1, 26241
(304) 636-1684; (888) 211-9123
www.wvonline.com/shareourbeds/tunnelmtn

This charming three-story fieldstone home is nestled on the side of Cheat Mountain on five private wooded acres, surrounded by scenic mountains, lush forests, and sparkling rivers. The interior is finished in pine and rare wormy chestnut woodwork. Tastefully decorated throughout with antiques, collectibles, and crafts, it extends a warm and friendly atmosphere to guests.

Hosts: Anne and Paul Beardslee
Rooms: 3 (PB) $65-80
Full Breakfast
Credit Cards: None
Notes: 2, 5, 9, 10, 11, 12, 13

Tunnel Mountain

## The Warfield House

318 Buffalo Street, 26241
(888) 636-4555

The Warfield House, a grand shingle-and-brick house built in 1901, is nestled on a quiet corner in a scenic small town. Facing the forested city park, it is within walking distance of restaurants, shops, and theaters. It contains spectacular woodwork and stained glass and has been faithfully restored with turn-of-the-century reproduction carpets and wallpapers

---

7 No smoking; 8 Children welcome; 9 Social drinking allowed; 10 Tennis nearby; 11 Swimming nearby; 12 Golf nearby; 13 Skiing nearby; 14 May be booked through a travel agent; 15 Handicapped accessible.

The Warfield House

designed to transport guests back in time. Five antique-appointed guest rooms provide comfort and privacy.

Hosts: Connie and Paul Garnett
Rooms: 5 (PB) $75-95
Full Breakfast
Credit Cards: None
Notes: 2, 5, 7, 9, 10, 11, 12, 13

## HARPERS FERRY

### Fillmore Street Bed & Breakfast

Fillmore Street, 25425
(304) 535-2619

With a clear mountain view, this antique-furnished Victorian home is known for its hospitality, service, and gourmet breakfast. Private accommodations and baths, TVs, air conditioning, complimentary sherry and tea, and a blazing fire on cool mornings. Closed Thanksgiving, Christmas, and New Year's Day. Smoking is permitted outside on the porch only. Children over 12 are welcome.

Hosts: Alden and James Addy
Rooms: 2 (PB) $75-80
Full Breakfast
Credit Cards: None
Notes: 2, 5, 7, 9

## HEDGESVILLE

### The Farmhouse on Tomahawk Run

1 Tomahawk Run Place, 25427
(304) 754-7350 (phone/FAX)
e-mail: tomahawk@intrepid.net

This beautiful, restored Civil War-era farmhouse, on 280 acres of hills and meadows, is rich in history and charm. Enjoy bountiful three-course breakfasts, spacious guest rooms with balcony or suite and king- or queen-size beds, and antiques. During the day relax on a rocking chair on the large wraparound porch, stroll the walking paths on the grounds, or visit the shops and historical sites within a short drive. In the evening luxuriate in the Jacuzzi on the back porch within earshot of the rippling brook nearby.

Hosts: Judy and Hugh Erskine
Rooms: 5 (PB) $85-125
Full Breakfast
Credit Cards: A, B, C, D, E
Notes: 2, 5, 7, 8, 12, 14

## HILLSBORO

### The Current Bed & Breakfast

HC 64, Box 135, 24946
(304) 653-4722; e-mail: current@inetone.net
www.carrweb.com/thecurrent

Tucked into a high mountain valley near the Greenbrier River Trail, the Current offers a

The Current

---

NOTES: Credit cards accepted: A MasterCard; B Visa; C American Express; D Discover; E Diner's Club; F Other; 2 Personal checks accepted; 3 Lunch available; 4 Dinner available; 5 Open all year; 6 Pets welcome;

relaxing getaway. Nearby state parks and national forest provide opportunities for hiking, mountain biking, fishing, and canoeing, while the outdoor hot tub and deck beckon the star gazer and bird watcher. The 1904 farmhouse is furnished with antiques, collectibles, and quilts. Adjoining country church is available for weddings and receptions. Facilities for horses.

Host: Leslee McCarty
Rooms: 6 (1 PB: 5 SB) $60-80
Full Breakfast
Credit Cards: A, B
Notes: 2, 5, 7, 8, 9, 11, 12, 13

## HUTTONSVILLE

### Hutton House

General Delivery, P.O. Box 88, 26273
(304) 335-6701
www.bbonline.com/wv/huttonhouse

Enjoy the relaxed atmosphere of this historically registered and antique-filled Queen Anne Victorian. Guest rooms are individually styled, and each guest has his/her own personal favorite. Breakfast varies from gourmet to hearty. Sometimes it is served at a specific time, while at other times it is served at guests' leisure. Children can play games on the lawn. Guests can lose themselves in the beauty of the Laurel Mountains as they lounge on the wraparound porch.

Hosts: Dean Ahren and Loretta Murray
Rooms: 6 (PB) $75-80
Full Breakfast
Credit Cards: A, B
Notes: 2, 5, 7, 8, 9, 12, 13, 14

## LOST RIVER

### Blue Ridge Bed & Breakfast

2458 Castleman Road, 22611
(540) 955-1246; (800) 296-1246
FAX (540) 955-4240; e-mail: blurdgbb@shentel.net
www.blueridgebb.com

This outstanding log house comes complete with conference rooms, hot tub room, swim-

ming pool. washer/dryer, Jacuzzi, six guest bedrooms with cable TVs, and private baths. Fabulous view of Allegheny Mountains. Land borders George Washington National Forest. $108-116.

## MARTINSBURG

### Boydville, The Inn at Martinsburg

601 South Queen Street, 25401
(304) 263-1448

This 1812 stone plantation mansion is on a 10-acre park with 100-year-old trees and boxwood. Originally part of a Lord Fairfax grant. The land, once part of a large plantation, was purchased by General Elisha Boyd in the 1790s and was a retreat for Stonewall Jackson and Henry Clay. Enjoy beautiful craftmanship from a past era, including woodwork, window glass, French chandeliers, and foyer wallpaper handpainted in England in 1812. Great porch with rockers. Continental plus breakfast. In the National Register of Historic Places. Just off of I-81, one and one-half hours from Washington, D.C., in the heart of Civil War country. Closed during the month of August.

Hosts: LaRue Frye, Bob Boege
Rooms: 7 (5 PB; 2 SB) $100-125
Full Breakfast
Credit Cards: A, B
Notes: 2, 7, 9, 12, 13, 14

### Pulpit & Palette Inn

516 West John Street, 25401
(304) 263-7012

Oriental ambiance in a Victorian home. Two bedrooms share a bath. Morning coffee/tea with shortbread and newspaper served in bed. Full breakfast, afternoon tea, evening drinks, and hors d'oeuvres. Fifty-store outlet one block away. Other attractions and golf nearby. Children over 12 welcome. No smoking allowed.

7 No smoking; 8 Children welcome; 9 Social drinking allowed; 10 Tennis nearby; 11 Swimming nearby; 12 Golf nearby; 13 Skiing nearby; 14 May be booked through a travel agent; 15 Handicapped accessible.

Hosts: Bill and Janet Starr
Rooms: 2 (SB) $80
Full Breakfast
Credit Cards: A, B
Notes: 2, 7, 9, 12

## MIDDLEWAY

### Blue Ridge Bed & Breakfast

2458 Castleman Road, 22611
(540) 955-1246; (800) 296-1246
FAX (540) 955-4240; e-mail: blurdgbb@shentel.net
www.blueridgebb.com

**A.** Beautiful stone mansion built in 1760 in an
18th-century village. Close to Harpers Ferry.
Romantic rooms and suite. Working fireplaces
in bedrooms. Great hospitality. Walking tours
and lectures given. In the National Register of
Historic Places. $90-150.

## MILTON

### The Cedar House

92 Trenol Heights, 25541
(304) 743-5516; (800) CALL WVA
e-mail: vickersc@marshall.edu
www.bbonline.com/wv/cedarhouse/

The Cedar House is a hilltop, air- conditioned,
trilevel ranch-style house that gives a
panoramic view of surrounding hills. The five
and one-half acres provide quiet and privacy
within .8 of a mile of I-64, exit 28. Relax in
front of the family room fire or play pool,
games, or piano in the game room and use the
treadmill or roller traction table. Watch skilled
glass blowers at Blenko Glass, visit the covered flea market, explore the small-town shops,
or attend Saturday performances at the Moun-
taineer Opry House.

Host: Carole Vickers
Rooms: 3 (PB) $65-75
Full Breakfast
Credit Cards: A, B, C, D
Notes: 2, 5, 7

## PENCE SPRINGS

### The Pence Springs Hotel

P.O. Box 90, 24962
(304) 445-2606; (800) 826-1829
FAX (304) 445-2204
e-mail: pencehotel@newwave.net

Known as the Grand Hotel, this national register inn was one of the historic mineral spas of
the Virginias. From 1897 through the Great
Depression, Pence Springs was the most popular and expensive hotel in West Virginia. From
1947 to 1985, Pence Springs was the State
Prison for Women. Restoration started in 1986
and the Grand Hotel came full circle. Now it is
a fine country inn on a 400-acre plantation and
has attracted national attention.

Hosts: O. Ashby Berkley and Rosa Lee Miller
Rooms: 15 (4 PB; 11 SB) $80-100
Full Breakfast
Credit Cards: A, B, C, D, E
Notes: 2, 4, 6, 8, 9, 11, 12, 13, 14

Pence Springs Hotel

## SHEPHERDSTOWN

### Thomas Shepherd Inn

Box 1162, 25443
(304) 876-3715; (888) 889-8952
FAX (304) 876-3313
e-mail: mrg@intrepid.net
www.intrepid.net/thomas_shepherd/

Small, charming inn in a quaint, historic Civil
War town that offers that special hospitality of
the past. Guests find fresh flowers at their bed-

---

NOTES: Credit cards accepted: A MasterCard; B Visa; C American Express; D Discover; E Diner's Club;
F Other; 2 Personal checks accepted; 3 Lunch available; 4 Dinner available; 5 Open all year; 6 Pets welcome;

Thomas Shepherd Inn

sides, fluffy towels and special soaps in their baths, complimentary beverages by the fireside, memorable breakfasts. Picnics available. Children over eight welcome. Smoking permitted in designated areas only.

Host: Margaret Perry
Rooms: 7 (PB) $85-140
Full Breakfast
Credit Cards: A, B, C
Notes: 2, 3, 5, 9, 12, 13

## VALLEY CHAPEL/WESTON

### Ingeborg Acres Bed & Breakfast

Millstone Road, P.O. Box 199, 26446
(304) 269-2834
www.tiac.net/users/mann

Guests can have a unique experience at this scenic 450-acre horse and cattle farm seven miles from Weston. The three air-conditioned guest rooms have shared bath. Private, secluded cottage with bath and kitchenette, king-size or two single beds, plus one single bed and two single sleeper loveseats, covered porch, central air and heat. Enjoy patio, deck, and pool. Casual atmosphere, private pond for fishing, seasonal hunting, hiking, and bird watching. Full breakfast. No smoking.

Hosts: Inge and John Mann
Rooms: 3 (SB) $59
Cabin: $80
Full Breakfast
Credit Cards: None
Notes: 2, 5, 7, 8, 9, 11, 12

## WHITE SULPHUR SPRINGS

### Blue Ridge Bed & Breakfast

2458 Castleman Road, 22611
(540) 955-1246; (800) 296-1246
FAX (540) 955-4240; e-mail: blurdgbb@shentel.net
www.blueridgebb.com

Mansion built in 1819 just three blocks from famous Greenbrier resort and spa. Outside Greenbrier State Forest. Close to federal fish hatchery. Trout-stocked rivers. Skiing and white-water rafting. $80-140.

7 No smoking; 8 Children welcome; 9 Social drinking allowed; 10 Tennis nearby; 11 Swimming nearby; 12 Golf nearby; 13 Skiing nearby; 14 May be booked through a travel agent; 15 Handicapped accessible.

# Puerto Rico
# Virgin Islands

# Puerto Rico

## BOQUERON

### Parador Boquemar

P.O. Box 133, 00622
(787) 851-2158; (888) 634-4343
FAX (787) 851-7600

Parador Boquemar is in walking distance to Boquerón Beach and village, one of the most visited places for local and non-local tourists year-round for its beautiful beach and warm climate. All rooms feature air conditioning, mini-refrigerators, color TVs, and private balconies (second and third floor). Also swimming pool and an excellent seafood restaurant, La Cascada Restaurant and Cocktail Lounge. Enjoy kayaking, snorkeling, swimming, fishing, scuba diving, and sailing or just relax and feel the Caribbean wind while swinging in a hammock under palm trees in this piece of paradise. Lunch available on weekends. Dinner available except Wednesdays.

Hosts: The Rodríguez Family
Rooms: 75 (PB) $65-80
Continental Breakfast
Credit Cards: A, B, C, E
Notes: 5, 8, 9, 11, 12, 14, 15

## CABO ROJO

### Parador Perichi's

Road 102, KM 14.3, Playa Joyuda, 00623
(787) 851-3131 (0590, 0560, 0620)
FAX (787) 851-0590

Parador Perichi's hotel, restaurant, and cocktail lounge in Joyuda, the site of Puerto Rico's famous resorts on the west side. Excellence has distinguished Perichi's in its 20 years of hospitality and service. The 49 air-conditioned rooms have wall-to-wall carpeting, private baths, balconies, color TVs, and telephones. Perichi's award-winning restaurant features the finest cuisine. After sunset, meet friends in the well-stocked and cozy lounge. The spacious and comfortable banquet room can accommodate up to 300 people—for those who like to combine business with pleasure.

Rooms: 49 (PB) $69.55-90.95
Full Breakfast
Credit Cards: A, B, C, D, E
Notes: 3, 4, 5, 7, 8, 9, 10, 11, 12, 13, 14, 15

## CEIBA

### Ceiba Country Inn

Road 977, KM 1.2, P.O. Box 1067, 00735
(787) 885-0471 (phone/FAX); (877) 885-1002

In the hills on the east coast, in a pastoral setting with a view of the sea. Quiet, serene atmosphere with a cozy cocktail lounge. Convenient for trips to El Yunque, Luquillo, San Juan, Vieques,

Ceiba Country Inn

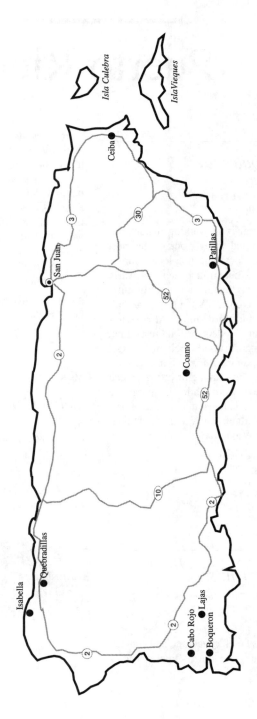

Puerto Rico

Culebra, and St. Thomas. Recommended by Frommer's, 1996. Continental plus breakfast.

Rooms: 9 (PB) $70
Continental Breakfast
Credit Cards: A, B, C, D
Notes: 5, 8, 9, 14, 15

## COAMO

### Parador Baños de Coamo

Bo. San Ildefonso Carr 540 Final, P.O. Box 540, 00769
(809) 825-2239; (809) 825-2186
(800) 443-0266 (US); (800) 981-7575 (PR)
FAX (809) 825-4739

The Parador Baños de Coamo is blessed for its lush, flowering vegetation, panorama, therapeutic baths, and so forth. Ponce de León missed it in his search for the Fountain of Youth. Known since 1847 (earlier by the Taino Indians). Restored to its 19th- century splendor by the Puerto Rico Tourism Company, using old aromatic wooden structures. Its 48 rooms are fully equipped to enjoy spa-style living. Individual wooden terraces; sweetwater pool for adults and children; therapeutic baths containing natural healing ingredients. Creole or international foods served. Country site. Beach nearby.

Host: Antonio Umpierre
Rooms: 48 (PB) $76
Continental Breakfast
Credit Cards: A
Notes: 3, 4, 5, 8, 9, 11, 12, 14

## ISABELA

### Costa Dorada Beach Resort

Emilio Gonzalez #900, 00662
(787) 872-7255; (888) 391-0606
FAX (787) 872-7595

Hotel in a tropical setting covered by palm trees on a mile-long stretch of white-sand beach in the lovely town of Isabela, next to a fishing village. All ocean-view rooms with air condition-

ing, color cable TV, direct-dial telephones. Two pools, tennis and basketball courts. Restaurant and bar. Live music on Saturdays.

Host: Mr. Carlos R. Fernandez
Rooms: 52 (PB) $112-140
Continental Breakfast
Credit Cards: A, B, C
Notes: 3, 4, 5, 8, 9, 10, 11, 12, 15

## LAJAS

### Parador Villa Parguera

P.O. Box 273, 00667
(787) 899-7777; (787) 899-3975
FAX (787) 899-6040

A tropical paradise in Puerto Rico! It's a 70-room resort hotel in La Parguera, Lajas. Home of the world-famous Phosphorescent Bay. Most of the rooms face the Caribbean Sea. Fine cuisine, local and international. Convention hall, seminar rooms, souvenir shop, night club, and swimming pool. Surrounded by beautiful patios with flowers and palm trees. Delightful tropical weather year-round. Fishing, diving, and snorkeling excursions nearby.

Rooms: 69 (PB) $95-104
Full Breakfast
Credit Cards: A, B, C, D, E
Notes: 3, 4, 5, 8, 9, 11, 14, 15

## PATILLAS

### Caribe Playa Beach Resort

HC 764, Box 8490, 00723
(787) 839-6339; (787) 839-7719
FAX (787) 839-1817; e-mail: geobeach@coqui.net

Thirty-two spacious beachfront studios equipped with air conditioning, refrigerator, private bathroom, ceiling fan, color cable TV, coffee maker, and patios or balconies. The restort features a guest library, TV/music lounge, and the sea-view terrace is open for breakfast, lunch, cocktails, light food and snacks. Hammocks and outdoor barbecues are

---

NOTES: Credit cards accepted: A MasterCard; B Visa; C American Express; D Discover; E Diner's Club; F Other; 2 Personal checks accepted; 3 Lunch available; 4 Dinner available; 5 Open all year; 6 Pets welcome; 7 No smoking; 8 Children welcome; 9 Social drinking allowed; 10 Tennis nearby; 11 Swimming nearby; 12 Golf nearby; 13 Skiing nearby; 14 May be booked through a travel agent; 15 Handicapped accessible.

available for guests' enjoyment and relaxation. The free-form pool has a sun deck, whirlpool, children's wading pool, and is surrounded by lush tropical greenery. Watersports, scuba diving, boatrides for fishing or pleasure are available and complement the services, for a truly relaxing and unforgettable getaway.

Hosts: Frances or George
Rooms: 32 (PB) $95-110
Continental Breakfast
Credit Cards: A, B, C
Notes: 3, 4, 5, 6, 8, 9, 10, 11, 12, 14, 15

## QUEBRADILLAS

### *Parador Vistamar*

Road 113 N #6205, 00678
(787) 895-2065; (888) 391-0606
FAX (787) 895-2294

On a hilltop with a breathtaking view of Puerto Rico's northwest Gold Coast. Rooms have ocean views, air conditioning, color cable TV, private bath; most with balconies. Two pools, tennis, basketball courts. Restaurant and bar. Live music on Saturdays.

Host: Mrs. Iris Myrna Cancel
Rooms: 55 (PB) $71-95
Continental Breakfast
Credit Cards: A, B, C
Notes: 3, 4, 5, 8, 9, 10, 11

## SAN JUAN

### *El Canario Inn*

1317 Ashford Avenue, Condado, 00907
(787) 722-3861; (800) 533-2649

San Juan's most historic and unique bed and breakfast. All 25 guest rooms are air conditioned, with private baths, telephones, and cable TVs. Beautiful tropical patio areas for relaxation. Only one block to beautiful Condado Beach, casinos, boutiques, and many fine restaurants. El Canario is perhaps the best deal for the vacation dollar in the Caribbean.

El Canario Inn

Hosts: Jude and Keith Olson
Rooms: 25 (PB) $75-100
Continental Breakfast
Credit Cards: A, B, C, D, E
Notes: 5, 8, 9, 10, 11, 14

### *El Consulado Hotel*

Ave Ashford #1110, 00907
(888) 300-8002; FAX (787) 723-8665

An elegant European-style bed and breakfast, El Consulado preserves all the fine qualities of the Spanish mansion it has been built upon. It offers 29 ample rooms with air conditioning, cable TV, and telephone. In the most centralized and accessible point in the Condado, it is only steps from first-class restaurants, casinos, night clubs, shops, and beautiful Condado Beach.

Rooms: 29 (PB) $95-115
Continental Breakfast
Credit Cards: A, B, C, D, E
Notes: 5, 8, 11, 14, 15

### *El Prado Inn*

1350 Luchetti Street, 00907
(787) 728-5925; (787) 728-5526; (787) 728-5134
(800) 468-4521; FAX (787) 725-6978

In front of park in the most elegant section of San Juan, this small and cozy, exclusive inn is the perfect place to use as a base in the

NOTES: Credit cards accepted: A MasterCard; B Visa; C American Express; D Discover; E Diner's Club; F Other; 2 Personal checks accepted; 3 Lunch available; 4 Dinner available; 5 Open all year; 6 Pets welcome;

Caribbean. Three-minute walk to beach, major hotels, casinos, restaurants. All rooms have private baths, air conditioning, ceiling fans, and a Spanish-style patio and pool. Self-contained apartments available. Complimentary Continental breakfast available.

Hosts: Nydia Hernández Pérez and Riaz Mawani
Rooms: 22 (PB) $59-79
Continental Breakfast
Credit Cards: A, B, C, D, E, F
Notes: 5, 8, 9, 10, 11, 14

## Tres Palmas Inn

2212 Park Boulevard, 00913
(787) 727-4617; (888) 290-2076
FAX (787) 727-5434; e-mail: tresplam@coqui.net
www.trespalmasinn.com

Centrally positioned on one of the most beautiful sandy beaches in the San Juan area. Just 10 minutes from the airport or Old San Juan and five minutes from entertainment centers, casinos, and restaurants. All rooms include air conditioning, private baths, color cable TV, touch-tone telephones, and electronic safes. Suites with kitchenettes are available. A brand new swimming pool is available as well as oceanfront sun deck and Jacuzzi. Handicapped facilities are available. Smoking permitted in designated areas only.

Hosts: Eileen and Manuel Peredo
Rooms: 15 (PB) $55-150
Continental Breakfast
Credit Cards: A, B, C
Notes: 5, 7, 8, 9, 10, 11, 12, 14, 15

7 No smoking; 8 Children welcome; 9 Social drinking allowed; 10 Tennis nearby; 11 Swimming nearby; 12 Golf nearby; 13 Skiing nearby; 14 May be booked through a travel agent; 15 Handicapped accessible.

St. John Island

St. Thomas Island

St. Croix Island

Virgin Islands

# Virgin Islands

## ST. CROIX—CHRISTIANSTED

### The Breakfast Club

18 Queen Cross Street, Christiansted, 00820
(809) 773-7383; FAX (809) 773-8642

The Breakfast Club is a comfortable and convenient bed and breakfast just six blocks from the heart of Christiansted and minutes away from beaches, diving, water sports, dining, golf, tennis, sailing, tours, or even shopping. Upon a ridge at the top of Queen Cross Street in an old West Indian neighborhood, the Breakfast Club is the perfect setting to relish the full, complimentary breakfast in the restored 19th-century commandant's house or to "lime" on the deck and savor the cooling trade winds by the hot tub. Children over six welcome. Groups inquire about the villa.

Hosts: Toby and Barb Chapin
Rooms: 9 (PB) $60
Full Breakfast
Credit Cards: B, C
Notes: 5, 9, 10, 11, 12

## ST. JOHN—CRUZ BAY

### St. John Inn (formerly Cruz Inn)

P.O. Box 37, 00831
(340) 693-8688; (800) 666-7688

Completely refurbished 13 units, including Junior Suites with full sofa beds and kitchenettes. All new four-poster beds, Ralph Lauren bedding, wardrobe armoires, and new carpeting. Brand new courtyard and swimming pool. TV/VCRs and cable TV in every room. New telephone system in every room. Custom-built bar with 61-inch big screen TV (largest on the island) featuring satellite TV including sports and movies two nights per week. Walking distance to town and the main port of entry. Fifteen dollars per each extra person. Commission to travel agents.

Hosts: John, Robb, and Gloria Hoffman
Rooms: 14 (12 PB; 2 SB) $105-200
Credit Cards: A, B, C, D, E
Notes:? 2, 5, 7, 8, 9, 10, 11, 14

## ST. THOMAS

### Pavilions and Pools Hotel

6400 Estate Smith Bay, 00802
(340) 775-6110; (800) 524-2001

A small villa hotel on the quiet east end of St. Thomas, 400 yards away from beautiful Sapphire Beach. Each villa has its own private swimming pool within its own garden. Featured are king-size beds, garden showers, fully equipped galley-style kitchen, air conditioning, and cable TV. Personal checks accepted for deposit only.

Hosts: Tammy Waters, general manager;
   Becca Nelsen, sales/reservations
Rooms; 25 (PB) $180-259
Continental Breakfast
Credit Cards: A, B, C
Notes: 4, 5, 6, 8, 9, 10, 11, 12, 14

---

NOTES: Credit cards accepted: A MasterCard; B Visa; C American Express; D Discover; E Diner's Club; F Other; 2 Personal checks accepted; 3 Lunch available; 4 Dinner available; 5 Open all year; 6 Pets welcome; 7 No smoking; 8 Children welcome; 9 Social drinking allowed; 10 Tennis nearby; 11 Swimming nearby; 12 Golf nearby; 13 Skiing nearby; 14 May be booked through a travel agent; 15 Handicapped accessible.

# RECOMMENDATION FORM

As *The Annual Directory of American and Canadian Bed & Breakfasts* gains approval from the traveling public, more and more bed and breakfast establishments are asking to be included on our mailing list. If you know of another bed and breakfast which may not be on our list, give them a great outreach and advertising opportunity by providing us with the following information:

1) B&B Name _____

Host's Name _____

Address _____

City _____ State _____ Zip Code _____

Telephone _____ FAX _____


2) B&B Name _____

Host's Name _____

Address _____

City _____ State _____ Zip Code _____

Telephone _____ FAX _____


3) B&B Name _____

Host's Name _____

Address _____

City _____ State _____ Zip Code _____

Telephone _____ FAX _____

Please return this form to: Barbour Publishing, Inc.
P.O. Box 719, Uhrichsville, OH 44683
(740) 922-6045; FAX (740) 922-5948